Equality in the Primary School

Also available from Continuum

Equality in the Secondary School, Mike Cole

Education and Community, Diane Gereluk

Values in Education, Graham Haydon

Educational Attainment and Society, Nigel Kettley

Equality in the Primary School

Promoting Good Practice across the Curriculum

Edited by
Dave Hill and Leena Helavaara Robertson

continuum

Continuum International Publishing Group

The Tower Building
11 York Road
London
SE1 7NX

80 Maiden Lane
Suite 704
New York
NY 10038

www.continuumbooks.com

British Library Cataloguing-in-Publication Data
A catalogue record for this book is available from the British Library.

ISBN: 9781847061003 (hardcover)

Library of Congress Cataloging-in-Publication Data
Equality in the primary school: promoting good practice across the curriculum/
edited by Dave Hill and Leena Helavaara Robertson.
        p. cm.
    1. Education, Elementary–Social aspects–Great Britain. 2. Educational
equalization–Great Britain. 3. Education and state–Great Britain.
4. Neoliberalism–Great Britain. I. Hill, Dave, 1945– II. Robertson, Leena Helavaara, 1958–.
III. Title.

LC4704.74.E78   2009
372.24′1–dc22

2009020204

Typeset by BookEns, Royston, Herts.
Printed and bound in Great Britain by the MPG Books Group, Bodmin King's Lynn

Contents

Chapter 1

Notes on Contributors

Gavin Baldwin is a principle lecturer at Middlesex University, UK, where he teaches on both primary and secondary programmes. He is responsible for the PGCE Secondary Citizenship course. He has published on history and citizenship education including *Living The Past* with Beth Goodacre (Middlesex University Press, 2002) and Combatting Homophobia and Heterosexism in *Gender in Education*, edited by Hilary Claire for the ATL 2004.

Kate Blackmore is a teacher and dance specialist in a Northamptonshire primary school. She completed a Diploma in Dance Theatre with Music at The Laban Centre and has freelanced as a children's dance teacher and entertainer. At Middlesex University she gained a combined degree in Geography, Environment and Society with Education and a PGCE in the Early Years. Kate is currently undertaking a Masters degree in Education at Northampton University.

Emily Beadle is a primary school teacher in Northamptonshire. She completed her degree in Business Administration at Cardiff and then went on to study her PGCE at De Montfort University, Bedford, UK. Emily is currently undertaking a Masters degree in Education at Northampton University. Following the untimely death of Rosie Turner-Bisset, Emily worked on finalizing the history chapter in this volume.

Chris Carter started teaching maths in East London in 1984. He now teaches maths in a North Bristol comprehensive school. Always an active member of the NUT, he left the Labour Party in the 90's when it became too right wing, but continues to be involved in Left politics. He is an active member of the alternative football club, Red Star Bedminster.

Mike Cole is Research Professor in Education and Equality, Director of the Centre for Education for Social Justice, and Head of Research at Bishop Grosseteste, University College, Lincoln. He has published extensively in the field of education and equality. His latest books are *Education, Equality and Human Rights: issues of gender, 'race', sexuality, disability and social class*, Routledge 2nd Edition (2006); *Marxism and Educational Theory: origins and issues*, Routledge

(2008); *Professional Attitudes and Practice: meeting the QTS standards*, Routledge 4th Edition (2008); and *Critical Race Theory and Education: a Marxist Response*, Palgrave Macmillan (2009). He is the editor of the companion volume to this book, *Equality in the Secondary School: Promoting good practice across the curriculum*, also published by Continuum in 2009.

Jessica J. P. Haberman is an elementary school teacher living and working in Toronto, Ontario, Canada. Previously, Jessica was both literacy coordinator and teacher in a state primary school in Wandsworth Borough, London. A specialist in both literacy and creativity in the primary school setting, Jessica received her MA, with distinction, from Kings' College London, University of London. The title of her dissertation was 'A Critical Analysis of Education Policy for the Knowledge Economy and its effects upon the English Primary School Setting'.

Jo Hardman is currently a principal lecturer in the Faculty of Sport, Health and Social Care at the University of Gloucestershire, UK. She teaches modules in adapted physical activity, inclusive physical activity, sport pedagogy and practical modules at the University. Prior to her university work, Jo taught in variety of teaching establishments in the UK and the USA. Jo's particular interest is in disability sport and inclusion issues related to PE in the National Curriculum.

Dave Hill is currently Professor of Education Policy at the University of Northampton, UK, and Chief Editor, *Journal for Critical Education Policy Studies*, at www.jceps.com. He is Routledge Series Editor for the *Education and Neoliberalism*, and *Education and Marxism* series. He has authored around a hundred articles and book chapters, and edited/co-edited 16 books. He is a Marxist/ Socialist political and Labour movement activist, stood twice for parliament for the Labour party when it was more left-wing, led a Labour group of councillors, and was an elected trade union regional leader. Dave Hill lectures worldwide on Marxism and Education, on Neoliberal Capitalist Education globally, on Radical/Socialist/Marxist Education/ Critical Pedagogy, and on 'Race' and Class. His most recent edited books, all Routledge, 2009, are *Contesting Neoliberal Education: Public Resistance and Collective Advance; The Rich World and the Impoverishment of Education: Diminishing Democracy, Equity and Workers' Rights;* (edited with Ravi Kumar) *Global Neoliberalism and Education and its Consequences;* (edited with Ellen Rosskam), *The Developing World and State Education: Neoliberal Depredation and Egalitarian Alternatives.* Other books he has co-edited in 2009 are, *Teaching Class: Knowledge, Pedagogy, Subjectivity* (Routledge, edited with Deb Kelsh and Sheila Macrine), and *Organizing Pedagogy: Educating for Socialism Within and Beyond Global Neo-liberalism* (Palgrave Macmillan, edited with Sheila Macrine and Peter McLaren).

Gillian Hilton has worked in Teacher Education for many years and is now Head of Education at Middlesex University, UK. She has a keen interest in education in Europe, particular teacher education in the Baltic States. These European connections have aided her specific research interests in teacher education, gender and education and in Personal, Social and Health Education (PSHE), in particular, sex education. She has undertaken a considerable amount of field work in the area of Sex and Relationship Education (SRE), particularly related to the needs of boys.

Gareth Honeyford is a principal lecturer and course leader of the Primary PGCE programme at the University of Northampton, and formerly lecturer in ICT in Education at the University of Northampton, UK, where he worked on a number of undergraduate and postgraduate courses. Prior to this, Gareth worked in the London Borough of Waltham Forest as part of the Excellence in Cities Team. Based at a City Learning Centre he ran a number of ICT supported projects for pupils, teachers, parents, learning mentors, teaching assistants and 'disaffected youth.' He has also worked for Becta and taught for a number of years in primary and middle schools. His interests lie in the use of ICT for Teaching and Learning, particularly as a communication tool with video and Web 2.0 technologies such as blogs and wikis. Primarily he believes that technology should be fun! When not working, he is a loving husband to Kate, doting parent to Beth and in an apparent contradiction, a keen long-distance cyclist.

Carole Hsiao works as a consultant in Seattle, Washington State, USA. She is primarily interested in promoting situations in which young people find ways of expressing themselves through the Arts. She has found that the community, as well as the school, can provide interesting as well as supportive spaces for these experiences to take place. She received her EdM in Arts in Education at Harvard Graduate School of Education and her PhD in Curriculum and Instruction at University of Wisconsin-Madison, USA.

Gianna Knowles is a senior lecturer at the University of Chichester, UK. She has experience of being a primary school teacher and OfSTED inspector. Whilst Gianna lectures in subject areas across the curriculum, her main area of writing, research, interest and expertise is in the field of social justice.

Philip Kovacs is an assistant professor in the Department of Education at the University of Alabama, Huntsville, USA, where he teaches courses on Educational Foundations, Curriculum Theory, and Methods. He is co-founder of the Educator Roundtable, a non-profit organization working to inform US citizens about the detrimental effects of the No Child Left Behind Act. While his work primarily focuses on the critique of neoliberal think tanks, institutes, and foundations, he also spends time exploring and articulating what a democratic education might look like and do. Recognizing that the world has been made and can be remade, Dr Kovacs spends a great deal of time trying to get citizens involved in educational reconstruction.

Henry Kum was educated in Cameroon and the UK and has remarkable experience with refugees at various levels. He has also researched various aspects of settlement, integration, community cohesion and inclusive practice. His research interests fall under issues of Class, Social Status, Gender, Equality and

Diversity, Social, Human, Cultural and Educational Capital and Neoliberalism and Resistance. His MA and PhD studies deal with issues of refugee integration and good practice. He has presented several papers in national and international conferences. He has taught in schools in Cameroon and the UK and is currently Research Officer at Strathclyde University, Scotland, and finishing his PhD at the University of Northampton, UK.

Tamar Margalit has a PhD in Operations Research. She is a graduate of the elementary teachers' preparation program, 'Education for Social Change, Environmental Change and Peace Education' given at the Kibbutzim College of Education, Israel. In the last few years, she has been conducting research in Mathematics Education and is developing a maths program that integrates concepts of social justice, human rights, and peace education into the maths curriculum and lessons. She has taught mathematics in a mixed-ethnic (Jewish and Arab) public elementary school in Jaffa, Israel, and she is currently a lecturer in mathematics courses at the Technion and at the Open University of Israel.

Meg Maguire is Professor of Sociology of Education in the Centre for Public Policy Studies at King's College London, UK. Previously she taught for some time in urban primary schools. She has a particular interest in urban policy and practice and has researched and published on these issues, including *The Urban Primary School* (2006), with Simon Pratt-Adams and Tim Wooldridge.

Curry Stephenson Malott earned his PhD in Curriculum and Instruction in 2004 from New Mexico State University, USA, where he examined the relationship between capitalism, as the process of value production, and Chicano student resistance and non-resistance within the official state-sponsored process of knowledge production. Dr Malott is currently assistant professor in the Social and Philosophical Foundations of Education at D'Youville College in Buffalo, New York State, USA. Dr Malott's scholarly contributions are predominately in the interrelated areas of social and cultural theory, critical pedagogy, popular and youth cultures, cognition, the social studies, liberation studies, urban education, teacher education, and educational leadership. His most recent books include *The Destructive Path of Neoliberalism: An International Examination of Urban Education* (2008) edited with Bradley Porfilio and *A Call to Action: An Introduction to Education, Philosophy, and Native North America* (2008).

Ruth Mantin is a senior lecturer at the University of Chichester and the Subject Co-ordinator for Religious Education. Her doctoral thesis was on the relationship between religious language and feminist spiritualities and she has published several articles on this subject. Her educational research interests are in issues of inclusion relating to gender and sexuality, with particular reference to religious education. Ruth has also co-authored the Heinemann Think RE series for Key Stage 3 Religious Education.

Uvanney Maylor is senior research fellow at IPSE (the Institute for Policy Studies in Education) at London Metropolitan University, UK. She is particularly interested in research that focuses on issues of ethnicity, racism and culture as they impact on educational practice and student experience. Her work includes 'minority ethnic students' experiences' in initial teacher training, and the experiences of Black staff in teaching and further education. She is currently managing an evaluation of the 'Black Children's Achievement Programme' (a national targeted programme) for the Department for Children, Schools and Families, and was project manager for the Department for Education and Skills *Diversity and Citizenship: Research Review* of the curriculum.

Peter McLaren is internationally recognized as one of the leading architects of critical pedagogy and known for his scholarly writings on critical literacy, the sociology of education, cultural studies, critical ethnography, and Marxist theory. He has developed a reputation for his uncompromising political analysis influenced by a Marxist humanist philosophy and a unique and poetic literary style of expression. His scholarship and political activism have taken him throughout Latin America, the Caribbean, Europe, the Middle East, and Southeast Asia. His numerous works have been translated into twelve languages. McLaren is the author, co-author, editor and co-editor of approximately forty books and monographs. Several hundred of his articles, chapters, interviews, reviews, commentaries and columns have appeared in dozens of scholarly journals and professional magazines worldwide. His most recent books include: *Pedagogy and Praxis* (with Nathalia Jaramillo, Sense Publishers, 2007), *Rage + Hope* (Peter Lang, 2006); *Capitalists and Conquerors* (Rowman and Littlefield, 2005); *Teaching Against Global Capitalism and the New Imperialism* (with Ramin Farahmandpur, Rowman and Littlefield, 2005); *Red Seminars: Radical Excursions into Educational Theory, Cultural Politics, and Pedagogy* (Hampton Press, 2005); *Marxism Against Postmodernism in Educational Theory* (with Dave Hill, Mike Cole, and Glenn Rikowski); *Che Guevara, Paulo Freire, and the Pedagogy of Revolution* (Rowman and Littlefield, 2000). He is also author of *Life in Schools: An Introduction to Critical Pedagogy in the Foundations of Education* (Allyn & Bacon) which is now in its fifth edition (2007). *Life in Schools* has been named one of the twelve most significant writings worldwide in the field of educational theory, policy and practice by an international panel of experts assembled by the Moscow School of Social and Economic Sciences. McLaren is Professor of Education, Graduate School of Education and Information Studies, University of California, Los Angeles, United States.

Dina Mehmedbegovic currently works as a researcher at the London Education Research Unit, the Institute of Education, University of London, UK. Her research interests focus on bilingualism, ethnic minority pupils, minority languages and attitudes to languages in general. In her previous job as an Ethnic Minority Achievement Adviser in the City of Westminster she led on promoting student voice through student consultations, student conferences and publications. Previously she worked in the London Borough of Camden as a teacher.

Nick Peim teaches and researches in the College of Social Science at the University of Birmingham, UK. His main interests are in contemporary theory and philosophy applied to the imperial drives of education as governance. Recent work has addressed school history, school improvement, assessment and curriculum issues through perspectives drawn from Walter Benjamin, Heidegger, Lacan and Derrida.

Simon Pratt-Adams is principal lecturer in education at Anglia Ruskin University. He has taught about urban education at both undergraduate and postgraduate levels and has researched and published in this area. Before working in higher education, he was deputy head of a London primary school.

Leena Helavaara Robertson is a principal lecturer at Middlesex University, UK. She started her career as an Early Years teacher in Watford, England, and her research interests and publications focus on multilingualism in urban schools, community languages and early literacies. Her current research project examines the work of bilingual classroom assistants. Her recent book, edited with Jean Conteh and Peter Martin, is *Multilingual Learning Stories in Schools and Communities in Britain*. Stoke-on-Trent: Trentham Books Ltd. (2007).

Jen Smyth is course leader for primary science at London Metropolitan University, UK, where she is also director of the Hands-On Workshop Unit. She has long experience of teaching at different levels in schools in Sheffield and London, from part-timer to headteacher before leaving to follow a university career. She has worked as a curriculum consultant in London and Scotland, and has helped to develop primary school science clubs, for which she received a Millennium Fellowship. Her research interests are in the early acquisition of science concepts and she has written widely on science in the early years.

Steve Smyth is manager for Diversity and Development with STEMNET, the National Network for Science Technology Engineering and Mathematics Education, in the UK. He has wide experience of curriculum development in both science and technology, working with the ILEA on both *Science in Process* and *Technology in Process*. He was Heinemann Fellow at University of York, where he helped develop *Science: the Salters' Approach*. He was science education officer at the National Maritime Museum and has been a consultant for a number of other museums, including the Historic Dockyard at Chatham and the Tall Ship in Glasgow. He has managed the Young People's Programme at the British Association and the Shell Education Service. He is a visiting lecturer in technology education at London Metropolitan University.

Rosie Turner-Bisset had a broad experience of working in education, spanning primary- and secondary-age phases and teacher education. For nine years she was a History teacher educator at the University of Hertfordshire, UK, where she became a University Learning and Teaching Fellow. In 2003 she won a National Teaching Fellowship; then moved to Middlesex University, England, as Reader in Education and on to Newcastle University. She published numerous articles and chapters on teachers' knowledge bases, curriculum, learning and teaching, history, history and literacy, reflection, creativity and creative teaching, including two books: *Creative Teaching: History in the Primary Classroom*, London: David Fulton (2005); and *Expert Teaching: Knowledge and*

Pedagogy to Lead the Profession, London: David Fulton (2001). Rosie died at an untimely early age in January 2009.

Emma Whewell is senior lecturer in physical education at the University of Northampton, UK, lecturing on undergraduate and postgraduate initial teacher training courses. Prior to this, she has taught physical education in various schools in Leeds, Bradford and Newcastle employed as a head of girls' physical education and head of year.

Linda Whitworth is a senior lecturer in citizenship and religious education at Middlesex University, UK, where she teaches on primary and secondary initial teacher education courses. Prior to this she taught religious education in a variety of schools. Her research interests are in promoting teachers' understanding of intercultural and inter-religious dialogue and she is currently a member of the Warwick University REDCo Community of Practice.

Acknowledgements

This is to thank Tina Foulser at BookEns, and Naomi Hill, Administrator of the Institute for Education Policy Studies (www.ieps.org.uk) for their indefatigable, expert and speedy proofing and copyediting. And thanks to Allison Clark and Ania Leslie-Wujastyk at Continuum for their forbearance and support during this process. And to Naomi Hill and Josh Akehurst (Editorial Assistant at the Institute for Education Policy Studies, www.ieps.org.uk) for their indexing of this book.

Not least, thanks to all the chapter writers – on both sides of the Atlantic! And readers. And most of all, those teachers and student teachers who find this book useful in helping to theorize and analyse and further understand the reasoning behind and impacts of their own and others' teaching and school practices. And who improve/add to their practice re promoting equality in the classroom – and staffroom. (And, by implication, in the wider society too).

Dave Hill
Professor of Education Policy at the University of Northampton, UK
Director of the e-institute, the Institute for Education Policy Studies, www.ieps.org.uk

Leena Helavaara Robertson
Principal Lecturer, Primary Education, Middlesex University, UK
Programme Leader PGCE Foundation and Key Stage 1 - Early Years

Preface

Peter McLaren

Ever since the sweeping changes imposed on schools and education following the Education Reform Act of 1988, and the persistent and tendentious encroachment of neoliberal educational policy, teachers and the teaching profession have increasingly come under public scrutiny from elected officials, the press and the general public. A new public managerialism has been seen at work in the ongoing surveillance of teachers and students; a project that includes the imposition of a tightly-monitored testing of knowledge deemed to be best suited for the global expansion of capitalist enterprises and values.

As numerous, vociferous and thoughtful as the attempts have been to address the increasing problems facing the educational system, there have been few attempts to address the structural determinations and historically prevailing systems of exploitation inexorably impacting the schooling process as our youth experience an ever-worsening alienation from the neoliberal social order. Debates over prescriptive curricula, standards, the national curriculum and publishable assessment have drawn attention away from the struggle for educational equality and social justice, including the sociological, political and psychological aspects and contexts of teaching and schooling.

This is a serious concern, especially given the fact that the current *mise-en-scène* for educational reform is now the rag-and-bone-shop of a decaying capitalist world system and the cataclysmic social and political changes of our time. And this is what makes *Equality in the Primary School* such a timely and significant work.

Hill and Robertson are depressingly skilful editors, and by this I mean that they do not spare raising the tough questions that peel back the surface beneficence of social democracy to reveal a complex skein of entanglements involving the creation of privileging hierarchies of exploitation maintained and reproduced by capitalist schooling. Furthermore, they understand that education is more reproductive of an exploitative social order than a constitutive challenge to one precisely because it rests on the foundations of capitalist exchange value. This is because, as Glenn Rikowski (2007) writes, the inequalities of labour-power quality generated within the capitalist labour process require re-equalization to the socially average level *in order to attain the equalization of labor-power values that is the foundation of social justice in capitalism.* There is clearly a capitalist plan for education, requiring the production of labour power with the skills and ideologically-compliant attitudes to develop a workforce for surplus value. Corporations now profit immensely from international privatizing, franchizing and marketing activities related to all aspects of educational services and training.

Equality in the Primary School foregrounds the unfinishedness of the modernist project of social emancipation and, as such, does not let go of the universal character of its struggle for liberation from the constraints of capital. This is a book that is astir with questions and challenges that makes capitalism froth at the mouth because it sets itself in opposition to customary ways of thinking about the education process – and to those who claim to know *ex officio* about what needs to be done to reform the education system – and what is too often a craven conformity to capital's law of value, a conformity that is inseparable from the fateful alienation that oxygenates the soil of human interaction in capitalist society.

Hill and Robertson set out to explore the diremption between the manifest goals of the education system (cynically camouflaged as the handmaiden of democracy) and its tacit outcomes – that agonistic space that has spawned what has come to be called the hidden curriculum. The editors have pitched their overall agenda in concert with what Istvan Meszaros calls socialist education: 'the social *organ* through which the *mutually beneficial reciprocity* between the individuals and their society becomes real' (2008:347).

In a neoliberal world, all efforts at bringing about equality court a certain impotence; there is always an unmasterable character to all reform efforts, an uncomfortable impass between the facts of schooling and the value we place on it. But education does not maintain a compact with failure. Not all education is about uncritically affirming inequality, turning one's back on social issues under unfolding conditions of unemployment, abandoning the interests of students and peculating public funds. It is not that capitalist schooling exercises some formal prohibition on social justice, it is more the case that the constitutive logic that operationalizes the divisive legacy of capital and capitalist schooling prevents social justice from becoming actualized.

Not only are the editors of *Equality in the Primary School* fully aware of the magnitude of the task and the long-term implications of the issues that they raise, they are also aware that addressing the vital structural determinations of capital's social universe cannot be done in individualistic terms. They are acutely conscious of the ways in which education – with its hierarchical command structure – needs to be refashioned in order to meet the continually shifting historical challenges that face us in accordance with the unfolding dynamics of social development. Theirs is a concrete proposal, one that goes well beyond what Istvan Meszaros calls a 'wishfully stipulated abstract moral "*ought-to-be*"' (2008:336) – a type of 'abstract and individualistic moral appeal which could yield only unrealizable utopian projections' (2008:338).

It is precisely in the area of social justice that education holds out against domination. But it must hold out beyond the realm of an abstract morality alone, where righteous rhetoric trumps concrete proposals – beyond the kind of educational equivalent of the Stakhanovite exhortations for transforming the work ethic of Soviet society. Does this mean that social justice and socialist education does not rest upon a moral foundation? On the contrary, it means that socialist and social justice morality is linked to far-reaching social change. Meszaros expands on this idea as follows:

... the morality in question is not an imposition on the particular individuals from outside, let alone from above, in the name of a separate and rather abstract moral discourse of 'ought-to-be,' like the inscription chiseled into marble in many English churches: '*Hear thy God and obey the King!*' Nor is it the secular equivalent to such half-religious external commands superimposed on the individuals in all societies ruled by capital's imperatives. On the contrary, the morality of socialist education is concerned with rationally conceived and commended far-reaching *social change*. Its tenets are articulated on the basis of the concrete evaluation of the chosen tasks and of the share required by the individuals in their conscious determinations to accomplish them. This is how socialist education can define itself as the *ongoing development of socialist consciousness* inseparable from and closely interacting with the overall historical transformation in progress at any given time. In other words, the defining characteristics of socialist education arise from, and deeply interact with, all of the relevant orienting principles of socialist development ... (2008:338–339).

In addition to fighting for concessions in the legal and political sphere that might temporarily favour the educational left, the contributors to *Equality in the Primary School* seek more permanent, long-range changes in areas such as curriculum models and policies, urban education, refugee education, English and literacy education, mathematics and numeracy, sex education, physical education, design and technology, religious education and religious diversity, foreign languages, citizenship education, and the national curriculum. While not all forms of address in this marvellous book are explicitly socialist, the spirit of the contributions contained therein unmistakably captures a social justice agenda, what Meszaros describes as activating 'the increasingly more conscious dialectical reciprocity between ... individuals and their society' (2008:348). The contributions unleash aspirations in teachers and in pedagogical realms, not only by igniting a transgressional impulse, but by seeking more permanent, structural changes in the educational system.

What is to be created atop the ruins of capital is both a political and an educational project that cannot be ignored nor denied. Capitalism – which has extra-parliamentary power – will resist all efforts to counter its efficacy, let alone its very existence, to be sure. And those who deny the legitimacy of these efforts, extolling instead the virtues of capitalist schooling, will be taking us into an imperilled future.

As social justice educators we cannot circumvent the contradictions of capitalist schooling or submit to them by clinging to some salvic impulse. We must transcend them by recognizing the impossibility of liberation under capitalism. To fail to recognize this is to tread perilously into a neoliberal future. But it is not enough to recognize this insight. Teachers and students together must join in creating a post-capitalist alternative education and fight to make it hegemonic. *Equality in the Primary School* is a major step towards this goal.

Peter McLaren
Professor
Graduate School of Education and Information Studies
University of California, Los Angeles

References

Meszaros, I. (2008) *The Challenge and Burden of Historical Time: Socialism in the Twenty-First Century*. New York: Monthly Review Press.

Rikowski, G. (2007) *Critical Pedagogy and the Constitution of Capitalist Society*, A paper prepared for the 'Migrating University: From Goldsmiths to Gatwick' Conference, Panel 2, 'The Challenge of Critical Pedagogy', Goldsmiths College, University of London, 14th September 2007. Online at http://www.flowideas.co.uk/?page = articles = Critical%20Pedagogy%20and%20Capitalism

Introduction

Dave Hill and Leena Helavaara Robertson

There are different sets of responses to the inequalities we have in our primary schools and society. One is to flatly deny inequality is a problem, to see it as 'only natural', or perhaps even desirable. Some policy makers may see it this way, believing that large inequalities are not a problem for societies. For example, the Thatcherite Conservatives, originally responsible for many current school reforms, starting with their Education Reform Act of 1988, deliberately widened social class inequalities in Britain (Hill 2004, 2006a; Harvey 2005), and New Labour's Peter Mandelson famously declared that he was 'extremely relaxed' about the super-rich getting richer.

Others do see there is a problem. The 2009 book, *The Spirit Level: Why more equal societies almost always do better* (Wilkinson and Pickett 2009, and for a summary, see Hansley 2009) shows the social ills – such as mental illness, teenage pregnancy, violence, rates of illness, general unhappiness, murder – that result from and are statistically linked with high levels of social inequality. And, there are different ways, different ideological response to this high level (and increasing) inequality.

A liberal-progressive way is to look for and work towards tolerance, mutual respect and multiculturalism and to develop empathy and to treat people with dignity. A number of the chapters in this book lay particular emphasis on developing love, tolerance, mutual understanding, kindness, and see that as a way of advancing social justice, reducing inequalities and hurts caused by personal and institutional racism, sexism, homophobia, and discrimination against working class and disabled children and adults. This type of approach works at the interpersonal level.

A social democratic way is to engage in reforms, with some income redistribution, and to use positive discrimination policies – such as SureStart, Education Maintenance Allowances, Free School Meals (in some areas) for all children who want them and to reduce the class sizes in poor areas. Teachers who see the need for these reforms – probably a majority of primary school teachers? – do wish to reduce the levels of injustice and structural discrimination (against, for example, some minority ethnic groups or working-class children in general, see Hill 2009, of this volume). This type of approach works at the level of reforming the existing (capitalist) society and its structures, such as schools, the labour market, the welfare benefit system, and the taxation system.

A fourth approach is what is widely known (among educators) in the USA as Critical Pedagogy (see Hill 2009, in this volume, and Hill 2010). This approach, drawing on educators such as Paolo Freire, Peter McLaren, Henry Giroux, Antonia Darder, Joe Kincheloe and Shirley Steinberg, urges teachers and educators (and other workers, such as media workers) to develop a critique of the way capitalist society works, to expose racism, sexism, homophobia, and discrimination against the disabled. Thus 'critique' becomes an important word in concepts and practice. A number of chapters in this book have been deliberately co-written with US and other critical educators, in order to bring these concepts more to the attention of primary school student teachers and teachers.

A fifth and final approach to inequalities in schooling is the Marxist, or socialist one. As is set out in Chapter 20, the principal exponent, at least in his writings since the mid-1990s, is Peter McLaren, who has written the Preface to this book. In the USA, this approach is known as 'revolutionary critical pedagogy' or critical revolutionary pedagogy. This approach welcomes the redistributive and positive discrimination reforms of the social democratic approach, (such as are evident in some of New Labour's education policies since 1997 (see Tomlinson 2005; Hill 2006b). This approach also welcomes the liberal-progressive stress on tolerance, mutual understanding, dignity, compassion, and seeing each other's points of view. But it sees these as not going far enough. It calls for not only the critique of racism and other forms of structural and widespread discrimination, but the critique of a capitalist society that privileges greed, consumerism, ultra-individualism, and 'beggar thy neighbour' philosophies and ways of behaving – it seeks to replace that system by a democratic socialist system.

This approach and form of analysis of what goes on in schools and society, is also the approach of Dave Hill, one of the two editors of this book. Dave has been 'political' – in the sense of being a political and trade union activist – since his teens. Being brought up in a cockney family from London's historically multi-ethnic East End, as a teenager in a single-parent working class home in some poverty, sensitized him to issues of social class inequality and discrimination (Dave's wiki entry is at http://en.wikipedia.org/wiki/Dave_Hill_(Professor)). His political activism led to him becoming a Labour parliamentary candidate in 1979 and in 1987 (when New Labour did not exist, the Labour Party was then 'Old Labour' – a mix of socialists, social democrats and trade unions), and becoming a local and a regional trade union leader, and a Labour group leader on East Sussex County Council in the 1980s. More recently, in June 2009, he stood for election to the European Parliament for a Socialist/trade union-backed coalition.

This concern for social justice – and for (much more) economic equality – extended into hostility to and activism over other forms of discrimination and oppression. Thus, for example, into anti-racism (in the Anti-Nazi League, for example), into a concern for (and political action as a councillor) issues of violence against women, and women's rights. Dave also has, as a hearing disabled person, a commitment to equal opportunities and equality regarding disabilities.

Leena Helavaara Robertson was born in Finland and moved to England as an au pair in 1978. She married a Londoner in 1979 and brought up her two boys bilingually and biculturally in London and in Hertfordshire. For many years she was involved in local playgroups and other early years settings, but it was the absence of support for bilingualism in English primary schools – and often the negative associations and the deficit model that surround bilingual children's school learning – that sensitized Leena to various forms of discrimination, injustice and under-expectations. She also became highly active in establishing and running a community language school for Finnish-speaking children in St Albans, Hertfordshire.

Following her qualification as a primary school teacher, Leena worked in urban multilingual schools in Watford, Hertfordshire, and for many years taught young children in predominantly British-Pakistani classes. Leena's initial teacher training course had prepared her to teach 'language' and 'English' as well as 'speaking, listening, reading and writing', but not 'literacy', and it was not until later when she encountered Paolo Freire's (1972) work that she began to develop a broader understanding of 'literacy'. Her experiences led her to complete a PhD in an area of multilingual literacy. Working with Eve Gregory (2008) she became much influenced by the work of Shirley Brice Heath (1983), Jim Cummins (2000), and Tove Skutnabb-Kangas (2000). Building on commitment to social justice and equality and coming from Finland, one of the fairest countries in the world, her work as a teacher educator continues to focus on issues of diversity and equality.

References

Cummins, J. (2000) *Language, Power and Pedagogy*. Clevedon: Multilingual Matters.

Freire, P. (1972) *The Pedagogy of the Oppressed*. Harmondsworth: Penguin.

Gregory, E. (2008) *Making Sense of the New World*. 2nd edn. London: Routledge.

Hansley, L. (2009) 'The way we live now: A hard-hitting study of the social effects of inequality has profound implications'. *The Guardian*, 14 March. Online at http://www.guardian.co.uk/books/2009/mar/13/the-spirit-level

Harvey, D. (2005) *A Brief History of Neoliberalism*. Oxford, UK: Oxford University Press.

Heath, S. B. (1983) *Ways With Words*. Cambridge: Cambridge University Press.

Hill, D. (2004) 'Books, Banks and Bullets: Controlling our minds – the global project of imperialistic and militaristic neo-liberalism and its effect on education policy'. *Policy Futures in Education*, 2, 3–4, pp. 504–522 (Theme: Marxist Futures in Education). Online at http://www.wwwords.co.uk/pdf/viewpdf.asp?j=pfie&vol=2&issue=3&year=2004&article=6_Hill_PFIE_2_3-4_web&id=81.158.104.245

Hill, D. (2006a) 'Class, Capital and Education in this Neoliberal/ Neoconservative Period'. *Information for Social Change*, 23. Online at http://libr.org/isc/issues/ISC23/B1%20Dave%20Hill.pdf

Hill, D. (2006b) 'New Labour's Education Policy' in D. Kassem, E. Mufti and J. Robinson (eds) *Education Studies: Issues and Critical Perspectives*. pp. 73–86. Buckingham: Open University Press.

Hill, D. (2009) 'Theorizing Politics and the Curriculum: Understanding and Addressing Inequalities through Critical Pedagogy and Critical Policy Analysis' in D. Hill and L. Helavaara Robertson (eds) *Equality in the Primary School: Promoting good practice across the curriculum*. London: Continuum.

Hill, D. (2010) 'Critical Pedagogy, Revolutionary Critical Pedagogy and Socialist

Education' in S. Macrine, P. McLaren, and D. Hill (eds) *Critical Pedagogy: Theory and Praxis*. London: Routledge.

Skutnabb-Kangas, T. (2000) *Linguistic Genocide in Education – or Worldwide Diversity and Human Rights?* New Jersey: Lawrence Erlbaum Associates Publishers.

Tomlinson, S. (2005) (2nd edn.) *Education in a post-welfare society*. Maidenhead, Berks: Open University Press.

Wilkinson, R. and Pickett, K. (2009) *The Spirit Level: Why more equal societies almost always do better*. London: Allen Lane.

Part 1

The Wider Context

Chapter 1

In the Crossfire: Early Years Foundation Stage, National Curriculum and Every Child Matters

Leena Helavaara Robertson

Introduction

A number of children from the early years unit have gone outside. 4-year old Zeynep is on her own and free to follow her own interests. She sits on a bench and blows bubbles. She watches carefully – again and again – as the bubbles rise and suddenly burst. Zeynep is of British-Turkish background and going through a non-verbal/silent stage, typical of many children who speak another language at home and who are at an early stage of learning the school's language. As the bubbles burst and disappear, she smiles and looks around to see if anyone has noticed. Her teacher approaches and comments, 'That's lovely, Zeynep. Can you see the rainbow colours on that bubble? What is that colour? That colour there? Colour?' Zeynep looks away.

This chapter presents a brief overview of recent changes in early years and primary curriculum and analyses their impact on equality. In the last 13 years or so, early years and primary school teachers, and particularly those who teach 4–5-year-old children in Reception classes (now class R), have witnessed in rapid succession the introduction and implementation of different types of curricula. While all of them have in various different ways purported to address the needs of *all* children – including children like Zeynep in the above vignette – the changes have also created various tensions and dilemmas for teachers, which have had a serious knock-on effect in the organization and management of teaching and learning. And on equality.

Zeynep's teacher, Marina, is a case in point as the above vignette shows. Marina is keen to encourage Zeynep's independence and motivation to learn as the new Early Years Foundation Stage (DfES 2007) states, and she provides regular opportunities for Zeynep to engage in self-initiated play inside and outside. She mentions Zeynep's enjoyment in her learning as one of the five outcomes identified by the Every Child Matters (DfES 2003a) agenda. Marina recognizes that Zeynep is interested in exploring soap bubbles and seems to be presenting problems for herself that extend her learning. Marina says, 'It is as if Zeynep is asking and checking to see whether all bubbles will eventually burst:

problem solving. She is learning to learn. You know, identifying a goal for herself, and then persevering to achieve that goal. Fantastic!' She also talks about Zeynep's process of learning English and recognizes that hurrying her to speak English is counterproductive. She admits, 'She needs to develop her confidence, to sort herself out, before she tries to use English. You know, the same way I can never speak French on my first day on holiday in France. I feel self-conscious and shy, and the words just don't come out. She needs time rather than this pressure to conform.'

Marina, however, feels trapped by the assessment requirements (DfES 2007; DCSF 2008). She feels that she has no other choice but to 'push her on': 'Push, push, push. She's got to know the colour words. It's in our plan. And there is an expectation that by the time they go to the Year 1 class, all this basic stuff has been learnt, and that they can then move on to read and spell different colour words. If I can't show the basic stuff, what can I show? The Year 1 teachers will think I've let them down, and Zeynep will fall behind other children.'

This teacher, like so many others, feels that there is an urgent need to show rapid progress both in Zeynep's English and in clearly defined areas of learning. When Zeynep learns to identify and use colour names accurately, Marina can show evidence of progress, and this will go towards demonstrating that Zeynep is ready for the demands of the National Curriculum (DfEE 1999a), and in particular for phonics teaching (DfES 2006a). Marina will have done her job well.

At the same time Marina has to cope with some very contradictory beliefs and values. She is aware that 'pushing' bilingual children, who are going through a non-verbal/silent stage, is counterproductive (Barrs *et al.* 1990; Tabors 1997) and, in fact, in opposition to the ways in which Marina believes Zeynep learns. These kinds of tensions in practice and pedagogy arise from the competing and often contradictory curriculum models that are based on different models of learning and from the overall educational agendas set by the Department of Children, Schools and Families, that draw on different ideological perspectives. Consequently, many teachers feel that it is impossible to fulfil many of the aims. They feel they have been caught in the crossfire.

This chapter reviews the main changes in the early years and primary curriculum in recent years, and focuses on Curriculum Guidance for the Foundation Stage (DfEE/QCA 2000), replaced by the Early Years Foundation Stage (DfES 2007), National Curriculum (DfEE 1999a) and Every Child Matters (DfES 2003a). It also evaluates the impact of the National Literacy and Numeracy Strategies (DfEE 1998; DfEE 1999b) and the 'Independent Review of Reading' (DfES 2006a) on early years and primary curriculum.

Keeping each curriculum in mind, this chapter aims to ask the following questions:

- who is this document aimed at?
- what view of the child as a learner does it present?
- what view of the society – and the child as a citizen – does it present?
- what impact has it had on equality issues?

Early Years Foundation Stage

Early childhood education covers the period between birth and 8 years (see, for example, Nutbrown *et al.* 2008). This period of children's development is characterized by rapid changes, both physical and intellectual, and by transitions, many of which are highly influential for learning and for later achievement. Today there is an agreed consensus that this is an important stage of development, and therefore of education, and consequently authorities in different parts of the world have conceptualized the education and care of young children in various different ways and forms. The New Zealand model, developed in 1996, for early years education is called Te Whāriki ('whāriki' meaning 'a mat for all to stand on' in Maori) and it presents four overlapping and interlocking aspects of children's learning (empowerment, holistic development, family and community, and relationships) (Soler and Miller 2003). Te Whāriki is an interesting intercultural attempt to develop a new approach to early years education, and important to mention here because societal diversity in New Zealand is seen as the basic starting point – and the norm – rather than something that needs to be tagged on once the overall aims and structure of the model have been developed.

Another interesting approach is that of Reggio Emilia, developed in northern Italy, where children are seen as protagonists in the educational process (Rinaldi 2005). The Reggio Emilia pre-school approach was developed soon after the Second World War by Loris Malaguzzi, and the surrounding community. From its early days onwards it has involved ordinary local people in all kinds of decision-making processes, as well as parents and teachers. Malaguzzi believed that there was an urgent need to ensure that never again would the people of Italy be tempted by fascist ideals (as they had been during Mussolini's time) and Malaguzzi firmly believed that the key was in early years' education. Today teaching in Reggio Emilia settings starts from the children's own ideas which are firmly anchored in their real lives and in the surrounding community, rather than from teachers' or indeed government's – preconceived ideas of what they should learn. The role of the Reggio Emilia teacher is to provide time and experiences that support children in making new connections.

In England early childhood education and care has recently undergone various and significant changes. Before 1996 there had never been a formal curriculum imposed by the government for those who work with children between birth and 5 years of age. This changed in 1996 when the Conservative government introduced Desirable Outcomes for Children's Learning and the Baseline Assessment (DfEE/SCAA 1996) as well as 'Nursery Vouchers' and OFSTED inspection for this phase of schooling. Desirable Outcomes for Children's Learning were directly linked to the National Curriculum, and were generally thought as ill-conceived (Wood 2007). They were soon replaced by the new Labour government's Curriculum Guidance for the Foundation Stage (DfEE 1999a).

The Curriculum Guidance for the Foundation Stage (DfEE 1999a) was implemented in 2000. It was a welcome document that for the first time identified 'early years' as an area of education in its own right. It covered the teaching and learning of all children between the ages of 3 and 5 years, and received some praise from teachers in its initial conception (Duffy 2006). It was a document for teachers, and it listed some sound principles for early years practice. It also divided the curriculum into six areas of learning (Social and Emotional Development, Communication, Language and Literacy, Mathematical Development, Physical Development, Knowledge and Understanding of the World and Creative Development). Each of the six areas had its own list of 'Stepping Stones' that identified more specific aspects of learning, and 'Early Learning Goals' that provided a bridge between this curriculum and the National Curriculum. There was an expectation that most of the children would achieve the Early Learning Goals by the end of their time in the Reception class.

The assessment document, the Foundation Stage Profile (DfES/QCA 2003), was introduced three years after the Curriculum Guidance for the Foundation Stage. It used both Stepping Stones and Early Learning Goals and presented a set of 13 assessment scales, each of which had 9 points, totalling 117 different items. This profile was a disappointing document as it forced teachers' attention away from the sound principles to a long list of assessment items. The responsibility of finding evidence for each one of the 117 assessment items, and for each child in the Foundation Stage, was sometimes seen as cumbersome, unmanageable and a meaningless process. It had a serious impact on teaching as many teachers now felt compelled to teach, or cover in some way or form, all 117 items. At the same time, however, it could be seen as fitting in with – and in fact formally promoting – a more focused and detailed observation routine for assessment in early years. Nutbrown viewed it from this angle and noted that it 'held out hope of a more flexible approach to ongoing assessment of young children's learning through observation' (Nutbrown 2006:100).

In the light of the assessment processes, it is evident that the starting point of this curriculum was not young children's interests or their real life experiences. Diversity in the society was also something that had to be considered separately from the rest of the curriculum. It prescribed the learning that needed to take place in order to build a 'foundation' on which later primary school learning would take place. Like Zeynep's teacher Marina, many others, too, felt forced to justify their practice in terms of the primary school demands. These later demands, and especially the demands of SATs (national tests), had seeped into the early years practice. It was as if the children of this age group were in danger of losing their right to exist as young children with their unique interests and approaches, and were already perceived as data for future league tables. But as Zeynep showed in the opening vignette, 4-year-old children are already competent learners; they have a right to have their learning needs considered in terms of who they are now, and not what they might become later.

This direction of movement (towards highly prescribed assessment scales) went against other early years developments, too. Internationally there had been a growing acceptance that young children are not simply citizens of the future, or 'becomings', but 'beings' (as in human beings, rather than 'human becomings' (James and Prout 1997)), and therefore competent experts in their own lives and willing and able to be involved in their communities and early years settings (Clark and Moss 2001; Paley 2004; Rinaldi 2005). This kind of positive approach, also called the New Sociology of Childhood (Kjørholt et al. (2005) had been developing alongside the attempt to build on the United Nation's Convention on the Rights of the Child (www.unicef/org/crc/).

It is also interesting to note that the term 'literacy' was firmly lodged in the Curriculum Guidance for the Foundation Stage. It is one key part of Communication, Language and Literacy, one of the six areas of learning. The embedding of the new Foundation Stage took place soon after the National Literacy Strategy (DfEE 1998) was established, and 'literacy' had become one of the new buzz words of education. In primary schools literacy as a curriculum subject was given a new high status at a time when the surveillance and management mechanisms were increased (see also Peim and Hill of this volume, that is Chapters 6 and 20). Literacy, more than any other subject, was seen 'at the heart of the drive to raise standards in schools' (DfEE 1998:2). Ofsted inspections and school league tables continued. Performance-related pay became a reality and was linked to raising literacy standards. Target setting in each school and class was tightened, and all this had an irretrievable impact on Foundation Stage. Furthermore, this increased emphasis on literacy paved the way for the more recent – and more aggressive – developments in phonics teaching.

The current Early Years Foundation Stage (EYFS) was implemented in September 2008 and this new document was to many practitioners a logical and cohesive development from the previous curriculum. The main differences between the earlier document (Curriculum Guidance for the Foundation Stage) and the current one, is that the new framework covers care, learning and development for children in all early years settings from *birth* to the August after their fifth birthday. It has also brought together the existing Birth to Three Matters Framework (DfES/Sure Start 2002), the Curriculum Guidance for the Foundation Stage (DfEE 1999a) and the National Standards for Under 8s Day Care and Childminding (DfES 2003b) Its agenda of inter-agency work and joined-up practice fits in very well with the recommendations made in the Every Child Matters (DfES 2003a).

The Early Years Foundation Stage is written, not just for teachers, but for a range of practitioners who work with young children, including childminders, playgroup leaders or workers in day care centres or crèches. It has aimed to move away from the long list of 'Stepping Stones' that had, in practice, been used like the termly learning objectives of the National Literacy and Numeracy Strategies (DfEE 1998; DfEE 1999b). It aims to emphasize some sound principles – once again – and this time presents four themes: Unique Child, Relationships, Enabling Environments and Learning and Development. Each of these has four commitments, and they highlight an individual child's holistic development and self-initiated learning and play. There is no space here to examine what these somewhat cherished terms of the early years pedagogy ('holistic' or 'play') signify, suffice to say that they are also highly problematic as they tend to be used with very little critical evaluation. (A good starting point for exploring this topic is Wood 2007; see also Wood and Attfield 2005). Criticism aside, a focus on self-initiated play and the way this document locates the child at the heart of the curriculum, is a good starting point for Zeynep and for all children who come from non-dominating or marginalized backgrounds.

It is also useful to note that the four themes (Unique Child, Relationships,

Enabling Environments and Learning and Development) and the four sets of commitments specifying each theme (totalling 16 important commitments) are at the forefront of this document (see also www.standards.dfes.gov.uk/eyfs). The six areas of learning and development have largely remained the same, apart from Mathematical Development which is now conceptualized as Problem Solving, Reasoning and Numeracy. (The other five areas of learning and development are as before: Social and Emotional Development; Communication, Language and Literacy; Physical Development; Knowledge and Understanding of the World; and Creative Development.) These six areas constitute as the final and 16th commitment. Thus, the document makes an important value judgement; while it is critical that a broad range of areas of learning, or subjects, is considered, the organization, management, planning and teaching, has to consider the other 15 commitments as well. It is also worth remembering that in policy terms the teaching of reading and early phonic work is only one tiny subsection of one of the six areas of the 16th commitment. But will teachers like Marina be able to perceive it as such? Are all these 16 commitments equal or is there a hierarchy between them, and to what extent are headteachers or Ofsted inspectors focusing on one small subsection, on phonics?

Assessment in the Early Years

The new assessment tool, now called the Early Years Foundation Stage Profile (DCSF 2008) is in many ways much the same as its predecessor; it has retained its 13 assessment scales in the six areas of learning. It is, however, a document that reveals its own tensions. On the one hand, it seems to be making some bold and innovative recommendations. First, it recognizes children as competent experts in their own lives and states that the evidence for the assessment must come from practitioners' observations of children's self-initiated activities. This is potentially exciting as children's play is, therefore, accepted as an important part of the curriculum and its assessment, and not just something children do by themselves after teacher-led or teacher-directed activities have taken place. Second, it also notes that practitioners should involve children fully in their own assessment by encouraging them to talk about their own learning. Third, it formally validates the use of home languages in both teaching and assessment:

> All the scales in personal, social and emotional development, problem solving, reasoning and numeracy, knowledge and understanding of the world, physical development, and creative development *can be assessed in the home language*. The first three points in all the scales for communication, language and literacy can also be assessed in this way. Scale points 4–9 of the communication, language and literacy scales must be assessed in English. This has implications for provision. Children must have opportunities to engage in activities that do *not depend solely on English for success*, and where they can participate in ways that *reveal what they know and can do in the security of their home language*. (DCSF 2008, emphasis added)

This is important because it has the potential to ensure that teachers, like Marina in the opening vignette, will no longer feel pressurized for pushing children like Zeynep to speak English – and *only* English. Rather the opposite. Zeynep is now entitled to use and hear her mother tongue in her Reception class. In addition the assessment of Zeynep's learning in its broadest sense can take place in Turkish.

On the other hand, disappointingly, the pressure of SATs and 'raising standards' in literacy have not disappeared from Key Stage 1 and hence the hierarchy between the six different areas of learning continues to shape and dominate the Foundation Stage practice. The Early Years Foundation Stage Profile (DCSF 2008) also reveals a clear focus on phonics – and on English phonics – and in fact the demand for phonic work has in many ways been tightened as the following scale points reveal:

Scale point 7 Uses phonic knowledge to read simple regular words;
Scale point 8 Attempts to read more complex words, using phonic knowledge;
Scale point 9 Uses knowledge of letters, sounds and words when reading and writing independently (DCSF 2008).

The Profile warns that the assessment scale points are not equivalent to any National Curriculum levels, or sub-levels, and that no such comparison should be made, but there is also a clear expectation that these scale points have been addressed – that is taught – even if they have not been achieved by all children at the end of the Reception class. It is also important to remember that the above scale points *must* be taught and assessed in English only, and that children's achievement in literacy (rather than say, in Knowledge and Understanding of the World or in Physical Development) is an indicator of the teacher's success.

Undoubtedly some 4-year-old children will be delighting in 'using phonic knowledge to read simple regular words', but many will not find 'phonic knowledge' interesting, and others will find it downright difficult. In fact it is deeply worrying that *all* children are expected to read for example 'more complex words', and in *English,* during their time in the Foundation Stage, or at least by the time they leave the Reception class. The expectation that all young children will conform and achieve these highly contested and formal aspects of the curriculum sits uncomfortably with general research evidence of literacy; there is no evidence that demonstrates that the earlier young children are given formal phonic lessons, the faster they will learn to read. Or that the earlier they start, the higher the literacy results will be later on in school.

The Finnish system is a case in point. In Finland schooling and the formal process of teaching children to read starts at the age of 7 years, and yet according to the PISA research the overall Finnish literacy results are the highest in the world (Hautamäki *et al.* 2008). The Finnish pre-school class ('esikoululuokka') for 6–7-year-olds provides some opportunities to learn about the letters of the alphabet and about numbers, but the assessment takes into consideration an individual child's interests and preferences. Generally the education and care for all young children (from birth to 7 years) emphasizes the development of a strong learner identity which is dependent on critical thinking, expression of creativity, imagination and independence. The provision for early childhood education and care, as well as the pre-school year, come under the remit of the Ministry of Social Affairs and Health (2004), unlike primary schools (from 7 years onwards) that fall under the auspices of the Ministry of Education. The statutory guidance for early childhood education and care identifies six 'orientations' for all children up to the age of 7 years; these are mathematical, natural sciences, historical-societal, aesthetic, ethical and religious-philosophical orientations:

> The concept of orientation underlines the notion that the intention is not for children to study the content of different subjects but to start acquiring tools and capabilities by means of which they are able to gradually increase their ability to examine, understand and experience a wide range of phenomena in the world around them. Each orientation has its own specific way of critical thinking and expressing creativity, practising imagination, refining feelings and directing activity. (STAKES 2004:24)

These orientations are conceptually very different from the English six areas of learning and development that have a very specific content and long list of assessment items. There are no ability groups in Finnish schools, either, and the orientations provide no specific guidance on teaching children to read (or on early phonics) and, therefore, there are no formal literacy lessons. However, some broad areas of language and literature are accepted and explicitly acknowledged:

> Children are naturally disposed to playing with words. Rhymes and funny non-sense words draw the child's attention to the form of the language in place of its meaning, and provides [sic] practice in the area of linguistic awareness. Children also enjoy stories. Both storytelling by children themselves and creative activities inspired by fairy tales and stories told by educators increase children's confidence in their own capabilities and help them continuously express themselves. Different types of literature belong to the world of even the youngest children. Literature offers children a wide range of insights into the world around them and the richness of language, and provides practice in listening skills. [...] The environment should allow the child to observe both spoken and written language. (STAKES 2004:18)

Thus, it seems that the Finnish system provides a solid base on which later school learning will be built upon: a true foundation. At the age of 7, children will arrive at school as learners – some undoubtedly more knowledgeable about reading and writing than others, some with greater levels of confidence, others with individual difficulties – but they will not arrive as already well-established and formally acknowledged success stories or failures.

National Curriculum

Since many of the chapters in this book provide a brief historical overview of the conception of the National Curriculum subjects and how they have developed over the years, there is no need to repeat any of that here. Rather, the focus here is on identifying tensions that these two different types of curricula (Early Years Foundation Stage and the National Curriculum) have created.

The current early years' curriculum and its related agenda (DfES 2007; DCSF 2008) for children from birth to 5 years and the National Curriculum (DfEE 1999) for children between 5 and 11 years in Key Stages 1 and 2 (as well as Key Stages 3 and 4 of the secondary phase) have been developed from very different ideological stances. The early years' curriculum is based on a liberal, more progressive child-centred view of education (Wood 2007; Tutt 2006). For example, the Early Years Foundation Stage advocates the use of observations in assessing children's learning and the detailed observations of self-initiated activities are perceived as critical. The National Curriculum, and its regime of 'tables, targets and tests' (Tutt 2006), continues to be fixated on subjects, especially literacy and numeracy, and on measurable lesson learning objectives or success criteria that can be ticked off after each lesson.

Much has been written about the two different types of curricula, that is, about the play-based early years curriculum and the more formal subject-based National Curriculum. (A good starting point for finding out more is Dunlop and Fabian (2007) and Brooker (2008)). The stark differences between the two have also generated a motley collection of documents and research projects that deal with 'transition' between the Foundation Stage and Key Stage 1. DfES (2006b) recognizes that the transition between the two stages is not 'smooth' or 'seamless', and provides guidance and advice for schools for making it better. Others, such as Sanders *et al.* (2005), explore the dilemmas between the two and identify some key differences. These consist of a change from active play that emphasizes a range of skills in the Foundation Stage to static participation in Key Stage 1, where the emphasis is on listening and writing, and where children lose the opportunity to have any influence over the direction of their own learning.

However, there is no need to look far for alternative solutions. In Wales, and in response to similar tensions and problems between the two different types of curricula, the Welsh Assembly has introduced a new model, Foundation Phase, for all 3–7-year-old children (Davidson 2004). The Key Stage 1 is disappearing from Welsh primary schools, and at the same time all SATs tests have also been abolished. The Welsh Foundation Phase is introduced in all schools, but this process is taking place relatively slowly, so that evaluations can take place and be acted upon (Siraj-Blatchford *et al.* 2006). The Foundation Phase is organized around seven areas of learning that are very similar to those of the English Early Years Foundation Stage; they are Personal, Social Development and Well-Being; Language, Literacy and Communication; Knowledge and Understanding of the World; Creative Development; Mathematical Development; Physical Development; and Bilingualism and Multicultural Understanding. Personal, Social Development and Well-Being is located at the centre of the Welsh curriculum map, and thus, at least in its policy terms, it is perceived at the heart of young children's learning.

Reception Class

In most European countries, formal education begins at the age of 6 or 7 years (Riggall and Sharp 2008). In England, compulsory schooling starts the term after children are 5, but in practice children tend to start school in the Reception class the term before their 5th birthday. For many years the length of time children spend in the Reception class has varied between one to three terms. Children whose birthday falls between September 1st and December 31st have a full year, whereas those whose birthday is in the spring term have two terms, and the summer-born children have only one term in Reception. Increasingly, many schools and Local Authorities have abolished the staggered entry and have opted for one annual intake of children. Today, large numbers of children start school at the age of 4 years, nearly 2–3 years earlier than their European counterparts.

The summer-born children are one group that require particular attention as there is a steadily growing body of research that suggests that they underachieve in relation to autumn-born children (Martin *et al.* 2004). The current system clearly favours those who are born early on in an academic year and discriminates against summer-born children (Payler and Whitebread 2007). However, the main question is not so much, as Brooker (2008) has pointed out, 'when do they start?' but rather 'what do they start?' What kind of curriculum, pedagogy and practice will young 3–4-year-old children meet when they first start school?

The Reception age group has recently experienced more changes in curriculum than any other group, and the provision and practice for this single age group has continued to be problematic and fraught with documents that have contradictory aims. When the new Primary National Curriculum for England and Wales was introduced in the late 1980s, Reception class was firmly part of this new legislation. This class was, as the name suggests, a phase of education for receiving and preparing young children for primary schools, and from the early 1990s to September 2000 this practice continued unchanged; Reception classes were part of the Key Stage 1 and its assessment procedures. In 2000, when the new Foundation Stage was established, Reception became for the first time part of the Foundation Stage. Table 1 on statutory guidance presents the main changes discussed here.

Initially the whole class Literacy and Numeracy Hours, as the key part of the National Literacy and Numeracy Strategies (DfEE 1998; DfEE 1999b), were also introduced in all Reception classes. The termly lists of learning objectives that had to be achieved quickly became a reality in Reception classes. Children throughout the primary school were now typically organized in ability groups because of the explicit recommendations of the National Literacy Strategy (DfEE 1998). It became acceptable to label many 4- and 5-year-old children on entry to school as 'low ability' or 'low achieving' (David 2003) simply because of their lack of engagement in or previous knowledge of formal aspects of literacy. Young bilingual learners were particularly vulnerable and were typically placed in 'low ability' groups because of their perceived or actual lack of English knowledge (Robertson 2007). Summer-born children, children with Special Educational Needs (SEN) or those from low socio-economic backgrounds and some children of minority ethnic backgrounds (notably Gypsy, Roma and

Table 1: Statutory guidance for pupils aged 0–11 years in England since 1989

Statutory guidance for pupils 0–11 years in England since 1989

	Children's Ages											
	0	**1**	**2**	**3**	**4**	**5**	**6**	**7**	**8**	**9**	**10**	**11**
1989	No statutory guidance					National Curriculum: Key Stage 1 (Reception, Y1–2)			National Curriculum: Key Stage 2 (Y3–6)			
1996	No statutory guidance			'Desirable Outcomes' for Nursery		National Curriculum: (Key Stage 1 Reception, Y1–2)			National Curriculum: Key Stage 2 (Y3–6)			
1998–1999	No additional literacy or numeracy guidance				National Literacy and Numeracy Strategies: Key Stages 1 and 2 (Reception class and Y1–6)							
1999	No statutory guidance			Curriculum Guidance for Foundation Stage for Nursery and Reception.	Transition from the CGFS to the NC takes place Reception.	National Curriculum: Key Stage 1 (Y1–2)			National Curriculum: Key Stage 2 (Y3–6)			
2000	No additional literacy or numeracy guidance			Reception class is no longer part of KS1; subsequently Literacy and Numeracy Hours	become slightly shorter.	National Literacy and Numeracy Strategies: Key Stages 1 and 2 (Y1–6)							
2003	Every Child Matters (0–19 years)											
2007	Early Years Foundation Stage: Covers all educational provision for children 0–5 years (including the Reception class)					National Curriculum: Key Stage 1 (Y1–2) Transition from the EYFS to the NC to take place in Y1 spring term tern.			National Curriculum: Key Stage 2 (Y3–6)			

Traveller and African-Caribbean pupils) have consistently been over-represented, in 'low ability' groups (Ireson and Hallam 1999; Boaler *et al.* 2000).
Children's movement between different groups is by now recognized as another
persistent problem: once labelled as 'low ability' or 'low achieving', these labels
tend to stick regardless of changes in children's aptitude, interest or levels of
maturity, or even changes in children's actual progress. Boaler (2005) reveals a
particularly chilling statistic: 88 per cent of all 4-year-olds placed in ability
groups will remain in the same group until they leave school.

In 2000, when the Curriculum Guidance for the Foundation Stage was
introduced (DfEE 1999a), Reception classes were no longer part of Key Stage 1
and many settings began to make big changes. Literacy and Numeracy hours
became shorter, the opportunities to be outside were increased, and play was an
accepted part of the curriculum. Schools that had a nursery class (for rising 4-
year-olds) often established Early Years Units, and in many cases Nursery and
Reception children began to share the same space and resources. Schools where
there was no nursery provision sometimes struggled to establish the new
Foundation Stage ethos. Various authors (David 2003; Drummond 2004)
identified problems with Reception classes and pointed out that generally
Reception classes provided a poorer range of 'activities' and 'facilities' than
Local Authority early years settings (David 2003).

Reception classes have remained an anomaly; it is as if schools are unsure
whether 4–5-year-old children belong to the Foundation Stage or to Key Stage 1
and, in fact, the recent changes in statutory guidance (Table 1) exemplify this.
The lines drawn between the curricula aimed at 4–5-year-old children keep
shifting. Initially, in 2000, the transition to Key Stage 1 took place in Reception
classes and in the summer term, whereas a few years later the transition had
shifted to Year 1 and its autumn term, and currently it is taking place in Year 1
spring term.

It is clear that in spite of the major change of including the Reception class in
the Foundation Stage in 2000, the Strategies have continued to have a powerful
impact on general early years pedagogy. In Reception classes teachers have
continued to provide fewer play-based and practical, first-hand learning
experiences, all of which have a negative impact on children's spontaneity and
independence (Moyles *et al.* 2002).

Boisterous and exuberant children – often boys – have also become a steadily
increasing 'problem' in early years' classrooms (as well as in primary schools in
general) because they find it difficult to conform to teachers' expectations and
refuse to listen passively for the required length of time. This is particularly true
of literacy sessions which still often follow the conventions of a three-part
Literacy Hour lesson. Typically the one-hour lesson consists of an initial whole
class teaching input, which is followed by shorter independent tasks, and
concludes in whole-class 'plenary' or discussion. In the last seven years the
Curriculum Guidance for the Foundation Stage (DfEE 1999a) has not succeeded
in reducing the impact of the Strategies or improved the organization of the
teaching of literacy and, consequently, the new Early Years Foundation Stage
Profile recognizes 'boys' and their interests and energy levels as an area of
concern:

National data shows that boys attain less well than girls across all areas of learning and that more girls are working securely within the early learning goals than boys. The difference is particularly marked in communication, language and literacy, and may in part reflect that the learning experiences on offer may not capture the interests or allow for the energy of some children. When building provision, practitioners should consider whether they are incorporating a wide enough range of activities to address these issues. [...] This requires provision that enables them to flourish regardless of their learning style, whether quiet or exuberant, preferring the outdoors or the classroom, methodical or favouring trial and error. (DCSF 2008)

It remains to be seen how these recommendations are taken up by teachers, schools and Ofsted inspectors.

Every Child Matters

The Every Child Matters (ECM) agenda was first introduced in 2003 in the Green Paper 'Every Child Matters' (DfES 2003a) and a year later it became a part of the Children Act 2004. The ECM covers all educational settings for children between birth and 19 years, and aims to ensure that all services work more closely together. At the heart of ECM are five outcomes:

Every Child Matters is all about improving the life chances of all children, *reducing inequalities* and helping them achieve what they told us they wanted out of life:
- Be healthy [...]
- Stay safe [...]
- Enjoy and achieve [...]
- Make a positive contribution [...]
- Achieve economic well-being. (DfES 2003:2 emphasis added)

From the onset the stated aim of the ECM is to reduce inequalities. This may not be enough in developing a more equal society (Hill 2009, this volume) but it is a start. The five outcomes also relate to the government's recent social or community cohesion agenda. The Education and Inspections Act 2006 introduced a duty on all maintained early years settings and schools in England to promote community cohesion, and on Ofsted to report on the ways in which schools engage with this agenda (DCSF 2007). Both ECM and the community cohesion agenda are positively bold and exciting aims for all early years' settings and primary schools. The changes for example in developing extended schools – providing wrap-around care in children's centres, or breakfast, after-school or homework clubs in schools, and opening schools and collaborating more with local communities – are already beginning to take place. In policy terms this marks a shift in locating children's educational needs more closely with families, communities and the society at large, rather than inside a single classroom.

The Every Child Matters agenda is positive and ambitious and will require years of consistent collaboration to ensure that its outcomes are being achieved.

There are some further positive moves that will work towards making school learning a more equal and positive experience for a wide range of children. Personalized learning, inclusion and collaboration are key aspects of the ECM agenda (Tutt 2006), and it would seem inevitable that a whole school approach in fostering these, together with other agencies and families and communities, will improve *all* children's learning. As Tutt notes:

> This programme on its own [*personalized learning, inclusion and collaboration*] would provide enough for schools to get their teeth into and holds out the promise of increased choice for pupils, better support for families, and schools taking collective responsibility for all students in the area. (Tutt 2006:213)

However, these aims of striving towards equality, and thereby improving all children's learning experiences, are in direct competition with the government's other aims, namely with the raising standards agenda and its hard-line focus on performativity – on tests, league tables and formal literacy and numeracy targets that are related to children's year groups. For example, the aim to personalize learning in Key Stages 1 and 2, as well as the first principle of Unique Child of the Early Years Foundation Stage (DfES 2007), are in direct opposition with the year-group targets and expectations.

In the light of the ECM, it is also curious to note the recent – and highly aggressive – emphasis on phonics teaching which also seems to work towards blocking the schools' attempts to engage with and work towards the ECM outcomes. In 2006 Jim Rose's controversial report, 'Independent Review of the Teaching of Reading' (DfES 2006a) recommended that synthetic phonics are to be taught as discrete lessons from Reception class onwards, and the following summer 'Letters and Sounds' (DfES 2007) (the government's own synthetic phonic guidance pack) was distributed free to all schools. In September 2007, the new style of synthetic phonics teaching became statutory. The statutory expectations were altered and now the National Curriculum and its Key Stage 1 English programme of study has been amended to reflect the report's conclusion that 'children should learn to employ their phonic knowledge as their first strategy in reading'. Similarly, the early learning goals were amended to include a systematic phonic approach.

The report and its 'simple view of reading' have been highly contested (Clark 2006; Wyse and Jones 2007) because they lack theoretical substance and sound international research evidence. While the activities promoted within Letters and Sounds (DfES 2007) are often fun and interesting for young learners, the expectation that all children should reach similar levels of reading, and at the same time in the same year group, is puzzling and goes against Early Years Foundation Stage principles. Similarly, teaching decontextualized bits of knowledge to young children, does not match up with general theories of learning (Donaldson 1978).

Meanwhile, every year, new groups of children start school for the first time. Will their teachers continue to muddle through competing and contradictory educational aims? Will the children, like Zeynep, be met by unrealistic expectations and a need to conform? What impact will this pressure have on their learning and on their learner identity? Will they maintain their resilience and a high level of motivation to continue to explore the word around then?

Zeynep's bubbles, pretty as they were, burst a long time ago. What will happen to the ECM outcomes?

Conclusion

Competing and contradictory aims and a need for teachers to muddle through these aims seem to be set to last for some years to come. At the time of writing, two influential reports on primary schools are beginning to publish their main recommendations. The first, the Cambridge review of primary education – set up independently from the government and led by Robin Alexander (Alexander 2009) – calls for major changes in education. The three-year review involved more than 70 academics, thousands of children, parents and teachers and produced 29 reports. It called for SATs and league tables to be scrapped, and the final report (to be published in 2009) is to provide suggestions for managing the suggested transition period. It lists 12 aims for primary pupils (well-being, engagement, empowerment, autonomy, encouraging respect and reciprocity, promoting interdependence, citizenship, celebrating culture, exploring fostering skills, exciting imagination and enacting dialogue).

At the same time, another review – this time set up by the government and led by Sir Jim Rose (knighted soon after his 'Independent Review of Teaching of Reading' (DfES 2006a)) – is beginning to publish its preliminary findings (Rose 2008). This review, once fully published, is also likely to be calling for major changes such as the primary curriculum to be organized in six areas of learning (very similar to those of the Early Years Foundation Stage) and maintaining a strong focus on literacy and numeracy. It is also likely to recommend that all children will start in the Reception class the term after their 4th birthday. As earlier discussed, the problem of the school starting age is not so much 'when' they start, but rather 'what' they start (Brooker 2008), and as a highly prescribed teaching programmes for phonics is likely to last for some years in all early years classrooms, the changes to the Reception year are deeply worrying.

Regardless of the possible changes taking place in future schools, the central aim of Reggio Emilia pre-schools is still as well-timed and significant for early years and primary school teachers in England as it was during Loris Malaguzzi's time in Italy (Rinaldi 2005). Malaguzzi wrote about listening to and learning to understand 'the hundred languages of children'. This notion of 'hundred languages' was used as a metaphor for understanding the various idiosyncratic and contextualized ways in which young children convey meaning. Zeynap was fluent in her hundred languages, none of which yet included the English language, and her smiles and gazes towards the adults demonstrated a curiosity to know more and to share her learning experiences.

References

Alexander, R. (2009) *Cambridge Primary Review*. Online at http://www.primaryreview.org.uk/index.html (Accessed 6 July 2009).

Barrs, M., Ellis, S., Hester, H. and Thomas, A. (1990) *Patterns of Learning*. London: CLPE.

Boaler, J. (2005) 'The "Psychological Prisons" from which They Never Escaped: the role of ability grouping in reproducing social class inequalities'. *Forum*, Vol. 47, (2–3), 135–143.

Boaler, J., Wiliam, D. and Brown, M. (2000) 'Students' Experiences of Ability Grouping – disaffection, polarization and the construction of failure'. *British Educational Research Journal*, 26, (5), 631–648.

Brooker, L. (2008) *Supporting Transitions in the Early Years*. Maidenhead: Open University Press.

Clark, M. (2006) 'The Rose Report in Context: What will be its impact on the teaching of reading?' *Education Journal*, 97, 27–29. Online at http://www.tactyc.org.uk/pdfs/response_Rose.pdf (Accessed on 22 January 2009).

Clark, A. and Moss, P. (2001) *Listening to Young Children, The Mosaic Approach*. National Children's Bureau and Joseph Rowntree Foundation.

Curtis, P. (2009) 'Where now after damning indictment of education?' *Guardian*, 20 February, p.17.

David, T. (2003) *What do we know about teaching young children?* Online at http://www.standards.dfes.gov.uk/eyfs/resources/downloads/eyyrsp1.pdf. (Accessed 4 April 2008).

Davidson, J. (2004) 'Distinctive Education Policies in Wales'. *Forum*, 46, (2), 46–51.

DCSF (Department for Children, Schools and Families (2007) *Guidance on the duty to promote Community Cohesion*. London: DCSF Publications. Online at http://www.teachernet.gov.uk/_doc/11635/Guidance%20on%20the%20duty%20to%20promote%20community%20cohesion%20pdf.pdf. (Accessed 12 December 2008).

DCSF (Department for Children, Schools and Families) (2008) *The Early Years Foundation Stage, Profile Handbook*. London: QCA.

DfEE (Department for Education and Employment) (1998) *The National Literacy Strategy: Framework for Teaching*. London: HMSO.

DfEE (Department for Education and Employment) (1999a) *The National Curriculum Handbook for primary teachers in England*. London: DfEE and QCA.

DfEE (Department for Education and Employment) (1999b) *The National Numeracy Strategy: Framework for Teaching*. London: HMSO.

DfEE/QCA (Department for Education and Employment/Quality and Curriculum Authority) (2000) *Curriculum Guidance for the Foundation Stage*. London: DfEE/QCA.

DfEE/SCAA ((Department for Education and Employment/School Curriculum and Assessment Authority) (1996) *Desirable Outcomes for Children's Learning*. London: DfEE/SCAA.

DfES (Department of Education and Skills) (2002) *Birth to Three Matters; a framework for supporting children in their earliest years*. London: DfES.

DfES (Department of Education and Skills) (2003a) *Every Child Matters*. London: DfES.

DfES (Department of Education and Skills) (2003b) *National Standards for Under 8s Day Care and Childminding*. London: DfES.

DfES/QCA (2003) *Foundation Stage Profile*. London: QCA.

DfES (Department of Education and Skills) (2006a) *Independent Review of Reading*. London: DfES.

DfES (Department of Education and Skills) (2006b) Seamless transitions: supporting continuity in young children's learning. London: DfES.

DfES (Department of Education and Skills) (2007) *Letters and Sounds, principles and practice of high quality phonics/*. London: DfES. Online at http://nationalstrategies.standards.dcsf.gov.uk/node/84969. (Accessed 5 May 2008).

Donaldson, M. (1978) *Children's Minds*. London: Fontana.

Drummond, M. J. (2004) 'Inside a Foundation Stage: a good life for 4 and 5 year olds?' *Forum*, 46, (3), 104–105.

Duffy, B. 'The Curriculum from Birth to Six', in Pugh, G. and Duffy, B. (eds) (2006) *Contemporary Issues in the Early Years*. 4th edn. London: Sage Publications.

Dunlop, A-W. and Fabian, H. (2007) 'Informing Transitions in the Early Years, research, policy and practice'. Maidenhead: Open University Press.

Hautamäki, J., Harjunen, E., Hautamäki, A., Karjalainen, T., Kupiainen, S., Laaksonen, S., Lavonen, J., Pehkonen, E., Rantanen, P., Scheinin, P., with Halinen, I. and Jakku-Sihvonen, R. (2008) *PISA06 Finland: Analyses, Reflections and Explanations*. Helsinki: Ministry of Education Publications. Online at http://www.minedu.fi/export/sites/default/OPM/Julkaisut/2008/liitteet/opm44.pdf?lang = en. (Accessed 22 January 2009).

Ireson, J. and Hallam, S. (1999) 'Raising standards: is ability grouping the answer?' *Oxford Review of Education*, 25, (3), 343–358.

James, A. and Prout, A. (1997) *Constructing and Reconstructing Childhood*. 2nd edn. London: Falmer.

Kjørholt, A.T., Moss, P. and Clark, A. (2005) 'Beyond Listening: future prospects', in Clark, A., Kjørholt, A.T. and Moss, P. (eds) *Beyond Listening, children's perspectives on early childhood services*. Bristol: Policy Press.

Martin, R. P., Foels, P., Clanton, G. And Moon, K. (2004) 'Season of birth is related to child retention rates, achievement and rate of diagnosis of specific LD'. *Journal of Learning Disabilities*, 37, (4), 3–17.

Ministry of Social Affairs and Health (2004) *The Early Childhood Education and Care in Finland*. Helsinki: Ministry of Social Affairs and Health. Online at http://pre20090115.stm.fi/cd1106216815326/passthru.pdf. (Accessed on 22 January 2009).

Moyles, J., Adams, S. and Musgrove, A. (2002) *Study of Pedagogical Effectiveness in Early Learning (SPEEL)*. Research Report No363 DFES. London: HMSO.

Nutbrown, C. (2006) 'Watching and Listening: the Tools of Assessment', in G. Pugh and B. Duffy (eds) *Contemporary Issues in the Early Years*. 4th edn. London: Sage Publications.

Nutbrown, C., Clough, P. and Selbie, P. (2008) *Early Childhood Education: History, Philosophy and Experience*. London: Sage Publications.

Paley, V. G. (2004) *A Child's Work, importance of fantasy play*. London: Chicago University Press Ltd.

Payler, J. and Whitebread, D. (2007) *Summer-born children deserve equal opportunities*. Online at http://www.tactyc.org.uk/pdfs/Reflection_payler_whitebread.pdf. (Accessed 15 January 2009).

Riggall, A. and Sharp, C. (2008) 'The Structure of Primary Education: England and Other Countries' (Primary Review Research Survey 9/1) Cambridge: University of Cambridge Faculty of Education. Online at http://www.primaryreview.org.uk/Downloads/Int_Reps/6.Curriculum-assessment/Primary_Review_RS_9-1_report_Primary_education_structure_080208.pdf. (Accessed 15 January 2009).

Rinaldi, C. (2005) *In dialogue with Reggio Emilia*. London: Routledge.

Robertson, L. H. (2007) 'Bilingual Children's Story of Learning to Read', in J. Conteh, P. Martin, and L. H. Robertson, (eds) *Multilingual Learning Stories in Schools and Communities in Britain*. Stoke-On-Trent: Trentham Books Ltd.

Rose, J. (2008) *The Independent Review of Primary Curriculum: The Interim Report*. Online at http://publications.teachernet.gov.uk/default.aspx?PageFunction = productdetails &PageMode = publications&ProductId = BLNK-01010-2008& (Accessed 15 January 2009)

Sanders, D., White, G., Burge, B., Sharp, C., Eames, A., McEune, R. and Grayson, H. (2005). *A Study of the Transition from the Foundation Stage to key stage 1*. DFES: London.

Siraj-Blatchfrod, I., Sylva, K., Laugharne, J., Milton, E. and Charles, F. (2006) *Monitoring and Evaluating the Effective Implementation of the Foundation Phase (MEEIFP) Project Across Wales: Foundation Phase Pilot, Final Evaluation Report*. Cardiff: Welsh Assembly Government.

Soler, J. and Miller, L. (2003) 'The Struggle for Early Childhood Curricula: a comparison of the English Foundation Stage Curriculum, Te Whäriki and Reggio Emilia'. *International Journal of Early Years Education*,11, (1), 57–67.

STAKES (2004) *National Curriculum on Early Childhood Education and Care in Finland*. Helsinki: STAKES.

Tabors, P. (1997) *One Child, Two Languages: a guide for Preschool Educators of Children Learning English as a Second Language*. Baltimore: Paul Brookes Publishing.

Tutt, R. (2006) Reconciling the Irreconcilable: coping with contradictory agendas. *Forum*, 48, (2), 209–216.

Wood, E. (2007) Reconceptualising Child-Centred Education: contemporary directions in policy, theory and practice in early childhood. *Forum*, 49, (1–2), 119–133.

Wood, E. and Attfield, J. (2005) *Play, Learning and the Early Childhood Curriculum*. Second Edition. London: Paul Chapman Publishing.

Wyse, D. and Jones, R. (2007) *Teaching English, Language and Literacy*. 2nd edn. London: Routledge.

Chapter 2

Conceptual and Practical Issues for the Primary/Elementary School Teacher

Mike Cole

Introduction

This chapter is in two parts.[1] The first part deals with the conceptual issues of 'race' and racism; gender; disability; sexual orientation; and social class and capitalism. In the second part, I look at practical issues, specifically strategies we might use to overcome what I refer to as 'isms/phobias. In this part of the chapter, I address personal issues and institutional issues, and how the two might be connected. The chapter is based on the premise that we should develop the learning of all students without limits rather than entertain vague notions of 'to their full potential'; that we should reject ideas of fixed ability; enable students to make rational and informed decisions about their own lives; enable them to make rational and informed decisions about the lives of others; that we should foster critical reflection with a view to transformative action; and help empower students to be in a position to take transformative action.

Conceptual Issues

'Race' and racism

There is a consensus among certain geneticists and most social scientists that 'race' is a social construct rather than a biological given. That this is the case is explained succinctly by Steven Rose and Hilary Rose (2005). As they note, in 1972, the evolutionary geneticist Richard Lewontin pointed out that 85 per cent of human genetic diversity occurred *within* rather than *between* populations, and only 6–10 per cent of diversity is associated with the broadly defined 'races' (*Ibid.*). As Rose and Rose explain most of this difference is accounted for by the readily visible genetic variation of skin colour, hair form and so on. The everyday business of seeing and acknowledging such difference is not the same as the project of genetics. For genetics and, more importantly, for the prospect of treating genetic diseases, the difference is important, since humans differ in their susceptibility to particular diseases, and genetics can have something to say about this. However, beyond medicine, the use of the invocation of 'race' is increasingly suspect. Rose and Rose conclude that '[w]hatever arbitrary boundaries one places on any population group for the purposes of genetic research, they do not match those of conventionally defined races'. For example, the DNA of native Britons contains traces of multiple waves of occupiers and migrants. 'Race', as a scientific concept, Rose and Rose conclude, 'is well past its sell-by date' (*ibid.*). For these reasons, I would argue that 'race' should be put in inverted commas whenever one needs to refer to it.

Racism, however, is, of course, self-evidently real enough, and, indeed, like inequalities associated with the other conceptual issues discussed in this chapter, a major worldwide problem. In order for teachers to deal with racism, they need to have an awareness of what it means. My view is that we should adopt a wide-ranging definition of racism, rather than a narrow one based, as it was in the days of the British Empire, for example, on biology. Racism can be institutional or personal; it can be dominative (direct and oppressive) as opposed to aversive (exclusion and cold-shouldering) (Kovel 1988); it can be overt or covert; intentional or unintentional; biological and/or cultural. Attributes ascribed to ethnic groups can also be seemingly positive, as, for example, when whole groups are stereotyped as having strong cultures or being good at sport. Such stereotypes may well be followed up, respectively, with notions that 'they are taking over', or 'they are not so good academically'. The point is to be wary of attributing any stereotypes to ethnic groups. All stereotypes are *at least potentially* racist.

Non-colour-coded racism and religious hatred

Racism directed at white people is not new and has a long history, for example, anti-Irish racism in Britain (Mac an Ghaill 2000) and, of course, anti-Jewish and anti-Slavonic racism are predominant factors in twentieth-century history. The continued persecution of Gypsy Roma Travellers in Britain is also a factor. In addition, Sivanandan has identified a new form of racism, primarily directed at people from the NJCEU coming to the UK: xeno-racism. He defines it as follows: 'it is a racism ... that cannot be colour-coded, directed as it is at poor whites as well ... [it] ... bears all the marks of the old racism. (Sivanandan 2001:2). There has been evidence in the media of xeno-racism directed at NJCEU people (e.g. Belfast Today 2006; BBC News 2007), and of racism of NJCEU pupils directed at Asian and black pupils in the UK (Glenn and Barnett 2007). Certain tabloids (in particular *The Sun*) have unleashed anti-Polish rhetoric on a regular basis in recent years. Xeno-racism and xeno-racialisaton: the process of falsely categorizing people from the NJCEU (Cole 2008b:124–126) thus need careful attention from antiracists in the UK and elsewhere.

Islamophobia, which has greatly increased in a number of countries worldwide, is also not necessarily based on skin colour. Moreover, though often triggered by (perceived) symbols of the Muslim faith, Islamophobia is not necessarily religion-based, and, though a form of racism, needs to be addressed as a discrete phenomenon. However, more generally, discrimination on religious grounds also needs serious attention. In this regard, it is important and significant that The Racial and Religious Hatred Act was passed in the UK in 2006 (Office of Public Sector Information 2006), making provision about offences involving stirring up hatred against persons on racial or religious grounds.

The implications for education are as follows. Education plays a role in reproducing racism (monocultural and much multicultural education), but also has a major role to play in undermining racism (antiracist education). Monocultural education in the UK is to do with the promotion of so-called British values;[2] multicultural education is about the celebration of diversity and has often been tokenistic and patronizing, and antiracist education focuses on undermining racism (Cole 1998; Cole and Blair 2006).

Modern technology has major implications for delivering antiracist multi-cultural education, in that it allows people to speak for themselves, via websites and email. It is highly likely that xeno-racism will filter down into schools in the UK, and impact on day-to-day pupil interaction. How this will affect intra- and inter-ethnic relations in schools is largely unforeseen. What is clear is that anti-xeno-racist multicultural education must feature largely in UK schools' priorities. Unfortunately, antiracist multicultural education appears to be under threat from the Education and Inspections Act (2006) which came into effect in September, 2007. The Act introduced a duty on the governing bodies of maintained schools to promote 'community cohesion'. Following Wetherell, Lafleche & Berkeley (eds) 2007, Andy Pilkington (2007:14) distinguishes between 'hard' and 'soft' versions of community cohesion, the former viewing community cohesion and multiculturalism as ineluctably at loggerheads and insisting that we abandon the divisiveness evident in multiculturalism and instead should adhere to British values. The hard version of 'community cohesion' is thus monocultural. The 'soft' version, on the other hand, views community cohesion as complementing rather than replacing multiculturalism. In addition, the 'soft' version recognizes that the promotion of community cohesion requires inequality and racism to be addressed. Unsurprisingly, the then New Labour Secretary of State for Communities, Ruth Kelly favours the hard version (for a discussion, see Cole 2009:74–75). The resolve of antiracist educators to keep antiracism as the priority is thus more important than ever.

Gender

Generally speaking a distinction is made between 'sex' and 'gender', with sex being biological and gender being constructed. These essentialized categories of male and female have important consequences in society, for you are either 'in' the category or 'outside' of it (Woodward 2004). Within a patriarchal society the male is the norm and women are the 'other' (Paechter 1998) However, it is argued that gender roles are learned and are relative to time and place. In other words, what are considered 'acceptable modes of dress' or body language for males and females vary dramatically through history and according to geographical location (this is not to say, of course, that everyone in a given society conforms to such norms – there are many examples throughout history, and, of course, today, of people who have refused to conform).

Davies (1993) has shown that, from their earliest years, children hold strong views about their gender positioning and that gender identities are constructed and learned throughout schooling. Schools have traditionally reproduced gender categorization and, as Francis (1998) suggests, children work hard at constructing and maintaining their gender identities. However, she also points out that gender constructions are only one part of the children's identities and that for example 'race', ethnicity (e.g. Connolly 1998; Archer 2003) and social class (see Reay 2006) are also part of their identities and these can compete with or reinforce gender stereotypes. For example, there are undoubtedly differences between boys' and girls' development and progress in reading and writing. However, there is sometimes an oversimplification of the debate about gender and achievement in English as it is not all boys *per se* who are underachieving but particularly those from lower socio-economic groups (Coultas 2007; Francis and Skelton 2005; Hill 2008).

Many schools today are aware of their role in providing a curriculum free of bias and a curriculum which is emancipatory. Many schools are also aware of the power that the structures, rules and regulations can have in promoting sexism. The curriculum, actual and hidden, can be non-sexist, or it can be anti-sexist (George 1993). In other words, schools can make sure that they do not promote sexism, or they can actively promote anti-sexism. Traditionally, there has been concern among feminists and their supporters about the way in which schooling has reproduced gender inequalities, particularly with respect to female subordination. More recently, since the late twentieth century, now that it has become apparent that many boys are now being out-performed academically by girls, there has been more general media and government concerns about boys. It is important to note that for many years girls had been disadvantaged by the education system with very little media attention being given to the problem. Indeed, in the 1950s and 1960s in the UK, it was acknowledged that girls' literacy and numeracy skills were superior to those of boys and that, as a consequence, to achieve a grammar school place, girls had to score far higher than boys in the 11 + (Gaine and George 1999; George 2004). In England and Wales, it has only been with the compulsory assessment and testing following the introduction of the National Curriculum that girls' superior achievement has become visible, provoking a minor 'moral panic'. In fact boys are actually improving year on year. Head (1999) points to a much more serious issue in relation to a number of adolescent boys which is their alienation from not only schooling but from society in general.[3] He notes the disproportionate number of boys who are excluded from schools, are deemed dyslexic, suffer from ADHD and attempt suicide. It is not all plain sailing for girls either. Much of the recent work which focuses on girls, indicates that they are now caught between two competing discourses. They are valued for being caring and selfless, putting the concerns of their friends first, but at the same time they have to be competitive and individualistic in order to maintain their current successes in school (e.g. George 2007).

If many boys are now being out-performed by girls, this is not to say, of course, that schooling does not continue to reproduce other forms of sexism, of which females are at the receiving end. For example, boys often still dominate space and talk in mixed-sex classrooms, and schools and university education departments suffer from an over-representation of men in higher positions, which is a reflection of the wider society. Women despite their 'schooling success' still occupy the low ranks in most areas of work and their earning potential is still far worse than it is for men, with women in the UK earning approximately 80 per cent of a man's wage. Indeed, nearly 40 years after the first Women's Liberation Conference, held at Ruskin College, Oxford, in 1970, as Jane Kelly (2006:7) argues, women are still far from having achieved equality. This is with respect to the demands made at that conference which included equal pay, the availability of childcare facilities for women at all times, free contraception, and abortion on demand (Kelly's chapter provides a comprehensive Marxist analysis of gender; for discussions on the way in which sexism impacts on schooling, on differential achievement and what can be done about it; see also Gaine and George 1999; Hirom 2001; Martin 2006; and Skelton *et al.* 2006).

Disability

Richard Rieser (2006a:135–7) has made a distinction between what he calls the 'medical' and 'social models' of disability. The 'medical model' views the disabled person as the problem. Disabled people are to be adapted to fit into the world as it is. Where this is not possible, disabled people have historically been shut away in some specialized institution or isolated at home. The emphasis is on dependence, and calls forth pity, fear and patronizing attitudes (*ibid*:135). Rather than the focus being on the person, it tends to be on the impairment (*ibid.*). With the 'medical model' peoples' lives are handed over to others (Rieser 2006a:135). The 'medical model' creates a cycle of dependency and exclusion from which is difficult to break free (*ibid.*)

The 'social model' of disability, on the other hand, views the barriers that prevent disabled people from participating as being that which disables them (*ibid*). This model was first developed by Mike Oliver (1990) to counter what Oliver refers to as 'the personal tragedy theory of disability' (*ibid*:3). The 'social model' makes a fundamental distinction between *impairment* and *disability*. Impairment is 'the loss or limitation of physical, mental or sensory function on a long-term, or permanent basis' (Rieser 2006a:135), whereas The Disabled People's International (2005) defines disability as 'the outcome of the interaction between a person with an impairment and the environmental and attitudinal barriers he/she may face'. Supporters of this model are of the view that the position of disabled people and the oppression they face is socially constructed (Rieser 2006a:135). It is up to institutions in society to adapt to meet the needs of disabled people. This is the model favoured by disabled people.

The educational implications for each of these are the 'fixed continuum of provision' and the 'constellation of services' (Rieser 2006b:159–167). Under the former, associated with the 'medical model', the disabled person is slotted and moved according to the assessment of (usually non-disabled) assessors. This model is based on segregation (Rieser 2006b:159). With respect to the 'constellation of services', associated with the 'social model', provision is made for the disabled child in mainstream school. The child and the teacher under this model are backed up by a variety of support services (*ibid*:167).

Currently, there is a wide consensus among disability activists, many educational institutions and the British Government that the way forward is inclusion, which, of course, relates to the 'social model' and the 'constellation of services'. Rieser (2006b:174) commends the London Borough of Newham as a 'useful indicator of how such moves towards inclusion can occur in a poor, multicultural, inner-city area'. Newham's (undated) aims for an inclusive education are as follows:

- A policy of welcoming all children and young people whatever special educational needs or disability they have;
- Governors and staff trained in disability awareness issues;
- A policy which ensures recruitment and training of staff who will support and are committed to inclusion;
- An inclusion policy which is an integral part of the school development plan;
- A special needs policy which is rigorously implemented and reviewed.

Newham aims to promote high levels of achievement for all children and young people by:

- offering a wide range of learning and teaching experiences
- developing and implementing Individual Education Plans
- valuing the contribution of all children and young people
- having high expectations of all children and young people
- training staff to equip them to teach all children and young people.

It further aims to include all children and young people in all the activities of the school by:

- fostering supportive friendships among children and young people
- having clear codes of behaviour that take account of the particular difficulties that certain children and young people face
- working to enable children and young people to become more independent
- finding ways to overcome any difficulties caused by the physical environment, school rules or routines
- promoting diversity, understanding difficulties, recognizing and respecting individual differences
- taking positive steps to prevent exclusions, especially of children and young people with statements of special educational needs.

It aims finally to work in partnership with parents and carers by:

- welcoming parents and carers into the school
- making written and spoken language accessible
- dealing with parents and carers with honesty, trust and discretion.
- taking time, sharing information, listening and valuing contributions in meetings.

(for more information, see London Borough of Newham 2007)

There is an urgent need for all mainstream state schools to follow Newham's lead, and for major investment, both financial and social, to make genuine inclusion a reality.

Sexual orientation

Sexual orientation has often been ignored in education. There are a number of reasons why it should be central. First, sexual orientation is an issue for every teacher, primary as well as secondary; for example, there is evidence that some children identify as gay or lesbian in the primary years (NUT 1991:7; Epstein 1994:49–56; Letts IV and Sears 1999). For this reason and to militate against the normalization of homophobic attitudes, it is important that sexualities education starts at an early age. In this respect, an important project is *No Outsiders: Researching Approaches to Sexualities Equality in Primary Schools*, a 28-month research project based in primary schools and funded by the UK-based Economic and Social Research Council. It involves a team of primary teachers from three areas of the UK who will develop ideas and resources to address lesbian, gay, bisexual and transgender equality in their own schools and their communities. The outcomes will be disseminated via the Teacher Training Resource Bank, a documentary film and an edited book of teaching ideas.[4]

Second, in most schools, lesbians, gay men and bisexuals will be members of the teaching and other staff. In some schools, there will be transgender members of staff. Some parents/carers will lesbian, gay, bisexual or transgender (LGBT), and some pupils will be open about their sexual orientation. Virtually all children will be aware of issues of sexual orientation. To this end, a project at Bishop Grosseteste University College Lincoln (Morris and Woolley 2008), undertaken by academic and support staff and undergraduate students, has produced the *Family Diversities Reading Resource*, an annotated bibliography of over one hundred quality children's picture books showing diverse families (including single parent, two and three parent, lesbian and gay parent and extended families). These texts explore ways of valuing difference in families and among children. Making such resources available to children in schools is essential if they are not to feel that their own family background is undervalued or even invisible within the formal learning environment.

Third, ignoring sexual orientation and homophobia is unprofessional and illegal in the UK. Harassment on the grounds of sexual orientation is unprofessional conduct. New equalities regulations will outlaw discrimination towards LGBT people in the provision of goods and services as well as employment.

Homophobia is an unacceptable feature of society and there is evidence that lesbian and gay young people experience bullying at school, including physical acts of aggression, name calling, teasing, isolation and ridicule (see Ellis with High 2004; see also Forrest 2006; and the Stonewall website: http://www.stonewall.org.uk/stonewall). There is also evidence that young people who experience homophobic violence are likely to turn to truancy, substance abuse, prostitution or even suicide. Lesbian, gay and bi-sexual pupils should be listened to and should be encouraged to seek parental/carer advice and/or encouraged to refer to other appropriate agencies for advice. Their experiences of homophobia and harassment should not be dismissed as exaggerated or exceptional. Homophobic 'jokes', remarks or insults should always be challenged.

It should be pointed out here that, given growing research into boys, girls and heterosexualities, and the links between homophobia and misogyny, sexual

bullying (from homophobia to heterosexual harassment) encompasses more than issues connected to LGBT identities (Renold 2000a, b, 2005, 2006).[5]

The curriculum should tackle homophobia and transphobia,[6] as well as other forms of discrimination. Just to give some examples: in order to promote equality for lesbians, gays, bisexuals and transgendered people, a range of family patterns and lifestyles can be illustrated in fiction used in English lessons, while drama can help to examine feelings and emotions. Reference can be made to famous lesbian, gay, bisexual and transgender writers, sports personalities, actors, singers and historical figures. (For a fuller discussion of sexual orientation, see Forrest and Ellis 2006; for fuller discussions of sexual orientation and education, see Williamson 2001 and Forrest 2006 and Ellis 2007; for a discussion of transphobia, see Whittle *et al.* 2007).

Social class and capitalism

Social class defines the social system under which we live. For this reason, among others, social class has tended to be left out of teacher education programmes, except in the narrow, though nonetheless fundamentally important, sense of more opportunities for working class children. This is because discussion of social class and capitalism poses a threat to the *status quo*, much more profound than the other equality issues discussed in this chapter.

There are two major ways in which social class is classified. First, there is 'social class' as based on the classification of the Office for Population Census Studies (OPCS), first used in the census of 2001. Based on occupation, life-style and status, it accords with popular understandings of social class differentiation; in particular, the distinctions between white-collar workers, on the one hand, and blue-collar workers and those classified as long-term unemployed, on the other. However, it is not without its difficulties:

- it masks the existence of the super-rich and the super-powerful (the capitalist class, and the aristocracy);
- it glosses over and hides the antagonistic and exploitative relationship between the two main classes in society (the capitalist class and the working class); and
- it segments the working class and thereby disguises the ultimate common interests of white-collar, blue-collar and long-term unemployed workers (Hill and Cole 2001:151–3; Kelsh and Hill 2006).

Thus, while for sociological analyses in general, it has its uses, its problematic nature should not be forgotten.

The other way to conceive social class is the Marxist definition, in which those who have to sell their labour power in order to survive are the working class, *whatever their status or income*, and those who own the means of production and exploit the working class by making profits from their labour are the capitalist class (see Cole 2008b for an analysis; see also Hickey 2006).

In post-World War II Britain, the economic system was generally described as a mixed economy; that is to say, key sectors (e.g. the railways, gas, water and electricity and the telephones) of the economy were owned by the state and other sectors were owned by private capitalist enterprises. This is no longer the case and not only is globalized neoliberal capitalism nearly universal, it is openly exalted as the only way the world can be run, even if, with the 2008–2009 'credit crunch', there is more recognition that neoliberal capitalism needs a degree of regulation.

With respect to education, it is my view that instead of commodifying knowledge in the interests of global capitalism, education should be about empowerment, where visions of an alternative way of running the planet (Venezuela is a good example; see Cole 2008c) become part of the mainstream curriculum. As Peter McLaren (2002) concludes his book, *Life in Schools*, schools should cease to be defined as extensions of the workplace or as frontline institutions in the battle for international markets and foreign competition. Paulo Freire (1972) urged teachers, to detach themselves and their pupils from the idea that they are agents of capital, where *banking education* (the teacher deposits information into an empty account) is the norm, and to reinvent schools as democratic public spheres where meaningful *dialogue* can take place. No space is provided for a discussion of *alternatives* to neoliberal global capitalism, such as world democratic socialism (see Cole 2008b for a discussion; see also Hill 2008). Discussing socialism in schools may be seen as one of the last taboos (Cole 2008d). It is time to move forward and bring such discussions into the classroom.

Practical Issues

Educators, in my view should:

- develop the learning of all pupils without limits rather than entertain vague notions of 'to their full potential'[7]
- reject ideas of fixed ability
- enable pupils to make rational and informed decisions about their own lives
- enable pupils to make rational and informed decisions about the lives of others
- foster critical reflection, with a view to transformative action
- help empower pupils to be in a position to take transformative action.

Equality and equal opportunity issues have both an institutional and legislative dimension and an individual dimension.

The personal challenge

It needs to be stressed that people's positions *vis-à-vis* the equality issues outlined in this chapter are not *natural*, but reflect particular social systems. Inequalities are not *inevitable* features of any society; they are social constructs, crucial terrains between conflicting forces in any given society. In other words, societies do not *need* to be class-based; to have racialized hierarchies; to have one sex dominating another. I do not believe that people are *naturally* homophobic or transphobic, or prone to marginalizing the needs of disabled people. On the contrary, we are socialized into accepting the norms, values and customs of the social systems in which we grow up. This is a very powerful message for teachers. If we *learn* to accept or to promote inequalities, we can also *learn* to challenge them. Schools have traditionally played an important part in socializing pupils to accept the *status quo*. They have also played and continue to play a major role in undermining that process (e.g. Hill (ed.) 2009).

In the personal challenge it is first important to distance oneself from the notion of 'political correctness', a pernicious concept invented by the Radical Right, and which, unfortunately, has become common currency. The term 'political correctness' was coined to imply that there exist (Left-wing) political demagogues who seek to impose their views on equality issues, in particular appropriate terminology, on the majority. In reality, nomenclature changes over time. To take the case of ethnicity, in the twenty-first century, terms such as 'negress' or 'negro' or 'coloured' were nomenclatures which at one time were considered quite acceptable, and are now considered offensive. Anti-racists are concerned with *respect* for others' choice of nomenclature and, therefore, are careful to acknowledge changes in it, changes which are decided by oppressed groups themselves (bearing in mind that there can be differences of opinion among such groups). The same applies to other equality issues. Thus, for example, it has become common practice to use 'working class' rather than 'lower class'[8] 'lesbian, gay, bisexual and transgender' rather than 'sexually deviant'; 'disability' rather than 'handicap'; and 'gender equality' rather than 'a woman's place'. Using current and acceptable nomenclature is about the fostering of a caring and inclusive society, not about 'political correctness' (Cole and Blair 2006).

Haberman (1995:91–2) suggests five steps which he considers to be essential for new teachers to overcome prejudice. I have adapted and considerably expanded Haberman's arguments and replaced his psychological concept of prejudice with the more sociological concept of 'ism/phobia'[9] in order to encompass racism, xeno-racism, sexism, disablism, classism and homophobia/ transphobia/ Islamophobia/ exenophobia. I have also provided my own examples of how each step might develop. It is important to point out that these steps apply to all members of the educational community, as well as new teachers, as specified by Haberman. I have also created a sixth step.

The first step is a thorough self-analysis of the content of one's ism/phobia. What form does it take? Is it overt or covert? Is it based on biology or is it cultural? Is it dominative (direct and oppressive) or aversive (excluding and cold-shouldering) (Kovel 1988)? Is it intentional or unintentional?[10] Are my attitudes patronizing? This is, of course, a *process* rather than an event. In many ways, this step is the most crucial and difficult of the steps.

The second step is to seek answers to the question of source. How did I learn or come to believe these things? Did I learn to be ist/phobic from my parents/ carers? Did I become ist/phobic as a result of experiences at primary school or at secondary school? Was it in further education or in higher education? Did I pick up ism/phobia from my peers; from the media: from newspapers; from magazines; from the Internet? Was it a combination of the above? Why was I not equipped to challenge ism/phobia when I came across it?

Step three is to consider to what extent I am on the receiving end of, or how do I benefit from ism/phobia? How does it demean me as a human being to have these beliefs? On the other hand, how do I benefit psychologically and/or materially from holding these beliefs?

Step four is to consider how one's ism/phobia may be affecting one's work in education. Am I making suppositions about young people's behaviour or attitudes to life based on their social class, ethnicity, impairments, gender, sexual orientation, religion or belief, or nationality? Am I making negative or positive presumptions about their academic achievement? If there is evidence of low achievement, am I taking the necessary remedial actions? Am I making assumptions about the parents/carers of the young people in my care? Am I making assumptions about other members of the school community, based on the above?

Step five is the phase in which one lays out a plan explicating what one plans to do about one's ism/phobia. How do I propose to check it, unlearn it, counteract it and get beyond it? This can involve reading a text or texts and/or websites which address the issues. It should mean an ongoing update on equality/equal opportunities legislation.[11] It must certainly mean acquainting oneself with differential rates of achievements, and a critical analysis of the various explanations for this, centring on the explanations given by those who are pro-equality. It should mean acquainting oneself with various forms of bullying related to isms/phobia and their effects. It might mean going on a course or courses.

It is not being argued that these five steps will necessarily occur in an individual's psyche (although they might), or spontaneously. Indeed, they can often be better addressed in group situations. I am suggesting that, as in this chapter, encouragement should be given for individuals to take these steps. Such encouragement could be done in the form of an introductory session for student or new teachers (and other educational workers). Also it is not being suggested that this is *merely* an individual process. It could be followed up with the sharing of questions and answers in groups and publicly. This could then progress (in practice) to an exploration of how a shared analysis of the five steps relates to the work of the school and the community; local, national and international.

The personal and the institutional

After or during these five steps, the sixth step should be to connect the personal with the institutional, in order to undermine isms/phobia, and to promote equality. This might involve becoming active in one's school and/or community and/or becoming a trade union activist.[12] It might involve joining and working for a socialist/Marxist political party. It might also involve becoming active in local, national or international lobby groups. It should involve making the combating of isms/phobia and the promotion of equality central to one's work in educational institutions, in both the actual curriculum (what is on the timetable) and the hidden curriculum (everything else that goes on in educational institutions). It might involve writing and lecturing about isms/phobia and equality.

Conclusion

In this chapter, I have outlined the main conceptual issues with respect to equal opportunity and equality issues in schools. Schools and other educational institutions should be places where personal and group reflection on *and action on* equality issues is central, and an integral part of the institutions' ethos. If we are to relate to and empower our pupils, if we are to engage in meaningful and successful teaching, we need to begin with the pupils' comprehension of their daily life experiences, whether in pre-school or university. From their earliest years, children's self-concepts are tainted by cultures of inequality. By starting from *their* description of these experiences, we are able to ground our teaching in concrete reality, then to transcend common sense and to move towards a critical scientific understanding of the world. This is the process by which teachers can support the process of the self-empowerment of tomorrow's children and young people. As stressed above, I firmly believe that we are not born ist/phobic. The way we think is a product of the society in which we live.[13] We can make important changes in societies as they are. However, in order to fully eradicate oppression of all forms, we need to change society, and indeed the world.

Acknowledgements

I would like to thank Viv Ellis, Rosalyn George, Emma Renold and Krishan Sood for their very helpful comments on an earlier draft of this chapter. As always, responsibility for any inadequacies remains mine.

Notes

[1] This is an updated version of a chapter that appeared in expanded form as the Introductory chapter in Cole 2008a

[2] There are a number of problems with the notion of 'British Values'. First, it assumes a parity of circumstance for all Britons, whereas the populace is deeply unequal in terms of ethnicity, social class and gender; second, it implies a consensus of values, when in fact these vary considerably according to ethnicity, social class and gender; third, it renders the economic system of global neoliberal capitalism and imperialism unproblematic – 'we all believe in this, because we are British' (see the discussion on social class below).

[3] In a social class-based society, where there is little hope for millions of young working-class people, such alienation often leads to anti-social behaviour. Young people need hope for the future, and expectations of a decent and fulfilling life, something apparent in countries such as Venezuela, but severely lacking in Britain (e.g. Cole 2008c).

[4] The project is led by Elizabeth Atkinson and Renée DePalma at the University of Sunderland, in collaboration with researchers at the University of Exeter and the Institute of Education (University of London), and a team of three research assistants. The project started on 1st September 2006 and will run until 31st December 2008. For further details, see http://www.nooutsiders.sunderland.ac.uk/

[5] However, it is not all bad news. Renold 2005 has explored the ways in which some young boys are playing around with homoerotic discourses in fun and pleasurable ways

(in contrast to the vast literature on homophobic talk) and girls queering heterosexuality through 'tomboyism'. The ability to queer normative gender and sexuality, however, remains restricted to the middle-classes.

6   Transphobia has been defined as 'an emotional disgust towards individuals who do not conform to society's gender expectations' (Hill and Willoughby 2005:91, cited in Whittle *et al.* 2007:21). Transphobia (by analogy with homophobia) refers to various kinds of aversions towards transsexuality and transsexual or transgendered people.
    • It often takes the form of refusal to accept a person's new gender expression.
    • Whether intentional or not, transphobia can have severe consequences for the targeted person; also, many transpeople experience homophobia as well, from people who associate gender identity disorder as a form of homosexuality.
    • Like other forms of discrimination such as homophobia, the discriminatory or intolerant behaviour can be direct (e.g. harassment, assault, or even murder) or indirect (e.g. refusing to take steps to ensure that transgender people are treated in the same way as cisgender (non-transgender) people.) (Action Against Homophobia and Transphobia, undated)

7   The book *Learning Without Limits* aims to challenge notions of fixed ability, and 'to build a new agenda for school improvement around the development of effective pedagogies that are free from ability labelling' (Hart *et al.* 2004:21). For a critical Marxist appraisal of the Learning Without Limits paradigm, see Cole 2008d; Yarker 2008; Cole 2008e.

8   As a Marxist, I recognize, of course, that the working class are structurally located in a subordinate position in capitalist societies, and, *in this sense*, are a 'lower class'. However, the nomenclature 'working class' is used to indicate respect for the class as a whole, a class which, as noted above, sells its labour power to produce surplus for capitalists in an exploitative division of labour.

9   For grammatical clarity, I have put 'ism/phobia' in the singular. Clearly, for many people it will be 'isms/phobia'. I also recognize that there are a number of positive 'isms' – Marxism, socialism; feminism; trade unionism among them.

10 These considerations are adapted from my definition of racism (see the "'Race' and racism' section of this chapter).

11 I do not deal with equalities legislation in this chapter, but see Nixon 2008; for up-to-date ongoing information about equalities legislation in England, see the Equality and Human Rights Commission (http://www.equalityhumanrights.com/en/Pages/default.aspx); for Wales which has some particularly progressive features, see Welsh Assembly Government: Equality and Diversity (http://new.wales.gov.uk/topics/equality/?lang=en); see also Chaney *et al.* 2007. My trade union, UCU, has a very good website on such legislation http://www.ucu.org.uk/index.cfm?articleid=1742).

12 It should be pointed out here that, as a matter of principle, all socialists and Marxists join trade unions and honour strikes and do not cross any picket lines, believing that industrial action is essentially a struggle over surplus value appropriated from workers' labour (for a discussion, see Cole 2008b, chapter 2).

13 Having visited Cuba on three occasions, I became even more convinced of the importance of socialization. Nearly 50 years of socialization in socialist values has had a dramatic effect all over the island. The selfish Thatcherite values abundant in the West are generally not apparent. They are apparent, however, in the tourist resorts and hotels, and in some of the *casas particulares* (private rented accommodation). With respect to Venezuela, with the projected programme for socialist values to be promoted in schools and workplaces, we are likely to see a further consolidation of socialist values and attitudes in that country.

References

Action Against Homophobia and Transphobia (undated) 'What is transphobia?'. Online at http://www.homophobia.org.uk (Accessed 20th December 2008)

Archer, L. (2003) *Race, Masculinity and Schooling*. Buckingham: Open University Press.

Callinicos, A. (2000) *Equality*. Oxford: Polity.

BBC News (2007) 'Poles in Redditch hit by racism'. Online at http://www.bbc.co.uk/herefordandworcester/content/articles/2007/03/22/breakfast_polish_racism_feature.shtml. (Accessed 18th January 2008).

Belfast Today (2006) 'Polish man hurt in vicious attack'. Online at http://www.belfasttoday.net/ViewArticle2.aspx?SectionID = 3425&ArticleID = 1532979. (Accessed 24th July 2006).

Chaney, P., Mackay, F. and McAllister, L. (2007) *Women, Politics and Constitutional Change*. Cardiff: University of Wales Press.

Cole, M. (1998) 'Racism, reconstructed multiculturalism and antiracist education'. *Cambridge Journal of Education*, 28, (1), 37–48.

Cole, M. (2008a) 'Introductory chapter: education and equality – conceptual and practical considerations, in M. Cole (ed.) *Professional Attributes and Practice: meeting the QTS standards*, 4th edn. London: Routledge.

Cole, M. (2008b) *Marxism and Educational Theory: Origins and Issues*. London: Routledge.

Cole, M. (2008c) 'The working class and the State Apparatuses in the UK and Venezuela: implications for education' *Educational Futures* 2, 2008.

Cole, M. (2008d) 'Learning Without Limits: a Marxist assessment', *Policy Futures in Education* 6 (4), 453-463. Online at http://www.wwwords.co.uk/pfie/content/pdfs/6/issue6_4.asp. (Accessed 27th February, 2008).

Cole, M. (2008e) 'Reply to Yarker' *Policy Futures in Education*, 6, (4) 468-469. Online at http://www.wwwords.co.uk/pdf/validate.asp?j = pfie&vol = 6&issue = 4&year = 2008&article = 8_Yarker_PFIE_6_4_web. (Accessed 21st December 2008).

Cole, M. (2009) *Critical Race Theory and Education: a Marxist response*. New York: Palgrave Macmillan.

Cole, M. and Blair, M. (2006) 'Racism and education: from Empire to New Labour', in M. Cole (ed.) *Education, Equality and Human Rights: issues of gender, 'race', sexuality, disability and social class*, 2nd edn. London: Routledge.

Coultas, V. (2007) *Gender and Talk Constructive Talk in Challenging Classrooms*. London: Routledge.

Connolly, P. (1998) *Racism, Gender Identities and Young Children*. London: Routledge.

Davies, B. (1993) *Shards of Glass*. Sydney: Allen Unwin.

Disabled People's International. (2005) 'Position Paper on the Definition of Disability'. Online at http://v1.dpi.org/lang-en/resources/details.php?page = 74 (Accessed 27th February 2008).

Ellis, V. (2007) 'Sexualities and schooling in England after Section 28: measuring and managing "at risk" identities'. *Journal of Gay and Lesbian Issues in Education*, 13–30.

Ellis, V. and High, S. (2004) 'Something more to tell you: gay, lesbian or bisexual young people's experiences of Secondary Schooling'. *British Educational Research Journal*, 30, (2), 213–25. April.

Epstein, D. (1994) 'Introduction', in D. Epstein (ed.) *Challenging Lesbian and Gay Inequalities in Education*. Buckingham: Open University Press.

Forrest, S. (2006) 'Straight talking: challenges in teaching and learning about sexuality and homophobia in schools', in M. Cole (ed.) *Education, Equality and Human Rights: issues of gender, 'race', sexuality, disability and social class*, 2nd edn. London: Routledge.

Forrest, S. and Ellis, V. (2006) 'The Making of Sexualities: sexuality, identity and equality', in M. Cole (ed.) *Education, Equality and Human Rights: issues of gender, 'race', sexuality, disability and social class*, 2nd edn. London: Routledge.

Francis, B. (1998) *Power Plays: Primary School Children's Construction of Gender Power and Adult Work*. Stoke on Trent: Trentham Books.

Francis, B. and Skelton, C. (2005) *Reassessing Gender and Achievement: questioning contemporary key debates*. London: Routledge.

Freire, P. (1972) *Pedagogy of the Oppressed*. Harmondsworth: Penguin.

Gaine, C. and George, R. (1999) *Gender, 'Race' and Class in Schooling. A New Introduction*. London: Falmer Press.

George, R. (1993) *Equal Opportunities in Schools. Principles, Policy and Practice*. Harlow: Longman.

George, R. (2004) The Importance of Friendship during Primary to Secondary School Transfer, in M. Benn and C. Chitty (eds). *A Tribute to Caroline Benn*. London: Continuum.

George, R. (2007) *Urban Girls Friendships: Complexities and Controversies*. Rotterdam: Sense Publications.

Glenn, J. and Barnett, L. (2007) 'Spate of racist complaints against Polish pupils'. *Times Educational Supplement*. 30th March.

Haberman, M. (1995) *Star Teachers of Children in Poverty*. West Lafayette, Indiana: Kappa Delta Pi.

Hart, S., Dixon, A., Drummond, M. J. and McIntyre, D. (2004) *Learning Without Limits*. Maidenhead: Open University Press.

Head, J. (1999) *Understanding the Boys: Issues of Behaviour and Achievement*. London: Routledge.

Hickey, T. (2006) 'Class and class analysis for the twenty-first century', in M. Cole (ed.) *Education, Equality and Human Rights: issues of gender, 'race', sexuality, disability and social class*, 2nd edn. London: Routledge/Falmer.

Hill, D. (2008) 'Caste, Race and Class: A Marxist Critique of Caste Analysis, Critical Race Theory; and Equivalence (or Parallellist) Explanations of Inequality'. *Radical Notes* (Delhi, India) Online at http://radicalnotes.com/component/option,com_frontpage/Itemid,1/

Hill, D. (ed.) (2009) *Contesting Neoliberal Education: Public Resistance and Collective Advance*. London/New York: Routledge.

Hill, D. and Cole, M. (eds) (2001) *Schooling and Equality: fact, concept and policy*. London: Routledge.

Hirom, K. (2001) 'Gender', in D. Hill and M. Cole (eds) (2001) *Schooling and Equality: fact, concept and policy*. London: Routledge.

Kelly, J. (2006) 'Women thirty-five years on: still unequal after all this time', in M. Cole (ed.) *Education, Equality and Human Rights: issues of gender, 'race', sexuality, disability and social class*, 2nd edn, London: Routledge

Kelsh, D. and Hill, D. (2006) 'The Culturalization of Class and the Occluding of Class Consciousness: The Knowledge Industry in/of Education'. *Journal for Critical Education Policy Studies*, 4 (1). Online at http://www.jceps.com/index.php?pageID=article&articleID=59

Kovel, J. (1988) *White Racism: a psychohistory*. London: Free Association Books.

Letts IV, W. J. and Sears, J. T. (eds) (1999) *Queering Elementary Education: Advancing the Dialogue about Sexualities and Schooling*. Lanham, MD: Rowman and Littlefield.

London Borough of Newham (undated) *Inclusive Education – our aims*. Online at http://www.newham.gov.uk/Services/InclusiveEducation/AboutUs/inclusiveeducationouraims.htm. (Accessed 27th February, 2008).

London Borough of Newham (2007) *Inclusive education strategy 2004–7*. Online at http://www.newham.gov.uk/NR/rdonlyres/27813CF3-A71F-4235-8F58-94C7C4FF492F/0/IES_Booklet.pdf. (Accessed 27th February, 2008).

Mac an Ghaill, M. (2000) 'The Irish in Britain: the invisibility of ethnicity and anti-Irish racism'. *Journal of Ethnic and Migration Studies*, 26, (1), 137–147.

Martin, J. (2006) 'Gender, education and the new millennium', in M. Cole (ed.) *Education, Equality and Human Rights: issues of gender, 'race', sexuality, disability and social class*, 2nd edn. London: Routledge.

McLaren, P. (2002) *Life in Schools*, 4th edn. Boston, MA: Pearson Education.

Macpherson, W. (1999) *The Stephen Lawrence Inquiry, Report of an Inquiry by Sir William Macpherson*. London: The Stationery Office.

Morris, J. and Woolley, R. (2008) *Family Diversities Reading Resource*. Lincoln: Bishop Grosseteste University College Lincoln.

National Union of Teachers (NUT). (1991) *Lesbians and Gays in Schools: an issue for every teacher*. London: National Union of Teachers.

Nixon, J. (2008) 'Statutory frameworks relating to teachers' responsibilities', in M. Cole (ed.) *Professional Attributes and Practice: meeting the QTS standards*, 4th edn. London: Routledge.

Office of Public Sector Information (OPSI). (2006) 'The Racial and Religious Hatred Act 2006 (Commencement No.1) Order 2007'. Online at http://www.opsi.gov.uk/si/si2007/uksi_20072490_en_1. (Accessed 20 December 2008).

Oliver, M. (1990) '*People with Established Locomotor Disabilities in Hospitals*' paper presented at a joint workshop of the Living Options Group and the Research Unit of the Royal College of Physicians. Online at http://www.leeds.ac.uk/disability-studies/archiveuk/Oliver/in%20soc%20dis.pdf. (Accessed 27th February, 2008).

Pilkington, A. (2007) '*From Institutional Racism to Community Cohesion: The Changing Nature of Racial Discourse in Britain*'. Inaugural professorial lecture, University of Northampton, November 29.

Paechter, C. (1998) *Educating the Other: gender, power and schooling*. London: Routledge.

Reay, D. (2006) 'Compounding inequalities: Gender and Class in Education' in C.Skelton, B. Francis and L. Smulyan (eds) (2006) *The SAGE Handbook of Gender and Education*. London: Sage.

Renold, E. (2000a) 'Coming out: gender, (hetero) sexuality and the primary school', *Gender and Education*, 12, (3), 309–327.

Renold, E. (2000b) 'Presumed Innocence: heterosexual, homophobic and heterosexist harassment in the primary school', *Childhood*, 9, (4), 415–434.

Renold, E. (2005) *Girls, Boys and Junior Sexualities: Exploring Children's Constructions of Gender and Sexuality in the Primary School*. London: Routledge.

Renold, E. (2006) 'They won't let us play * unless you're going out with one of them: girls, boys and Butler's "heterosexual matrix" in the primary years', *British Journal of Sociology of Education*, 27, (4).

Rieser, R. (2006a) 'Disability equality: confronting the oppression of the past', in M. Cole (ed.) *Education, Equality and Human Rights: issues of gender, 'race', sexuality, disability and social class*, 2nd edn. London: Routledge.

Rieser, R. (2006b) 'Inclusive education or special educational needs: the challenge of disability discrimination in schools', in M. Cole (ed.) *Education, Equality and Human Rights: issues of gender, 'race', sexuality, disability and social class*, 2nd edn. London: Routledge.

Rose, S. and Rose, H. (2005) 'Why we should give up on race: as geneticists and biologists know, the term no longer has any meaning'. The *Guardian*, April 9 2005. Online at http://www.guardian.co.uk/comment/story/00,,1455685,00.html. (Accessed 8 August 2006).

Skelton, C., Francis, B. and Smulyan, L. (eds) (2006) *The SAGE Handbook of Gender and Education*. London: Sage.

Sivanandan, A. (2001) 'Poverty is the new Black', *Race and Class* 43 (2), 2–5.

Williamson, I. (2001) 'Sexuality', in D. Hill and M. Cole. (eds) *Schooling and Equality: fact, concept and policy*. London: Routledge.

Whittle, S., Turner, L., Al-Alami, M. (2007) *The Engendered Penalties: Transgender and Transsexual People's Experience of Inequality and Discrimination*. London: The Equalities Review. Online at http://www.theequalitiesreview.org.uk/upload/assets/www.theequalitiesreview.org.uk/transgender.pdf. (Accessed 25th April, 2007).

Woodward, K (2004) *Questioning Identity: Gender, Class, Ethnicity*. London: Routledge.

Yarker, P. (2008), 'Learning Without Limits – a Marxist assessment: a response to Mike Cole' *Policy Futures in Education*, 6, (4), 464–468.

Chapter 3

Policy Context: New Labour, Social Inclusion and the Curriculum

Uvanney Maylor

Introduction

This chapter is concerned with New Labour's education policies on social inclusion in the curriculum. It seeks to examine the ways in which issues of social inclusion are framed and understood within contemporary education policy discourse. By reviewing recent policy initiatives the intention is to tease out the tensions, contradictions and challenges surrounding social inclusion in the curriculum. The arguments presented are premised on the view that there are multiple and potentially contradictory educational policies targeting social inclusion that lead to practices that may work against each other. These policies in turn have to compete with other policy agendas (such as raising standards, school choice) which give rise to differential outcomes in terms of social inclusion in the curriculum and wider school context. New Labour's emphasis on curriculum social inclusion is somewhat contradicted by its desire for improved educational standards, while social inclusion in the curriculum is largely undermined by the school realities of parental choice, school selection, setting by ability, target setting, standard assessment tests, GCSE examinations and league tables. All of which have served to exclude some groups of pupils rather than include all groups. Moreover, the policy discourse on social inclusion masks inequalities in schooling and curriculum which make the delivery of a socially inclusive curriculum difficult.

This chapter begins by outlining New Labour's expectations of curriculum social inclusion. It then explores some of the contradictions inherent in delivering a socially inclusive curriculum when the school system is not necessarily socially inclusive. Before concluding, attention is given to highlighting what a socially inclusive curriculum might encompass.

Social Inclusion in the National Curriculum

With the advent of New Labour in 1997 social inclusion came into prominence to challenge social exclusion (a feature of previous Conservative government education policies) and tackle educational inequality. Social inclusion has been a national educational policy priority and key statutory objective which teachers have been encouraged to engender through the National Curriculum Inclusion Statement (DfEE 1999) since1999. Explicit within the National Curriculum Inclusion Statement is the expectation that teachers will take account of the diverse needs and experiences of all pupils in their planning and teaching, and in the resources that are used to deliver their lessons. Acknowledging the needs of all pupils requires teachers to consider:

> Boys and girls, pupils with special educational needs, pupils with disabilities, pupils from all social and cultural backgrounds, pupils of different ethnic groups including Travellers, refugees and asylum seekers, and those from diverse linguistic, religious backgrounds (DfEE 1999).

In their delivery of a socially inclusive curriculum (in each subject) teachers are statutorily entrusted to value pupil diversity and enable pupils to develop an understanding of different groups, and at the same time view positively differences in others. A socially inclusive curriculum should allow pupils to see their identities, histories and experiences positively incorporated in the curriculum. At the same time, teachers are expected to have high expectations of all pupils, set suitable learning challenges and overcome potential barriers to learning and assessment for individual pupils and groups of pupils (DfEE 1999). This is to be facilitated by schools implementing a curriculum that is relevant to all children regardless of their background and is 'responsive to changes in society ... and the impact of economic, social and cultural change' (DfEE 1999). Underpinning the implementation of a socially inclusive curriculum is an expectation that teachers will challenge assumptions/stereotypes, prejudiced attitudes and racism in relation to class, disability, ethnicity, gender, culture, religion, language and sexuality. Challenging such as this is considered conducive to fostering the participation of all pupils in lessons 'fully and effectively' (DfEE 1999). As part of an inclusive curriculum Ofsted (2005) argue that the inclusion of 'race' equality concepts in lessons ought to be regarded as a normal part of effective teaching and learning. This has the added benefit of enriching the curriculum and pupil attainment. There is also an expectation that teachers will look beyond adopting a Eurocentric approach and teach pupils about the contributions of non-European groups to the development of different subjects (e.g. mathematics) and their contributions to British society. The expectations and significance of educational social inclusion are reinforced in Ofsted (2000) guidance (see also Ainscow *et al.* 2007).

Where the school curriculum delivered fails to meet the needs of all pupils there is 'flexibility' (DfES 2003a; QCA 2003) within the National Curriculum for the curriculum to be adapted in order to better reflect the diversity of pupils in individual schools. In this way the school curriculum can be made more relevant to pupils' own experiences and more socially inclusive. However, it is evident that not all teachers are aware of this flexibility (DfES 2005).

Equality legislation aims to support educational social inclusion of all groups. Schools are statutorily bound by duties to promote race (Race Relations (Amendment) Act 2000), disability (Disability Duty 2006) and gender equality

(Gender Equality Duty 2007). These duties, like the National Curriculum Inclusion Statement encourage schools to remain aware of the needs and experiences of all pupils, and to facilitate their inclusion and equality of opportunities/outcomes. Government support of curriculum social inclusion is further evidenced in New Labour's 'Every Child Matters' (DfES 2003b) and 'personalization' (DfES 2005) educational agendas. The personalization education agenda promotes 'a tailored curriculum/education' for five- to 19-year-olds so as to meet individual educational need. Such a curriculum/ education is thought essential 'to tackling the persistent achievement gaps between different social and ethnic groups' (DfES 2005, para 4.1). It is expected to give pupils 'strength in the basics, stretch their aspirations and build their life chances ... create every opportunity for every child, regardless of their background' (DfES 2005, para 4.1). Social inclusion within the curriculum of the individual child would involve schools/teachers providing pupils with access to an 'engaging', 'rich and flexible' curriculum (DfES 2005). An accessible/ flexible curriculum for secondary-aged pupils would mean pupils being able to 'mix academic and vocational learning' (DfES 2005, para.4.2). The introduction of specialized diplomas in 2008 for secondary pupils should enhance this aim. The implementation of a personalized curriculum in primary and secondary schools is intended to allow pupils to 'benefit from the style and pace of learning that fits with their aptitudes, interests and learning styles' (DfES 2005, para. 7.25). It should additionally 'address the needs of the most gifted and talented just as much as those who are struggling' (DfES 2005, para. 4.21) or have 'fallen behind age related expectations' (DfES 2005, para. 4.45). Where pupils have become disengaged from school/learning there is a further expectation that 'an appropriate' curriculum will be found (if necessary through learning support units) to re-enthuse them.

As part of their discourse on social inclusion New Labour argue for pupils to experience an engaging 'rich, well designed and broad curriculum' (DfES 2004:34). However, Boyle and Bragg (2006) have called into question the delivery of such a curriculum. They contend that the curriculum at Key Stages 1 and 2 is 'skewed in the direction of English and maths to the detriment of science, the humanities and arts' (Boyle and Bragg 2006:576; see also Webb and Vulliamy 2006). Bragg and Boyle relate this change in emphasis to 'power exerted by the policy imperatives of hitting national government targets in English and maths'. Ofsted (see Coffield *et al.* 2007) are similarly critical of New Labour's target-driven culture for 'narrowing' the primary curriculum in favour of literacy and numeracy. Despite these criticisms, the concentration on literacy/ English and numeracy/mathematics appears to be central to New Labour's perspective on social inclusion in the National Curriculum. They suggest that:

> To overcome economic and social disadvantage and make equality of opportunity a reality, we need to give every child a good command of English and maths. Without a firm grasp of the basics, children will struggle to succeed. This has been a touchstone of our education reforms since 1997, from the introduction of the National Literacy and Numeracy Strategies in 1998 and 1999, to our proposals in the 14–19 Education and Skills White Paper to focus on young people's mastery of functional English and maths in GCSE

examinations, and in the Achievement and Attainment tables... (DfES 2005, para 4.3)

This expressed paper commitment to social inclusion in the curriculum in the subject areas of English and mathematics has not, however, resulted in all primary pupils being able to successfully benefit from the secondary curriculum:

... Despite all the progress we have made in improving the basics, it is still the case that almost a quarter of children leave primary school without the necessary skills in literacy and numeracy to make a success of the secondary curriculum (DfES 2005, para. 1.26).

It has also not led to wider curricula social inclusion and engagement in the primary and secondary school phases. The absence of an engaging and inclusive curriculum for secondary-aged pupils is reflected in New Labour's proposal to have in place by 2011 a 'new engaging curriculum for 14–19'-year-olds, with a particular emphasis on 'enhanc[ing] inclusion in sport and PE' (DCSF 2007a:13).

In addition to understanding government priorities for curriculum inclusion, it is salient to consider why New Labour's political commitment to curriculum social inclusion remains rhetoric as opposed to being integral to school/teacher practice. New Labour's statutory commitment needs to be situated within education debates as to what is the purpose of education? There are two sides to this argument. First, education is intended to prepare pupils for employment by equipping them with the skills (academic and vocational) necessary to aid their contribution to the economic development/prosperity of Britain (DES 1981; DfEE 1998). With an educated workforce Britain can compete effectively in a 'knowledge-based' economy locally and globally (DfEE 1998).Second, education is considered essential for supporting the development of an inclusive and stable society. The Race Relations (Amendment) Act 2000 requires schools to prepare pupils for living in a culturally and ethnically diverse but inclusive society through the promotion of tolerance and understanding of diverse groups. The desire for education to produce an inclusive/stable society took on greater significance and urgency in Britain after 9/11 and with the July 7th bombings in London in 2005. The failed bombing attempts in London and Scotland in 2007 arguably put some stress back on creating a socially inclusive society (in and outside of the classroom). This is encompassed in the new Community Cohesion Duty (DCSF 2007b; see also Education and Inspections Act 2006) placed on schools (enforceable from September 2008) through which pupils will be encouraged to respect, value and understand others.

Curriculum Social Inclusion/Exclusion

New Labour's aspirations for curriculum social inclusion is infused with contradictions as it produces an inclusion/exclusion dichotomy within school/ curriculum practice, with social exclusion being exacerbated at the expense of social inclusion. Instead of inclusion some minority ethnic groups find themselves more excluded than others (e.g. Cline et al. 2002; Commission on African and Asian heritage 2005; Tikly *et al.* 2006). This curriculum exclusion of minority ethnic groups/experiences is itself contradictory as in some curriculum areas some minority ethnic groups have been found to be more included. Tikly *et al.* (2006) for example, reported that the inclusion of African-Caribbean groups in the curriculum in some secondary schools was more evident in the English rather than the mathematics curriculum. This finding is supported by teachers who have argued that areas of the curriculum such as English, history and citizenship education lend themselves more 'naturally' to allowing greater diversity and (minority ethnic) inclusion (Maylor and Read *et al.* 2007). The citizenship education curriculum with its concern to educate pupils to become active citizens and to promote diversity, equality and social inclusion promotes recognition and inclusion of all groups (Ajegbo *et al.* 2007; QCA 1998). There is a question, however, as to how the delivery of citizenship education can be tailored to meet the needs of pupils from refugee and asylum-seeking backgrounds when some do not have British citizenship status (Rutter 2003).

Curriculum exclusion of minority ethnic groups seems to be implicit within educational policies. Demie (2005; 505) contends that 'colour-blind national priorities such as Excellence in Cities, Numeracy and Literacy strategies and the Ethnic Minorities Achievement Programme have not addressed the needs of black Caribbean pupils, particularly regarding teaching and learning styles' that impact on their attainment. Demie is additionally critical of the initiatives as lacking 'local innovations' and failing to recognize black Caribbean pupils' achievement as an issue.

The perceived lack of curriculum inclusion of some ethnic groups was largely responsible for the government's commissioning of a review of 'diversity' (and citizenship) in the curriculum in 2006. The commissioned reviews (see Ajegbo *et al.* 2007; Maylor and Read *et al.* 2007) supported the findings of previous research but also drew attention to the absence of white British pupils from the curriculum. This was due in part to some schools viewing white British pupils as the norm and as a homogeneous group and therefore not having different ethnic (e.g. Scottish, Welsh, English, mixed British) experiences (Maylor and Read *et al.* 2007). The curriculum in mainly white schools was less likely to include references to culturally, ethnically, linguistically and socially diverse groups (Maylor and Read *et al.* 2007; see also Gaine 2005). It is concerning also that mixed-heritage pupils (e.g. white and black Caribbean; white and black African) who are an increasing pupil population (DfES 2006b) remain largely invisible in the curriculum (Cline *et al.* 2002; Tikly *et al.* 2004; Maylor and Read *et al.* 2007).

Just as minority ethnic groups are not necessarily considered salient to delivering a socially inclusive curriculum, working-class pupils are often excluded from the curriculum (Cassen and Kingdon 2007). The concerns raised by existing research about the lack of curriculum inclusion of minority ethnic and working-class pupils could be viewed as irrelevant, given that the National Curriculum (as established by the 1988 Education Reform Act), was never intended to be inclusive of these groups. The National Curriculum was primarily designed to improve educational standards by facilitating pupils' access to a curriculum (of three core and seven foundation subjects) that reflected and inculcates English/British traditions, culture and history, without reference to or consideration of pupils' cultural and 'racial' identities (Ross 2000). For some (e.g. Minhas 1988; Tomlinson 1990; Menter 1992) the National Curriculum represented educational nationalism and a re-working of old assimilationist philosophies in that its purpose was to engender 'cultural assimilation (to English upper and middle-class male, heterosexist white values) (original emphasis, Hill 2001:4; see also Hill 1997) and 'preserv[ing] certain [class] interests (Boyle and Bragg 2006:571).

As well as being assimilationist and offering a 'Euro-centric' and 'traditionalist' (Hill 2001) curriculum, the National Curriculum represents an 'elitist' educational system which involves 'formal, test driven methods' (Hill 2001:4). As such it 'incorporates specific disadvantages [particularly] for ... working class and minority ethnic groups' (Hill 2001:4). These disadvantages have not subsided even with the delivery of a more vocationally-oriented curriculum in some secondary schools and the introduction of specialist secondary schools with a particular focus on areas such as drama and dance, arts and sports. Cassen and Kingdon (2007:29–30) suggest that 'there is [still] a problem of the young people whose aptitudes lie more on the practical side' in that they are not totally included within the curriculum. While specialist schools are more inclusive of some [working-class] pupils, there are also specialist secondary schools that place greater emphasis on a more academic curriculum (e.g. sciences, languages), and these by their very nature offer a less socially inclusive curriculum and consequently, are more exclusionary of some pupils. The increased number of specialist schools invariably means that more pupils can be 'chosen according to 'aptitude' and/or 'ability' (Gillborn 2005:496). Setting by ability brings with it a different curriculum experience for high and low achievers. Pupils in lower ability groupings encounter a more restricted curriculum with accompanying lower teacher expectations and they are more likely to be entered for lower-tiered examinations (Gillborn and Mirza 2000; Gillborn and Youdell 2000; Gillborn 2005). Setting by ability has been shown to particularly disadvantage lower attainers (Kutnick *et al.* 2005) especially black pupils who are often 'relegated to lower sets due to their behaviour, rather than their ability' (original emphasis – Bull 2006:22) whereas it advantages middle class pupils:

> Where you have two children with the same prior attainment – the middle class pupil is more likely to be in the higher set and the working class pupil is more likely to be in the lower set (BBC New 2007).

Boys, minority ethnic and pupils with special educational needs are over represented in lower sets (DfES 2006). The consequence of this is that 'pupils in lower groups can be more vulnerable to making less progress, becoming demotivated and developing anti-school attitudes, which is not conducive to narrowing achievement gaps or promoting race equality and inclusion' (DfES 2006a, para 5.16). Not only are black pupils over represented in lower ability sets, they are five times less likely than white pupils to be registered as gifted and talented (DfES 2006a).

Like other learners, disabled pupils have experienced discrimination in the school curriculum. They have found themselves 'frequently excluded from certain subjects, faced with low expectations and assumptions and often not given genuine choices' (Disability Rights Commission 2006). They also experience inconsistencies in the provision of support and curriculum resources (Disability Rights Commission 2006). In an attempt to counteract such criticism, New Labour has promised to reduce curriculum stereotyping of disabled groups and 'ensure that a range of programmes (including work related and work-based) [are] available' to 'enable disabled learners to choose the right course or training to progress and achieve' (DCSF 2007a).

The dichotomy between social inclusion in the curriculum and social exclusion is arguably a real dilemma for New Labour as to how it can balance the curriculum to incorporate social inclusion, raise standards and prepare pupils to meet challenges in the 21st century, against one that reproduces existing societal inequalities. These tensions beg the question as to whether they are recognized as such either by the government or schools?

School Social Inclusion/Exclusion

The contradictions and tensions identified above in the curriculum between social inclusiveness and exclusion is equally evident in wider school/educational discourse, with some groups experiencing greater social inclusion than others. As well as a lack of inclusion in some areas of the curriculum, it could be argued that the structural context within which pupils are educated has never been one of total inclusion. Middle class parents have long been able to choose more socially exclusive schools that represent their class interests. They have the educational, social, cultural and economic capital to secure their desired schools (Ball 2003; Vincent 2007) which are invariably higher performing. The operation of the neoliberal market in education and a series of educational reforms since the 1980s have increased the propensity of middle-class parents to select more socially exclusive schools (Ball *et al.* 1996; Burgess *et al.* 2007). The White Paper 'Higher Standards for All: More Choice for Parents and Pupils' (DfES 2005) has served to accentuate middle class parental choice, rather than challenging them to opt for more socially inclusive schools for their children. The government choice agenda, combined with its emphasis on raised standards, has inadvertently contributed to increased racial segregation:

> ... Britain is becoming increasingly racially segregated, driven in part by giving parents' choice in where they send their children to school. In central London, for instance, 75% of the population is white, so you might expect a broadly similar percentage of pupils in state schools to be white. But in fact only 35% are. Why? Because white parents increasingly send their children to private schools, if they can afford it, or schools in the suburbs (Easton, BBC *Newsnight*, 14 June 2006).

Inevitably, where segregation exists, pupils will have access to a less socially inclusive curriculum (Coffield *et al.* 2007).

New Labour commitment to the operation of the market in the education system has not only given parents greater choice of secondary schools, but has given schools greater freedom (without sanction) to adopt more exclusionary strategies (such as selection by religion or ability) in their pupil selection. Schools do not seem to have been deterred by the introduction of the new secondary school admissions code from fostering school segregation (Curtis and Andalo 2008). It has been argued that where parents choose schools according to league table rankings, this provides schools with 'an incentive to "cream skim" more able children, with [the] potential for increased ability and socio-economic segregation across schools' (Coffield *et al.* 2007:35). Schools applying religious selection criteria are known to admit 'over 50% more pupils in the top quarter of the ability distribution in Key Stage 2 tests than they would if they recruited a more locally representative intake' (Curtis and Andala 2008). Schools may justify their selection of the 'right' pupils as being essential for maintaining higher standards, league positions and in some cases beacon status, but this contributes to the exclusion particularly of minority ethnic and working-class communities from some schools, thus further privileging middle-class families (Crozier 2000). There is evidence to suggest that, 'ethnicity … [has] an independent significant association with whether or not parents [are] offered a place in their favourite schools', while 'parents in urban areas are more likely not to be offered a place in their favourite school than elsewhere' (DfES 2006a, para. 3.20). A Sutton Trust (2005) survey revealed that the number of pupils eligible for free school meals attending the top 200 state secondary schools was just 3 per cent compared to a national average of 14.3 per cent. In 2007, of 30,000 pupils who achieved 3 A* A levels, only 176 were eligible for free school meals (Curtis 2008). Despite the existence of the Excellence in Cities initiative (which was designed to encourage middle-class children to stay in comprehensive schools and raise the achievement of the socially excluded) some schools are unlikely to become more socially inclusive as New Labour has encouraged the development of more Academies to meet the needs of pupils from lower socio-economic backgrounds (DfES 2005).

On one level we have social class exclusion demonstrated by middle-class choice of schools and on another, social exclusion is played out in school exclusion systems whereby the pupils most likely to be excluded are working-class and minority ethnic. Disproportionate exclusion rates exist particularly among pupils of African-Caribbean heritage (Sewell 1997; Parsons *et al.* 2005; Bull 2006; DfES 2006a/b). Unfortunately, government commitment to reducing truancy and pupil exclusion fails to address why certain ethnic groups are more likely to be excluded.

In the middle of school choice and school exclusions, we have inequality in attainment outcomes for certain minority ethnic groups. Regrettably, the implementation of the Race Relations (Amendment) Act 2000 and the requirement of schools to develop race equality policies have not necessarily translated into equal educational outcomes for majority and minority ethnic pupils. Under New Labour, pupils from Bangladeshi, African, African-Caribbean and Pakistani backgrounds continue to fare the worst in their Key Stage 2 and 3 tests and GCSE examinations (Gillborn and Mirza 2000; DfES 2006a/b; DCSF 2007c):

In 2006 at KS2 Level 4 +, pupils of African, African-Caribbean, Bangladeshi and Pakistani backgrounds achieved below national averages in English and mathematics, with the gap being significantly wider in mathematics. The gap in mathematics was 12 percentage points in the case of pupils of African heritages, 13 for those of African-Caribbean heritage, 5 for those of Bangladeshi heritage and 11 for those of Pakistani heritage.

In 2006 at GCSE 5+ A*-C, pupils of African, African-Caribbean, Bangladeshi and Pakistani backgrounds achieved below national averages and the gap was particularly wide when attainment in English and mathematics was taken into account. The gap when these two subjects were taken into account was 9.4 percentage points in the case of pupils of Pakistani heritage, 5.2 for those of Bangladeshi heritage, 14.6 for those of African-Caribbean heritage and 6.6 for those of African heritages (DCSF 2008, seminar paper 10)

Similarly, pupils from lower socio-economic backgrounds have lower achievement than middle-class pupils with the social class gap being quite wide (Strand 2007). In addition to gaps in educational attainment associated with ethnicity and social class, there are clear gender gaps. Cassen and Kingdon (2007: xi) suggest that boys outnumber girls as low achievers by 20 per cent and white British boys comprise nearly half of all low achievers, but the gender gap is larger for Bangladeshi, Pakistani and black Caribbean groups. There is an even greater gap in disabled learners achievement with only 8.5 per cent of pupils in 2006 with a statement of special educational needs gaining five or more GCSE grades A*-C compared with 65.9 per cent of those without such a statement (DCSF 2008).

These differential educational outcomes illustrate the widening social exclusion in schools and lack of curriculum social inclusion for some groups. New Labour may be aware of their failure to reduce the attainment gap for pupils from more deprived backgrounds (DfES 2005). But they continue, nonetheless, to ignore the fact that the schools are not socially inclusive, and without such inclusion, the ethnic and social class attainment gaps 'will never close' (Equalities Review 2007:24; see also DfES 2006b).

'There is a long way, too, before every child, regardless of their ethnicity, has an equal chance of reaching their potential ... many white working class boys can also fail to fulfil their potential. Those in receipt of free school meals perform less at GCSE than almost any other group of pupils' (DfES 2005, paras 4.30– 4.31).

Delivering a Socially Inclusive Curriculum

Research evidence points to a consistency in the absence of a socially inclusive curriculum in several schools and a range of challenges that would need to be overcome in order to engender a more socially inclusive curriculum. The ability of schools to deliver a socially inclusive curriculum is to a large extent dependent on teachers' recognizing, comprehending and valuing cultural, ethnic, gender, linguistic, social and religious diversity and pupils with disabilities (with or without special educational needs). The Qualified Teacher Status Standards similarly emphasize the development of socially inclusive teacher practice. Teachers are, however, more likely to deliver a socially inclusive curriculum where they have the appropriate professional knowledge and understanding. This would include having the wherewithal to engage with the issues and the ability to support pupil acquisition of English as an Additional Language, challenge stereotypical and prejudiced views, address racisms and other discriminatory practices. However, it is known that only 35 per cent of newly qualified teachers feel confident to effectively educate pupils from minority ethnic backgrounds (TDA 2005). There is also evidence to suggest that teachers in predominantly white schools are less likely to have an understanding of cultural, linguistic and ethnic diversity or direct experience of interacting with individuals from cultures different than their own (Cline *et al.* 2002; DfES 2004; Gaine 2005; Maylor and Read *et al.* 2007). Consequently, they may find it difficult to address such issues in school.

Enhancing social inclusion in the curriculum would require schools to undertake curriculum reviews in order to develop a curriculum (including language and resources used) more conducive to enabling all pupils to feel included. Cross-curricula links would need to be made across subject areas and curriculum activities. A socially inclusive curriculum would be representative of all groups and recognize the diverse needs and experiences (including disability, gender, culture, ethnicity, heritage, social class, religion) of pupils. It would need to accessible by all, help to engage/enthuse pupils and facilitate their learning and social inclusion. Ultimately, a socially inclusive curriculum would facilitate pupil understanding of their own and others' experiences in a diverse society, and equip them with the skills necessary to live in a socially (and culturally) diverse society.

Conclusion

In spite of New Labour's policy commitment to 'broaden social inclusion' (Goodson (2005:145) in education and to 'benefit the many, not just the few' (Power and Whitty 1999:538), it is evident that in practice their policies have 'deepen[ed]' social exclusion (Goodson 2005:14). New Labour's education policies, rather than redressing the balance of class inequality, have in practice reinforced such inequality. Like schools, the goal for a socially inclusive curriculum has not been met. This is hardly surprising within the primary phase, especially as primary schools have been encouraged through the Excellent and Enjoyment policy initiative to 'take control of their curriculum, and ... be innovative' (DfES 2003c, para 2.4) which means they can design the curriculum to suit their own aims. New Labour's attempts to centrally dictate the development of a socially inclusive curriculum have not only failed, but have raised more questions than it has produced answers. A question that remains unanswered is how can the National Curriculum deliver social inclusion in 'a system that excludes at every level' (Hill 2001:12)?

Clearly, current educational policy discourse favours social inclusion in the curriculum. However, this discourse ignores the inherent contradictions in the policies themselves and the challenges in schools trying to implement a socially inclusive curriculum, such as the fact that a key function of schools is to identify difference and variety in terms of improving achievement and raising standards. Furthermore, raising standards does not necessarily mean addressing inequalities or engendering social inclusion, and addressing inequalities does not necessarily lead to greater social inclusion in the curriculum or improved standards. Importantly, New Labour's expectations of a socially inclusive curriculum ignores parental choice, school selection practices and hierarchy in school settings, which more often than not come down on the side of social exclusion rather than inclusion. These factors make a socially inclusive curriculum less forthcoming in some schools and New Labour has done little to make it incumbent on schools to comply with this statutory requirement. Indeed, it could be argued that New Labour has done more to ensure that schools pay lip service to the demands of social inclusion in the curriculum, with the resulting outcome that the school curriculum is one of social exclusion. The introduction of Academies, specialist schools, together with government emphasis on league tables, target setting and raising standards in English and mathematics (through the Primary National Literacy and Numeracy strategies) and a core curriculum that is underpinned by national testing have served to exacerbate curriculum social exclusion and educational inequality. This invariably has a larger impact on those who experience greater societal inequality. Ultimately, if a socially inclusive curriculum is to become a reality in all schools this would require recognition by the government that at a school level 'inclusive and equitable responses to [social inclusion] necessarily involve teachers working within their professional and institutional contexts to make sense of the complex situations they face' (Ainscow *et al.* 2007:16). And at a national level, the government would need to 'support and facilitate responses that can be made at a [local] school and classroom level' (Ainscow *et al.* 2007:16). They would also need to address the above concerns and develop strategies to ensure that schools not only have a socially inclusive curriculum, but are socially inclusive in all aspects.

References

Ajegbo, K., Kiwan, D. and Sharma, S. (2007) *Diversity and Citizenship: Curriculum Review.* Nottingham: DfES.

Ainscow, M., Conteh, J., Dyson, A. and Gallanaugh, F. (2007) *Children in Primary Education: Demography, Culture, Diversity and Inclusion* (The Primary Review Research Survey 5/1). Cambridge: University of Cambridge Faculty of Education.

Ball, S. (2003) *Class Strategies and the Education Market: The Middle Classes and Social Advantage.* London: Routledge Falmer.

Ball, S. Bowe, R. and Gewirtz, S. (1996) 'School Choice, Social Class and Distinction: The Realization of Social Advantage in Education', *Journal of Education Policy* 11, 89–112.

BBC News (2007) ' "Social Bias" in Setting Pupils', 7 September 2007.

Boyle, B. and Bragg, J. (2006) 'A Curriculum without Foundation', *British Educational Research Journal*, 32, (4), 569–582

Bull, M. (2006) Priority Review: Exclusion of Black Pupils 'Getting it. Getting it Right', EMA Unit. London: DfES.

Burgess, S., McConnell, B., Propper, C. and Wilson, D. (2007) The Impact of School Choice on Sorting by Ability and Socio-Economic Factors in English Secondary

Education, in L. Woessmann and P. Peterson, (eds) *Schools and the Equal Opportunity Problem.* Cambridge, MA: MIT Press.

Cassen, R. and Kingdon, G. (2007) *Tackling Low Educational Achievement.* York: Joseph Rowntree Foundation.

Cline, T., De Abreu, G., Fihosy, C., Gray, H., Lambert, H. and Neale, J. (2002) *Minority Ethnic Pupils in Mainly White Schools, RR 365.* Nottingham: DfES.

Coffield, F., Steer, R., Allen, R., Vignoles, A., Moss, G. and Vincent, C. (2007) *Public Sector Reform: Principles for Improving the Education System.* Bedford Way Papers 30, 42–51. London: Institute of Education.

Commission on African and Asian Heritage (2005) *Delivering Shared Heritage – The Mayor's Commission on African and Asian Heritage.* London: GLA.

Crozier, G. (2000) *Parents and Schools.* Stoke-on-Trent: Trentham Books.

Curtis, P. (2008) 'Free School Meal Pupils Lose Out in Race for Top A-levels'. *The Guardian,* 23 February.

Curtis, P and Andalo, D. (2008) 'Religious State Schools Accused of Fuelling Social Segregation', *The Guardian,* 13 March.

DCSF (2007a) *Single Equality Scheme.* London: DCSF.

DCSF (2007b) *Guidance on the Duty to Promote Community Cohesion.* London: DCSF.

DCSF (2007c) *National Curriculum Assessment, GCSE and Equivalent Attainment and Post-16 Attainment by Pupil Characteristics, in England 2006/07, SFR 38/2007.* London: DCSF.

DCSF (2008) 'Developing the Equalities Agenda, 2008 and Beyond: The Duties of Schools and Local Authorities, Equalities Seminar'. British Library Conference Centre, 28 February.

Demie, F. (2005) 'Achievement of Black Caribbean Pupils: Good Practice in Lambeth Schools', *British Educational Research Journal,* 31, (4), 481–508.

DES (1981) *The School Curriculum.* London: HMSO.

DfEE (1998) *The Learning Age: A Renaissance for a New Britain.* London: The Stationery Office.

DfEE (1999) *Social Inclusion: Pupil Support.* London: DfEE Circular 10/1999.

DfES (2003a) *Disapplication of the National Curriculum 0076 (revised).* London: DfES.

DfES (2003b) *Every Child Matters: Change for Children.* London: DfES.

DfES (2003c) *Excellence and Enjoyment: A Strategy for Primary Schools.* London: DfES.

DfES (2004) *Five Year Strategy for Children and Learners,* CM6272. Norwich: HMSO.

DfES (2005) *Higher Standards, Better Schools for All: More Choice for Parents and Pupils,* Cm 6677. Norwich: HMSO.

DfES (2006a) *Higher Standards, Better Schools for All White Paper and Education Bill 2006, Race Equality Assessment.* Online at www.dfes.gov.uk/publications/education and inspection bill/doc/race equality impact assess

DfES (2006b) Ethnicity *and Education: The Evidence on Minority Ethnic Pupils aged 5–16.* London: DfES.

Disability Rights Commission (2006) *Education Research in England and Wales: Highlights 2004-05.* Online at www.education.bham.ac.uk/research/projects1/drc/index.shtml

Easton, M. (2006) 'BBC *Newsnight* Report', 14 June. London: BBC.

Equalities Review (2007) *Fairness and Freedom: The Final Report of the Equalities Review.* Online at www.theequalitiesreview.org.uk.

Gaine, C. (2005) *We're All White, Thanks: The Persisting Myth about 'White' Schools.* Stoke-on-Trent: Trentham Books.

Gillborn, D. (2005) 'Education Policy as an Act of White Supremacy: Whiteness, Critical Race Theory and Education Reform'. *Journal of Education Policy,* 20, (4), 485–505.

Gillborn, D. and Mirza, H. (2000) *Educational Inequality: Mapping Race, Class and Gender – A Synthesis of Research Evidence.* London: Ofsted.

Gillborn, D. and Youdell, D. (2000) *Rationing Education: Policy, Practice, Reform and Equity.* Buckingham: Open University Press.

Goodson, I. (2005) 'The Exclusive Pursuit of Social Inclusion', *FORUM*, 47, (2 & 3), 145–150.

Hill, D. (1997) 'Equality in British Schooling: The Policy Context of the Reforms', in M. Cole, D. Hill and S. Shan (eds), *Promoting Equality in Primary Schools*. London: Cassell.

Hill, D. (2001) *The Third Way in Britain: New Labour's Neo-Liberal Education Policy*. Paper presented at Congres Marx International III Le Capital et L'humanite, Universite de Paris-X Nanterre-Sorbonne, 29 Septembre 2001.

Kutnick, P., Sebba, J., Blatchford, P., Galton, M. and Thorp, J. (2005) *The Effects of Pupil Grouping: Literature Review*. London: DfES.

Maylor, U. and Read, B., with Mendick, H., Ross, A. and Rollock, N. (2007) *Diversity and Citizenship: Research Review, RR 819*. Nottingham: DfES.

Menter, I. (1992) 'The New Right, Racism and Teacher Education: Some Recent Developments', *Multicultural Teaching*, 10, (2), 6–9

Minhas, R. (1988) 'The Politics Behind the National Curriculum', *Multicultural Teaching*, 6, 9–10.

Ofsted (2000) *Evaluating Educational Inclusion: Guidance for Inspectors and Schools, HMI 235*. London: Ofsted/HMI.

Ofsted (2005) Race *Equality in Education: Good Practice in Schools and Local Education Authorities, HMI 589*. London: Ofsted.

Parsons, C. G., Godfrey, R., Annan, G., Cornwall, J., Dussart, M., Hepburn, S., Howlett, K. and Wennerstrom, V. (2005) *Minority Ethnic Exclusions and the Race Relations (Amendment) Act 2000, RR 616*. Nottingham: DfES.

Power, S. and Whitty, G. (1999) 'New Labour's Education Policy: First, Second or Third Way?', *Journal of Education Policy*, 14, (5), 535–546.

QCA (2003) *Changes to the Key Stage 4 Curriculum, 1167*. London: QCA.

QCA (1998) *Education for Citizenship and the Teaching of Democracy in Schools, Final Report of the Advisory Group on Citizenship, 22 September*. London: QCA.

Race Relations (Amendment) Act 2000. London: Stationery Office.

Ross, A. (2000) *Curriculum, Construction and Critique*. London: Falmer Press.

Rutter, J. (2003) *Supporting Refugee Children in 21st Century Britain: A Compendium of Essential Information*. Stoke-on-Trent: Trentham Books.

Sewell, T. (1997) *Black Masculinities and Schooling: How Black Boys Survive Modern Schooling*. Stoke-on-Trent: Trentham Books.

Strand, S. (2007) *Minority Ethnic Pupils in the Longitudinal Study of Young People in England*. Nottingham: DCSF.

TDA (2005) *Results of the Newly Qualified Teacher Survey*. London: TDA.

Tikly, L., Cabellero, C., Haynes, J. and Hill, J. in assoc. with Birmingham Local Education Authority (2004) *Understanding the Educational Needs of Mixed Heritage Pupils, RR 549*. Nottingham: DfES.

Tikly, L., Haynes, J., Cabellero, C., Hill, J. and Gillborn, D. (2006) *Evaluation of Aiming High: African Caribbean Achievement Project, RR 801*. Nottingham: DfES.

The Sutton Trust (2005) *Rates of Eligibility for Free School Meals at the Top State Schools*. London: The Sutton Trust.

Tomlinson, S. (1990) *Multicultural Education in White Schools*. London: Batsford.

Vincent, C. (2007) 'Parental Voice in Education', in F. Coffield, R. Steer, R. Allen, A. Vignoles, G. Moss and C. Vincent, *Public Sector Reform: Principles for Improving the Education System*, Bedford Way Papers 30, 42–51. London: Institute of Education.

Webb, R. and Vulliamy, G. (2006) The Impact of New Labour's Education Policy on Teachers and Teaching at Key Stage 2, *FORUM*, 48, (2), 145–157.

Chapter 4

Urban Education, Equality and Inequality

Meg Maguire and Simon Pratt-Adams

Introduction

This chapter is concerned with equality and social justice issues in relation to a specific set of primary schools; those schools that have served and continue to serve the children of the 'urban poor' (Grace 1994:45). The chapter starts with a discussion of what is meant by urbanization and urban primary schools. Then it explores the relationship between urbanization and the historical foundations of elementary schooling. Then the chapter turns to the inequalities that continue to influence urban primary schools. Finally, the chapter considers some steps that could be taken to promote a more socially just form of education provision in urban primary schooling.

Urbanization and Its Consequences

In order to locate this chapter theoretically, first it is necessary to explain what we mean by urbanization. Initially, urban studies centred on the city as a spatial location – a specific place. Contrasts were drawn between urban and rural lifestyles and experiences. In consequence, a rural-urban binary emerged, where the city became demonized and the rural was idealized – and traces of this approach still remain in the popular consciousness. As the field of urban studies developed, research attempted to chart the ecology of the city and map the experiences of different urban communities (Mumford 1961). Another body of urban research, and one interwoven with post-modern approaches to social science research, has positioned the city as part of a cultural imaginary, a place of lifestyle, complexity and ambivalence (Sassen 1993). While we recognize that the urban is a contradictory and contested phenomenon, in this chapter we want to foreground the ways in which change in the modes of production, that is taking a politico-economic perspective, underpins and shapes the urban and urbanization. This approach is centrally concerned with the ways in which the urban and urbanization are deeply implicated in the production and reproduction of inequalities and social injustice.

In what follows, we argue that urbanization is bound up with changes in capitalism and the means of production (Harvey 1998). In order to chart the longevity of some of the outcomes of these changes, we start with the industrial revolutions of the eighteenth and nineteenth centuries in Europe which had massive consequences for social relations, lifestyle and the development of the city. In terms of changes in the modes of production, a seismic shift occurred where people moved away from the land where they had been subsistence farmers or the tenants of landowners, towards the cities where they could sell their labour for wages in the newly emerging factories. 'The need for a high concentration of industrial workers to live in close proximity to their places of work' (Stevenson 2000:75) accelerated as mass production methods were extended.

The rate of change was unprecedented (before and since) in the UK. This movement away from the land and towards the towns and cities put enormous pressure on what infrastructure existed. Unskilled manual work predominated and a 'casual residuum' was employed (or not) on a daily basis – thus rendering life haphazard for many families and workers. Rented housing was often of poor quality and, in any case, was in short supply, so that overcrowding was commonplace (Stedman-Jones 1992). Inadequate sanitation in these dwellings meant that infant mortality figures were high and poor health and contagious diseases were commonplace. As more and more people moved to the cities, these problems intensified (Fishman 1988).

One of the consequences of this population shift was that many of the professional middle classes, the factory owners and commentators of the day, were appalled and frightened by the threat to their existence that they believed was posed by uprisings and violence from the so-called unruly urban working classes. One result was their own move outwards and back towards the 'rural idyll' of the newly emerging suburbs as a form of escape; an early example of housing segregation (Maguire *et al.* 2006). Concerns were expressed about alleged high levels of crime, dissolute youth and a lack of moral fibre among the working-class urban populations. For all these sorts of reasons, the emerging cities presented challenges for middle-class society.

Stedman-Jones (1992:11) has argued that the nineteenth-century urban problem 'was not structural but moral'. There was widespread concern about the urban working classes who were viewed as degenerate, unfit and immoral. The middle classes feared the possibility of disease and contamination. In many ways, then as now, pauperism and not poverty was seen as the problem and the victims were seen as partly responsible for their own difficulties. All these 'fears', coupled with pressures for reform, eventually produced a set of responses to the 'problems of the city'. In the UK, these responses were part of the formation of the modern state through the emergence of state-welfarism; in particular housing, health-care and education.

What we want to claim in this chapter is that there are similarities between the nineteenth- and twenty-first-century experience of urban life, as well as social and cultural continuities between the processes of industrialization and contemporary changes in the modes of production. In the northern hemisphere, industrial modes of production have been overtaken by deindustrialization, the falling away of the manufacturing industry and the growth of the service sector (Massey 2007). For example, in Manchester, one of the UK's old Victorian cities, 'more people are employed in leisure activities operating after the hour of 8pm than are employed in manufacturing' (Byrne 2001:58). Much of this work is low-paid, unskilled and temporary, and thus, easy to control and manage, particularly in a period of global economic turmoil and recession.

People still move to large towns and cities in the UK in order to seek opportunities and escape from privation (Sassen 2006). Newly-arriving refugees and asylum-seekers are frequently housed in hard-to-let, run-down public accommodation where they frequently have reduced access to health care, social welfare and employment. Fears are still being expressed about youth crime, binge-drinking, scroungers, and feckless behaviour in public places – mostly of the working classes and 'urban poor' (Fionda 2005). There are striking similarities between the nineteenth- and twenty-first-century experiences of urban life, as well as some continuities between industrialization and deindustrialization – the employment of casual workers at low rates of pay with very little organized protection or capacity to withstand economic recessions.

The ways in which capitalist modes of production and consumption continue to produce inequality, exclusion and oppression in society are areas that have been explored by critical urban studies (Soja 2000). As these modes of production inflect policy and provision, regardless of place and space, to some degree the spatiality of the urban (the city as a focus of concern) is moved away from the lens of enquiry. Where the city comes back into the equation is through its capacity to illustrate, in an intense form, the consequences of social and economic injustice:

> The city concentrates and makes highly visible the contrasts between the rich and the poor. This concentration and visibility means that conflicts over scarce resources, not least education, between rich and poor are more likely, more extreme, and in turn, more visible in urban areas (Coulby 1992:221).

In order to explore some of these 'conflicts' in educational provision in more detail, we turn to the historical foundations of the urban primary school.

Historical Foundations of Urban Primary Schools

While we have not got enough space here to fully explore the origins of state schooling – the schools that were set up by the 1870 Elementary School Act – three points need to be remembered. These schools were segregated; that is, they were only intended for the urban working classes. Second, they were set up to control and 'civilize', not to educate children (Johnson 1976). Third, these schools were generally seen as 'difficult places' for unruly children. In talking of pedagogy and practice, it is better to think of 'schooling' rather than 'educating' – for this is what took place.

The Elementary School Act (1870) set up a segregated classed provision of schools in the towns and cities of the rapidly urbanizing nineteenth century. These schools were intended to produce a well-behaved and well-disciplined labour force; 'an orderly, civil, obedient population, with sufficient education to understand a command' (Tawney 1924:22, cited in Simon 1974:119). Thus, segregated and differentiated provision for the children of the poor and working classes was eventually set up – albeit with a small provision for 'rescuing' those talented enough to pass the scholarship exam. In fact 'rescuing' those selected as able to benefit from a more academic curriculum still enjoys a degree of policy continuity to this day. Working-class children were legally obliged to go to schools where they were regularly physically punished for fairly minor incidents, had a limited curriculum and where they were frequently taught, in large numbers, by poorly-educated teachers (Silver 1983). Some teachers, trade unionists and social reformers tried to challenge this harsh regime. Political struggles centred on the need to reduce child labour and to provide free meals for the 'large numbers of children ... attending school in a state of near starvation' (Simon 1974:133). The elementary schools were seen as 'difficult places' which catered for unruly children. They were not regarded as suitable for children from more economically-privileged families. What we want to claim, however, is that some of the dominant ideas that framed the provision of the elementary schools in the nineteenth century have persisted, albeit in slightly different forms, to influence the contemporary urban state primary school, as we shall see.

The Urban Primary School

In this section we now want to clarify more precisely what it is that we mean when we talk of an urban primary school today; those schools that are frequently referred to as 'high-poverty' schools in the US. Essentially, we are talking about schools that have high numbers of children who come from working-class families, many of whom will qualify for free school meals or whose parents/carers are on a low income (Power *et al.* 2002). As an aside, recently there have been reports that more than one million children who qualify for free school meals are not actually obtaining them (Curtis 2008). Many urban schools will be supporting higher than average numbers of children who have English as an additional language (EAL) (Datta 2007). Urban primary schools will generally record lower levels of attendance and higher rates of exclusions than a non-urban primary school and may have to deal with higher proportions of children experiencing emotional distress. All this is in a context of higher than average teacher turnover (Ofsted 2007). The point being made is that the urban primary school is a distinctive setting that will demand a different set of responses and sensitivities from its teaching staff. These schools may also demand an increased workload that would not be the case in primary schools with a more economically privileged intake (Riddell 2003). Paradoxically, while the demands of urban primary schools may require additional resources, both human and material, such schools will frequently be less able to respond to these needs. They will be less able to rely on additional income from fund-raising from their families and the local communities than primary schools with more advantaged intakes. They may find it harder to find the time to prepare and submit proposals for any additional funding streams.

Urban primary schools face distinctive sets of challenges (DETR 2000; Ofsted 2007). Some of these challenges are structural, such as higher levels of relative poverty. Other challenges may be school-specific. School buildings in need of repair, higher than average numbers of temporary teachers covering permanent teacher vacancies, difficulties in recruiting headteachers, can make it harder for urban primary schools to meet the needs of their children and parents. In consequence, greater consideration needs to be paid to the unique circumstances faced in urban localities and urban primary schools. Primary schools provide the foundations for educational progression for young children everywhere. If children are to have an equal chance in life and if social injustices are to be dismantled, primary schooling is a key stepping stone in this process.

Continuities Between the Past and the Present

As we have already suggested, there are continuities between the urban primary schools of the past and present time. In this section we want to briefly explore what we see as some of these similarities. One common factor relates to the complex social and economic conditions that some urban families will have to navigate. The families of the urban working classes, then as now, face higher levels of unemployment, precarious and volatile social conditions, and emotional difficulties and disruptions. In stressful settings like these, education may not always be the first priority.

The schools that serve these communities will have higher than average intakes of children who are being brought up in relative poverty (Toynbee and Walker 2008). Now as then, they will have higher than average numbers of children who are from refugee or asylum-seeking backgrounds, some of whom will have experienced debilitating trauma and upheaval (Rutter 2007). These schools will also experience higher levels of 'turbulence'. That is, they will have lower levels of teacher retention and some of these schools may well be being 'patched together' by a constant stream of supply teachers (Hutchings *et al.* 2007). Many of these schools, particularly those in urban areas, will also have higher than average levels of turnover in their intake. Families in temporary housing and families experiencing other disruptions will tend to be moved between different housing stock. Their children will likewise move from school to school. For instance, in some urban primary schools, less than 30 per cent of children in Year 6 will have started in the same school. This mobility makes continuity of teaching and learning much harder to organize and manage. For example, Ofsted (2002:6) reported that:

> in one London primary school, 135 pupils joined the roll in the course of a year. Of these, 40% were refugees, 30% were homeless and 28% had no previous schooling, with overlap between these categories. The health and welfare of many new pupils presented serious concerns.

Not surprisingly, the children who go to urban primary schools tend to experience higher levels of ill-health, lower levels of attendance and thus, potentially lower levels of attainment (Ofsted 2007a). What all this suggests is that it may be 'naive' to expect schools on their own to be able to overcome all these difficulties (Grace 2005).

One consequence, that is sometimes not always recognized or acknowledged, is that schools facing these 'challenging' circumstances can become positioned as 'part of the problem'. Schools that are seen as turbulent are more likely to be seen as difficult places in which to work. In a culture of managerialism and performance (Thrupp 2005) some teachers will actively seek to avoid working in these schools. These urban schools may well be more prone to becoming 'demonized' in their local area (Reay and Lucey 2000). Neglected environments and poorer facilities will contribute towards this process. However, other research has found that teachers had sometimes deliberately chosen to work in challenging but rewarding environments where they felt they could *make a difference* (Maguire *et al.* 2006).

As in the past, some working-class and middle-class parents may be far less likely to see these schools as 'acceptable' for their children. It is highly unlikely in any case that they will live in the catchment area of these primary schools. At the same time, many of the primary schools that have become demonized in these sorts of ways may also gain little recognition for the positive contribution that they are making. Almost by default, the children and their families and the schools they attend may become positioned as deficient or deviant.

Equality Issues and Social Justice

The picture we have wanted to create of urban primary schools is that they are typified by serving communities that experience higher levels of socio-economic disadvantage and, in some areas, this overlaps with higher percentages of children from minority ethnic backgrounds and children with EAL (Maguire *et al.* 2006). However, the critical variable in relation to inequality and lack of opportunity is economic, nothing else. Not surprisingly, many urban primary schools are 'under-performing' relative to schools in more privileged areas. As a recent study on social mobility in the UK has pointed out:

> Those from the poorest fifth of households but in the brightest group at age three drop from the 88th percentile on cognitive tests at age three to the 65th percentile at age five. Those from the richest households who are least able at age three move up from the 15th percentile to the 45th percentile by age five. If this trend were to continue, the children from affluent backgrounds who are doing poorly at age three would be likely to overtake the poorer but initially bright children in test scores by age seven (Sutton Trust 2007)

What then are the key equality issues that need to be considered in respect of urban primary schools? Many of the chapters in this collection will deal specifically and in detail with issues related to class, race, gender, sexualities, dis/abilities and other aspects of difference. They will be making recommendations for policy and practice in educational settings in terms of curriculum provision and innovations in primary schools, particularly in the light of the Rose recommendations for the primary curriculum (Rose 2008). Thus, in this chapter we want to concentrate on the urban primary school and social justice issues in the wider socio-political context. First, we will focus on matters that lie 'outside' the reach of schools' capacities to influence and control, but that need urgent attention. Second, we will identify some 'internal' issues that urban primary schools (and urban policy makers) also need to consider.

The most important 'outside' matter that needs to be addressed relates to the persistence of poverty that still scars the lives of many families in the UK and elsewhere (Hirsch 2006; Palmer *et al.* 2007; Toynbee and Walker 2008). Since New Labour was elected to office in 1997, they have pursued a policy of 'work as welfare' in their attempts to reduce poverty. They have developed policies like the New Deal to get some of the long-term unemployed back to work and into real jobs. They have designed redistributive policies such as family tax credits and have set a (too low) minimum wage. The 'problem' with these sorts of piecemeal approaches, as Jones (2003) has pointed out, is that there is still a large gap between the more- and less-advantaged in society. These policies are not about equalizing outcomes, they concentrate on inclusion, even if this simply means inclusion at the bottom of a hierarchically organized society. The bottom line is the persistence of high numbers of children in the UK who are poor and who overwhelmingly attend urban primary schools:

> Poverty shapes children's development. Before reaching his or her second birthday, a child from a poorer family is already more likely to show a lower level of attainment than a child from a better-off family. By the age of six a less able child from a rich family is likely to have overtaken an able child born into a poor family. (End Child Poverty 2008:1)

Any attempt to address issues of equality and inequality in urban primary schools needs to start by addressing poverty. One way forward would be to start to implement the sorts of policies that the poverty lobby in the UK has been advocating for some time; that is, quality state housing, decent and easily available health care, 'proper' jobs with good pay and a much higher minimum wage (most poor families are in work – it is just that their wages are low and only kept 'manageable' through small-scale means-tested benefits). Equal pay for women would also go a long way towards reducing and removing poverty, particularly, but not only, in families where women are sole-carers and in rural as well as urban settings (Women's Budget Group 2005). In a political culture of relative private interest, a growing number of citizens reject action in support of the disadvantaged (who are seen to be responsible for their own problems) and support policies designed to enhance their own interests (Grace 1994). This culture of 'blame' and 'individualism' needs to be challenged and dismantled.

In thinking about extending equality, it is useful to consider some of the different dimensions of justice that are involved. This is because different sorts of justice issues, need 'different' sorts of responses. One dimension of social justice involves the redistribution of goods and resources; a second concerns the need to reflect and respect social groups and diverse social identities. There is also a third dimension, associational justice that argues for the involvement of participants in reaching decisions; that is, those to whom the policy is 'to be done' (Cribb and Gewirtz 2003). Frequently 'expert' policy makers determine what is, or is not, in the interests of the 'socially excluded'. As Apple (2006:229) has suggested, part of the process of trying to assess policy in terms of social justice should involve seeing any proposals 'from the standpoint of those who have the least power'. Doing this would mean empowering and collaborating with different policy stakeholders. Whether the focus is on distributional, cultural or associational social justice, without the political will for a change in the political culture, urban primary school teachers might be left struggling to work towards social justice in overwhelmingly challenging circumstances.

Turning now to what goes on inside the urban primary school, we believe that questions need to be asked in relation to social and cultural relevance. For example, some questions for educationalists to pose might include: to what extent is the social world of the children outside school seen either as a restriction or, more positively, as a source for learning and empowerment by their teachers? What learning is involved in living in urban settings that is less likely to impact the contemporary primary classroom? Here we are thinking of the experiences of racisms, awareness of social injustices and oppressions, as well as what is involved in managing a school in complex emotional and economic circumstances. We are also thinking of the histories, cultures and languages that make up the situated lives of many urban communities and which are frequently sidelined from the 'official' curriculum of schools (Datta 2007). Would including the informal, local knowledge that children carry with them make school learning accessible for more of them? Would it respect, or even enhance, what they already know, rather than potentially positioning them as 'deficit' in terms of knowledge? Overall, what we are claiming is that the curriculum and pedagogy of urban primary schools needs to be made more 'relevant to the lived experiences of children from diverse backgrounds' (Corson 1998:25)

We have made the following point about the purpose of education elsewhere (Maguire *et al.* 2006) but we believe it is worth repeating again in this collection. Some time ago, Midwinter argued that urban children needed to do more than learn their place in society; they needed to learn how to change it. He advocated drawing on 'the potential and the experiences of the city child in his (*sic*) own right' rather than compensating the children for any alleged 'deficits' (Midwinter 1972, in Connor with Lofthouse 1990:120). He believed that a relevant curriculum would produce 'social criticism and action'. This did not mean that core skills would be sidelined. Instead, they would act as vehicles for exploring what the children knew and understood.

One of the complexities in planning for learning in urban primary schools has been the pressure to ensure that children succeed in the basics of literacy, numeracy and Information and Communication Technology alongside the desire to expose them to an enriching, diverse and challenging curriculum. In a period where schools have been judged and their teachers assessed on a limited set of curriculum activities (the SATs), there has been pressure on teachers to teach to the tests and concentrate on a limited part of the National Curriculum. This has sometimes meant that urban schools – potentially more likely to 'under-achieve' on national tests – were more likely to offer a restricted curriculum. As this book is going to press, changes are afoot in relation to the primary school curriculum in terms of attempting to assure that more children are exposed to a worthwhile, enriching curriculum that encourages a love of learning for itself, and not just a concentration on success in testing. In December 2008, Sir Jim Rose published 'The Independent Review of the Primary Curriculum: Interim report' (IRPC). This was in response to Secretary of State for Education Ed Balls' Remit Letter of 9 January 2008, where he charged Rose as follows:

> Building on the steady rise in primary school results in recent years, I would like your review of the primary curriculum to enable schools to have even greater flexibility to meet pupils' individual needs and strengths, including those with special educational needs, in order to further help them *narrow the attainment gap between disadvantaged pupils and their peers*. The content of existing programmes of study should be reviewed, *reducing prescription where possible.* (our italics)

In December 2008, Rose produced an interim response that has addressed all aspects of the remit in varying degrees. In the IRPC (Rose 2008) the primary curriculum is, in the main, approached in a general and non-contextualized manner. However, there are some small references to urban matters. For example, Rose (2008:60) recognizes that 13.5 per cent of children in primary schools speak languages other than English. What is not recognized is that this percentage is clustered in certain areas and particular schools in the country. Rose talks of the value of early years education as being 'of particular benefit for... disadvantaged children' (2008:50) although there is no indication that additional free access is being planned beyond the provision in Sure Start of 12.5 hours a week. However, the IRPC highlights the need for the primary curriculum to help schools in 'making the best of their local circumstances' (Rose 2008:25). Some time ago, Freire (1972) argued that teachers needed to use curricular themes that were familiar to their students in order to empower them and extend their motivation to learn. In what Rose is suggesting, it seems that there will be more legal scope for schools to do this. Thus, schools are going to be able to incorporate a perspective that recognizes that urban settings have distinctive cultures and values (Black 2000).

We recognize the value in detailing specific ways in which the curriculum can and should be responsive to issues of difference and diversity. These matters are addressed in detail elsewhere in this collection. However, here our overriding concern is to establish a culture of respect in urban primary schools for what the children themselves bring to school. We believe that this approach has to be the starting point, the genesis of a more radical and socially just curriculum for the urban primary school.

Urban Education, Equality and Inequality

We recognize that there are a range of issues that need addressing in order to improve urban primary schools. What we want to do in this final section is highlight three points. First, in this chapter, we have argued that such schools are distinctive for all the reasons that we have outlined. This distinctiveness of the urban primary school needs to be recognized in curriculum and pedagogy and also in terms of a realistic appraisal of what is, and what is not, possible in schools as they are currently constructed.

If we want to understand and explain persistent educational inequalities, and if we want to do something about them through policy, then increasingly the school is the wrong place to look and the wrong place to reform – at least in isolation from other sorts of changes in other parts of society (Ball 2008:1).

Second, in relation to the curriculum and pedagogy of urban schools, as Wrigley (2006:111) has argued, there is evidence of creative and innovative work taking place. With the reduction in prescription and overloading that seems promised in the IRPC, schools will have more scope for considering some of the points that we have raised in this chapter. As Hatcher (2007:1) says, 'the most obvious strategy available to teachers... is to pragmatically take advantage of whatever spaces are available within the neoliberal context' – a point that we endorse. But we want to argue that this advantage-taking needs to have a more progressive and radical agenda.

Finally, in this discussion of urban education and social justice, we are not just calling for more creative and innovative ideas in teaching and learning. We are calling for more socially critical teaching that really does engage with the world as urbanized children and their families experience it – not only to know it but to help towards changing it and making it socially just.

References

Apple, M. (2006) *Educating the 'Right' Way: Markets, Standards, God and Inequality*. New York: Routledge.

Black, M. (2000) 'Using your city as a multicultural classroom', *Teaching Education*, 11, (3), 343–351.

Byrne, D. (2001) *Understanding the Urban*. London: Palgrave.

Clark, D. (1996) *Urban World: Global City*. London: Routledge.

Connor, C. with Lofthouse, B. (eds) (1990) *The Study of Primary Education: A source book, Vol 1: Perspectives*. London: Falmer.

Corson, D. (1998) *Changing Education for Diversity*. Buckingham: Open University Press.

Cribb, A. and Gewirtz, S. (2003) 'Towards a sociology of just practices. An analysis of plural conceptions', in C. Vincent (ed.) *Social Justice, Education and Identity*. London: Routledge/Falmer, pp.15–29.

Coulby, D. (1992) 'Urban Civic Culture and Education', in D. Coulby, C. Jones, and D. Harris (eds) *World Yearbook of Education, Urban Education*. London: Kogan Page, pp. 219–228.

Curtis, P. (2008) 'Million poor pupils denied free meals'. *The Guardian*. Online at http://www.guardian.co.uk/education/2008/dec/16/school-meals-education-government-funding (Accessed 22.07.09).

Datta, M. (2007) (ed.) *Bilinguality and literacy: principles and practice*. London: Continuum.

Department of Employment, Training and Rehabilitation (DETR). (2000) *Indices of Deprivation*. London: DETR.

End Child Poverty (2008) *Why end child poverty*. Online at http://www.endchildpoverty.org.uk/why-end-child-poverty/the-effects. (Accessed 9 December 2008).

Fionda, J. (2005) *Devils and angels: Youth, policy and crime*. Oxford: Hart Publishing.

Fishman, W. (1988) *East End 1888: a year in a London borough among the labouring poor*. London: Duckworth.

Freire, P. (1972) *Pedagogy of the Oppressed*. Harmondsworth: Penguin.

Grace, G. (1994) 'Urban Education and the Culture of Contentment: The Politics, Culture and Economics of Inner-City Schooling', in N. Stromquist (ed.) *Education in Urban Areas. Cross National Dimensions.* Westport Connecticut and London: Praeger, pp. 45–59.

Grace, G. (2005) *Urban Education: confronting the contradictions.* Unpublished position paper for the staff of the London Centre for Leadership in Learning. 16 June.

Harvey, D. (1998) *The urbanization of capital: studies in the history and theory of capitalist urbanization.* Ann Arbor, MI: UMI Books on Demand.

Hatcher, R. (2007) ' "Yes, but how do we get there?" Alternative visions and the problem of strategy'. *Journal for Critical Education Policy Studies,* 5, (2). Online at http://www.jceps.com/?pageID = article&articleID = 98. (Accessed 20 December 2008).

Hirsch, D. (2006) *What will it take to end child poverty? Firing on all cylinders.* York: Joseph Rowntree Foundation.

Hutchings, M., James, K., Maylor, U., Menter, I. and Smart, S. (2007) *The Recruitment, Deployment and Management of Supply Teachers in England.* London: DfES.

Johnson, R. (1976) 'Notes on the schooling of the English working class 1780–1850', in R. Dale, G. Esland, and M. MacDonald, (eds) *Schooling and Capitalism. A Sociological Reader.* London: Routledge and Kegan Paul, pp. 44–54.

Jones, K. (2003) *Education in Britain: 1944 to the Present.* Cambridge and Malden, MA: Polity Press.

Maguire, M., Wooldridge, T. and Pratt-Adams, S. (2006) *The Urban Primary School.* Maidenhead: OUP.

Massey, D. (2007) *World City.* London: Polity Press.

Mumford, L. (1961) *The City in History: Its Origins, its Transformations and its Prospects.* London: Secker and Warburg.

Ofsted (2002) *Managing Pupil Mobility Report.* Online at http://www.ofsted.gov.uk/.../Managing%20pupil%20mobility%20(PDF%20format).pdf (Accessed 22.07.09).

Ofsted (2007) *The Annual Report of Her Majesty's Chief Inspector.* Online at http://www.ofsted.gov.uk/ (Accessed on 25 January 2008).

Ofsted (2007a) *Narrowing the Gap: the inspection of children's services,* (ref. no. 070041). Norwich: The Stationary Office.

Palmer, G., MacInnes. T. and Kenway, P. (2007) *Monitoring poverty and social exclusion.* York: Joseph Rowntree Foundation.

Power, S., Warren, S., Gillborn, D., Clark, A., Thomas, S. and Coate, K. (2002) *Education in Deprived Areas: Outcomes, inputs and processes.* London: Institute of Education, University of London.

Reay, D. and Lucey, H. (2000) ' "I don't like it here, but I don't want to live anywhere else": children living on inner London council estates'. *Antipode: A Radical Journal of Geography,* 32, (4), 410–28.

Riddell, R. (2003) *Schools for our Cities: urban learning in the 21st Century.* Stoke on Trent: Trentham Books.

Rose, J. (2008) *Independent Review of the Primary Curriculum.* Interim Report. Online at http://publications.teachernet.gov.uk. (Accessed 20th December 2008).

Rutter, J. (2007) *Worlds on the move: educational responses to changing migration patterns.* Stoke-on-Trent: Trentham.

Sassen, S. (1993) *The Global City.* Princeton, NJ: Princeton University Press.

Sassen, S. (2006) *Cities in a world economy.* Thousand Oaks, CA: Pine Forge Press.

Silver, H. (1983) *Education as history: interpreting nineteenth- and twentieth-century history.* London: Methuen.

Simon, B. (1974) *The politics of educational reform, 1920–1940.* London: Lawrence and Wishart.

Soja, E. W. (2000) *Postmetropolis: critical studies of cities and regions.* Malden, MA: Blackwell Publishers.

Stedman Jones, G. (1992) *Outcast London: a study in the relationship between classes in Victorian society.* London: Penguin Books.

Stevenson, D. (2000) *Cities and Urban Cultures*. Buckingham: Open University Press.

Sutton Trust (2007) *Recent Changes in Intergenerational Mobility in Britain: A Summary of Findings*. Online at http://www.Suttontrust.com/reports/summary.pdf. (Accessed on 11 January 2009).

Thrupp, M. (2005) *School improvement: an unofficial approach*. London: Continuum.

Toynbee, P. and Walker, D. (2008) *Unjust Rewards: Exposing greed and inequality in Britain today*. London: Granta.

Women's Budget Group (2005) *Women's and Children's Poverty: Making the links*. London: Fawcett Society/Women's Budget Group.

Wrigley, T. (2008) *Another School is Possible*. London: Bookmarks.

Chapter 5

Refugee Education

Henry Kum

Introduction

In Britain, there has been a coalescence of the politics of immigration and nationality on the one hand with the politics of asylum on the other hand. The specific educational needs for children from refugee communities is distinctive, especially as the children may have experienced considerable trauma through rapid relocation, often under physical threats, to a very new society where their own language is not understood (Menter *et al.* 2000; Rutter 2003). When dominant ethnicity in most British schools is white, it is difficult for cultural differences to be recognized, represented and respected in schools (Lynch and Lodge 2002).

This chapter discusses the concerns that affect refugee parents in relation to their ability to assist in their children's schooling. The themes under discussion respond to the context of equality in multicultural Britain. Given the objectives of the research, a multi-method strategy was employed in order to explore a number of dimensions. This report will discuss entitlement to refugee pupils, look at the research subject and discuss the methodology and results before providing a critical examination of these concerns. The survey concludes with the importance of the research as not solely exclusive to the specific subjects but applicable to the wider migrant population.

Immigration status makes no difference to educational entitlement up to the age of 16. The award of 'exceptional leave to remain' or refugee status makes no difference to entitlement to education for pre-16s. Schools and Local Authorities (LAs) are obliged to offer school places in accordance with their published admissions arrangements. LAs are obliged to provide education for all children resident in their areas.

Education in the UK is sometimes very different to that in other countries: often refugee children have been in schools where teaching is more formal than it is here. Many refugee children will need help in learning English. Often a specialist English as an Additional Language teacher will help the child, working alongside the usual class teacher and extra help is often needed from parents at home. Some LAs also have refugee support teachers who can help children who are experiencing difficulties in school. Children whose families are on income support or are being supported by the National Asylum Support Service (NASS) now managed by the Border and Immigration Agency (BIA) can receive free school meals. There is also much initiative now to encourage collaborative partnership between schools and parents in a drive towards excellence for all children in education and the effective access to the National Curriculum by all children without regard to need or ability.

The relative newness of the children in a new environment can most especially be helped by parental participation (Coll 2001). Participation is often desirable to middle-class parents who demonstrate this by attending meetings, volunteering for activities, helping their children with homework and ensuring their children begin school knowing their numbers and letters as preparation for school literacy instruction. This could be very difficult to some uneducated refugee parents who have just come from some remote war-torn zone in Africa or the Middle East. Bhachu (1985), Gibson (1988) and Bertossi (2007) acknowledge that children from such cultures where parents view their role as non-interventionist in nature can still attain high levels of academic achievement.

Many refugees have fled countries where serious human rights abuses occur. Some have witnessed massacres or individual killings and may also have been tortured or raped, or witnessed this happening to someone else. Some young refugees may have been directly involved in armed conflict and some recruited forcibly into militia groups; others driven into armed forces by poverty, alienation and discrimination. These children do not only risk physical injury, psychological trauma and death, but they also lose childhood and opportunities for education and development (Child Soldier 2001).

The escape from the home country is often characterized by risk either due to the means of transportation or the dangers of sexual or physical exploitation and abuse (Ayotte 2000). Some of the refugees may never have attended school or may have gaps in their learning and may also be managing difficult transitions at home as well as at their place of learning (Ayotte 2000). These factors lead to low self-esteem compounded by frequent disruptions to their schooling and their newness to the environment. As a result of psychological effects of war and persecution, refugee children manifest high levels of mental illnesses – their ability to function in normal social settings is severely and adversely affected (Hodes 2000; Fazel and Stein 2002). In addition, there are symptoms of intrusion, such as nightmares, flashbacks and intrusive thoughts involving constriction and avoidance, such as fear of places and activities that are reminiscent of the trauma, and symptoms of increased arousal such as poor concentration or insomnia. This often presents a difficult and challenging learning environment (Bracken 1998).

Research about the conditions of refugee children is often fraught with irregularities and inaccuracies especially as data collected is from parents, guardians, carers and other stakeholders. Rutter (2006) argues that literature about refugees is dominated by studies that examine the traumatic experiences of refugees and their psychological adaptation in exile. Data on trauma and psychological state of mind is often collected in clinics. None of the research subjects is observed in social or school settings, and this is very significant in the UK where refugees usually reside in areas of high deprivation. This argument is extended on the impact of how they are viewed by their teachers. In the same paper, Rutter states that the adjective 'traumatized' is widely used when talking about refugee children. As a result of this limitation, refugees' background and needs are framed by educationalists largely in terms of trauma.

Accompanied children rely on the decisions taken by their parents and find it easier to be looked after by their parents and LAs. When refugee children are in the care of local authorities, many local authorities lack the financial resources, skills and knowledge to meet the needs of these children. Richman (1993) indicates that such children may manifest feelings of loss, change and separation; through fear of loud noises or voices of groups of men, or men in uniform; sadness or irritability as they may appear worried, miserable or lacking in energy: poor concentration and restlessness and regularly being over-active and unable to settle at any one activity; aggression and disruptiveness which is a very common feature of distress. They may hit out in the absence of other ways of expressing their frustration, may act out inappropriate aggressive behaviour they may have witnessed or may simply try to keep away from adults or, alternatively, cling to them, terrified of abandonment. They may tend to manifest physical symptoms such as nightmares, aches and pains and loss of appetite. Most evidently, frustration and insecurity, as a result of unfamiliarity with new customs and scenery, takes control of them.

Research Participants

The research participants were initially refugees from French-speaking countries in Africa, but experiences from other refugee groups have also been rewarding to the project. The participants believe that the economic situation and social status of their families can be ameliorated through successful education. Yet, there is increased anxiety over research and media reports about black underachievement. There is a need to identify where the gaps come from in respect to the children, parents, teachers, schools, and government and whole communities. Throughout the research, evidence emerged that being a Francophone or African refugee is not so significant in the context of integration, settlement, education and social inclusion. Hence, the experiences of other refugee groups became very useful. Being a refugee exposes the individual to the same social and economic injustices, inequalities, alienations and social exclusions that go with the labelling. That is why the survey initially started with African refugees in the East Midlands but finally involved others from different ethnic groups, especially in Scotland. The participants were drawn from the skilled to the unskilled, from the newly arrived, the recently arrived and the long term settled.

Some Immigration Statistics by First Quarter 2009

In 2007 asylum claims rose by 9 per cent and there was a further increase of 3 per cent in 2008. In the first half of 2008, about 165,000 asylum claims were submitted in about 44 industrialized countries and it is estimated that between 330,000 and 360,000 asylum claims were lodged in 2008. About 120,000 were lodged in the first half of 2008 in the European Union. The United Kingdom ranked forth among 44 industrialized countries with 14,500 new cases in the first half – far below the peak year of 2002 when about 103,000 individuals requested refugee status in the United Kingdom. The Home Office (2009) recorded 8,380 asylum applicants in the first quarter of 2009 but does not have any data on the number of dependants of school age. From 2000 to 2007, it is recorded that about 120,500 dependants entered the UK with an addition of 37,250 children of settled migrants recognized as dependants. These figures are not spread over different countries, making it difficult to determine those from French-speaking African countries. In 2008, it was estimated that 16,338 Francophone Africans from former French-speaking African colonies claimed asylum in the European Union (UNHCR, The UN Refugee Agency 2008). The statistics document legally registered cases from Senegal, Mali, Guinea Algeria, Cote D'Ivoire, Burundi, Congo, and the Democratic Republic of Congo. Countries like Togo, Chad, Central African Republic, Gabon, and Burkina Fasso, which are also Francophone Africa, are not included in the statistics. These countries also have internal instability and this researcher has met refugees from these countries. This means that if a complete census is conducted, the total number of Francophone African asylum seekers will rise in the EU countries as well as in the UK for the year 2008. Added to the history of immigration and the peak year of 2002, these figures prove that there are many Francophone African families seeking refuge in the UK. These families have school-age children and the specific needs of refugees or asylum seekers in UK schools need to be addressed.

There is no completely accurate national and local data on numbers of asylum seeking and refugee children in the UK. This is partly because published data does not include numbers of dependants or break down dependants by age group. In 2003, the Refugee Council estimated that there were almost 99,000 children of compulsory school age (Bolloten and Spafford 2005). Inasmuch as there are concerns on the specific needs of refugee children from other regions, Rutter (2006) states that Congolese children were underachieving in national tests at 14 years. An over-represented number of Congolese children were judged to have special needs, 50 per cent compared with 22 per cent of pupils as a whole. A disproportionate number of Congolese children had been temporarily excluded from school for behavioural problems and underachievement. The reasons included the absence of education prior to arriving in the UK, poor links between parents and schools, and family welfare issues (Rutter 2006). How this related to other Francophone African children in the UK is also important to this study.

Methodology

The researcher adopted a multi-method strategy to triangulate original data (Korac 2003; Malde 2005; Ragu 2007; Rutter *et al.* 2007). Korac (2003:122) argues that 'since integration is individualized, contested and contextual, it requires qualitative methodologies which allow the voices of respondents to be heard in an unadulterated form'. The multiple strategies were intended to show how refugees feel about their experiences as an important indicator – just as important as objective indicators of adaptation such as employment, income and socio-economic mobility. Montgomery (1996) acknowledges that it exposes strategies aimed at revealing the subjective world of the refugees rather than social mappings of numerical data and statistical methods favoured by governments in evaluating the success of their policies. Unlike numerical data and statistical mapping, which rather present a 'tidier than life account' of social reality, the question of whether, when and how far the person identifies with those who share the same categorical status, is never proposed. To balance the sources of data collection, a literature search, focus group discussion, interviews and participant observation were employed. Two sessions were held with refugee focus groups and another focus group session was held with refugee case workers drawn from the British Red Cross, Peterborough and Cambridge, Gladstone Community Refugee Centre, the African Refugee Association in Peterborough and LINCS, Peterborough. The researcher felt the need to develop the research hypotheses by exploring the issues surrounding refugees' schooling in the UK, causes of their underachievement, as well as tackle such a set of controversial issues through active and loosely-controlled discussions.

Open-ended interviews were conducted with six refugees in Peterborough and 20 others in Glasgow. (Lofland 1971; Turner 1994; Gilham 2000). Three of the six interviews were conducted in French, translated and, as with the rest, transcribed and later validated by the respondents. The inability of most refugees to articulate in English disqualified the use of questionnaires. Four children in primary schools in Peterborough and four families outside schools were observed to evidence some of the themes. Since some of the issues dealt with identity, acculturation and bilingualism, the researcher carried out a one-month observation of a French-speaking African family in France and in a French primary school.

Results

The results of this survey indicate that all pupils need to develop skills and understanding to succeed in an increasingly global society. A great number of concerns preoccupied parents and easily translated into the lack of motivation which accounted for children from refugee households attending school irregularly or even dropping out of school after a while. The concerns discussed here include induction and IQ tests, class allocation, school events, parents' economic status, language needs, choice of subjects and future careers, child protection legislations and discipline, teacher and school perceptions of refugee children, bullying, racism and trauma.

Induction and IQ Tests

Refugee children are received by the coordinator of new arrivals and, after an initial assessment, the children are sent to the school to begin classes immediately. Parents reported that the children often get confused in the organization of the school, the planning for the day, the language and curriculum as well as methodology. Sometimes the children are given IQ tests using standards built on Western resources. They are often sent to the wrong class levels and even given special needs assessments due to wrong IQ results. Two of the parents made allusion to the system of education in their home countries modelled on the French system of education. Classes run as:

Petit Section – Nursery 1
Moyen Section – Nursery 2
Grande Section – Primary 1
Cour Preparatoire – Primary 2
Cour elementaire 1 – Primary 3
Cour elementair 2 – Primary 4
Cour Moyen 1 – Primary 5
Cour Moyen 2 – Primary 6.

The final exam written in Primary 6 by every pupil is Certificate Etudes Primaire (CEP) translated as The First School Leaving Certificate. In the UK, classes are assigned to age groups and the classes are labelled differently. In Scotland, primary studies run from 5 to 12 years. Parents complained that the direct immersion of their children into the classroom without proper induction often led to confusion, frustration and disengagements.

Class Allocation

Refugee parents were concerned that classes are assigned according to age groups rather than academic abilities. All the children aged 7 belong to one class, even though there are streams of different abilities. In their home country, as with their educational system, classes are determined by examinations. A child has to obtain an average of 10 + in an exam to move to the next class. This means that you could have children of 8 years, 10 years and 14 years all in the same class as defined by examination results. Parents were worried that their children are assigned into wrong classes with gaps in their schooling because of the age group criterion.

School Events

Parents complained that some school events were organized for the benefit of the indigenous population. They were invited to sporting events like skiing, ice skating and refreshments or lunch where menus usually did not consider the multicultural composition of the audience. Muslims, for example, will not sit where pork and alcohol are consumed and where dancing or spectacles involving girls exposing some parts of their bodies, as this would be against the teachings of their religion. These feelings often led the parents to stay away from school events which consequently affected their children. This affects primary children as their very young ages requires parental consent or that they must be accompanied during such school events and trips.

Parents' Economic Status

Asylum seekers are not allowed to work until they receive a positive decision about their application. They rely on a support token that is often very basic and cannot cater for transportation costs to accompany their children to schools, take care of participation in school events, afford proper clothes or enrol children to paid learning and social centres. Prejudice from employers, ignorance, a low level of English and lack of the required job skills often make it difficult for them to obtain employment. When they do get jobs, most of them end up in low-paid jobs, not good enough to guarantee them regular income to supplement the school needs of their pupils. They would hardly ever become financially able to get specialist education which cannot be met by LAs, or afford private tuition for their children. Two of the parents that were interviewed were cleaners and 17 of those that were interviewed in Scotland could not get jobs. Most of their children qualified for free school meals but did not appreciate the meals because the menu was always foreign to what they are used to.

Language Needs

The progress in learning written English is very slow. Some parents felt that English as an Additional Language was often directed at vocabulary and communication teaching that responded to the needs of the school rather than to the needs of the children. The training did not normally adapt to the divergent learning capacities of asylum seekers and refugees and did not convey key information about the host society and its functioning. The children could express themselves in specific phrases that did not apply beyond the school context. It was difficult to check the progress of the child and the children, in some cases, were used as interpreters by their parents. The mistakes and inaccuracies often increased, leading to wrong information, misunderstandings, difficulty in negotiating meanings and increased ignorance.

Choice of Subjects and Future Careers

Some parents had earmarked specific careers for their children. Some wanted their children to be doctors, engineers, pilots, and had always used existing structures in their countries to motivate their children towards these professions. They could not easily distinguish the curriculum in primary schools, unlike in their home countries where primary education fell into arithmetic, languages, geography, history, hygiene, nature study, rural sciences, farm work, sports, drawing, civics and general knowledge and education. Parents pointed out that they could not easily decide on which subjects their children should concentrate in order to develop an interest for a particular career. Their children chose subjects depending on their friends, especially the friends that had more experience about the system here. Parents complained that their children tended to lay emphasis on dance, music, drawing and so on, and tended to lose interest in core subjects which would be critical later on in determining the career that they wanted to do.

Child Protection, Legislation and Discipline

Most parents were concerned about child legislation that forbids parents from punishing their children. This was compared to their home countries where parents had the right to use physical punishment and beat their children. The fear expressed by most parents was about the frustrating situation where they could not effectively devise methods to discipline their children. They blamed child protection legislation and social services as well as the police who would intervene when a child was corrected with physical punishment. This was also blamed as the major cause for early smoking and alcohol addiction and lack of respect and discipline in schools in the UK.

Teacher and School Perceptions of Refugee Children

Most parents held the view that schools often had negative thoughts about refugee children. Schools often thought that refugee children were violent, subnormal and underachieving. A parent stated that a school gave up early on his daughter because they thought that she was not intelligent enough to be in a normal school. She was referred to a specialist school, but the parent refused to send her there and preferred her to work hard at home with a refugee teacher. The child 'picked up' and progressed very well into secondary school. Parents held that this perception affected the way the teachers related to the child; the way the child was singled out during classroom activities, the attention devoted to the child and the pastoral care offered to the child.

Bullying and Racism

Parents recognized that their children were new to the environment and were always looked at as 'different' or often considered as 'the other'. Most parents acknowledged the fact that their children cried regularly in school. They were often distracted with racist comments and were pushed about or beaten, had resources taken from them, their personal space encroached upon, and had their accents imitated and laughed at. Most parents felt that when these attitudes were reported, the teachers and the school often dismissed them as irrelevant. Parents themselves could enumerate regular racist incidents that they and their families suffered daily and how these were not often resolved by the police. Helpless under such circumstances, most parents simply withdraw and accepted the problem as uncontrollable. During the participant observation, this researcher could notice different reactions to racism in France and the UK. In the UK, children who did not speak English often silently walked away when racially abused. But in France, the researcher noticed a refugee from a French-speaking

African country fighting back to bullying and racial remarks. The child had the same cultural experience of assimilation in France.

Trauma

Persecution, exposure to brutality and violence, displacement and forced separation from family members and friends affected their stability and the ability of their children to learn. Inadequate social and economic resources, continued separation from friends and peers and difficulty in creating social ties, added to trauma. Most of them were affected by the absence of work, social exclusion and marginalization, stereotyping and being continuously branded as refugees, anxiety over immigration decisions, problems of relocation, debts owed to people back home, disintegration of home societies, humiliation from hostilities from the public and negative press reporting. Continuous debates on immigration combined to affect the parents and children negatively.

Discussion

The fact that some recently and newly-arrived refugees may be experiencing intense financial pressures, and working long hours doing physically exhausting tasks, has a bearing on the availability of refugee parents to assist their primary school children. Parents who work very hard to provide the bare essentials for their families find that participation in their children's education negatively affects their daily income and often causes them to remain on the extreme poverty ladder. Despite the heterogeneous class structures of the migrating population, refugees often occupy, overwhelmingly, the semi-skilled and unskilled positions in the English labour market (Smith 1977). They have been disproportionately concentrated in certain manual work, characterized by shift working, and sometimes in very unsocial hours. This often increases their interest in prioritizing their jobs, thereby leaving little or no time for issues like assisting their children in homework, or accompanying them to school events. It has generated a work culture among refugee parents which Lopez (2001) describes as the importance of work ethic.

Communication in the language of the host country is an effective tool for settlement and integration. Coll (2001), in a survey on immigrants and schools, concluded that rate of participation was relative to the ability to communicate in the language of the host country. The inability to communicate with staff and teachers alienated migrant parents from any group meetings (McCollum 1996). In most cases, lack of English skills, coupled with low levels of schooling, made parents feel ashamed to interact with school staff. Parents would prefer to send children to represent them in events and meetings, and this should not be considered as shifting their responsibility, but as an effort to resolve their language crisis in the most satisfactory way possible, given their resources. Viewed in a more positive light, abstaining and sending an English-speaking sibling is a successful functional adaptation strategy for interacting in a new social system where one does not speak the language. The limited use of English, added to the lack of knowledge about the education system, and even a lack of tradition in questioning professionals, inhibits interaction with the school.

Blair (1994) recognized the fact that schools do not communicate clearly what they expect of parents, nor do they always understand what the parents expect of them. The general pattern of communication includes newsletters, telephone calls, student reports, and letters, open evenings, which are often in English, despite the schools being multi-ethnic and linguistically driven. It is a serious threat to the morale of even educated refugee parents from Africa or Asia if they cannot read English. Most schools have a system of homework diaries which parents are expected to sign to ensure that the child has done the homework. Some educated refugee parents and most long-term settled refugee parents could assist in homework, but newly arrived and the uneducated could not. Some of the refugees can only use their own languages, originating in remote rural areas and used by small numbers of people, that do not relate to any of the more widely-spoken languages. Often these parents would not speak English at all, or only a little, and would not feel confident in speaking to their children's teachers (Crozier *et al.* 2003)

Racial harassment and abuse, as well as bullying, were prominent themes articulated by all the research participants. Respondents reported being verbally abused, and in some cases experienced physical abuse. Respondents felt powerless and unable to help themselves or their children from bullies or racial perpetrators. Beale-Spencer (1991) recognizes the fact that bullying is a serious problem in the UK and that racial bullying has distinctive causes and implications for the psychosocial wellbeing. For young people, it curtails their involvement in extracurricular school activities and has led many young people to spend most of their time in school with students from their own ethnic groups, which in turn has led to criticism. Many teachers refer to these associations as the formation of 'gangs' and some describe 'gangs' of boys, in particular, as intimidating, displaying 'assertiveness' and 'arrogance'. Hence, rather than asking support and sympathy, these young people are demonized with the implication that they are the perpetrators of trouble (Archer 2003). This adds to parents' concerns about children's safety; a numbers of attacks have been witnessed by black and Asian families, and this situation is not conducive for free and easy movement through the streets which is afforded to the white majority. It has forced refugee families to be relegated to their homes. The school, by association, may be seen as part of that unwelcoming and, at times, hostile environment.

Tibbetts (cited in Straker-Welds 1984) argues that young children's acquisition of racist attitudes – popularly believed to occur simply because parents teach their children such feelings – can more accurately be seen to result from a subtler and complex process of socialization affecting the minority group. If the play activities and the general ethos in schools only values the host community, then all children, irrespective of their cultural backgrounds, are channelled to play in a way which confirm to a white ethnocentric view of the world. Sivanandan (1970) states:

[T]hat it is a racism that is not just directed at those with darker skins, from the formal colonial territories, but at the newer categories of the displaced, the dispossessed and the uprooted, who are beating at Western Europe's doors, the Europe that helped to displace them in the first place. It is a racism, that is, that cannot be colour coded, directed as it is at poor whites as well, and is therefore passed off as xenophobia, 'a natural fear of strangers'. But in the way it denigrates and reifies people before segregating and/or expelling them, it is a xenophobia that bears all the marks of the old racism. It is racism in substance, but 'xeno' in form. It is a racism that is meted out to impoverished strangers even if they are white. It is xeno-racism. (Sivanandan 1970:348)

This unsympathetic disregard of human beings and negative perception further alienates the refugees even in issues surrounding their children. Miles (1986:165) has analysed the structure of the refugee population and his critique point to the notion that those immigrants occupy a structurally distinct position in the economic, political and ideological revelation of British capitalization, but within the boundary of the working class, and one that can be identified as a 'radicalized fraction'. It is not only in name calling or verbal abuse that refugees are targeted by their host counterpart. It has over-spilled into the economic domain as well (Smith 1977).

Some refugee parents felt that racial assumptions about their ethnic groups, cultures, dressing and so on, were prevalent and that this prevented teachers from relating to them and respecting them as partners in the education of their children. This is also a challenge on their educational or cultural capital (Ball 2003); they simply posses low volume capital to function in the place, time and system. Bourdieu (cited by Dunkwu in Hill and Cole (2001)) argues that the culture transmitted by the school confirms values and validates the culture of the ruling classes. At the same time and as a consequence, it disconfirms, rejects and invalidates the cultures of other groups. (See also Hill 2009 in this volume). That is the welcome that refugees receive in England.

Blair (1994) pointed out that despite responses within the education system, extensive discussions with African-Caribbean, Asian and other minority ethnic teachers and parents revealed that the black community became discontented because the Education Reform Act of 1988 lacked respect for the needs of black minority ethnic children. Regulation governing the teaching of religious education required school assemblies to be mainly and broadly Christian acts of worship. In addition, many schools attempting to implement anti-racist initiative faced suspicion from white parents, with little support from officials in most LAs. The few LAs that had attempted to represent black communities and control service delivery towards anti-racist ends were the object of frequent vilification and political attack. The open display of cultural superiority by English white parents over subordinate cultures is a huge barrier to refugee parents in their attempt to socialize in the wider community. Dunkwu states that:

All cultures – working class/middle class, urban/rural, Roman Catholic/ Protestant – have intrinsic validity and embody an intricate and often distinctive network of norms, values, and traditions. A social democracy committed to liberty and equality is committed to diversity and our schools have a responsibility to recognize it and further it. (Dunkwu in Hill and Cole 2001:57)

Dunkwu argues that the cultures of the minorities should be maintained and fostered, irrespective of their content and specific customs. The notion that these cultures should be exempt from critical comment, official disapproval or legislative interference may have arisen from the desire to compensate for the deprivation of ethnocentrism, which ethnic minorities have all too often been forced to contend with, as relatively powerless communities. Muslim parents, for example, provide further evidence of a strictly controlled and regulated culture where dressing codes and even eating habits are highly restrictive.

When indigenous white staff talk of involving people from the minority group, like refugee parents, it generally means involving them in something which is of the majority culture (Straker-Welds 1994). Minority group members are frequently expected to conform to the indigenous group's standards when they come to the community at large; standards which they may not understand too well or do not accept. This view could easily be looked at in another way, which could mean that the minority group is being exposed to majority culture in order not to be put at a disadvantage. Straker-Welds (1994:11) states that:

It is important to recognize that minority group parents are individuals with different circumstances, needs and ideas. For example, while many minority group parents are personally suffering from stresses of making the transition from one culture to another, while experiencing these stresses will find ways of coping with them. Others will have become acculturated. Some parents will consciously take the decision that they want themselves and their children to become fully integrated into the majority group's culture; some may choose to maintain their own culture by isolating themselves as much as possible from the host community, others feel that they want to acknowledge their identity by having their culture represented and valued in society. (Straker-Welds 1994:11)

While acceptable integration into a majority group's culture becomes incumbent on refugee parents, the majority or dominant white culture, and the way the indigenous people perceive non-English values, tend to be a barrier to refugee parents' involvement in their children's schooling. The Schools Council, (1985 cited in Ofsted 2003:45) in a school report, held that in a multicultural society like England, a two-way exchange of minority and majority cultures could be more beneficial in a whole school setting and that 'some English speaking parents in some schools might be known to be hostile to any form of cultural or linguistic diversity'.

In the same report, a head teacher commented about the celebration of a local dance:

Unfortunately a number of English parents were not happy about us celebrating DIWALI and withdrew their children from school for the day. They said they didn't want their children involved in any act of worship other than a Christian one ... other parents, although not withdrawing their children, did not approve and in fact spread malicious rumours insinuating that there were to be no Christmas celebrations in the school and that we were only interested in the Asian children. (Schools Council (1985) cited in Ofsted 2003:45)

This is the cultural clash that often benefits the majority culture.

Conclusion

The multi-method approach employed in this project generated data that is essentially of a qualitative nature. Although the research initially focussed on French-speaking African refugees, the views of participants were expanded to involve the research with refugees in Glasgow. With attention to concepts of equality, universality and inclusivity, such insights will provide key indicators of how to better support a diverse and representative educational community while fostering diversity in the future. The government is committed to securing improved access and additional educational support to enable all children to achieve their full potential. While this research recognizes the challenges of teaching asylum seeking and refugee pupils, it helps to highlight the conclusion that:

- Factors do exist that detract, inhibit or deter refugee parents and pupils from effectively participating in schools.
- It is the schools and LA's responsibility to ascertain which of these factors are present in the life of their schools and recognize them as legitimate concerns.
- School staff and related bodies must take action to minimize or prevent these obstacles.
- These issues should be recognized in the commitment to supporting schools to help refugee pupils settle in schools and to help refugee parents play an active role in assisting their children to enjoy full access to the National Curriculum.

References

Archer, L. (2003) *Race, Masculinity and Schooling*. Buckingham: Open University Press.

Ayotte, W. (2000) *Separated Children coming to Western Europe: Why they travel and how they arrive*. Save the Children.

Ball. S. J. (2003) *Class Strategies and Educational Market. The Middle Class and Social Advantage*. London: Routledge/Falmer.

Bhachu, P. (1985) *Parental Educational Strategies: The Case of the Punjabi Sikhs in Britain*. Research paper 3. Centre for Research and Ethnic Relations. University of Warwick.

Blair, M. (1994) 'Black teachers, black students and education markets'. *Cambridge Journal of Education*, 24, (2), 21.

Beale-Spencer, M. (1991) 'Class Pedagogies; Visible and Invisible', in A. Halsey, P. Lauder and A. Stuart-Wells (eds) *Education, Culture, Economy and Society*. Oxford: Oxford University Press.

Bertossi, C. (2007) *European Anti-Discrimination and the Politics of Citizenship: Britain and France (Migration, Minorities and Citizenship)*. Palgrave: Macmillan.

Bolloten, B. and Spafford, T. (2005) *Refugee and Asylum seeker children in UK schools*. Online at http://www.naldic.org.uk/ITTSEAL2/teaching/Refugeechildreninschool.cfm. (Accessed on 14 January 2009).

Bracken, P. J. (1998) 'Hidden agendas: Deconstructing post traumatic stress disorder', in P. J. Bracken and C. Petty (eds) *Rethinking the Trauma of War*. London: Free Association Books and Save the Children.

Child Soldier Global Report (2001) *Children used as soldiers in most major conflicts*. Online at http://www.thinkweb.hrw.org/en/node/68738.

Coll, G. (2001) *Parents Involvement in their Children's Education: Lessons from Three Immigrant Groups*. New Haven, CT: Yale University.

Crozier. G., Davies. J., Booth. D., Khatun, S. (2003) *School, Family and Community Relationship, with reference to families of Bangladeshi origin in the North East of England.* Paper presented at the British Educational Research Association Annual conference. Heriot-Watt University, Edinburgh, 11–13 September 2003. Online at http://www.leeds.a-c.uk/educol/documents/00003233.htm. (Accessed on 10 April 2006).

Dunkwu (2001) 'Policy, equality and the educational research', in D. Hill and M. Cole, (eds) *Schooling and Equality. Fact, Concept and Policy.* London/Sterling: Kogan Page Limited.

Fazel, M. and Stein, A. (2002) 'Mental Health of Refugee Children: Comparative Study'. *British Medical Journal,* July 17, 327 Online at http:/www.bmj.com/cgi/reprint/327/7407/134. (Accessed on 20 January 2008).

Gibson, M.A. (1988) 'Immigration Adaptation and Patterns of Acculturation'. *Journal of Human Development* 2001:44, 19–23.

Gilham, B. (2000) *The Research Interview.* London: Continuum.

Hill, D. (2009) 'Politics and the Curriculum: The National Curriculum, the Hidden Curriculum, Inequality, and Understanding and Addressing Inequalities through Critical Pedagogy and Critical Policy Analysis', in D. Hill and L. H. Robertson (eds) *Equality in the Primary School: Promoting good practice across the curriculum.* London: Continuum.

Hodes, M. (2000) 'Psychologically Distressed Refugee Children in the United Kingdom'. *Child Psychology and Psychiatry Review.* 5, 57–68.

Home Office (2009) Control of Immigration accessed on http://www.homeoffice.gov.uk/rds/immigration-asylum-stats.html.

Korac, M. (2003) 'Integration and How We Facilitate it: A comparative Study of the Settlement Experiences of Refugees in Italy and the Netherlands'. *Sociology,* 37(1): 58–68.

Lofland, J. (1971) *Analysing Social Setting; A guide to qualitative observation and analysis.* Belmont CA: Wodsworth.

Lopez, G. R. (2001) 'The value of hard work; Lessons on parent involvement from an (Im)migrant household'. *Harvard Educational Review* 71, 416–437.

Lynch, K. and Lodge, A. (2002) *Equality and Power in Schools.* London: Routledge Falmer.

Malde, A. (2005) '*Is it 'cos I is Black, Sir?' – African/Caribbean males and British Higher Education.* University of Oxford (Internal Dissertation). Online at http://www.anjool-co.uk/dissertation.htm. (Accessed on 24 January 2008).

McCollum, P. (1996) *Immigrant Education; Obstacles to Immigrant Parent Participation in Schools.* Online at http://www.questia.com/PM/qst.

Menter, I., Cunningham, P., Sheibani, A. (2000) 'Safe at Last? Refugee Children in Primary Schools', in M. Datta (ed.) *Bilinguality and Literacy; Principles and Practice.* London: Continuum.

Montgomery, R. (1996) 'Components of Refugee Adaptation'. *International Migration Review* 30, (3), 679–702.

Miles, R. (1986) *State, Racism, and Migration: The Recent European Experience.* Amsterdam: Centre for Economics and Political Studies, 23.

OFSTED (2003) *The Education of Asylum Seeker Pupils.* London: HMSO.

RAGU (Refugee Assessment and Guidance Unit) (2007) *Training Provision and Other Support for Refugee Teachers in the UK: Mapping the Field.* London: London Metropolitan University. Online at http://www.londonmet.ac.uk/londonmet/library/d56185_3.pdf.

Richman, N. (1993) *Communicating with Children; Helping in Distress.* Development Manual 2. London: Save the Children.

Rutter, J. (2003) *Working with Refugee Children.* Stoke-On-Trent: Trentham Books.

Rutter, J. (2006) *Refugee Children in the UK.* Buckingham: Open University.

Rutter J., Cooley, L., Reynolds, S. and Sheldon, R. (2007) 'From Refugee to Citizenship: Standing On My Own Two Feet'. *A Research Report on Integration, Britishness and*

Citizenship. London: Metropolitan Support Trust and the Institute of Public Policy Research.

Sivanandan, A. (1970) 'Race, Class and the State; the Black Experience in Britain'. *Race and Class*, 17, (4), 347–368

Smith, D. J. (1977) *Racial Disadvantage in Britain*. London: Penguin.

Straker-Welds, M. (1984) *Education for a Multi cultural Society. Case Studies ILEA Schools*. London: Welds Bell and Hyman.

Tibbetts, C. (1984) 'Working with Under-Fives' in Straker-Welds (ed.) *Education for a Multi cultural society. Case studies in ILEA schools*. London: Bell and Hyman.

Turner, B. S. (1994) *Qualitative Methods in Landscape ecology; the Analysis and Interpretation*. New York: Springer-Verlag.

UNHCR, The UN Refugee Agency (2008) *Asylum Levels in Industrialized countries, first half 2008. Statistical Overview of Asylum Applications Lodged in 38 countries and 6 Non European countries*. Geneva: UNHCR.

Part 2

Core Subjects

Chapter 6

English and Literacy

Nick Peim

Introduction: Pastoral Discipline and Technological Enframing

From the moment children enter the world of schooling they are beset by the machinery of education, framed by the remorseless logic of improvement. This means, in effect, that all they do will be charted according to the norms of development ensconced in the National Curriculum: their performance will be monitored, their status measured against those norms and against the performance status of their peers. Assessments will be made, grades awarded, reports written: they will take up their place within a systematic ordering of identity that will define where they stand in relation to publicly endorsed ideals of knowledge and culture (Peim and Flint 2009).

Of course, it's not only the performance of children in specific subjects that is subject to this endless charting of performance and achievement. Their behaviour will be closely monitored and constantly subjected to formation and, where necessary, reformation. Children in schools will be managed and controlled, subjected to the symbolic order that defines their very character and judges their conduct within a moral framework of conformity. More significantly, perhaps, children in schools will be encouraged, trained and guided in the arts of *self*-regulation and *self*-management, subtly directed to adopt the norms of development and aspiration the school projects. Children will be taught to review their own progress, and to align their desires with the proper aspirations of educational progress. They will be expected to learn how to become good citizens: to become self-conscious about themselves as social beings, to project positive futures for themselves, to celebrate the benefits of the social system, to avoid obesity, and to ingest the norms and values of the dominant symbolic order (Lacan 1977).

This is the logic of pastoral discipline that defines the nature of contemporary schooling. It constitutes an unprecedented, far-reaching and powerful social technology. It is supported by new electronic surveillance technologies, as well as historically deeply-embedded technologies of person management (Donald 1992; Hunter 1988, 1994). It has a relatively kindly face: it is pastoral and works in the name of 'care'; but it is also disciplinary: it demands obeisance to norms and threatens exclusion form social goods if that demand is rejected (Foucault 1977;

Willis 1979). What's more, with the introduction of a formal curriculum at nursery level and the threat of 'lifelong learning', children face a lifetime of potential enclosure within this 'enframing' (Heidegger 1978). Should children fall outside of the norms and values system of the school, a host of adjacent institutions stands ready to enfold them in a special embrace designed to keep them from the dark domain of social exclusion and to manage their existence within acceptable margins of social inclusion.

The Political Dimension of Curriculum

That the school is about learning more than specifications of the formal curriculum has become a truth universally acknowledged – and even celebrated by advocates of school extension (Bowles and Gintis 1976). It is also the case that the curriculum itself cannot be separated from the social function of order and control that the school so powerfully and universally enacts in our culture (Bernstein 2000; Hill 2009 in this volume). While specific elements of the curriculum represent forms of knowledge that carry with them the endorsement of the symbolic order, they also carry with them specific forms of conduct.

One of the interesting things about English is that is has become, *par excellence*, that element of the curriculum where self-expression is both encouraged and validated. To engage fully in subject English is not merely to learn about material that is external to the learner. In English, the learner is required to express herself, is required also to activate her own 'voice' and to express her own responses to various forms of textual material. The invitation to participate, of course, is not entirely free and open: it is highly conditional. In English, self-expression is charted against the norms of the curriculum. While these norms are represented as being self-evident and neutrally developmental, in fact, it turns out that they express a partial view of what both language and culture are.

It is in relation to language and culture that we confront the political nature of English and the political nature of the relation between subject identity and the social technology of the school. In recent times, English has adopted the guise of the most liberal subject on the curriculum, the area of school labour where children can express, in their own various idioms, their own different identities, heritages and can articulate their own cultural affiliations (Dixon 1967, 1991; Bullock 1975). This apparent openness may sit rather oddly with the regulation of content, the grid of specifications and the regime of norm related assessment and inspection that has characterized the order of things since the 1988 Education Reform Act.

The History of Subject Identity

The deeper history of subject identity, however, seems to tell a rather different story from John Dixon's warm account of the development of English as progressively liberal in essence (1991). One alternative version of that history, in fact, tells the story of a subject born from concerns about the spiritual health of the nation's population, becoming a national project at a time of fear of

Bolshevism, a time of concern for the corruption of the English language, fear of the popular, and a desperate need for socio-cultural cohesion (Baldick 1983; Doyle 1989). English in the 1920s was projected as the subject that could work against the depredations of popular culture, that could maintain the proper standard of standard English and that could promote a culture of national unity. There was good reason for the authors of the Newbolt Report (1921) to focus on English as a linguistic-cultural project with serious political mission. According to one scandalous version of subject history, English – yes, English, the subject that surely belongs most properly to England and the English – had its origins in India. According to this view, English as a curriculum subject first arose as a vehicle for the enculturation of subaltern populations. Imperial rule in India decreed that sections of the native population had to be learned in the ways of Englishness, lessoned in the language, culture and values of their rulers. Studies in English language and literature provided that function (Viswanathan 1989). Some would have it that English came to serve a parallel function in England and Wales after World War I, when the native population was looking increasingly restless, potentially Bolshevik and in need of pastoral discipline (Peim 2005) . If we take this history seriously, we must accept the fact that English has traditionally been a subject freighted with anxieties and concerns about the linguistic and cultural health of the nation, long before National Curriculum specifications occupied subject identity. On this view, English was always a ideologically loaded business (Doyle 1989).

Dixon's more sanguine view of English teaching represents a history of progress towards a liberal ideal. English may have begun as a state project concerned to enculturate the potentially wayward masses (Newbolt); it may have spent a significant section of its history defining its core values as belonging to 'the great tradition' of English literature in opposition to the corrupting influences of mass culture (Leavis 1942) and it may have endorsed an authority for standard English at odds with any sane linguistics (Chomsky 1979; Halliday 1978); but, according to Dixon, English gradually worked to make itself more open, more user-friendly, more tolerant of linguistic and cultural differences (Dixon 1967). In fact, English became *the* subject, above all others, that would redeem the project of state-sponsored education from the inequalities it had persistently enacted until the instigation of the comprehensive ideal (Dixon 1991). The coming of the National Curriculum and its general endorsement by the vast majority of practising English teachers put paid to this vision of English as the subject of enlightened political reform.

An alternative set of positions for English did emerge that challenged Dixon's history and challenged the very foundations of English to the core.

Theory and the Politics of Subject Identity

The 1980s saw a particularly virulent outbreak of questions directed at English, striking at the heart of subject identity (Widdowson 1982; Batsleer *et al.* 1985; Eagleton 1983; Day 2002). The 'new sociology of education' via Bernstein, Bourdieu, Young, Willis and Bowles and Gintis, in different ways, had re-examined the class bias in public education systems (Bernstein 1971, 1990, 1997;

Bourdieu and Passeron 1977; Young 1971; Willis 1979; Bowles and Gintis 1976). The language and the culture of the school, its dominant forms of pedagogy as well as the form and content of the curriculum were found to be socially loaded in favour of certain social class groups. Neither knowledge nor pedagogy could henceforth be regarded as neutral in relation to class and cultural differences. Some claimed authority from the new wave of continental 'theory': post-structuralism in particular and the rethinking of Marxism and culture by Althusser (1984) and Gramsci (1985). Some questions came from upstart disciplines, such as cultural studies and media studies, drawing on new and more inclusive forms of textual engagement and modes of knowledge far beyond the ken of English. Sociolinguistics, 'new literacy studies' and psychoanalysis also had their say (Ang 1985, 1991; Lapsley and Westlake 1988; Street 1984; Turner 1992; Peim 2003). Post-colonial discourses challenged the hegemony of Western metaphysics and the truth claims of established institutionalized forms of knowledge from a cultural and historical perspective. These discourses challenged the claims of enlightenment thought at their broadest and more modestly revealed the cultural and historical biases in the school curriculum. Practices, hitherto understood as offering goods in themselves, had been no more than the promotion of linguistic and cultural norms through the technologies of participation (Ahmad 1992; Said 1978). The very institutions of education could not be entirely freed from the colonial project – with all its varied forms of domination. The post-colonial perspective helped to remind us that English as a curriculum subject had not always been about free expression in one's own language, nor had it always been concerned with self- and world-discovery through the liberalizing effects of literature (Viswanathan 1989). Similarly far-reaching, feminism's challenge put the dominant assumptions of English into question with a strong focus on the politics of identity. Much feminist cultural critique, focused on the everyday business of language and textuality, was extremely powerful in displacing some of the dominant assumptions and practices of English as a subject – from the rethinking of the canon to the specific textual practices of criticism (Gilbert and Gubar 1979; Belsey 1985; Moi 1985; Weedon 1987; Butler 1990).

English, then, was diagnosed as both culturally biased in favour of a notional national elite culture and linguistically biased in favour of the norms of one dominant class group. English could never be the same again – having discovered that it was inescapably political. The unconcealed ideological history of English had revealed the subject's long-term complicity with the illiberal project of national unity. The subject had been interrogated to the core.

From questions came proposals for dissolution and redefinition. For a while it seemed that the end of English was on the horizon, a relatively near and necessary event. This was being hailed by its advocates not as catastrophic apocalypse but a necessary, positive destruction to be followed by a more self-conscious and informed reconstruction. Dramatic tropes of reconstruction were the order of the day (Batsleer *et al.* 1985:1–12; Easthope 1991; Peim 1993).

A new world order of English never arrived. No apocalypse materialized. Some changes to subject identity occurred but hardly effected the radical displacement promised by some of the bold titles of the time. From present perspectives, we can see that the present constitution of the subject has a strongly defined form. English didn't suddenly transform itself into something altogether more politically self-conscious nor did it gradually wither away. The new influx of ideas and perspectives on language and textuality offered by theory never quite took hold and certainly failed to make the drastic changes they had promised or threatened. After a brief moderately agonistic flurry over the setting up of the National Curriculum, English in schools became established along lines that remained significantly attached to a notional standard English and to a fairly unregenerate notion of literature with a strong flavour of cultural heritage (Cox 1994).[1] In the process, the work of English teachers became more controlled than ever.

Primary English Specified

In all its statements, the primary English curriculum indicates that it is unaware of its own political structure. From the outset, in terms of both what gets specified and what gets left out, the primary English curriculum betrays a reliance on a shared, but inexplicit set of values. While the curriculum purveys an approach to language textuality that is heavily ideologically loaded, the form of its expression is enigmatic and strongly coded. In order to understand much of what the curriculum means, it is necessary to be an insider, to have already acquired the linguistic habits, the textual orientation and the general attitude to both these things: to be, in Bourdieu's terms 'a fish in water'. The curriculum deploys a language that eschews all theory, that speaks of naturalized practices from a commonsense point of view. In effect, to understand and endorse the National Curriculum is to stand aside from the theoretical knowledge that must render all its statements in their minute forms of expression as politically questionable.

Of course, commonsense understanding will find no problem with the kinds of statements and assertions made in the National Curriculum. And commonsense will find no problem with the idea that children's linguistic and textual competences should be judged in relation to the requirements of performance that the curriculum expresses. Commonsense similarly will have no problem with the fact that children's linguistic and textual engagements in school are highly likely, in many cases, to be judged negatively in relation to these specifications and that in the long run, as patterns of performance set in and patterns of attainment become inscribed in individuals, that social destinies will be determined by these specifications. From the outset, the primary curriculum cannot operate in innocence of socially divisive effects.

That the primary English curriculum begins with 'speaking' is itself an interesting facet of its thinking. All the specifications concerning speech are prefaced with the injunction that 'pupils should be taught to . . .' In itself, within a phase of history, dating from the early eighties, when oracy became more and more a recognized aspect of a 'liberalized' English curriculum, this phrase may appear unexceptionable. Of course, it is redolent of a certain will-to-power that takes the form of a will-to-regulate. From the moment children enter the institution, their very language is to be subjected to both scrutiny and improvement. There are powerful reasons, rooted in linguistic knowledge, about the acquisition and development of speech and, rooted in sociolinguistic knowledge, about the development of the idiolect and its relations with socio-cultural differences. However, why this very formulation, this immediate assumption should appear is highly suspect. Post-Chomskyan linguistics affirms that the acquisition of language is extensive, subtle and complex, irrespective of individual variation in terms of inputs and contexts; post-Chomskyan linguistic also considers that the very idea that some idiolects might be preferable to others is patent nonsense, and would consider the very idea that you could teach language development to be absurd. Any form of sociolinguistics will also recoil at the idea of 'teaching' speech and will be suspicious of the social purposes of such a project, in terms of being likely to privilege certain ingrained forms of speech above others, along class-cultural lines (Chomsky 1979; Gumperz 1982; Halliday 1978; Hymes 1974).

What 'pupils should be taught to . . .' in relation to speaking includes: 'clear diction and appropriate intonation'; choosing words 'with precision'; pupils should also be taught to 'organize what they say'; to 'focus on the main points' (*sic*), 'to include relevant detail' and 'to take into account the needs of their listeners' (English Key Stage 1 2009). What becomes immediately apparent here is that a particular model of language and a particular model of language development are in play. This model, it is also immediately clear, has been informed by no recognized form of knowledge about language, apart from some general untheorized ideas that, despite being relatively powerful in the public sphere, hold absolutely no sway whatsoever in any well-developed linguistic ontology. In other words, the primary curriculum in English is founded in what can only be called prejudices about language and language development. These prejudices, of course, carry considerable force and are likely to be instrumental in how pupils are identified in terms of their linguistic and literacy competences and prospects. What the National Curriculum doesn't specify, but depends on for its implementation, is the kind of everyday judgments (misjudgments, in fact) that get made about linguistic differences among children. This is due to the fact that far from challenging what are, in the not very long run, eugenicist ideas about linguistic difference and overall 'ability' or 'intelligence', the National Curriculum has elevated such prejudices into a rational system, sustained by public criteria and the whole bureaucracy of assessment that defines contemporary education.

How do you teach children to 'speak clearly, fluently and confidently' and what constitutes any one of those key features? Labov's research, for example, long ago indicated that what was taken as the unclear and nonceptual speech of African-American children in US linguistic diagnoses was, in fact, in its own terms, sophisticated and just as conceptually powerful as the speech of any white researcher: hence the change of title for Labov's seminal paper: 'Black Intelligence and Academic Ignorance . . .' It is not as if this paper were rare or unknown; it has a long-standing authority and status and is freely available (Labov 1969).

How come, then, that the authors of English Key Stage 1 appear to know nothing of this position, and nothing of the wealth of material, also freely available, that constitutes modern linguistics and sociolinguistics (Trudgill 1975)? That they must know nothing of the ebonics movement in the USA (Smitherman 2000)? That they haven't attended to Halliday's long-standing account of linguistic difference and they are unaware of all that both Chomsky and Pinker have affirmed about the nature of language acquisition and language competence (Halliday 1978; Chomsky 1979; Pinker 2008)? Given this sustained unawareness, perhaps it is only fair that the English Key Stage 1 specifications should exhibit equal ignorance of much of the far-reaching thinking concerning language and identity that is associated with continental philosophy and theory, with the names of Lacan, Derrida, Wittgenstein, Foucault and others that have revolutionized understandings of what language is and how it works (Lacan 1977; Derrida 1976, 1981, 1987; Wittgenstein 1968; Foucault 1977a, 1977b, 1980; Coward and Ellis 1977). All of these positions negate all the premises that the English Key Stage 1 curriculum is founded on.

Even listening is subject to a series of specifications; but the central concern of the specifications for speech concern what is blithely referred to in the official documentation as 'standard English': 'Pupils should be introduced to some of the main features of spoken standard English and be taught to use them' (English Key Stage 1 2009) A note on standard English indicates what the key deviations are: 'they was', 'I done', 'ain't'. The section on the imperative of standard English is swiftly followed by an equally interesting and equally terse section on speech variety. Apparently, speech may vary according to 'different circum- stances' and 'different listeners': no reference, then, to regional or ethnic or social class differences, nor any reference as to why the forms of 'standard English' should be seen as preferable to the deviant forms that are identified as its negation. But what is this 'standard English' that is, entirely mysteriously in the documentation, given a privileged position without explanation? It is assumed, one imagines, that we all know what it is, why it should claim this special position and why it should be deemed superior to variation. And why is variation deemed legitimate only according to matters of circumstance and audience, having nothing at all to do with identity and life-world?

The specifications for reading, engaging as they must with questions about the determination of the textual field that comes within the remit of education, is no less troubling nor any less under-informed. English Key Stage 2, for instance, needs to offer no explanation as to why 'literature' occupies a privileged position in the textual field. Pupils are not required to understand the historical role of literature in education, of course; but they are required to assent to the special properties that the curriculum assumes belong to literature and to do so in a mode of 'appreciation'. No doubt, the curriculum doesn't consider 'appreciation' to be an appropriate or necessary element in engagements pupils might have with other textual forms. But the question: Why is literature so privileged? just never seems to arise. It is, in fact, foreclosed. In spite of the various questions that have beset the category of literature, including questions about its intrinsic value and its inevitable centrality in curricula, literature simply appears as an inevitable and necessary component of subject identity (Foucault 1988). The National Curriculum is not ambiguous about the necessity for literature: 'the range should include . . .' strikes the tone of the specifications. Pupils are expected to be confronted by 'stories, plays and poems' but these must be 'by significant children's authors' (English Key Stage 1 2009). Once again, there is no expansion on the injunction. We are to suppose, perhaps, again, that the 'truth' of this requirement is simply self-evident, that we all know both what this phrase 'significant children's authors' signifies and why it is itself significant. The general introduction to the official statement of the programme of study for English adds nothing to this gaping lacuna, aside from this kind of familiar, untheorized and unconfirmed platitude: 'Literature in English is rich and influential, reflecting the experience of people from many countries and times'; and a quotation from a 'famous novelist' – 'Studying English literature at school was my first, and probably my biggest, step towards mental freedom and independence. It was like falling in love with life.' Mental freedom and independence, however, do not figure largely in the National Curriculum specifications that follow: the requirements for the nature of responses, once again required to be 'appropriate' like semantic and syntactical choices in speaking, are prescriptive, and the requirement for response itself is non-negotiable. Certain kinds of freedom, clearly, are *not* on offer here.

The National Curriculum determines the textual field – that is, the whole world of text –first of all in terms of literature that takes precedence over all other text types. All other text types then fall into the category of 'non-fiction and non-literary texts', clearly less significant in terms of weight and significance. Here 'the range should include' first of all 'print and ICT-based information texts, including those with continuous text and relevant illustrations' and then 'dictionaries, encyclopaedias and other reference materials' (English Key Stage 1 2009). As a taxonomy of the textual field, these specifications looks distinctly odd, and suspiciously weighted towards a range of textual material that is represented as standing against popular culture. Why else specify 'information texts' to the exclusion of all forms of popular cultural material that extensively occupies the cultural field and that must, necessarily, we assume, surely, stand well beyond the place of what warrants 'appreciation'. Does not this systematic and comprehensive exclusion constitute a parallel to the kind of exclusion implicit in the specifications concerning speech of linguistic variations that might pertain to social class-based, ethnic differences?

Given the history of English as both a self-consciously promoted vehicle for social cohesion, it should not perhaps surprise us that it is highly norm saturated and that the norms it promotes in the whole field of language and textuality are redolent of particular class-cultural 'ethos'. The effective exclusion of large areas of linguistic and textual experience, knowledge and modes of engagement effectively works to exclude significant sections of the pupil population from being at home with the very stuff of the curriculum. In one sense, this shouldn't surprise anyone, given the consistent story of systematic exclusion that the sociology of education has promoted through key figures such as Bernstein and Bourdieu. The symbolic order of the curriculum is designed to validate certain kinds of meanings, certain forms of linguistic and textual orientations.

Of course, all the specifications of the National Curriculum are enfolded within the logic of normative development and 'proper' progression that characterizes what Bernstein refers to as 'framing'. Framing here signifies the whole cultural logic that structures the form of knowledge, the manner of its delivery and the social relations that are essential to its characteristic way of working. Any seriously alternative proposal for reform would have to call into question the whole machinery of assessment and improvement, the entire logic of performativity that the curriculum is at present entangled with.

Alternative Practices?

It is perfectly possible, nevertheless, to propose a whole range of principles for practice in relation to language and textuality that might inform a National Curriculum that would engage primary school pupils differently from the present order of things.

The following suggestions are imaginary, designed only to indicate what an alternative might look like, mainly in order simply to demonstrate that a radically different set of principles and practices *is* possible at both the conceptual level and the level of practice. The apparent commonsense that enables the National Curriculum to set out its requirements tersely as a series of unarguable necessities ... is indicative of a lack of theoretical awareness, but is also indicative of the extent that its ideas have become common currency and accord with professional habitus.

It is possible to conceive of a subject and a practice that approaches oracy, not as a set of prescriptions concerning what is 'appropriate', not in order to improve the 'native' speech of pupils, but as opening pupils towards an understanding of language and textuality as a varied field. Such a practice might encourage and enable pupils to explore rhetorics of speaking positions, for example, to engage in speech activities designed to explore social discourse, to become aware of positions taken, rhetorics available and used and to examine registers that operate in varied contexts. There is no reason, apart from mere prejudice, why very young pupils should not be encouraged to be aware of matters of positionality and ideology in everyday discourses, nor why they should not be encouraged to learn about conduct of speech on socially significant issues.

Linguistic role-play enables pupils to explore both analytically and practically language in the institutional contexts. The formal dimension of language as role-bound, pre-scripted and framed by context can thus be explored through play rather than experienced as a competence to be judged that the pupil stands before in a relation of assessment. Similarly, varieties of speech can be explored in relation to different modalities and idioms, including engaging in ethnographic work on speech differences: and this can be done, of course, without recourse to the idea that so-called 'standard English' represents the desired norm of a full competence that all other varieties fall short of.

The liberal practice of organizing small group discussion might be reconfigured to examine how discussion operates within certain specific types of social group context. Pupils can be directed to consider how speech operates in the family, the school, the workplace and other contexts of social encounter. If pupils can be inducted into the ways of liberal humanist textual response, there is no reason why they can't, alternatively, and from the outset, be inducted into learning some explicit aspects of sociolinguistics: about different ways of talking, different contexts and above all about social prestige and language use. Pupils might also explore the language of identity: the kinds of speech that people use to describe themselves and the kind of speech others use to describe them.

Pupils can also be encouraged to engage in talk around their own real media experiences, exploring the language of representation in media forms they encounter and discussing their own understanding of media-generated meanings. Very young pupils can engage in such practices and produce shared understandings of their own linguistic engagements with various media forms and texts. The whole business of engaging in group discussion and working towards shared meanings or shared recognitions of difference goes against the grain entirely of an assessment system that, from the beginnings of primary education to degree level, sees the individual as the essential unit of performance.

Perhaps one of the most remarkable features of literacy in English has been the absence of an understanding of reading above and beyond a notional view of a technical competence. Of course, reading is always a much more engaging process than that limited idea could represent. Approaches to reading can be formulated that enable pupils to become familiar with printed material while also engaging with a broad range of texts for 'reading' in a more full sense. The phenomenology of reading, although hardly featuring in the understanding of teachers and literacy strategists, that explores fundamental processes of meaning making can give rise to a series of practices looking at the relations between texts and readers that go well beyond present specifications and activities. Again, there is no reason why primary school children should not be encouraged to engage in questions about how meanings operate, about what different types of texts exist and about different ways we do and we might make sense of them. Pupils could also be encouraged to look more explicitly at definitions and categories of texts and the different contexts that texts inhabit and the different things they do in those contexts. While this does mean moving away from standard, stock and hegemonic 'definitions' of what learning to read involves, it promises also to enable pupils to engage in a greater range of texts than at present, including, significantly, texts that are familiar within their own life-worlds and that may afford, for many, more intimate forms of engagement. A teaching of English open to an awareness of subject positions and the role of institutions might also look in detail at *ideas about* reading, about the role of reading in contexts of contemporary culture: looking at different conceptions of reading, how it works, what it's for and so on. Very young pupils already get taught some aspects of textuality, and this could be extended to include explicit reference to genres, codes, contexts, time, representations, identities, gaps and ideology. Very young pupils can be made alert to the fact that ideas about the way the world is circulate in texts and in discourses that position reading subjects differently. All of this means going well beyond the liberal legacy of what literacy is and beyond technical conceptions of learning to read.

Similarly, young pupils can be encouraged to explore and engage in writing from a more phenomenologically-aware perspective. This implies reference to the social dimension of writing: exploring different types of writing, drawing up taxonomies of writing, exploring functions of writing and contexts of writing. The process of encouraging pupils to examine their own world of writing is much more likely to enable active participation and an engagement with their own immediate life-worlds and interests. As a consequence, very young children can also be enabled to explore writing as a social practice, to understand, discourses and texts of writing – to articulate constraints that structure writing as well as to begin to identify relations between writing and institutions and to become aware of markets of writing.

Why does hegemonic literacy not do more to interrogate writing and some of the key assumptions that inform practices of writing in education: writing as communication, writing as 'self'-expression? It is not too far-fetched I believe, as an alternative, to propose an introduction to 'grammatology' for young pupils, to promote understandings of key features of writing concerning reference, metaphor, presence/absence, dissemination, and repetition. A broader and more theoretically informed approach to writing might include reference to writing as technology, looking at specific forms of writing as technologies, but also engaging with 'the question concerning technology' and its various roles in our relations with the world and in defining what we are. A real engagement with writing and technology will also be an engagement with questions of meaning and sense making: ultimately, questions of reading and writing in the world. In the technical emphasis on writing as a standard procedure to be learned and acquired with different levels of competence, the fact that writing is something that intimately engages subjects must be forgotten or foreclosed. Examining subject positions in relation to writing and how these engage with, and are themselves, positioned by written discourses and the organization of knowledge and genres of knowledge can only serve to promote a more reflective, less competence-bound practice of learning and form of education. Pupils might be guided to understand the range of possible writing and written texts they may either encounter or produce, understanding the limits of texts and writing, the extent to which they both depend on meanings beyond themselves, becoming aware of the phenomenon, for example, of intertextuality and questions about 'authorship' – suggesting a more self-conscious relation to writing than the competence model, with its persistent threat of exclusion, could dream of. And isn't it necessarily the case that questions about writing and the representation of reality, matters concerning systems of meaning, production of meaning, orders of identity, writing and truth, writing and cultural differences, writing and regimes of power – all touch on matters that cannot be reduced to another module on the curriculum, or one other competence, to acquire.

Finally

English has long operated as the arbiter and promoter of culture in the school. Literature, regarded as a significant (*the* significant?) element in the cultural field has been central to the project of English from The Newbolt Report (1921) through various influential statements about subject identity (Bullock 1975; Cox 1991; Dixon 1991; The National Curriculum 2009). In spite of the theoretical recognition of its limits as a cultural form, literature remains central in the constitution of English teaching at all levels. English teaching both represents and enacts ideas about language and culture. The modern school is at a critical point in the cultural field: it represents culture with a peculiar generalizing power. The school projects values and ideas; but also *enacts* culture in its habitual regime of control and through the management of the language environment. Language in the school is organized and systematically differentiated by formal curricula discourses.

Language and culture are continuous. Issues of linguistic domination go hand in hand with cultural hegemony. In the context of contemporary global tendencies there is a proliferation of linguistic differences. And just as urban linguistic forms thrive and grow, so cultures continually produce new forms and amalgams. The postmodern condition, if we accept that set of notions as a provisional way of accounting for the contemporary order of things, with its emphasis on both diversity and hybridity, is both a linguistic and a cultural phenomenon. Schooling continues, perhaps of necessity, to resist or foreclose any active recognition of itself as a socially differentiated linguistic and cultural environment. The symbolic violence schooling enacts remains an unresolved and powerful problematic. In spite of liberal innovations and developments, it remains the case that linguistic and cultural differences are a key factor in differential levels of achievement for different social class groups. Non-standard language users are heavily penalized, often to the point of effective exclusion. Hence the ebonics movement in the USA, a serious attempt to address problems of stratified ethnic social exclusion by changing the cultural/linguistic milieu of the school (Smitherman 1998, 2000).

Historically, English teaching has been significantly under-theorized. Ideas that may have threatened to undermine the dominant concepts and practices of the subject have been kept at bay. The language practices traditionally promoted by English, even in its most liberal forms, have been limited and have been tied to institutional practices that have been culturally loaded in favour of an arbitrary standard. The privileging of literature in English indicates a similar failure. The liberal embrace, including the invitation to participate 'freely', is incompatible with the fact of differential achievement.

While it is perfectly possible to envisage a subject dealing with textuality and language organized around different assumptions and ideas from the conventional models of English, such a transformation is not likely in any foreseeable future. The very idea of 'English' – with all the assumptions carried in its title and its history – would have to be called into question. A rethinking of pedagogy tied to assessment and all the devices that go along with it would also be necessary.

It seems very clear that the means to produce a new curriculum in the field of language and textuality are readily available. Practices in Cultural Studies and Media Studies provide some models – as do discourses concerned with language and power. The richness of the field of theory (and its attendant practices) seems unquestionable. The problem remains, though, of the subject's enclosure within its institutional limits, its inherited purposes and modalities. These cannot so easily be swept aside. They are powerfully inscribed in the constitution of the subject. This operates at the 'juridical' level – in terms of the official and 'legal' definition of the subject; and it operates at the 'veridical' level – in terms of the beliefs and values of practitioners.

The question of how to institute alternative perspectives, how to engage in an effective politics of transformation in the context of English teaching in schools remains seriously problematic. The case for transformation, on the other hand, seems incontrovertible.

Note

1   Brian Cox, a former black paper author, ironically, or perhaps tellingly, became the ally of those trying to salvage a 'common-sense' liberal version of English. Cox promoted an 'establishment' view of literature and its value.

References

Ahmad, A. (1992) *In Theory*. London: Verso.

Althusser, L. (1984) 'Ideology and Ideological State Apparatuses' in *Lenin and Philosophy*, 1–60. London: Verso.

Ang, I. (1985) *Watching Dallas*. London: Methuen.

Ang, I. (1991) *Desperately Seeking the Audience*. London: Routledge.

Baldick, C. (1983) *The Social Mission of English Criticism 1848–1932*. Oxford: Basil Blackwell.

Batsleer, J., Davies, T., O'Rourke R., and Weedon, C. (1985) *Rewriting English: Cultural Politics of Gender and Class*. London: Methuen.

Belsey, C. (1985) 'Disrupting Sexual Difference: Meaning and Gender in the Comedies', in J. Drakakis (ed.) *Alternative Shakespeares*, London: Methuen, pp. 166–90.

Bernstein, B. (1971) 'Class, Codes and Control', *Volume I: Theoretical Studies towards a Sociology of Language*. London: Routledge and Kegan Paul.

Bernstein, B. (1990) *Class, Codes and Control, Volume. IV. The Structuring of Pedagogic Discourse*. London: Routledge.

Bernstein, B. (1997) 'Class and Pedagogies: Visible and Invisible', in A. H. Halsey, H. Lauder, P. Brown and A. Stuart Wells (1997) *Education: Culture, Economy, Society*, 59–79. Oxford: OUP.

Bernstein, B. (2000) *Pedagogy, Symbolic Control and Identity*. Oxford: Rowman and Littlefield.

Bourdieu, P. and Passeron, J.-C. (1977) *Reproduction in Education, Society and Culture*. London: Sage.

Bowles, S. and Gintis, H. (1976) *Schooling in Capitalist America*. London: Routledge and Kegan Paul.

Bullock, A. (1975) A Language for Life: Report of the Committee of Enquiry appointed by the Secretary of State for Education and Science under the Chairmanship of Sir Alan Bullock FBA, *The Bullock Report*. London: HMSO.

Butler, J. (1990) *Gender Trouble*. London: Routledge.

Chomsky, N. (1979) *Language and Responsibility*. Sussex: Harvester.

Cox, B. (1991) *Cox on Cox*. London: Hodder and Stoughton.

Cox, B. (1994) *The Battle for the English Curriculum*. London: Hodder and Stoughton.

Day, G. (2002) 'Revolutionary tracts that left us 'all shook up''' in *Times Higher Education Supplement*, November 1st, 2002, 28–29.

Derrida, J. (1976) *Of Grammatology*. London: The Johns Hopkins University Press.

Derrida, J. (1981) *Dissemination*. London: University of Chicago Press.

Derrida, J. (1987) *Positions*. London: Athlone Press.

Coward, R. and Ellis, J. (1977) *Language and Materialism*. London: Routledge and Kegan Paul.

Dixon, J. (1967) *Growth through English*. Oxford: Oxford University Press.

Dixon, J. (1991) *A Schooling in English*. Milton Keynes: OUP.

Donald, J. (1992) 'Well-Regulated Liberty' in *Sentimental Education, 1-16*. London: Verso.

Doyle, B. (1989) *English and Englishness*. London: Routledge.

Eagleton, T. (1983) *Literary Theory: an Introduction*. Oxford: Basil Blackwell.

Easthope, A. (1991) *Literary into Cultural Studies*. Routledge: London.

Foucault, M. (1988) 'What is an Author', in D. Lodge (ed.), *Modern Criticism and Theory*. London: Longman.

Foucault, M. (1977a) *The Archaeology of Knowledge*. London: Tavistock.

Foucault, M. (1977b) *Discipline and Punish*. London: Allen Lane.

Foucault, M. (1980) *Power/Knowledge*. London: Harvester Wheatsheaf.

Gilbert, S. M. and Gubar, S. (1979) *The Madwoman in the Attic: The Woman Writer and the Nineteenth-Century Literary Imagination*. London: Yale University Press.

Gramsci, A. (1985) *Selections from Cultural Writings*. London: Lawrence and Wishart.

Gumperz, J. (1982) *Language and Social Identity*. Cambridge: Cambridge University Press.

Halliday, M.A.K. (1978) *Language as Social Semiotic*. London: Edward Arnold.

Heidegger, M. (1978) *Being and Time*. Oxford: Blackwell Publishers.

Hill, D. (2009) Theorising Politics and the Curriculum: Understanding and Addressing Inequalities through Critical Pedagogy and Critical Policy Analysis. In D. Hill and L. Helavaara Robertson (eds) (2009) *Equality in the Primary School: Promoting good practice across the curriculum*. London: Continuum

Hymes, D. (1974) *Foundations in Sociolinguistics*. Philadelphia: University of Pennsylvania Press.

Hunter, I. (1988) *Culture and Government*. London: Macmillan.

Hunter, I. (1994) *Rethinking the School*. Sydney: Allen and Unwin.

Labov, W. (1969) 'The Logic of Nonstandard English', in P. Giglioli, (ed.) (1990) *Language and Social Context*. Harmondsworth: Penguin.

Lacan, J. (1977) *Ecrits: A Selection*. London: Tavistock.

Lapsley, R. and Westlake M. (1988) *Film Theory: An Introduction*. Manchester: Manchester University Press.

Leavis, F. R. (ed.) (1942) *Scrutiny: A Quarterly Review*, 22, 1942–43. Cambridge: Cambridge University Press.

Moi, T. (1985) *Sexual/Textual Politics*. London: Methuen.

Peim, N. (1993) *Critical Theory and the English Teacher*. London: Routledge.

Peim, N. (2005) 'Deconstructing Curriculum Politics – English Teaching in England: a History of Ideas', *English in Australia*, 141, 62–76.

Peim, N. (2003) *Changing English? Rethinking the Politics of English Teaching*. Sheffield: NATE.

Peim, N. and Flint, K. (2009) 'Testing Times: Questions concerning assessment for school improvement', *Educational Philosophy and Theory*, 41, 3, 342–361. Online at http://www.ingentaconnect.com/content/bpl/epat/2009/00000041/00000003/art00012-aff_2.

Pinker, S. (2008) *The Stuff of Thought*. Harmondsworth: Penguin.

Said, E. (1978) *Orientalism*. New York: Pantheon Books.

Smitherman, G. (1998) 'Ebonics, King, and Oakland: Some Folk Don't Believe Fat Meat Is Greasy', *Journal of English Linguistics*, 26, (2), 97–107.

Smitherman, G. (2000) *Talkin' That Talk: Language, Culture, And Education In African America*. London: Routledge.

Street, B. (1984) *Literacy in Theory and Practice*. Cambridge: Cambridge University Press.

Trudgill, P. (1975) *Accent, Dialect and the School*. London: Edward Arnold.

Turner, G. (1992) *British Cultural Studies: An Introduction*. London: Routledge.

Viswanathan, G. (1989) *Masks of Conquest*. New York: Columbia UP.

Weedon, C. (1987) *Feminist Practice & Poststructuralist Theory Challenge of English in the National Curriculum*, 164–181. London: Routledge.

Widdowson, P. (ed.) (1982) *Rereading English*. London: Methuen.

Willis, P. (1979) *Learning to Labour*. Aldershot: Gator.

Wittgenstein, L. (1968) *Philosophical Investigations*. Oxford: Basil Blackwell.

Young, M. F.D. (1971) *Knowledge and Control*. London: Collier-Macmillan.

English Key Stage 1, 2009 The National Curriculum for England www.nc.uk.net

Chapter 7

Mathematics and Numeracy

Tamar Margalit and Chris Carter

Introduction

In this era of widening economic gaps between classes, of globalization and of human rights violations, we need to examine the role and influence of mathematics education in preserving inequalities in society, and to explore different attitudes towards teaching and learning mathematics that might be used to challenge this role, alter mathematical pedagogy and effect change.

Recent documents and standards for school mathematics reform in different countries are calling for equity in mathematics education (e.g. the American standards book (NCTM 2000)). To achieve this goal, teachers and researchers alike need to better understand the origins and implications of the current inequalities between diverse groups of pupils; for example, in which ways are ethnic, racial, gender and language minorities (frequently) discriminated against and marginalized in mathematics lessons? We need to analyse the political dimensions of mathematics education, and reveal issues of power that influence mathematics reforms, curriculum, resource allocation and other policies.

This chapter addresses these issues: it refers to different aspects of mathematics education, analyses the most common existing situations and surveys critical theories and pedagogical ideas developed and published in the literature in recent years, together with practical ideas and examples, aimed to promote equality and lead to a more socially-just society. Note that although these aspects are broken down into different sections for the purpose of analysis, they are all related and interconnected. But first, it might be useful to consider the recent history of mathematics teaching in England and Wales.

A Brief History

At the end of the 1970s there was concern in England and Wales that mathematics education was in need of review. So in 1978, a group met under the leadership of Dr Cockcroft, and in 1982 'Mathematics Counts' was published, although often referred to as the 'Cockcroft report'. The report quotes, 'In

arithmetic, I regret to say worse results than ever before have been obtained ...
the failures are almost invariably traceable to radically imperfect teaching'
[found in an HMI report from 1876!], (Cockcroft Report 1982). However, there
was nothing new in such concerns and the report ended up with some fairly
progressive ideas on teaching '...we do not believe it should ever be necessary ...
to commit things to memory without at the same time seeking to develop a
proper understanding of the mathematics to which they relate' (238:70).

> The primary mathematics curriculum should enrich children's aesthetic and
> linguistic experience, provide them with the means of exploring their
> environment' [287:84], 'practical work is essential' [289:84].

Armed with this report, mathematics education in the early 1980s had the
potential to develop a more progressive mathematical education. The
Association of Teachers of Mathematics (ATM)[1] developed its pupil-centred
philosophy, and programmes like SMILE[2] involved teachers developing their
own CSE and 'O'[3] level teacher-led certifications. Along with all strands of
progressive education, some of these initiatives were attacked. (For example, the
Daily Telegraph ran a story attacking an exam question set in a SMILE CSE
exam that asked pupils to calculate with data from the arms race and compare
costs to those of providing clean water in third world countries.)

Then in 1988, the Education Reform Act (ERA) introduced the National
Curriculum and SATs. There was little fight from most teachers' unions against
this attack on teacher autonomy (although the NUT did launch a campaign).
The 'left' in Britain were in limbo. The right-wing government of Margaret
Thatcher had been in power for nine years,[4] and the Labour party was divided
and the unions likewise showed no unity in fighting the ERA (Jones 1989).

The dogma of the right-wing government in the UK at that time was that
'private was good, public bad'.[5] Market forces had to be introduced into
education if its shortcomings were to be addressed. The customers (parents) had
to be able to choose where they could obtain the service (schooling). Up until
that time there had been no real way to be able to choose, except by anecdotal
opinions circulating the local communities. The National Curriculum would
force all schools to teach the same and so they could be 'fairly' measured using
testing combined with published league tables and a powerful mechanism was
created: the effect of the Act was for central government to control the education
in England and Wales as never before.

When the first league tables were published, it was clear to any rational
observer that performance was closely correlated to poverty. Schools with mostly
middle-class intakes did well, while schools in areas of relative poverty did badly.
(Interestingly rural schools, where there is little choice and schools could be said
to be more comprehensive, also did well.) Rather than make the obvious
conclusion that schools with poor records needed more support and help, the
Conservative government chose a policy that had the effect of a direct attack on
working-class communities – closing 'failing' schools. After the 'league tables' of
results were published in the local newspaper a pupil asked: 'Does that mean
we're the worse school in the country, sir?' Within five years that school was
closed, and that working-class area of Bristol is further deprived.

During this time, the Labour party in the UK had been hijacked by the Blairite[6] faction who talked of a 'third way' in party politics, creating 'New Labour' whose education policies looked to appease middle-class voters. When they came to power in 1997, parental choice was to continue, and with it league tables and Ofsted reporting which would increase the naming and shaming of 'failing' schools.

Another layer of control was to be introduced – first in primary schools and then 'rolled out' to secondaries – the National Numeracy Strategy (NNS) (together with the National Literacy Strategy). The effect was to further reduce the creativity of teachers and continue a process of de-professionalization. Teachers were programmed in the introduction of the 'numeracy hour', and some erroneous research was produced to imply that it would be best if lessons took the form of a 'three-part' format: they must have a 'starter', a main activity – which has a 'learning objective' that is shared with pupils, and a 'plenary' when pupils' understanding of the learning objective should be assessed. The lessons should be 'interactive', i.e. that teachers lead discussion with the pupils.

As this chapter is being written, it is still the case that this is the expected delivery of mathematics/numeracy lessons in primary and secondary schools. Indeed, teachers will probably be assessed in classroom observations, internally and externally. It is, therefore, too simplistic and unrealistic for teachers to ignore the strategy.

Anything that a capitalist government introduces to education has to be understood for what it is – a mechanism to maintain that capitalist system. But within big bureaucratic systems, complex strands interplay and some positive possibilities exist. Indeed, at this point it is important to point out the NNS can be considered progressive compared to some practices that exist in some schools. Often the rhetoric of the establishment tries to give the illusion of equality and aspects of the progressive, even if they do not really intend to effect positive change.

Consultants working for LEA's were able to develop positive pedagogical themes. Head of Departments in secondary schools could do likewise. Many progressive primary teachers who were not confident in delivering mathematics now had a structure. What is missing is a unifying vehicle of the left that gives support and a lead to teachers in the classroom. One of the aims of this chapter is a plea for such a vehicle to be developed. There are then possibilities for us in practice to use available openings, as will be illustrated later in the chapter. 'An objective-led 3-part lesson delivers passivity and superficiality' (Blair 2007). Criticism and resistance are growing in the profession, some of it from surprising places. A recent Ofsted report[7] into the teaching of mathematics made these observations:

> Evidence suggests that strategies to improve test and examination performance, including 'booster' lessons, revision classes and extensive intervention, coupled with a heavy emphasis on 'teaching to the test', succeed in preparing pupils to gain the qualifications but are not equipping them well enough mathematically for their futures.

and

It is of vital importance to shift from a narrow emphasis on disparate skills towards a focus on pupils' mathematical understanding. Teachers need encouragement to invest in such approaches to teaching.

It goes on to suggest that

The fundamental issue for teachers is how better to develop pupils' mathematical understanding. Too often, pupils are expected to remember methods, rules and facts without grasping the underpinning concepts, making connections with earlier learning and other topics, and making sense of the mathematics so that they can use it independently.

The nature of teaching and assessment, as well as the interpretation of the mathematics curriculum, often combine to leave pupils ill equipped to use and apply mathematics. Pupils rarely investigate open-ended problems which might offer them opportunities to choose which approach to adopt or to reason and generalize. Most lessons do not emphasize mathematical talk enough; as a result, pupils struggle to express and develop their thinking.

Now it would be quite right to point out that the Office for Standards in Education, Children's Services and Skills (Ofsted) was the very regime that presided over this narrowing of curriculum and concentration on exam results, as schools desperately sought to avoid being at the bottom of the league table that would attract so much negative attention. But it is important to see this as a major shift in policy from Ofsted: they cannot go so far as to say that the last decade or so has been something of a failure – their political bosses could never allow that to happen, but reading between the lines, this is clearly the case.

It is interesting that the comments made in this report and the previous 'Futures in action' development are so resonant with critical theorists in education like Vygotsky (1962, 1978) and Freire (1970) – even though they dare not say so!

'Futures in action', a development from QCA, seemed to be an acknowledgement that the present curriculum is in need of review, and schools were being encouraged to develop their own twenty-first-century curriculum. It seemed unbelievable that the organizations that had strangled education for so long were suggesting that schools could have their own autonomy! But it is true: visit the site (www.qca.org.uk) and navigate your way to 'Futures in action' and you will even see a programme designed to help individual schools develop their own curriculum.

The Gap in Mathematics Achievements

Hill and Cole make a distinction between equal opportunities and equality. They emphasize that promoting equal opportunity policies alone is important, but not sufficient – an overall framework and long-term commitment to equality is needed. They argue that:

Most children leave school with the belief that the class system is inevitable. Many consider that women should have different roles in society than men;

many think that Asian, black and other minority ethnic groups are odd or peculiar or alien; that gays and lesbians are not normal; that disabled people are to be pitied. Teachers are failing to promote equality unless they challenge these beliefs. (Cole *et al.* 1997:4).

Mathematics education has a dual role in that it can be aimed at promoting aspects of both equal opportunities and equality. When discussing equity in mathematics education, one of the first issues that arises is the existing gap between the achievements of pupils from minority groups and dominant groups. The analysis of performances focuses on the end result, and it is important to understand the underlying reasons and processes which cause and preserve inequalities (Ladson-Billings cited in Nasir and Cobb 2002). However, it is no less important to pinpoint the deep social and economic implications of these gaps in achievement, especially for those pupils who belong to minority groups.

In the early primary grades, pupils are already classified into different levels in the mathematics classroom, and this categorization generally sticks throughout school: pupils do not move easily from a low grouping level to a higher one. The subject of mathematics serves as a gate-keeper and filter in the educational system. High achievements in mathematics are a gateway to the path of higher education, which in turn improves opportunities for employment in high-status occupations and well-paid jobs. Many pupils from the working class and other marginalized groups exhibit low performance in school and standardized mathematics tests, and they therefore have a lesser chance of being able to compete in this race. Hence, mathematics as a school subject plays a critical role in preserving the existing social and economic inequalities.

One aspect of promoting equality in mathematics education is to address the gaps in achievement among the different social groups so that poor and minority children will have the same educational and economic opportunities as white, middle- and upper-class children. Note that equality does not mean that all pupils should reach the same achievements. Gutierrez (2002) emphasizes the inability to predict pupils' outcomes, or participation patterns in the classroom, based solely on their characteristics, such as race, class, ethnicity, gender and language:

> Only when there is sufficient variation within groups and no major clusterings that are associated with power or status in society between groups can we suggest that one level of equity is being addressed (Gutierrez 2002:154).

Providing high-quality mathematics education to children from marginalized groups is also important in granting accessibility to an understanding of economic knowledge. Moses and Cobb (2001) compare mathematics literacy and civil rights, arguing that both lead to empowerment and equality:

> The most urgent social issue affecting poor people and people of color is economic access. In today's world, economic access and full citizenship depend crucially on math and science literacy. I believe that the absence of math literacy in urban and rural communities throughout this country is an issue as urgent as the lack of registered voters in Mississippi was in 1961. (Moses and Cobb 2001:5).

Mathematics instruction should show pupils how mathematics' analytical tools can be helpful in their own decision-making and improve their ability to take an active part in public discussions which require mathematical knowledge and understanding (Tate 1994).

Critical Mathematics Literacy

Mathematics is grasped as a neutral subject; however, the uses to which it is put, for instance, the questions that appear in school mathematics textbooks, are mostly non-neutral; rather, they carry political messages, some overt and some hidden. For example, a central connection between mathematics learned in primary school and reality is based on consumerism. Typical questions in early grades' mathematics textbooks deal with the selling and buying of different products, with discounts and sales. These questions, considered to be real-life problems, reflect and support the Western trend of consumerism. Numerical data that connect consumption, poverty, inequality and global environment issues are almost never explored or discussed in mathematics lessons. A distinction should be made between practical and critical mathematics problems. While practical problems can be relevant and engaging for pupils, they will not promote social change and they will not lead to a critical awareness of the current social order. Moreover, when talking about 'real-life' problems, we need to make the following critical assessments: Whose vision of real life counts? Whose interests are being served? Who benefits? (Apple 1995:337, 339).

School mathematics content and contexts can be different. The mathematics curriculum can be aimed at promoting equality by addressing human rights, social justice and environmental issues. There is a wealth of real-world data on social justice and human rights issues (local and global) that can be explored with mathematical tools, including number operations, algebra, geometry, measurements, data analysis and probability. Analytical mathematical tools can be used to reveal and analyse inequalities in society. Social, economic and political processes, such as racism, sexism, militarism, poverty and others, can be addressed in the context of mathematics.

The interest of young children in what is 'fair' and what is 'unfair' can be used in mathematics lessons to explore examples from their local experience and daily lives, as well as from a global perspective (Peterson 2006): government budgets – military vs. social spending (operations with large numbers), unequal distribution of world wealth (percentages, ratios), environmental racism (geometry, measurements, density, ratio), life expectancy in different areas of the world (probability, statistics, data analysis), and more (see the list of resources at the end of this chapter for more ideas and detailed examples). Children also like to develop and conduct surveys. Different social justice issues can be analysed by using fractions, percentages and graphical representations of data. Through exploration of numerical data, pupils can learn to understand the importance of how questions are constructed and how data are presented. Basic concepts in probability and statistics such as chance, randomness, sampling, and bias can be further studied. Mathematics can also be used to confront prejudices and stereotypes. For example, pupils can conduct surveys on gender stereotypes and other biases in books, TV shows, advertisements and other media (Peterson 2006). The context of word-problems can also promote equality, for instance, by referring to children with physical disabilities in situations such as diving or skiing in the fog, in which the disability is not a weakness but an advantage (Margalit 2008).

In recent years, a number of mathematics educators and researchers have written about the theoretical and practical aspects of critical mathematics education (Frankenstein 1987, 1998; Skovsmose 1994, 2004; Gutstein 2003, 2006). Following Paulo Freire, Frankenstein and Gutstein apply the idea of reading the world, from literacy (Freire and Macedo 1987) to mathematics, and connect learning mathematics to developing a socio-political consciousness: 'Reading the world with mathematics means to use mathematics to understand relations of power, resource inequities, and disparate opportunities between different social groups and to understand explicit discrimination based on race, class, gender, language, and other differences' (Gutstein 2003:45).

Developing critical socio-political awareness is an essential step toward cultivating activism for social change. Gutstein advances the next step of 'writing the world with math', in which pupils attempt to change their reality. Though promoting activism with young pupils is not an obvious step, it is possible; young children can influence their families, their schools and their neighbourhoods. It is a 'developmental process, of beginning to see oneself capable of making change, and developing a sense of social agency' (Gutstein 2006:27), and teachers in primary schools should help young pupils develop 'a belief in themselves as people who can make a difference in the world' (Gutstein 2003:40). A starting point for the promotion of activism might be by coupling the mathematical questions with a discussion: How can the situation be improved? How can we have an influence on this situation in the school, neighbourhood, and community? Which alternatives can we offer?

When discussing issues of inequality, poverty, racism, etc. with their young pupils, teachers must be aware of the danger of reinforcing negative stereotypes instead of demolishing them, as this will disempower the children who experience these realities for themselves (Gutstein 2003; Osler 2007).

Ethnomathematics and Culturally Relevant Mathematics

Aside from a few token illustrations or use of names from ethnic-minority communities, traditional Western mathematics textbooks reflect the hegemonic white, middle-class culture. They give little recognition to mathematical knowledge which has been developed in other societies throughout the world (Shan and Bailey 1994).

Practical cultural implementations of mathematical ideas are rarely introduced in the classroom, leading to the perception of mathematics as an abstract subject. The historical development of mathematical knowledge is almost never discussed in class and pupils often get the impression that most mathematical ideas originated in Greece. Mathematical word-problems tend to reflect situations from the daily reality of the middle class, and an analysis of pupils' answers to 'real-world' word-problems reveals that some of their 'mistakes' are caused by a different interpretation of the question, which is based on the pupils' own everyday knowledge and experience (Tate 1994; Cooper and Dunne 2000).

Pedagogies of ethnomathematics and culturally relevant mathematics address these issues and are oriented toward equity and justice. Culturally relevant pedagogy, originally used with African-American pupils in the United States, is aimed at improving pupils' abilities to learn mathematics by connecting it to their own lives and cultures and to their communities' knowledge and experience (Ladson-Billings 1995; Tate 1995). Ethnomathematics studies the relationship between culture, mathematics and power relations. It explores diverse mathematical knowledge, created and developed in different societies and cultures around the world (Africa, India, China, South America) and challenges the notion that most mathematical ideas were originated and developed by Europeans. Moreover, ethnomathematics sees mathematics as a product of human activity, the development of which is based on practical knowledge and everyday uses (D'Ambrosio 1985; Powell and Frankenstein 1997).

Various cultural practices can be integrated into the mathematics curriculum. For example, Al Khorizmi's contribution to the development of algebra and computation can be highlighted; Islamic patterns in art and architecture can be used to study basic concepts in geometry, symmetry and measurements; Mayan mathematics can be given as an example of calculations in the base-20 numerical system, and diverse mathematical games from different cultures can be introduced and played in the classroom (see the list of resources at the end of this chapter for more ideas and detailed examples).

Ethnomathematics and culturally relevant mathematics can empower pupils from minority groups: girls who learn about women mathematicians may develop a more positive image of themselves as mathematics learners; immigrant children and children from minority race and ethnic groups who meet their culture in mathematics lessons may value mathematics, seeing it as meaningful and relevant. At the same time, these approaches can teach pupils to value diversity, and can develop respect and solidarity among pupils from diverse cultures and backgrounds.

Mathematics Pedagogy

Most pupils form their attitudes towards mathematics and their abilities in this subject in the early stages of primary school and this influences their subsequent learning patterns. For example, a common public opinion is that succeeding in mathematics requires special talent. Many pupils view mathematics as an enemy and have a low self-image about their abilities in this subject. Since mathematics is a high-status subject, their opinion of and desire for proficiency are sometimes set accordingly. Another point is that mathematics is usually grasped as an absolute, with one correct solution, making use of true/false statements. Questions which may arise in other subjects such as: What is your opinion about ...? What can you add to ...? are mostly absent in mathematics lessons and textbooks. The absolute knowledge in mathematics is regularly brought to class by the teacher and for the most part is not based on pupils' former knowledge and practice (Zalmanson-Levi and Margalit 2008).

These stereotypes and attitudes reflect different aspects of the power relationships that are present in the mathematics classroom: between the pupil and the subject, between the pupil and the teacher, and between the pupils themselves. Pupils' self-image as mathematics learners is influenced, among other things, by these perceptions, as well as by their feelings and experiences in the classroom. An important task for the primary school mathematics teacher is to be aware of these attitudes and to challenge them, with the aim of improving the mathematics learner's self-image, thereby encouraging equality.

The power relationships in the mathematics classroom can be shifted in several directions. For example, the stereotype that any mathematics problem has only one correct answer can be challenged at several levels. One way is to introduce mathematics problems with multiple solutions, for example: 'Look at the following numbers: 15, 20, 23, 25; which number does not belong? Why?' (Hershkovitz *et al.* 2004). The ATM has a wealth of ideas and resources to promote positive mathematical pedagogies.

Real-world problems provide another opportunity to present mathematical problems that have several possible answers. One example is the activity: 'Using maths to take a look at how the unemployment rate is determined' proposed by Frankenstein in Gutstein and Peterson (2006). Different choices about who is counted as unemployed and who is counted as part of the labour force give different answers for the unemployment rate. The activity involves operations (addition and division) with large numbers, and is appropriate for Stage-2 pupils.

Power relationships can be changed by giving pupils the opportunity to compose their own mathematics problems, a task which is usually reserved for the teacher or textbooks. The posed problems can be shared and solved by other pupils in the classroom. For example, first-grade pupils can draw pictures and ask mathematical questions about them. A similar culturally-relevant activity is described in Jacqueline and Smita (2002): African American children in grades 2–5 walked around their neighbourhood and took photographs. Later, in class, they wrote word-problems based on their photos. This activity empowered the pupils and made the mathematics more relevant and enjoyable for them.

Examples of Mathematics Lessons for Social Justice

This section includes several examples and suggestions for mathematics lessons that address issues of social justice. Numbers and numerical data can be found everywhere and these are just a few examples to give some idea of how the mathematics curriculum can be aimed at promoting equality. Teachers can also identify main social issues in their pupils' community and try to refer them.

The cost of the war in Iraq (2003–)[8]

What is the cost of the war in Iraq? In a lesson about large numbers, pupils can consider the financial cost of the war in Iraq, and look at some alternative options for spending the same amount of money on global humanitarian issues.

Other questions, such as how many people have died in this war and how many of them were civilians can be also addressed.

For example:

1. UK spending on the Iraq war is estimated to be £31 per second.[9] How much money is spent by the UK on the war in Iraq in a year? Which number is easier for you to grasp, the cost per second or the cost per year?
2. The amount spent by the United States and UK together is much larger, estimated at $600 billion (up to 2008).[10] Table 1 suggests several alternatives that might be funded instead.

Suggest how the money spent on the war in Iraq so far could be invested in the given options. Decide how many years you will fund each project, and calculate the total cost. (This question can be addressed in groups, and followed up by a class discussion to recognize the existence of different answers).

Table 1   Funding Humanitarian Goals

Social or Economic Goal	Additional Annual Investment Needed to Achieve this Goal
Reproductive health care for all women	$12 billion
Elimination of hunger and malnutrition	$19 billion
Universal literacy	$5 billion
Clean drinking water for all	$10 billion
Immunizing every child	$1.3 billion

Source: Worldwatch Institute[11]

Wealth distribution in the UK[12]

How wide is the gap between rich and poor families in the UK? Tables 2 and 3 contain data on wealth and income sharing in the UK. The inequalities can be presented and discussed in mathematics lessons about percentages, fractions, and decimals. For example:

1. The total marketable wealth in the UK, in 2003, was £3,783 billion. The wealth owned by the wealthiest 1 per cent was £795 billion. What is the percentage of UK wealth held by the wealthiest 1 per cent? Does this number surprise you? Why?
2. Look at Table 2 (Distribution of wealth, UK). Complete the following sentences:
   a)   One-half of the population shares _____ per cent of the total wealth, while the other half of the population shares _____ per cent of the total wealth.
   b)   Half of the wealth in the UK is owned by the wealthiest _____ per cent of the UK's population.
   What do you think and feel about this data? Which questions arise?
3. Draw a 10 × 10 squares table. Follow the data in Table 3 (share of total

income, UK), and paint the percentage of income of the different deciles in different colours. Show in your painting that the income of the richest tenth is more than the combined income of the bottom five-tenths.

A similar analysis can be performed on the world's unequal distribution of wealth by considering the population and wealth distributions on the six continents. A simulation with cookies demonstrates the sharp inequality: children are first divided into groups representing the world's population distribution among the six continents; they then receive cookies according to the world's wealth distribution. Children who represent, during the simulation, North America and Europe get many more cookies even though there are far fewer of them than in the groups representing Asia and Africa (Gutstein and Peterson 2006).

Table 2 Distribution of Wealth, UK, 2003

Percentage of wealth owned by	Percentages
Most wealthy 1%	21
Most wealthy 5%	40
Most wealthy 10%	53
Most wealthy 25%	72
Most wealthy 50%	93
Total marketable wealth (£ billion)	3,783

Source: Office for National Statistics, UK[13]

Table 3 Share of Total Income, UK, 2005/6

Deciles	Percentages
Poorest tenth	2%
2nd	4%
3rd	5%
4th	6%
5th	7%
6th	9%
7th	10%
8th	12%
9th	15%
Richest tenth	30%

Source: The Poverty Site[14]

The price of our clothes – sweatshops and globalization[15]

Many of the consumer products traded in Western societies are handmade by exploited workers in less economically developed countries. This lesson gives a different look at the clothes we wear and refers to the working conditions of the people who make them. The main mathematical topics are decimals and fractions.

Start by asking the pupils to check the labels on their clothing and shoes: China, Vietnam, the Philippines, etc. What can we learn from the labels, and what do the labels not tell us about the people who make the clothes that we wear and their working conditions?

1. A Filipino worker who sews T-shirts works 14 hours a day. If he/she starts at 7:00 a.m., when will he/she finish? Does this seem reasonable? Is it consistent with UK law?
2. The worker is paid £0.2 per hour. How much is he/she paid for a working day of 14 hours?
3. The same T-shirt, in a clothing store in England, costs £7. How many hours does the worker need to work in order to earn enough money to buy the T-shirt that he/she made from the clothing store?
4. Suppose it takes the worker 15 minutes to sew a T-shirt. What is the relative pay for a T-shirt that he/she has sewn? What part of the price that we pay in the store for the T-shirt goes to the worker who made it? Who do you think earns the rest of the amount? What can you/we do in order to change this situation?

Climate change

The following activities are part of an interdisciplinary project run at a secondary school in Bristol in 2007. The activities were designed to meet the following broad learning processes:

- investigating the evidence;
- coming to an understanding about the topic;
- arriving at conclusions about the issue;
- gathering information to discover wider attitudes on the issue;
- encouraging pupils to **act** as a result of what they have learned.

Pupils were given the following activities:

Look at the changes in the average temperature of the Earth over the years, and plot it against different scales to see what effect this will have on the impact of the graphs. Discuss who would be likely to present the graph in a particular way (compare, for example, graphs 1 and 2), and what interests each particular presentation might reflect.

The graphs ended up looking like these:

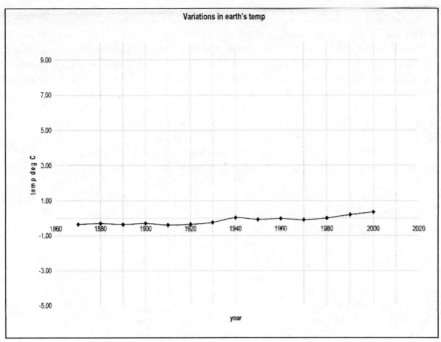

Graph 1 Variations in Earth's Temperature

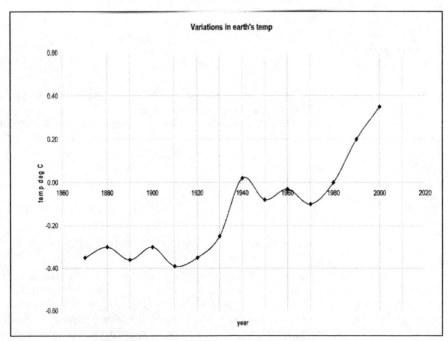

Graph 2 Variations in Earth's Temperature

Additional factors that could be analysed include changes in carbon emissions and percentage change over time.

Pupils were asked to measure their carbon footprint by calculating what they and their families use in their daily lives, from data provided. This allowed for much discussion and provided opportunities to problem solve, for instance: How can central heating be calculated over a whole year and averaged out? Would a journey to the shops by car be averaged over all family members or applied only to those who went? Why is it impossible for girls to shower for only 15 minutes?

Pupils went on to design, conduct and analyse a questionnaire to discover attitudes to climate change in the community at large.

The Human Race – the Migrant Species

The following activities are part of an interdisciplinary project run at a secondary school in Bristol in 2008. The mathematics department created a resource/booklet called 'The Human Race – the Migrant Species' which allowed pupils to examine the history (and pre-history) of the migration, not just of peoples throughout time, but also the inevitable movement of mathematical concepts (this booklet drew on the excellent book 'The Crest of the Peacock' by Gheverghese 1992).

The project went on to ask the pupils to examine two statements:

Some people say:
   Statement 1: 'too many refugees are coming into this country'
   Statement 2: 'our country cannot afford to help refugees'
Other people disagree.
How could we use data to help us decide?

Pupils were then able to use data to help them critically examine contentious issues based upon hard facts and not preconceived notions. As Louis, a Year 9 pupil, said 'I always thought that there were lots of refugees coming to this country, but I see that was wrong'. Pupils were able to calculate that the difference refugees make to our population is 0.03 per cent! Unless we are able to develop critical faculties within our young people, they will always be at the mercy of the misinformation deliberately fed to them by the political right who own the media.

Closing Comments – Working Together Towards Change

Working alone in a small primary school with little moral support can clearly be difficult, no matter how committed one is. It may also be potentially awkward if the environment is a hostile one. Therefore, as is always the case, there is strength in unity. Seeking support from colleagues in other schools is beneficial. One example is the 'Alternative Futures Group' – a collaborative group of teachers at a secondary school in Bristol. Teachers in that group wanted pupils to begin to act in a more critical way and worked together to find ways in which this could be implemented in the classroom.

The National Critical Mathematics Education Group, http://www.shu.ac.uk/ education/cmeg/index.html, is another example of collaborative work on issues of social justice and how they are promoted or inhibited in the mathematics classroom. The group provides an effective national network for promoting critical engagement with social and political concerns in mathematics education.

Additional groups of teachers, seeking and forming alternative critical mathematics curricula, can be found in countries all over the world. Since many problems and questions are common and global, there is a benefit in developing international collaborative and networking groups. The internet is a useful source for this, and some links appear in the list at the end of this chapter.

Notes

[1] The Association of Teachers of Mathematics (ATM), whose second guiding principle is 'The power to learn rests with the learner. Teaching has a subordinate role. The teacher has a duty to seek out ways to engage the power of the learner'.

[2] The Secondary Maths Independent Learning Experience (SMILE) was a largely London-based curriculum development that has a large resource of mathematical activities (mostly work cards). The resources were written mostly by classroom teachers who trialled materials and wrote exam papers. The system allowed a mixed-ability, pupil-centred pedagogy, but was effectively destroyed by the NNS.

[3] CSEs and 'O' levels were the dual certification for 16-year-olds in England and Wales before GCSEs were introduced.

[4] First elected in 1979.

[5] This has continued with New Labour who have used private companies to clean schools, work in the kitchens and even build schools, effectively mortgaging buildings and services for decades. The introduction of 'Academies' is a further erosion of comprehensive schooling – taking schools out of local democratic control.

[6] Tony Blair's ideas on education can be read in his book, 'New Britain', Blair, T. (1996) New Britain Fourth Estate Ltd., London.

[7] Found on www.ofsted.gov.uk – 'mathematics – understanding the score'.

[8] Adapted from Gutstein and Peterson (2006) and Stocker (2006).

[9] http://www.dailymail.co.uk/news/article-472524/Iraq-war-costs-US-UK-2-000-second.html

[10] http://www.nationalpriorities.org/costofwar_home

[11] Worldwatch Institute, State of the World 2004, Tables 1-6 http://www.worldwatch.org/node/1783

[12] The idea for this activity was adopted from Gutstein and Peterson (2006).

[13] Office for National statistics, http://www.statistics.gov.uk/cci/nugget.asp?id = 2

[14] The Poverty Site – http://www.poverty.org.uk/09/index.shtml

[15] This activity is based on Gutstein and Peterson (2006) and Stocker (2006).

Acknowledgements

Tamar Margalit would like to thank Galia Zalmanson-Levi and Hagit Gor-Ziv, founders and teachers at the Center of Critical Feminist Pedagogy, for their guidance.

Resources

The following resources include examples and lesson plans which integrate human rights, social justice and environmental issues into the mathematics curriculum.

Gutstein, E. and Peterson, B. (2006), *Rethinking Mathematics: Teaching Social Justice by the Numbers*. Milwaukee, WI: Rethinking Schools, Ltd.

Shan, S.-J. and Bailey, P. (1994), *Multiple Factors: Classroom Mathematics for Equality and Justice* (2nd edn). Stoke-on-Trent: Trentham Books.

Stocker, D. (2006), *Maththatmatters: A Teacher Resource Linking Math and Social Justice*. Ottawa: Canadian Center for Policy Alternatives.

Center of Critical Feminist Pedagogy, < http://criticalpedagogy.org.il/critfemlibrary/mathematicsforsocialjustice/tabid/317/Default.aspx >

Ethnomathematics, < Digital Library http://ethnomath.org/ >

Radical Math, < http://www.radicalmath.org >

Rethinking School, < http://www.rethinkingschools.org/publication/math/ >

References

Apple, M. W. (1995) 'Taking power seriously: new directions in equity in mathematics education and beyond', in W. G., Secada, E. Fennema and L. B. Adajian (eds), *New Directions for Equity in Mathematics Education*, 329–348. New York: Cambridge University Press.

Blair, A. (2007) 'Mathematics Teaching, 202'. Derby: Journal of the ATM.

Cockcroft, W. H. *et al.* (1982) *Mathematics Counts*. London: Her Majesty's Stationery Office.

Cole, M., Hill, D. and Shan, S. (1997) *Promoting Equality in Primary Schools*. London: Cassell.

Cooper, B. and Dunne, M. (2000) *Assessing Children's Mathematical Knowledge: Social Class, Sex and Problem-Solving*. Buckingham: Open University Press.

D'Ambrosio, U. (1985) 'Ethnomathematics and its place in the history and pedagogy of mathematics'. *For the Learning of Mathematics*, 5, 44–48.

DfEE (and Ofsted) (1997) in *Department Report*. London: HMSO. March.

Frankenstein, M. (1987) 'Critical mathematics education: an application of Paulo Freire's epistemology', in I. Shor (ed.), *Freire for the Classroom: A Sourcebook for Liberatory Teaching*, 180–210. Portsmouth, NH: Boyton/Cook.

Frankenstein, M. (1998) 'Reading the world with math: goals for a critical mathematical literacy curriculum', in E. Lee, D. Menkart and M. Okazawa-Rey (eds), *Beyond Heroes and Holidays: A Practical Guide to K-12 Anti-Racist, Multicultural Education and Staff Development*, 306–313. Washington D.C.: Network of Educators on the Americas (reprinted in Gutstein and Peterson 2006).

Freire, P. (1970) *Pedagogy of the Oppressed*. London: Penguin.

Freire, P. and Macedo, D. (1987) *Literacy: Reading the Word and the World*. South Hadley, MA: Bergen & Garvey.

Gheverghese, J. G. (1992) *The Crest of the Peacock: Non-European Roots of Mathematics*. London: Penguin Books.

Gutierrez, R. (2002) 'Enabling the practice of mathematics teachers in context: toward a new equity research agenda'. *Mathematics*, 4, (2&3), 145–187.

Gutstein, E. (2003) 'Teaching and learning mathematics for social justice in an urban, Latino school'. *Journal for Research in Mathematics Education*, 34, 37–73.

Gutstein, E. (2006) *Reading and Writing the World with Mathematics: Toward a Pedagogy for Social Justice*. New York: Routledge.

Gutstein, E. and Peterson B. (2006) *Rethinking Mathematics: Teaching Social Justice by the Numbers*. Milwaukee, WI: Rethinking Schools, Ltd.

Hershkovitz, S., Rubineck, H. and Nesher, P. (2004) *Promoting creativity in mathematics through non-standard problems*. Global Conference in Education and Training 20–22 May, Singapore. Online at http://storage.cet.ac.il/CetForums/Storage/MessageFiles/6707/22873/Forum22873M101I0.ppt. (Accessed September 20, 2008).

Jacqueline, L. and Smita, G. (2002) 'Creating cultural relevance in teaching and learning mathematics'. *Teaching Children Mathematics*, 9, (2), 114–118.

Jones, K. (1989) *Right Turn – the Conservative Revolution in Education*. London: Hutchinson Radius.

Ladson-Billings, G. (1995) 'Toward a theory of culturally relevant pedagogy'. *American Educational Research Journal*, 32, 465–491.

Margalit, T. (2008) 'Educating for human rights through math lessons'. Manuscript submitted for publication.

Moses, R. P. and Cobb, C. E. (2001) *Radical Equations: Math Literacy and Civil Rights*. Boston: Beacon Press.

Nasir, N. and Cobb, P. (2002) 'Diversity, equity, and mathematical learning'. *Mathematical Thinking and Learning, 4*, (2&3), 91–102.

NCTM (National Council of Teachers of Mathematics) (2000) *Principles and Standards for School Mathematics*. Reston, VA: NCTM.

Osler, J. (2007) *A guide for integrating issues of social and economic justice into mathematics curriculum*. Online at http://www.radicalmath.org/docs/SJMathGuide.pdf (Accessed October 17th, 2007)

Peterson, B. (2006) 'Teaching math across the curriculum', in E. Gutstein and B. Peterson (eds), *Rethinking Mathematics: Teaching Social Justice by the Numbers*, 9–13. Milwaukee, WI: Rethinking Schools.

Powell, A. B. and Frankenstein, M. (1997) *Ethnomathematics: Challenging Eurocentrism iin Mathematics Education*. Albany, New York: State University of New York Press.

Shan, S.-J. and Bailey, P. (1994) *Multiple Factors: Classroom Mathematics for Equality and Justice* (2nd edn). Stoke-on-Trent: Trentham Books.

Skovsmose, O. (1994) *Towards a Philosophy of Critical Mathematical Education*. Dordrecht: Kluwer Academic Publishers.

Skovsmose, O. (2004) *Critical Mathematics Education for the Future*. Aalborg, Denmark: Aalborg University, Department of Education and Learning.

Tate, W. F. (1994) 'Race, retrenchment, and the reform of school mathematics'. *Phi Delta Kappan*, 75, (6), 477–484 (reprinted in Gutstein and Peterson 2006).

Tate, W. F. (1995) 'Returning to the root: a culturally relevant approach to mathematics pedagogy'. *Theory into Practice*, 34, (3), 166–173.

Vygotsky, L. S. (1962) *Thought & Language*. Massachusetts: MIT.

Vygotsky, L. S. (1978) *Mind in Society*. London: Harvard University Press.

Zalmanson-Levi, G. and Margalit T. (2008) *'Educating for Social Justice and Peace Education in mathematics Lessons'*. Manuscript submitted for publication (in Hebrew).

Chapter 8

Science

Jen Smyth and Steve Smyth

Introduction

Science teaching and learning is an area of the curriculum that often causes anxiety for practitioners, as few primary teachers have studied it in depth. This is a great pity, as science can be a very powerful tool for addressing all aspects of inequality. At its best, science is an expression of the rational, enquiring mind, and rational enquiring minds are exactly what is needed to achieve a society based on social justice and equality. But not necessarily what the government want!

Unfortunately, science can also be a subject beset by problems for the primary teacher. Without science as a specialism, just achieving a basic understanding of concepts such as electricity and forces can be difficult enough. Ethnocentric viewpoints can creep unnoticed into the curriculum in schools and schemes of work. Then there is the practical nature of science, where hands-on work differs from activity in most other areas of the curriculum because there may be an explicitly expected outcome (a set of results that confirm something). Finally, there are the problems of societal perception, from the high value the outside world places on scientific knowledge through to the nerdy and other-worldly image of those who study science, as personified by Professor Frink or the 'superfriends' in *The Simpsons* (an American TV cartoon).

This chapter looks at each of these areas in turn. We start with a general survey of science in schools and its relationship to racism and prejudice. Next we consider the content of primary science, and the pitfalls that may arise in teaching it. Following this we look at practical work and the implications that may have for equality, especially with regard to gender issues, followed by a consideration of how to implement this practically in the classroom. Next, we turn our attention to perceptions, the status that science holds in society, the elevation of Western 'high-tech' science within that perception, the relationship of science to capitalism and globalization, and ways that primary teaching can avoid embedding pre-conceptions. The final section provides advice for good practice and enjoyment.

Avoiding Prejudice

The generally accepted view about science is typified by the stereotypical image of a scientist who is a slightly odd man, eccentric and clever, toiling away at something that nobody else can quite understand because the subject itself is 'hard'. It is, consequently, a subject that is one of the most challenging to teach. This perception of exclusivity serves to reinforce the 'elitist' world of the scientist and even very young children are faced with media coverage that reinforces this idea, so from early on in their lives many children are already beginning to disassociate themselves from scientific matters.

Talking in the context of racial identity, the MacPherson report (MacPherson 1999) on the Stephen Lawrence Inquiry stressed that 'radical thinking and sustained action is needed from pre-school onwards [...] with (positive) education and examples [given] at the earliest age'. There is a need for this type of thinking to also address the problems encountered by other minority groups within the classroom.

Until the introduction of the National Curriculum (DfEE 1999), and subsequently the Curriculum Guidance for Foundation Stage (QCA/DfEE 1999), the delivery of science within the school was usually dependent upon the enthusiasm of the individual teacher. If a teacher felt reasonably secure within the subject, then the class would experience science lessons, but the insecurity felt by some practitioners in this area of the curriculum meant that some children experienced very little discrete science learning during the early years and primary stages of their school career.

Both documents emphasize the necessity to provide an appropriate science-based curriculum for the child. The documents also emphasize the necessity to ensure that the planning allows for each child to have access to the learning.

The Curriculum Guidelines for the Foundation Stage (QCA/DfEE 1999) document, still influential in early years' settings and schools today, states in the opening paragraph the commitment that is required of all early years practitioners:

> This guidance is intended to help practitioners plan to meet the diverse needs of all children so that most will achieve and some, where appropriate, will go beyond the early learning goals by the end of the foundation stage.(QCA/DfEE 1999:5)

It goes on to state that:

> No child should be excluded or disadvantaged because of ethnicity, culture or religion, home language, family background, special educational needs, disability, gender or ability. (QCA/DfEE 1999:11)

Again the National Curriculum for Key Stage 1 Science states that:

The importance of science
Science stimulates and excites pupils' curiosity about phenomena and events in the world around them. It also satisfies this curiosity with knowledge. Because

science links direct practical experience with ideas, it can engage learners at many levels. Scientific method is about developing and evaluating explanations through experimental evidence and modelling. This is a spur to critical and creative thought. Through science, pupils can understand how major scientific ideas contribute to technological change – impacting on industry, business and medicine and improving quality of life. Pupils recognize the cultural significance of science and trace its worldwide development. They learn to question and discuss science based issues that may affect their own lives, the direction of society and the future of the world. (DfEE 1999:76)

So How Do We Achieve This?

By achieving this as successfully as possible the child should feel confident in the classroom setting. It is essential that we, as practitioners, recognize this important part of the child's life and seek to make the work we carry out in the classroom/nursery reflect this understanding and our respect for others.

Early years' children may have already acquired negative attitudes towards issues of race, disability, gender, social class and other stereotypical stances (Lane 2007). The teacher must confront these attitudes and challenge them while, at the same time, acknowledging that the parents may have differing views on such subjects.[1] This requires sensitive handling as there is a real need to build up successful partnerships with home. We have often found that the most useful way of dealing with such situations is to explain to the child that, although such things may be said at home, it is not acceptable in school or nursery (Brown 2001). The ways in which we deal with such situations have an impact on the child who may be left feeling confused, and it is vital then that we continue to display a positive stance towards this aspect of the child's learning.[2]

In order to create an environment that provides for equality of access to all the children in the nursery or school, the relationship between home and school needs to be fostered at every possible opportunity. When entering school for the first time, the child brings skills and abilities already acquired at home. In order for the child to continue to develop successfully there is a need on the part of the school to provide continuity in this learning process, acknowledging the importance of the home.

This can be achieved in various ways, starting with the relationship between home and school. This means much more than having the occasional special celebration evening where 'multiculturism'/cultural diversity (in the sense of 'race'/ethnicity and also in the sense of social class cultures) is celebrated, or a welcome sign is provided in different languages. Claire expands on this:

> It is important to go beyond projects which exoticize minority communities, or highlight the ways in which they are different from the majority. In some schools minority communities get a look in through curriculum work in RE, focusing on festivals and specific beliefs. Best practice is not the celebration after which you revert to a monocultural curriculum but always looking for opportunities to include different ethnicities in the ordinary range of resources and activities. (Claire 2006:309–310)

Working with parents and encouraging them to join in lessons when appropriate, creating times in the timetable when parents, grandparents and other family members can come into the class and talk to the children about their own cultural and linguistic heritage, asking older people to come in and talk about their own life experiences, are all helpful strategies. There is a need to continually develop the child's own self-esteem and identity and parents can play a part in this. It is necessary to provide experiences that enable children to think about other areas of inclusion such as disability, gender and social class. It is important to address issues of social power in raising self-esteem. There is a crucial connection between esteem and social power in terms of both knowledge selected for the curriculum and cultural behaviour. (Hill 2001).[2]

Once a child is able to feel secure about their own identity, there is an increased chance that they will be able to respect children who are different from them. One way of helping the child to respect his own identity is to provide opportunities for the children to look at themselves and others in the class, looking at differences in shoe sizes, type of hair or what they looked like as babies. By examining the differences and similarities, children are given the opportunity to find a sense of their own identity by seeing themselves reflected in others. The acknowledgement that there are differences in us all, and that these differences should be respected rather than ignored or resented, should provide a good starting point for the child to develop as a caring, respectful person.

Developing children's respect for each other is an important aspect of equality of access. This respect can be developed by the teacher who should be seen to challenge any negative views some children may have about another child in the class. By careful modelling of appropriate reactions and continually reinforcing the ideas of inclusion for all, children should gradually begin to develop respect for each other, regardless of race, culture, language, gender or disability (Claire 2006).

When visiting a primary school in Northern England, we were privileged to be part of a special day focusing on hearing impairment. There were a number of children throughout the school who had various types of hearing loss and the staff had decided to organize a day where these children would be the VIPs for the day. By deciding to highlight rather than play down the problems encountered by this type of need, and to provide opportunities for the group to lead various activities rather than be just included, the school appeared to have embraced their responsibilities and reacted in a positive manner. The day finished with the children delivering an assembly using signing. This seemed to us a very good example of providing equality of access. By taking positive steps, the school was able to acknowledge the needs of these particular children, while at the same time not patronizing them. Most children and many of us adults have the need to feel that we belong and that we are accepted. Hopefully, this type of event is helpful in achieving this and will in the future become less of a 'one-off' event and more of a regular feature on the timetable.

The Content of Primary Science

There are many different primary science curricula throughout the world (Ninnes 2002). But, although they may differ in detail, there is great agreement in the majority of what they cover. Most will focus on basic human biology and the growth of plants. They will cover basic materials and their properties. There is some coverage of forces and movement, light and sound, and an introduction to electricity. Most will also cover the concept of planet Earth and the Solar System, although the ways in which these are taught will vary, and in fact most of this topic is covered without practical investigation.

Within our experience, primary teachers feel more comfortable with the biological aspects of the curriculum than with those dealing with physical science. However, this does not mean that a more relaxed attitude can be taken in dealing with biology in the primary curriculum. Some of the biggest scandals in science have been through researchers falsifying data to imply connection between race and intelligence or other characteristics (for example, see Cyril Burt's infamous work on IQ testing (Parrington 1996).[3] There is a parallel trap for teachers in gathering data from a class of children for any mathematical exercise – data about physical characteristics such as height, weight, foot size, pulse rate – as small sets of data may reinforce preconceptions. However, most teachers are sensible enough to treat these as individual data and not to attempt to group them in ways that could be misinterpreted.

Similarly, plants provide an excellent topic of study for the diverse classroom. Many varieties of plants can be grown from seed in the warmth of a classroom. Discussions exploring which crops grow where, and why, can give a good starting point for celebrating diversity. For example, the fact that wheat is sensitive to late frosts, while barley and rye thrive on long hours of summer sunshine, can begin to explain some of the differences between English and Scottish culinary traditions. Bringing in parents and other members of the community to discuss different ways of preparing rice, cassava and maize can further support children's learning.

It is in the physical aspects of primary science that tend to present the trickiest difficulties. The problem is not so much with the concepts themselves, but in the way the topics are enlivened for children. Many physics topics are told in terms of stories, of the men who solved problems and made discoveries ... Did you notice the mistake that crept into our writing above? We said 'men' and surely we ought to have been gender neutral and written 'people'. It is a historical and undeniable fact that the people associated with the development of topics, that are on the primary science curriculum, are men, and indeed white and European (think about Newton, Watt, Ampere, Volta, Galileo, Faraday) but some, like Faraday and Telford had humble beginnings which is a useful point to make. The Herschels are also a good example of eventual recognition of the female contribution to work in Astronomy.

So these areas pose a dilemma for teachers. Do we abandon the notion of personifying science? Science is already considered abstract and colourless, and leaving people out of the story would mean abandoning cherished anecdotes, such as Newton and the apple and Watt and his kettle, as well as the drama of the conflict between Galileo and the church. Besides, such an approach would be impossible, given the support books, videos and websites that exist. Of course, there is much available information on black or women scientists, but the nature of the curriculum does not demand their inclusion. Therefore, they are easily sidelined.

Do we mention the names briefly and rush on, hoping that children will not notice the gender of the people behind the names? Or do we include a little historical and societal analysis each time we mention a famous scientist, to explain the prevalence of white, middle-class men in the pantheon, concluding with an exhortation that life and society isn't like that now and that opportunity awaits all who accept the challenge of research? This latter suggestion would seem a good way forward, and indeed there are more and more resources available that will include a whole range of scientists.

Practical Work

As mentioned earlier, the need to provide positive and appropriate learning situations is especially important in science. In this area of the curriculum there is often a greater need to allow and encourage inclusion for all. There is a need for practitioners to actively seek to address all areas of social inclusion. The stereotypical images of science are often seen as precluding certain sectors of society, and it is therefore necessary to positively reinforce the all-inclusive approach, encouraging all children to take part in the sessions.

Practitioners need to seek out and build on planning around children's existing knowledge. As in all areas of good primary practice, it is essential to establish what existing knowledge the children in class already have and to use this information to inform future planning. The constructivist approach to teaching (Vygotsky 1978) is often found to very effective in the delivery of science teaching and learning (Littledyke and Huxford 1998). The suggested first step taken by the teacher is to provide an opportunity for the children to discuss their personal understanding and for the teacher to help the child construct and extend their own understanding. This is an essential part of the role of the teacher, and the action taken after gaining this crucial knowledge is especially important if the teaching is going to provide equality of access to all the children in the class. Using the information gained initially whether it be by classroom discussion or through the provision of a suitable activity – the teacher needs to provide an appropriate activity to enable the children to investigate their own understanding. There is also a need to ask questions in such a way that children can discover how much they know, even when they do not know that they know it.

However, in spite of the perceived problematic nature of this curriculum area, it is possible to use science as an excellent means of providing a vehicle for all children to achieve their best. The practical nature of the subject allows for children to succeed at learning in a way that is most useful for them as individuals. Children with English as an Additional Language (EAL) may typically find it easier to undertake a practical task than communicate verbally the findings of an investigation. EAL children will often succeed in practical tasks, and it is this practical context of exploring something interesting and meaningful that which will give rise to the development and learning of their new school language. This is also helpful in assessing a child's understanding of a particular concept..

Providing an enjoyable activity, such as investigating the properties of bubbles, serves as a useful introduction to scientific investigation for children (and adults) of all ages.

Some children – often girls – are sometimes still seen as being disadvantaged in terms of their science learning as they take on a more passive role in schools. For example, recording the classroom investigation is a task that may often be undertaken by a girl, rather than carrying out the more exciting or active part of the investigation. Sadly, we have witnessed this kind of situation often occurring among groups of teacher trainee students who have not challenged these kinds of discriminatory practices. Teaching situations such as these have also led to long and useful discussions about the need to provide equality of access to all the children in a class during a science session. One possible solution to this problem is to make sure that each child is assigned a precise role within the activity; the roles will vary according to the age and abilities of the children involved. An example of this type of group work would be to identify the roles of manager, worker, secretary and presenter and these would be designated to each of the group. Or the roles could also include an encourager (who makes sure that everyone contributes and everyone's contributions are considered democratically), and time-keeper (who can hold on to the egg timer). Each member of the group would be given a badge with the role written on it. In each subsequent session the roles would be divided in a different way, therefore allowing each child an opportunity to experience each of the specified roles. There are obviously issues of sensitivity surrounding this type of classroom management; for instance, an introverted child may find it tortuous to have to present their findings to the class – in which case the child may want to write down or draw the activity.

Resources

One of the major problems of teaching any practical activity in school is that of resourcing. This problem is amplified in science because, even in the primary school, specialist equipment may be required. Specialist equipment requires storage and maintenance, neither of which is readily available in many primary schools. The availability of equipment then becomes a significant factor in the teaching approach used. A teacher may spend half a day in search of resources and testing them out, and still have only six sets of electrical equipment working. So, with a class of thirty children, that often implies groups of five, presenting constraints upon the teacher's organization and management of the session.

Equipment shortage may be of particular significance in areas of economic deprivation. As reported by one teacher at a school in area of severe economic deprivation 'these children just grab what they can – it isn't malicious... It's just 'I must have it in case I don't get it" (Solomon 1993). However, 'all is not lost': it is possible to provide ample, useful materials at reasonable cost. For example, when purchasing electrical components to carry out work on circuits, it is very cost-effective to source suppliers who buy in bulk, and who do not provide glossy brochures, but will sell to schools at costs which are usually considerable lower than some big supply firms. 'Kitchen sink' science is also very effective and perhaps more meaningful to the primary children than elaborate equipment often found in secondary schools.

This problem surrounding equipment and resources can also be resolved in a number of other ways. Some primary schools have contacted the science department of their local secondary schools for sharing equipment and working together during practical sessions. Others make good use of recyclable materials. For example, Pringles tubes make good pinhole cameras, bubble wrap makes a good insulator and margarine tubs of different sizes with different surfaces attached to the bottoms can be used for exploring friction

It is also important to ensure that books, educational toys and ICT provision reflect the school community; there are excellent resources which we list at the end of this chapter. There is never a right answer to the problem of resourcing primary science. But, however a teacher attempts to solve the problem, all issues of equality should be at the forefront of the teacher's mind. Individual success for a child is more likely if he/she is able to relate to the context in which the learning takes place.

Multilingualism

A major feature of schools serving diverse communities is the number of languages spoken. Many schools set down a policy that formal lessons are carried out in English, on the grounds that this will speed the child's learning of English, which in turn is necessary for success in English-speaking societies.

However, while this may be a reasonable policy for the learning of English, it is poor practice for learning science. In order to embed their learning practical activities, children need to discuss their experiences (Newton 2001). Talk needs to be in the language the child is most comfortable with – and that may very well be the child's home language. (See the chapters in this volume by Leena Robertson and Dina Mchemedbegovic). Being able to consolidate conceptual understanding in the child's own language has benefits, and in classes with a number of representatives from a particular linguistic minority community, this is easily arranged. It is often possible to pair children who are at different stages of their English language development, to their mutual benefit, when it becomes necessary to switch between languages.

However, where there is only a single child with a particular language, discussion and talk become more difficult. One strategy may be to invite parents or other members of the community to join the class as helpers; this can often be a useful strategy for integrating isolated families, quite apart from the benefit to science learning.

Practical work, with its many observations, inferences and conclusions, is an ideal starting point for many forms of talk. A teacher with confidence will allow this talk to develop, sometimes in a number of languages, often in a language she herself does not speak. What should not be forgotten is that science has very precise language requirements. Although a primary child with English as an Additional Language may learn colloquial English in 18 months, the language of science may take far longer to assimilate. Children may be able to instinctively feel that a test is unfair long before they can articulate the reasons that make it so. Similarly, an understanding of science words, such as force, current or cell, is bedevilled by their alternative usages. As to the distinction between mass and weight – hard enough for adults with excellent linguistic skills, let alone an 11-

year-old with only a year's experience of English. Science does have its own language, but a further problem is the non-scientific use of these words, such as 'battery' for 'cell', 'weight' for 'mass'.

Teaching for Equality

Providing resources of books or CDRoms which depict female scientists, and maybe encouraging any known local female scientist to come in and talk to the class, will help to reinforce the anti-sexist message as Claire argues:

> Aim for a more inclusive approach through all the curriculum subjects, not just RE. For example in art, design and technology, children might learn about cultural and scientific achievements from outside Europe – the Taj Mahal built by Shah Jehan, the Great Wall of China, Great Zimbabwe, the Egyptian or the Mayan pyramids; sculptors from Mesopotamia (now Iraq) who made the great friezes commemorating their rulers' victories; the bronzes and sculptures of Benin craftworkers in the sixteenth century, the magnificently decorated monasteries carved into the mountains in Ethiopia, built by early Coptic Christians (Claire 2006:310)

Although some of these structures are outside the context of many young childrens' understanding, talking about magnificent buildings found outside Britain will also help to introduce the idea that there are great things in other countries of the world.

Teachers will find it useful to collect images from the cultures represented in their classroom. Interactive whiteboards are a useful resource that can be used to provide relevant images that can be shared comfortably by a whole class of children. Teachers will also need to avoid associating some images (such as spacecrafts, high-speed railways or gleaming hospital equipment) with Western nations and others (horse-powered water pumps or sail-powered boats, to mention a few) with developing nations.

Inner city areas, where there are diverse cultural and lingual situations, may also consist of smaller monolingual and monocultural environments. Glauert states:

> This kind of approach is equally vital in mono-lingual, mono-cultural situations if the development of stereotyped attitudes and assumptions about black and other minority groups is to be avoided and if all children are to share the wealth of experience and understanding that this approach to science can offer. (Glauert 1991)

If we are to achieve truly inclusive classrooms, it is vital that we are seen to behave in a positive manner towards all the children. Siraj-Blatchford argues that:

> The greatest challenge for educators in the early years may therefore be to provide positive role models in terms of science and design and technology themselves. (Siraj-Blatchford 1999:34)

The Curriculum Guidance for the Foundation Stage is explicit in its promotion of inclusion for all:

> Young children are finding out more and more about the world they live in and the people they encounter. Children acquire a range of skills, knowledge and attitudes related to knowledge and understanding of the world in many ways. They learn skills necessary to this area of learning by using a range of tools, for example computers, magnifiers, gardening tools, scissors, hole-punches and screwdrivers. They learn by encountering creatures, people, plants and objects in their natural environments and in real life situations (DfEE/QCA 2000:82)

The Classroom Environment

If we are to provide an environment that is inspiring for all the children in the class, there is a need to resource it from an all-inclusive angle. Provision of appropriate books and ICT resources should reflect the children working there. Encouraging parents to come into the nursery or classroom to talk about their own experiences at school, sharing of food, again from representative countries, is helpful, as already mentioned. Toys that are not just Eurocentric, and dual or multilingual labelling of classroom items in appropriate languages, are just a few of the many ways of creating a classroom or nursery where all children can feel that they belong.

Disinterest and under-achievement in science can be the result of a child experiencing negative attitudes at a very early age, therefore it is essential that the experiences a child has in the early years are positive and trigger a long-term interest in this area of the curriculum. Science should be seen as an exciting, attainable area of learning and it is the teachers' responsibility to reinforce this attitude and fight the old, but still prevalent, idea that science is an elite discipline that is only open to a small select part of society. By promoting the enthusiasm and confidence for science in primary schools, we will provide a firm basis for future successful learning.

The Status of Science

As one of the three core subjects of the primary curriculum (the other two are English and mathematics), science has a high status in English schools. It is seen as key to the government's ambition for Britain to have a 'knowledge economy' (Roberts 2002), and various government reports have urged the need for investing in producing more science graduates and a more scientifically-literate society (Lord Sainsbury 2007).

Science gains its status from the belief that it has an empirical method of research leading to systematic laws. These laws allow us to understand and make use of the natural world. However, closer inspection of the working of science leads to the question of whether there is such a thing as 'scientific method'. The idea that individual observations could be generalized to wider theories (inductivism) has long been discredited. Sir Karl Popper introduced the idea that science was a creative process, with any explanation that fitted observed facts being permitted until undermined by observation, together with the idea that a useful theory would generate predictions that could be tested. More recent philosophers have further dismantled the notion of science as a series of logical, methodical steps (Chalmers 1982).

Does this brief incursion into philosophy have any relevance to the primary class teacher struggling with practical science? Indeed it does, because primary science is full of investigations. It is the unique feature of science as one of the high-status subjects that it encourages hands-on, active and practical investigations. Primary science is often categorized as being 'about investigations'.

Yet, if we encourage children in the belief that we teach them investigations because that shows them the way science works, we encourage them (and their parents) to subscribe to the belief in empirical research methods outlined above. We need to be careful in our own claims for investigative science, saying that it is a part of the way science works, and that practical work is a good way of learning and remembering. As teachers, we need to divorce ourselves from the claim that all problems are soluble by the reductionist method.

In teaching science, we also need to acknowledge that the reductionist and inductivist approaches to science have caused much harm, from the false results of Burt on comparative racial intelligence, to Western capitalist approaches to mineral extraction and deforestation. These issues may be considered too complex to approach in the primary classroom, but teachers also need to begin to introduce young children to a range of societal phenomena. And in any case, should these questions arise in classrooms, teachers need to be prepared to discuss such matters (Reiss 1993).

Apart from philosophical issues, we must also guard against the triumphalism of Western approaches and the way that the history of recent science has been distorted to enhance the role of Britain within it. Nowhere is this better exemplified than in the history of vaccination. Many science writers and educators before us have pointed out that vaccination has been practised in China for over two thousand years and was widely known across Asia before 1700 (Shan 1997). Yet the label on a major exhibit in the National Museum of Science and Industry (London's Science Museum) was still stating in 2008 that 'Edward Jenner introduced vaccination to the world'. The Science Museum is regarded as *the* authority on science matters by many primary teachers; it is also closely linked into the network of Science Learning Centres set up across the UK in 2005.

This kind of distortion is even more serious if we consider it within schools and the micro-organisms section of the QCA Scheme of Work (the work of Jenner is specifically mentioned) (The Standards Site) which is taught in Year 6 in many schools, just prior to SATs and transfer to secondary school. The problem is not only that Jenner is credited with this, but that everyone else who has challenged this view, has been ignored. Science has its own prejudice.

The Status of Scientists

It may seem paradoxical to follow a section in which we claim that problems with science teaching may arise because of the *high* status of the subject with a section that addresses problems arising from the *low* status of scientists. But, in fact, there is a causal relationship: society has conferred high value on scientific knowledge and a concomitant priesthood-like status on practitioners of science. The elite clique of scientists is portrayed by the media as a series of stereotypes, characterized as male, pale and stale, perhaps leavened with a dash of world dominating vindictiveness. It is not an attractive image for primary children.

As scientists are portrayed so negatively, and there are few black, minority ethnic, women or economically-disadvantaged scientists to act as role models and counter the images, this constitutes as an image problem for many children in school. This is exacerbated by the scientific community's attempts to popularize science by showing it as a career, rather than a non-job-specific learning opportunity (Hamman 2008). Science is shown as something you do, so you can be a scientist, and at the same time scientists are shown as being something alien to black and minority ethnic groups or women. Scientists are also shown as middle-class, pottering along on average salaries, and certainly not in the same league as footballers or models, nor even the second division of lawyers or accountants, so the potential earnings are hardly attractive.

In an attempt to counter this negativity, the UK government has set up a scheme of Science and Engineering Ambassadors (SEAs). 18,000 ambassadors (STEMNET 2008) are available to go into primary and secondary schools in the UK, and they are recruited with an eye to being attractive to young people. 40 per cent of SEAs are women, but less than 10 per cent are from BME groups. Even though the ambassadors themselves are unpaid volunteers, the administration of such a huge effort costs in the region of £2 million a year. The government has absorbed the message that something needs to be done to counteract the negative image of scientists – it remains to be seen whether this effort is sufficient or whether further spending will be necessary. There may not be many 'super scientists' but then there are not that many 'super footballers' either. However, any large town probably has had some successful scientists.

The ambassador concept has a drawback that leads us into one other problematic area regarding equality. The companies that can afford research scientists working for them are inevitably large. To encourage part of this workforce to spend time voluntarily in schools also means that the companies are rich. So the majority of ambassadors that go into schools to enhance the teaching of science are inevitably from large national or multi-national companies that are part of the global capital network. In turn, this inevitably fixes the subject of science as part of the agenda of capitalization and globalization for both pupils and primary teachers alike.

Is science inevitably a major part of globalization and capitalism? Not necessarily, but it is very easy to make it appear so. The original proposal for a Science National Curriculum (Thompson 1988) included a much more balanced approach with sections on social justice. However, this was dropped entirely in the National Curriculum published in 1989, with its emphasis on knowledge and understanding (see, for example, the parliamentary debate between Jack Straw and Kenneth Baker, respectively the Labour Education spokesman in the House of Commons and the Conservative Minister for Education, responsible for the Education Reform Act (Straw 1989)).

The present curriculum, in emphasizing relevance and 'How Science Works', has taken science well away from neutrality and positioned it as a major contributor to the growth of capitalist hegemony. The 'knowledge economy' that is the vision of the present government is a euphemism for the unequal distribution of scientific knowledge, driven by the dynamic that capital will flow from those without to those with 'knowledge' (exemplified by the prohibitively high prices that Africans are expected to pay to get hold of anti-Aids drugs produced by Western pharmaceutical companies (Mathiason 2001).

And, In Conclusion . . .

The average teacher, having read through the preceding 6,000 words, may well feel close to despair – so many difficulties, so many hidden pitfalls, and all in a subject in which only a minority of teachers feel any confidence. But science teaching can also be a great, positive asset to primary teaching. Many children love the loosening of formal learning that comes with practical work. The kinaesthetic experience of moving around, touching and interacting with objects makes science lessons instantly memorable. The discussion promoted by something spectacular or unexpected can be enormously valuable.

Most of all, children love to enquire. They like to experiment with objects and systems, try things out and so to understand them. In the primary school we are privileged to watch the way children learn to transform from play to rational enquiry. And the greatest privilege is to see this transformation spreading equally among all the young minds in our charge.

Notes

[1] For a useful summary of negative stereotyping and its early acquisition, see Lane (2007). She writes that 'Putting inclusion into practice means recognizing and supporting every child's potential and worth equally and removing any barriers that prevent this being realized.'

[2] Another useful source of published research on stereotyping is by Babette Brown who discusses the use of 'Persona Dolls' to work with children on issues of inequality: 'Using Dolls while telling stories makes it easier for children to make connections with their own lives. They are empowered to reflect on who they are and on the identities and feelings of those around them.' (Brown 2001).

[3] Sir Cyril Burt (1883–1971) was an educational psychologist (indeed, the first psychologist to be knighted) who was professor of psychology at University College, London for 20 years from 1931. Much of his work was on intelligence, inheritance and race. However, many of his controversial findings have subsequently been discredited and his research shown to have been falsified. Many of his papers were mysteriously burnt shortly after his death.

References

Brown, B. (2001) *Combating Discrimination – Persona Dolls in action*. Stoke-On-Trent: Trentham Books

Chalmers, A. F. (1982) *What is this thing called science?* Buckingham: Open University Press.

Claire, H. (2006) 'Education for Cultural Diversity and Social Justice' in J. Arthur, T. Grainger and D. Wray (eds) *Learning to Teach in the Primary School*. Oxford: Routledge.

DfEE/QCA (1999) *The National Curriculum: Handbook for Primary Teachers in England*. London: DfEE/QCA.

DfEE/QCA (2000) *The Curriculum Guidance for the Foundation Stage*. London: DfEE/QCA.

Glauert, E. (1991) 'Science Teaching for Equality', in S. Thorpe (ed.) *Race, Equality and Science Teaching*. Hatfield: Association for Science Education.

Hamman, N. (2008) *Careers from Science*. London: Royal Society.

Hill, D. (2001) 'The National Curriculum, the Hidden Curriculum and Equality', in D. Hill and M. Cole (eds) *Schooling and Equality: Fact, Concept and Policy*. London: Kogan Page.

Lane, J. (2007) *Embracing Equality*. Online at http://www.multiverse.ac.uk/attachments/e45687e4-ae2f-4922-993e-8f3ca94a47bc.pdf

Littledyke, M. and Huxford, L. (1998) *Teaching the Primary Curriculum for Learning Constructively*. Abingdon: David Fulton Publishing

Lord Sainsbury of Turville (2007) *Race to the Top*, HM Treasury, 2007. Online at http://webarchive.nationalarchives.gov.uk/+/http://www.hm-treasury.gov.uk/d/sainsbury_review051007.pdf.

Mathiason, N. (2001) 'South Africa fights Aids drugs apartheid'. *The Observer*, 14th January. London.

MacPherson, W. (1999) *The Stephen Lawrence Inquiry*. London, TSO. Online at http://www.archive.official-documents.co.uk/document/cm42/1262/1262.htm

Mehemedbegovic, D. (2009) 'Community/Foreign Languages', in D. Hill and L. Helavaara Robertson (eds) *Equality in the Primary School: Promoting good practice across the curriculum*. London: Continuum.

Newton, L. (2001) 'Teaching for Understanding in Primary Science', in *Evaluation and Research in Education*, 15, (3), 143–153.

Ninnes, P. (2002) 'Spaces in Science Curriculum Materials in Canada, Australia and New Zealand'. *Journal of Curriculum Studies*, 34, (5), 557–570.

Parrington, J. (1996) 'The Intelligence Fraud'. *Socialist Review*, 196. Online at http://pubs.socialistreviewindex.org.uk/sr196/parrington.htm

Reiss, M. (1993) *Science Education for a Pluralist Society*. Buckingham: Open University.

Roberts, G. (2002) *SET for Success*, London: HM Treasury. Online at http://www.hm-treasury.gov.uk/ent_res_roberts.htm

Shan, S. (1997) *Promoting Equality in Primary Schools*. London: Cassell.

Siraj-Blatchford, J. (1999) *Supporting Science, Design and Technology in the Early Years*. Maidenhead: Open University Press.

Solomon, J. (1993) 'Science Teaching in Areas of Social Deprivation', in E. Whitelegg, J. Thomas and S. Tresman (eds) *Challenges and Opportunities for Science Education*. London: Paul Chapman.

The Standards Site. Online at http://www.standards.dfes.gov.uk/schemes2/science/

STEMNET (Science, Technology Engineering and Maths NETwork) Online at www.stemnet.org.uk

Straw, J. (1989) *Hansard*. Online at http://hansard.millbanksystems.com/commons/1989/apr/17/national-curriculum

Thompson, J. J. (1988) *National Curriculum Science Working Group: Final Report*. London: Department of Science/Welsh Office.

Vygotsky, L. (1978) *Mind in Society*. Cambridge, MA: Harvard University Press.

Part 3

Foundation Subjects

Chapter 9

ICT

Gareth Honeyford

Introduction

Information Communication Technologies (ICTs) are pervasive in society and schools, but ICT is often surrounded by confusion. It can be seen to be a subject in its own right, but it is also a tool for teaching and learning in other subjects. Any consideration of ICT and equality must recognize these twin roles that ICT plays and take these into account.

It should also be recognized that in a conventional school-based teaching and learning scenario there are two key players, the pupils and the teacher, along with other facilitators such as teaching assistants. ICT impacts on both teachers and learners and this chapter seeks to address some of the equality issues for both. It is also worth considering that in 'the information age', when we talk about teaching and learning with ICT, this does not stop at the school gates and we therefore should also consider access elsewhere, including at home.

Access to good quality ICT is a right of pupils and teachers and therefore there are important equality issues around that access. This chapter explores why that right should exist, and highlights some of the aspects of inequality with consideration for how some of these might be addressed. I do not subscribe to the view that 'Placing technology in schools leads to automatic learning gains' – a view that is explored and strongly contested by Waller (2007) but I do believe that ICTs can give teachers and pupils access to different ways of teaching and learning and that *sometimes* these will be better ways, at least, for some.

What are ICTs?

Information Communication Technologies (ICTs) is an all-encompassing term for the myriad of devices that exist today. Most people immediately think of the computer and, if pushed, in a primary school context, will often mention the interactive whiteboard (IWB). In a Key Stage 1 or Foundation Stage setting one might also include electronic toys such as cash registers or metal detectors, as well as programmable floor robots such as Pips, Pixies, Roamers and Bee-Bots.[1]

In such a large and rapidly changing arena, any attempt to provide a comprehensive list is doomed to fail, so here I simply include some illustrative examples. In addition to the relatively school-specific examples listed above, ICTs also include digital cameras, MP3 players such as iPods, games consoles, hand-held devices such as PDAs[2] and audio-visual technologies such as DVDs and videos. In conclusion, ICTs are wide-ranging and so commonplace that it is virtually impossible to avoid them, yet this is precisely what occurs in some classrooms. As Reynolds *et al.* state, 'ICT remains a contentious issue for many teachers at the point of implementation. Attitudes to whether, how and why it should be used for teaching and learning are very varied.' (Reynolds *et al.* 2003:1).

ICT as a Curriculum Subject

According to Teachernet, 'Information and communication technology (ICT) is one of the National Curriculum non-core foundation subjects', and indeed is seen by some as being 'the fourth core subject' (DCSF 2008).

During Key Stage 1, pupils explore ICT and learn to use it confidently and with purpose to achieve specific outcomes. They start to use ICT to develop their ideas and record their creative work. They become familiar with hardware and software. [...] During Key Stage 2, pupils use a wider range of ICT tools and information sources to support their work in other subjects. They develop their research skills and decide what information is appropriate for their work. They begin to question the plausibility and quality of information. They learn how to amend their work and present it in a way that suits its audience. (http://www.nc.uk.net).

In addition to the statutory guidance outlined in the National Curriculum, a range of non-statutory materials are produced by the Qualifications and Curriculum Authority (QCA) in the form of the 'QCA Scheme of Work for ICT' (www.standards.Dfes.gov.uk/schemes).

This scheme of work is effectively a series of medium-term plans that could be used (they are non-statutory) for teaching the various aspects of the (statutory) National Curriculum for ICT. It is generally well received although not without its critics. Potter and Darbyshire (2005) provide a useful overview for the general reader including an analysis of 'its underlying pedagogical basis, a behaviourist sub-skills approach to teaching, very reminiscent of the principles of instructional design as outlined by Gagne and his co-workers.' (Potter and Darbyshire:117) They also provide a model for an alternative 'Vygotskian' approach. The prime difference between the two approaches is that the Gagnerian approach favoured by the QCA culminates in an integrated task that should be achievable independently by all pupils. A Vygotskian approach, however, would situate this task within individual pupil's 'Zone of Proximal development' (ZPD) – that is unable to be achieved independently but achievable with 'scaffolding'.

The above can be viewed as a gradual move from the teaching of ICT skills to the application of those skills used in support of other areas of learning. In the QCA Scheme this is characterized by a series of short focused tasks culminating in an integrated task that applies previously learnt skills. Those skills must be 'taught not caught' so that pupils can make efficient and appropriate use of ICT both in the integrated task and in other areas. To deny pupils the opportunity to develop these skills, either by not providing access to technology or failing to support them in their development of these skills, is at best, 'marginalizing.'

ICT as a Tool for Teaching and Learning

Lord Stevenson, in reporting on the state of ICT in UK schools in 1997 outlined a vision, 'We wish to see a society within ten years where ICT has permeated the entirety of education (as it will the rest of society) so that it is no longer a talking point but taken for granted – rather as electricity has come to be.' Furthermore, the report made the recommendation to 'Central Government is that they must make the act of faith and encourage the education sector to start using technology rather than talking about it!' (Stevenson *et al.* 1997). The government has taken a 'leap of faith' on the potential of funding the provision of ICT equipment and connectivity in UK schools through the National Grid for Learning (NGFL) programme and later focus on the use of interactive whiteboards. According to Waller (2007:1), 'over the past 5 years the government has spent in excess of £2.5bn on ICT equipment for schools and in 'training' teachers to use the technology'.

ICT clearly has potential as a tool for teachers and pupils, although as Reynolds *et al.* note, the evidence base of academic research to back up the realization of this potential is still very limited, often existing in the form of anecdotal evidence and *optimist-rhetoric*. (Reynolds *et al.* 2003).

The best evidence we have to date is the line, 'Schools that were judged by OfSTED to have very good ICT resources had better achievement than schools with poor ICT' (Becta 2002, cited in Reynolds 2003:2) but this is clearly open to a number of different interpretations.

However, if we maintain this leap of faith, it does seem 'commonsense' that good quality ICT provision can be a useful resource for teachers and pupils. The key here is that the resources should be of good quality and well designed, unlike a lot of the materials that one can find on the World Wide Web. To ensure the best provision for pupils, it is important that teachers critically review the quality of any materials that they download to use with pupils. This may seem obvious but there are many resources that at first glance appear to be of good quality, but with further analysis, are not. It is also clearly important to ensure that ICT resources, like all classroom materials, are free from stereotypes (intentional or otherwise) and are not alienating to any members of the classroom. The use of ICT can make for a more inclusive classroom and access to interactive whiteboards can allow teachers to display rich multimedia resources to illustrate difficult concepts for pupils. This is not universally the case, but materials can be designed to be attractive and accessible to all pupils, including those with visual or auditory difficulties, or in different languages, or suit different learning styles, etc. Resources may be designed with whole-class interactivity in mind, but could also be provided for small group or individual use, both in a classroom situation or outside, e.g. at home or an after-school club. Materials can also be made available to those pupils that were unable to be present at a particular time, perhaps because of illness or another barrier to attendance. Materials can also be adapted by teachers, or teaching assistants, to tailor them to the needs of specific groups or individuals. The fact that the software to run these presentations is generally free to distribute is also important here and schools that are committed to equality have a responsibility to support parents/guardians that have ICT access in gaining access to this software, and thus, learning materials.

ICT and Young People

The World Wide Web was invented by the English scientist Tim Berners-Lee between March 1989 and November 1990 (Naughton 1999) and the word 'Internet' had become commonplace by 1996 (http://en.wikipedia.org/wiki/Internet)/.[3] This means that pupils in our primary schools have been born into a society in which ICTs, including the Internet, are a normal part. There are issues of access and digital divides which will be explored later, but it is worth considering the role that technology has in the life of many pupils. Marc Prensky dubs these individuals Digital Natives and contrasts them with those born before technology was so commonplace – the digital immigrants (Prensky 2001).

It is my opinion that we owe it to our 'digital native' pupils to encourage and empower them to make use of the technologies that they are comfortable with and to address the issues of digital divides to give them access to learning tools. I do not think that the situation is as cut-and-dried as suggested by certain computer retailers keen to sell their machines into the education sector:

The Differences Between Digital Native Learners and Digital Immigrant Teachers

Digital Native Learners	Digital Immigrant Teachers
Prefer receiving information quickly from multiple multimedia sources.	Prefer slow and controlled release of information from limited sources.
Prefer parallel processing and multi-tasking.	Prefer singular processing and single or limited tasking.
Prefer processing pictures, sounds and video before text.	Prefer to provide text before pictures, sounds and video.
Prefer random access to hyperlinked multimedia information.	Prefer to provide information linearly, logically and sequentially.
Prefer to interact/network simultaneously with many others.	Prefer students to work independently rather than network and interact.
Prefer to learn 'just-in-time.'	Prefer to teach 'just-in-case' (it's on the exam).
Prefer instant gratification and instant rewards.	Prefer deferred gratification and deferred rewards.
Prefer learning that is relevant, instantly useful and fun.	Prefer to teach to the curriculum guide and standardized tests.

Jukes and Dosaj, (2003) in Apple advertising materials online.

I am, however, convinced that we cannot afford to have 'neo-Luddites' in our classrooms, and to reject technology out of hand does a disservice to our pupils. Technology is not always the answer to 'improving learning', but it can usually provide an alternative approach and sometimes this may be better, at least for some pupils. Stephen Johnson (2005) in his book *Everything Bad is Good for You: Why Popular Culture is Making Us Smarter*, takes a wonderfully sideways look at popular culture. He suggests a thought experiment where we, 'Imagine a world identical to ours save one techno-historical change: video games were invented and popularized before books' (Johnson 2005:19). He then goes on to ask what teachers and parents would have to say about these new 'books' that have became all the rage. His analysis is too lengthy to include in full here but he suggests we might hear the following:

> Reading books chronically underestimates the senses. Unlike the longstanding tradition of game playing – which engages the child in a vivid, three-dimensional world filled with moving images and musical soundscapes, navigated and controlled with complex muscular movements – books are simply a barren string of words on the page. [...] Books are also tragically isolating (Johnson 2005:19).

While I do not accept all of Johnson's contentions, I do believe that we cannot reject technology just because it is new, rather we should embrace it, use it and perhaps most importantly, fight to give access to those who might otherwise be denied it.

The importance of access for all is particularly important in an early years' context. Jackie Marsh in her extensive study on the use of technology by young people from birth to six states that, 'The introduction of popular culture, media and/or new technologies into the communications, language and literacy curriculum has a positive effect on the motivation and engagement of children' (Marsh *et al.* 2005:6).

The Problems of Access to Technology – the Digital Divide

> The term 'digital divide' refers to the gap between those people with effective access to digital and information technology and those without access to it. It includes the imbalances in physical access to technology, as well as the imbalances in resources and skills needed to effectively participate as a digital citizen. In others words, it's the unequal access by some members of the society to information and communications technology, and the unequal acquisition of related skills.' (http://en.wikipedia.org/wiki/Digital_divide)

Waller (2007) makes a clear case for the existence of multiple digital divides: 'There are clear divisions based on class, 'race', gender, age and geography. Waller also quotes Castells (2001) and states,

> Core economic, social, political and cultural activities throughout the planet are being structured by and around the internet, and other computer

networks. Exclusion from these networks is one of the most damaging forms of exclusion in our economy and our society.' (Castells 2001, cited in Waller 2007:5).

For more on digital divides and further analysis of Castells' work, see also Suoranta (2003).

The following figures, collated mainly by Waller, illustrate the problem.

There is a tendency to assume that the 'World Wide Web' means that the whole World is connected to the internet but approximately 96% of the world's population is not. (Waller 2007:5).

In wealthy countries there are 563 computers per 1,000 people, but in less wealthy countries only 25 per 1,000 people (Social Watch 2006, cited in Waller 2007:5).

White families are more far more likely to own a computer. Black people living in deprived neighbourhoods have less access to home computers than their white neighbours (Owen 2003, cited in Waller 2007:6).

Children of single parent families were significantly less likely to have access to home computers and the internet. Just over half the children in lone parent families were likely to have a computer, compared to eight out of 10 in two-parent households. Only 36 per cent of children in single-parent households had internet access with almost double that able to surf the net in two-parent homes (Office for National Statistics 2002, cited in Waller 2007:6).

The top three income groups show an 85 per cent home computer ownership level and 75 per cent internet connection, while the bottom three groups are just 23 and 16 per cent respectively (DCSF 2007).

There is not even full equity between schools, 'a substantial minority of schools still do not have broadband access, while others have lower specifications with bandwidth that is insufficient for their needs' (Becta 2006, cited in Waller 2007:6). In my experience of visiting primary schools to observe student teachers, I would argue that it is fair to say some schools and some classrooms within schools make very little use of ICT. It is not uncommon for student teachers to say – 'my teacher does not use the computer' or 'there is an interactive whiteboard but he/she never uses it, hasn't had any training or it doesn't work'. The aim here is not to criticize teachers, we have Ofsted[4] and the *Daily Mail*[5] to do that, but rather to raise the issue of inequality of provision or 'institutional digital divides.' ICT is a statutory curriculum entitlement, arguably the fourth core subject and also, many would contend, a powerful tool for teaching and learning in other subjects. Therefore, I believe that it is our duty to make good use of it **when** it is appropriate.

In summary then, there is a serious disparity in the access to technology among different groups of teachers and learners with those that are most marginalized being found furthest from the white middle-class Western norm. This raises the question of 'What can be done about this in a classroom context?' and, indeed, the whole school, LA or national context.

Implications of the Digital Divide or Divides for the Classroom

Even with the numbers of computers in homes increasing over time (Kominski and Newburger 1999; BBC 2008), pupils are likely to be competing for access within the home. For example, while many middle-class homes may have more than one computer, many of these homes will have competition for access with individuals vying for time online, or using a particular piece of software, the printer or scanner and so on. This situation will obviously be even more pronounced in homes with only a single computer and it is likely that younger, primary-aged pupils may be particularly marginalized in this 'battle for access' as they have to give way to older siblings and parents who need access for their work or leisure. And, of course, there are homes where there is no computer.

This inequality of opportunity is highly likely to spill over into the classroom as pupils without home access may be less confident or capable. They may be less likely to put themselves forward to use the computer or they may take longer to complete a given task. This raises some interesting questions of equality because for some, conventional wisdom would imply that all pupils should be given the same amount of access in the classroom to ensure 'fairness'. This 'equality of access' argument is, of course, not used by egalitarians who are concerned at achieving more equality of outcome through the use of positive discrimination and targeted resources. In reality, though, those pupils who are marginalized by lack of access elsewhere may fall further behind without extra support and time. As always, there is no simple solution to the problem but focused support, loan machines, open access facilities (including libraries, learning centres and the like) and targeted computer clubs, may go some way towards redressing the balance. And here the Local Authorities have a national role to play in targeting funding and resources to those in the greatest need, redistributing resources where appropriate and supporting schools in developing their ICT infrastructure.

There has been a long history of research into gender issues in the classroom. One area of long-standing concern is that of 'boys hogging computers', monopolizing them, particularly when a free choice is given or there are not enough machines for one per child (see, for example, Holdness 1994; Grundy 1996). Recent research also suggests that the inclusion of interactive whiteboards in primary classrooms may increase the dominance of boys rather than improve the situation (Smith *et al.* 2007).

In an attempt to address this issue the Department for Children, Schools and Families (DCSF) are currently funding access to the Computer Clubs for Girls (cc4g) with online materials for all English state schools (http://www.cc4g.net). It is also supported by the Welsh Assembly and many of the resources are also available in Welsh. The cc4g website lists a large number of education and industry partnerships along with testimonials from schools. While it would be difficult to argue against the spirit of this intervention, and the materials seem to be popular with schools and pupils, they may well perpetuate a stereotypical view of the interests of girls, and perhaps some alternative content or at least colour scheme would be preferable. It seems strange – and somewhat counterproductive in terms of societal stereotypes – that the material targeted at girls is largely delivered through a pink and pastels website through themes of celebrity and fashion. There certainly appears to be an assumption, in the rationale behind the intervention, that girls do not find the tasks they are generally set appealing. On the other hand, they may well be interested in the tasks but feel marginalized or intimidated by the boys. It also concerns me that we are not seeing resources targeted at other marginalized groups.

Inequality of Content (Freedom of Access Versus Child Safety or School Censorship)

When considering the issue of young people and access to computer content, particularly materials delivered via the internet, appropriateness of content is an important area. Many schools, and indeed parents, make use of some form of internet filtering to 'protect children.' While there is clearly a place for this, it is by no means a straightforward matter. Dr Victoria Nash of the Oxford Internet Institute, speaking on BBC Radio 4, 'You and Yours Programme' (2008) talked about the issues around the use of internet filters, and especially the problems of under-blocking and over-blocking. In essence, no filtering system is 100 per cent effective and some inappropriate material will often slip through the net, while useful material may be incorrectly blocked. She likened the use of the internet to crossing the road and made the point that adults have responsibility to supervise pupils initially, and then to educate them in how to proceed safely. Filters may both lure schools or parents into a false sense of security and also tempt them to skip the education step, leaving children untrained and potentially vulnerable.

As filters are not 100 per cent effective, schools need to have internet safety policies in place to help keep pupils safe online, and parents and teachers have a responsibility to work with pupils to teach them about online safety. A number of materials exist to help with online safety training for pupils. Two sites that are particularly worthy of note are http://www.thinkuknow.co.uk/default.aspx (From Child Exploitation and Online Protection Centre(CEOP)) and http://www.kidsmart.org.uk (from Childnet).

The increasing use of social networking sites (for example, www.Facebook.com, www.MySpace.com and www.Bebo.com) further illustrates the need to work with young people on issues of internet safety as these sites are based on sharing of personal information, and this clearly exposes young people to potential risks. Some games aimed at very young children also present problems as they contain elements of chat or instant messaging (for example www.clubpenguin.com/)

While access to unsafe materials or potential exposure to 'online-predators' are both clear issues of online safety, another risk is access to materials that are simply biased either by design or accident. Suoranta (2003) states that, 'In a mediated culture, it can be difficult for young people to know whose representations are closest to the truth, which representations to believe and whose images matter' (Suoranta 2003:4–5). This highlights the importance of training pupils in evaluating the validity of websites – a vital aspect of training pupils to be intelligent information consumers. A large number of information literacy materials are available online (see, for example, November 2008). One site, referred to by November that clearly illustrates Suoranta's point is www.martinlutherking.org. This site, currently the 7th hit on a Google search for 'Martin Luther King', reports to contain 'The truth about Martin Luther King: Includes historical trivia, articles and pictures. A valuable resource for teachers and students alike', but which is, in fact, run by 'Stormfront', a 'White Pride' organization.

This is an extreme example of an issue that affects all web users: trying to evaluate quickly and accurately the merits of a particular site as an information source is challenging. Training in this area may be particularly important for those pupils who are affected by the digital divide and who have less experience of working online.

Another aspect of school censorship is that it is not uncommon for schools to block sites that are not 'educational' or that pupils might use simply for their own enjoyment. The video sharing website www.youtube.com is a good example. Teachers taking the decisions about which sites are blocked have their own agendas and may wish to maintain their own cultural norms. This 'censorship' will particularly affect those pupils that are already marginalized by the digital divide as they may not gain access elsewhere. Kellner (1998) contends that in a media culture it is important to learn multiple ways of interacting with social reality. Children and young people must be provided with opportunities to develop skills in multiple literacies in order for them to be able to better work on their identities, social relationships and communities, whether material, virtual or combinations of the two (Kellner 1998, cited in Suoranta 2003). It is worth considering that the use of social networking sites is a cultural phenomenon of our time, and the blocking of access for those young people who have no access elsewhere could be very marginalizing. I believe that blocking access to social networking and media-rich sites could deny marginalized groups important social and cultural capital, particularly as they move into secondary school. This may also silence an important aspect of a pupil voice that is important in fighting oppression (BBC 2007; Aune 2008).

Some schools do embrace technology to enable them to hear their pupils voices. One Shropshire secondary school makes use of a blog (online diary) to encourage pupils to make anonymous comments on issues important to the school, such as those ranging from the quality of online testing to gender equality (Lacon-Childe 2007). Another school, a Bristol primary school, allows pupils to communicate details of their work with a worldwide audience, including their parents (Teyfant Community School 2007).

Web 2.0 and the Democratization of Content

Web 2.0 is the term, coined in 2004 by Tim O'Reilly, used to encompass a number of recent internet phenomena including social networking, blogs, wikis and so on (O'Reilly 2005). These centre on the concept of 'the web as platform' and the freedom for anyone to publish. This certainly gives all manner of people a voice as Suoranta suggests;

It is hardly surprising that the majority of the content of current media culture is of Western-origin and is produced mainly in the US by Hollywood entertainment industry. Its contents are blind to the consuming young person's cultural, economic, and educational background as well as her or his social status (Suoranta 2003:4)

The potential for anyone to be an author and publisher means that teachers and pupils can do just that. Pupils and teachers can make short films and with a few clicks of a mouse upload these to video sharing websites such as YouTube and potentially have an audience of millions. They can also share these videos with their social networks, via sites such as Facebook, or even using much older technologies such as email. The same can be said of audio recordings or podcasts and writings in the form of blogs, or collaborative work through wikis. Putting such powerful publishing tools in the hands of pupils can be empowering and can allow schools to help pupils publish personal, local and relevant content. This can also allow schools and pupils to publish in their own languages and thus move away from the ever-present domination of English-language content. This ease of publishing means that there are also potential risks and care needs to be taken around the nature of content that pupils publish, including seeking to avoid teachers being harassed by the publication of covert films made by pupils in classrooms (Meikle 2006; Fitzsimmons 2007; Torney 2007).

Again, the issue of information literacy is critical but pupils who have written and published their own content will be better equipped to understand the need to carefully vet online sources. The potential to develop specific content for local situations rather than only using mainstream sources can help prevent a potentially one-sided voice that does not take into account the cultural heritage of the pupils involved.

ICT as an Access Medium

ICT can be used to give curriculum access to pupils that would otherwise be marginalized by special needs. This is an important area that cannot be explored fully here but from an equality aspect it is worth considering that appropriate interventions can be very powerful. Furthermore, failing to make appropriate provision could be both damaging and discriminatory. A vast array of hardware devices is now available to support pupils with multiple special needs. From high-contrast and big-key keyboards for those pupil with visual impairments to alternative access devices such as foot pedals and switches for those with other barriers to conventional access. (ICT Test Bed 2005; http://www.keytools.co.uk/, http://www.donjohnston.com/)

Excellent software is already available to support pupils with specific SEN, from talking word processors and screen readers to screen magnifiers, switch accessible word banks and so on. There are also a host of modifications that can be made to a conventional Windows or Apple Mac set up that will assist those with particular SEN. One potential problem in many schools is that systems are blocked and therefore the pupil (and often the teacher) can make no changes to settings without administrator rights which they may not have, thus missing valuable support opportunities.

ICT also has an important role in terms of online translation services, (such as http://www.google.com/translate or http://uk.babelfish.yahoo.com/) These services can prove useful to schools working with new-arrival pupils in translating materials for their use and for their parents or carers. The role of multilingual word processors in providing materials in home language is also significant. Both of these areas need careful consideration though; online translation systems can provide a transliterated return, with an anglicized version of the original, and multilingual word processors are expensive.

Conclusion

ICT plays a major role in many pupils' lives today and it has the potential to allow them to complete their work in different ways, to provide other ways for teachers to teach and pupils to learn. Access to quality teaching of ICT skills is a curriculum entitlement of pupils, vital for making effective and efficient use of technology in an ICT-rich world. It is also not available to all pupils and this disparity of access leaves some pupils potentially marginalized. Teachers need to embrace technology when it is the appropriate resource for their pupils and must avoid a 'neo-Luddite' stance just because it is new. Web 2.0 provides excellent opportunities for pupils and teachers to develop and publish their own content but this opportunity also brings with it risks and responsibilities, from information literacy to online safety. The range of material on the internet also presents a number of risks and consequently internet safety should be clearly considered by all teachers, but any solution should have education at its core, developing skills in pupils to analyse risks and to make carefully informed decisions in a safe and supportive environment.

We need to:

- ensure schools are equipped with adequate numbers of high spec computers;
- ensure schools have high speed connectivity to the internet;
- where appropriate, use the technology to enhance teaching and learning, when inappropriate, use something else;
- ensure software is appropriate for the pupils and the tasks being set;
- ensure hardware is well maintained and appropriate modifications are in place for those pupils who need them;
- educate pupils to use resources appropriately rather than block access;
- take steps to provide additional access for those pupils who do not have access outside school;
- within the context of differentiated activities, allocate computer time to finish tasks not on strict time allocation;
- take steps to support and provide for anytime, anywhere learning while protecting teachers from excessive workloads;
- provide ICT opportunities and learning space for all pupils (irrespective of gender, cultural background, race, home language) that are interesting, engaging, relevant and challenging;
- value ICT sources from digital natives as much as more conventional sources that may be favoured by 'digital immigrants';
- above all, enjoy the diversity and enjoyment that ICT can bring to the classroom.

Notes

¹ These are four of the most commonly-found programmable floor robots used in UK primary schools. They are controlled by pupils using simple button presses to build up LOGO procedures, enabling the robot to move around the floor. LOGO supports constructivist teaching approaches and was invented by Seymour Papert in the 1960s. Further exploration can be found in his ground-breaking book *Mindstorms* (Papert 1980).

² The acronym PDA has effectively become the name of 'Personal Digital assistants,' small, hand-held computers or 'palmtops' that usually include diary software and, increasingly, are integrated with mobile phones, such as Blackberry.

³ Wikipedia references are used here unapologetically. The online encyclopaedia is controversial because 'anyone can edit it.' This leads people to claim that it is totally unreliable. This somewhat misses the point of the collective power of the net as the intention is that any mistakes will quickly be rectified by the community of users. It is true that mistakes happen, and these are widely documented, but Wikipedia is truly egalitarian in its approach and often is a useful source, particularly in fast-moving areas such as technology. It is widely used by large organizations, including the BBC, and is an example of a technology that is often misunderstood. Writers, readers and pupils should be aware of the reasons why Wikipedia, like all online sources, could be unreliable and make an informed decision about whether to accept the validity of the materials presented. This critical evaluation should be a part of ICT teaching and learning.

⁴ Office for Standards in Education (OfSted) is the Government's inspection regime

⁵ The *Daily Mail* is a tabloid newspaper in the UK popular with the 'middle classes.' Famously supportive of Oswald Mosely and the British Union of Fascists (aka Blackshirts) in the 1930s it still takes a hard right stance today. Immigration and 'liberal policies' are popular topics for abuse, and teachers are often lambasted for 'being soft' or for political correctness.

Useful Websites

www.Bebo.com – Social networking site, apparently popular with younger users.
http://www.cc4g.net – Computer Clubs for Girls.
www.clubpenguin.com/ – Online game aimed at very young pupils.
http://www.donjohnston.com/ – SEN materials.
www.Facebook.com – Popular social networking site – fastest growing in UK currently.
http://www.keytools.co.uk/ – SEN materials.
http://www.kidsmart.org.uk – Online safety.
http://www.martinlutherking.org – Racist site allegedly providing information about Martin Luther King, contains highly offensive materials.
www.MySpace.com – Social networking site, popular with music fans.
http://www.nc.uk.net – National Curriculum online.
http://www.standards.dfes.gov.uk/schemes – QCA schemes of work.
www.stormfont.org – Publishers of Martin Luther King site above. Warning, contains highly offensive materials.
http://www.thinkuknow.co.uk/default.aspx – Online safety
www.youtube.com – Popular video sharing website

References

Aune, S. (2008) *Kids use facebook to organize protest against South African law.* Online at: http://mashable.com/2008/01/06/kids-use-facebook-to-organize-protest-against-south-african-law/ (Accessed 12 February 2008).

BBC (2008) *Half of pupils have own computer.* Online at: http://news.bbc.co.uk/1/hi/education/7174885.stm (Accessed 31 January 2008).

BBC (2007) *Bank's U-turn on student charges.* Online at: http://news.bbc.co.uk/1/hi/education/6970570.stm (Accessed 31 January 2008).

Becta (2002) *Primary Schools – ICT and standards.* Coventry: Becta.

Becta (2006a) *The Becta Review 2006. Evidence on the progress of ICT in education.* Coventry: Becta.

Castells, M. (2001) *The internet galaxy. Reflections on the internet, business and society.* Oxford: OUP.

DCSF (Department for Children, Schools and Families). Online at: http://www.teachernet.gov.uk/teachingandlearning/subjects/ict/ (Accessed 31 January 2008).

DCSF (Department for Children, Schools and Families) *Parents Centre.* Online at: http://www.parentscentre.gov.uk/educationandlearning/whatchildrenlearn/learningathomeoutsideschool/theelearningfoundation/ (Accessed 4 December 2007).

Fitzsimmons, C. (2007) PCC *Makes first video ruling.* Online at: http://www.guardian.co.uk/media/2007/aug/15/digitalmedia.pupilbehaviour (Accessed 31 January 2008).

Grundy, F (1996) *Women and Computers.* Bristol: Intellect Books

Holdness, M (1994) *Want pay? Play!* Online at: http://www.poptel.org.uk/nuj/mike/articles/gdn-edu1.htm (Accessed 12 February 2008).

ICT Test Bed (2005) *Several case studies.* Online at: http://www.evaluation.icttestbed.org.uk/learning/research/primary/interest/sen (Accessed 12 February 2008).

Johnson, S. (2005) *Everything bad is good for you: why popular culture is making us smarter.* London: Penguin.

Jukes, I and Dosaj, A. (2003) *The differences between digital native learners and digital immigrant teachers.* Online at: http://www.esc-cc.org/_upload//documents/professional_development/Digital%20Natives%20and%20Immigrant%20Teachers.pdf.

Kellner, D. (1998). 'Multiple Literacies and Critical Pedagogy in a Multicultural Society'. *Educational Theory,* 48 (1), 102–122.

Kominski, R and Newburger, E. (1999) *Access Denied: Changes in Computer Ownership and Use: 1984–1997.* Online at: http://www.census.gov/population/socdemo/computer/confpap99.pdf (Accessed 25 January 2008).

Lacon-Childe (2007) Online at: http://lacon.ethink.org.uk/2007/06/18/improving-lacon-childe-gender-equality/

Marsh, J. Brooks, G. Hughes, J. Ritchie, L. Roberts, S. Wright, K. (2005) *Digital Beginnings: Young children's use of popular culture, media and new technologies.* Online at: http://www.literacytrust.org.uk/Research/popularreviews.html#Marsh2005what's (Accessed 13 May 2008).

Meikle, J. (2006) *Teachers want ban on cyber-bully pupils.* Online at: http://education.guardian.co.uk/pupilbehaviour/story/0,,1946299,00.html) (Accessed 31 January 2008).

Naughton, J. (1999) *A brief history of the future: the origins of the internet.* London: Phoenix.

November 2008, Online at: http://novemberlearning.com/index.php?option=com_content&task=category&sectionid=5&id=27&Itemid=93. (Accessed 19 December 2008).

O'Reilly, T. (2005) *What Is Web 2.0.* Online at: http://www.oreillynet.com/pub/a/oreilly/tim/news/2005/09/30/what-is-web-20.html (Accessed 12 February 2008).

Papert, S. (1980) *Mindstorms: Children, Computers, and Powerful Ideas.* New York: Basic Books.

Potter, F. and Darbyshire, C. (2005) *Understanding and teaching the ICT National Curriculum.* London: David Fulton Publishers.

Prensky, M (2001) *Digital Natives, Digital Immigrants.* Online at: (http://www.marcprensky.com/writing/Prensky%20-%20Digital%20Natives,%20Digital%20Immigrants%20-%20Part1.pdf) (Accessed 12 February 2008).

Reynolds, D., Treharne, D. and Trip, H. (2003) 'ICT – the hopes and the reality'. *British Journal of Educational Technology.* 34,(2), 151–167.

Smith, F, Hardman, F and Higgins S (2007), 'Gender inequality in the primary classroom: will interactive whiteboards help?' *Gender and Education.* 19, (4), 455–469.

Suoranta, J. (2003) 'The world divided in two: digital divide, information and communication technologies, and the "youth question"' *Journal for Critical Education Policy Studies*.1, (2). Online at: http://www.jceps.com/index.php?pageID = article& articleID = 16 (Accessed 31 January 2008)

Teyfant Community School (2007) Online at: http://teyfanty1.ethink.org.uk (Accessed 12 February 2008).

The Stevenson Committee (1997) *Information and Communication Technology in UK Schools, An Independent Enquiry.* Online at: http://rubble.heppell.net/stevenson/default.html (Accessed 31 January 2008).

Torney, K.(2007), Mobile phone ban urged as teacher humiliated on 'net. Online at: http://www.belfasttelegraph.co.uk/news/local-national/mobile-phone-ban-urged-as-teacher-humiliated-on-net-13422801.html (Accessed 31 January 2008).

Waller, T. (2007) 'ICT and social justice: educational technology, global capital and digital divides'. *Journal for Critical Education Policy Studies.* 5, (1). Online at: htp://www.jceps.com/index.php?pageID = article&articleID = 92 (Accessed 3 September 2007).

Chapter 10

History

Rosie Turner-Bisset with Emily Beadle

Introduction

This chapter presents a view of promoting equality in the teaching of history which is grounded in a deep understanding of the nature of history. To know that history is an enquiry-based discipline, dealing with the interpretation of evidence and the imaginative reconstruction of the past, is to transform history from a parade of facts and concepts into a powerful vehicle for promoting equality. The enquiry-based nature of history generates a pedagogy which encourages children to question, to examine and interpret evidence, and to detect bias and manipulation. At the same time, the exercise of the historical imagination helps children to put themselves into other peoples' shoes in the past and the present. The chapter argues for strong links between the skills, aptitudes and values of citizenship, and the skills and processes of history. Indeed, many links can be made with citizenship and also Personal, Social and Health Education (PSHE) – both of which have a firm place within the curriculum of schools. An excellent example of this link is a book titled 'Journey to Jo'burg' by Beverly Naidoo which deals with the apartheid history in South Africa, together with the challenges and choices that everyone faces in their lives. Selection of topics focusing on 'history from below' can help children to question inequalities in society. History is an excellent vehicle with which to deal with racism, as it is a subject that children enjoy and are fully engaged in. They are inspired when investigating, learning and discovering about the past.

The 'stuff' of history concerns people, societies and cultures in the past. It is thus a superbly appropriate vehicle for promoting equality in primary and elementary schools. Furthermore, the nature of history as an enquiry-based discipline makes it wholly suitable for pedagogies which promote equality. If it is well-taught, children can confront evidence about the past themselves and form their own interpretations.

This chapter tackles the question: 'What is good practice in promoting equality in history teaching in primary and elementary schools?' In order to address this question, several issues and aspects need to be discussed. These comprise: the nature of history; the National Curriculum for history; equality issues; citizenship education and controversial issues; and recent developments such as 'Every Child Matters'. The final section offers some examples of how history can be used to promote equality, while preserving academic rigour. By way of introduction, here are two vignettes of teaching the Victorians to Year 6 classes, where children are 10 or 11 years old.

Class A

This teacher followed the Standards site scheme of work for the Victorians (maintained by the Department of Children, Schools and Families), the third in a medium-term plan of six lessons. She showed the children pictures of school life at the end of the nineteenth century and talked to them about how school appears different from today, e.g. uniforms, architecture and interiors of classrooms. Referring to the time line, she talked briefly about the 1870 Education Act, and how schooling was not free until 1891. She had sources on display to illustrate aspects of school life at this time, e.g. extracts from stories, school logbooks, inspection reports. She asked the children to write a conversation between two children, one established in school and the other a new arrival who had been working in a factory, mill or mine for years. Despite this, in part, being based on last week's lesson on working children, the children struggle to write their conversations. Most of the lesson she circulates, suggesting sentences the children might say. She selected two children from the most able group to present their work to the class. She finally tried to lead a discussion on the differences in the views of school and work and why the children in the nineteenth century would have interpreted school life differently. However, the children did not have enough evidence to contribute and teacher talk dominated the 'discussion'. Within this lesson the children also failed to achieve in terms of the lessons objectives due to the lack of modelling provided by the teacher – something that is vital in all subjects.

Class B

This teacher devised a plan adapted from the schemes of work, substituting other topics in order to promote equality and give a richer picture of society. . She also wished to practise literacy within a meaningful context. She presented three carefully-selected sources on maidservants in Victorian times. The first, an extract from 'Lark Rise to Candleford' is about a twelve-year-olds' interview for her first job as a maid. She employed the pedagogical approaches of story-telling and drama, using freeze-framing parts of the story, before showing them the extract and reading it together. The children worked with the text, highlighting all the references to time, and to the different tasks the maid would have to accomplish between 6 a.m. and 10 p.m. The teacher introduced the next text by asking them if they were going to run a home and cook for a family, what book would they use to help them? The children settled on Delia Smith (referring to a famous television personality and chef and one of her many published cookery books). The teacher showed them the extract from Cassell's *Book of Household Management* and told them it was a kind of instruction book for women who were going to run households with servants. This extract gave a detailed account of a maid's day, again from 6 a.m. to 10 p.m. The same highlighting exercise was carried out. The third piece of evidence was a song: 'The Serving-Maid's Holiday.' The class sang the song through twice and carried out the same highlighting exercise. The teacher gave the children a grid with three columns, one for each piece of evidence: from the book of memoirs written by an eye-witness; from the book of household management published in 1880, and the song, from a slightly earlier period. The teacher checked that the children understood 'chronological order' and they wrote down the jobs they had highlighted in order from each piece of evidence. This was in answer to the question: what was it like to be a maid? The final task was for the children to write 'A day in the life of a Victorian serving maid.' All the children were able to engage with the task, regardless of ability in writing. I asked the question: why do some people have to work so hard for others on very low wages, while their employers lead lives of relative luxury. The children offered ideas about rich and poor people, and how people come to be rich or poor.

The first of these vignettes is an example of weak practice in teaching history in general and in promoting equality in particular. It is dull and teacher-dominated. The instructions in the scheme of work suggest that the teacher leads discussions at various points in the lesson, but it is not clear how, without investigating and interpreting the evidence, the children would be able to contribute to a discussion, other than to answer low-level questions. The evidence is in the classroom, but at no point are the children able to access it directly, apart from the pictures. However, the reasons for its weakness go deeper than the surface issues, and it is those underlying reasons which we explore in this chapter. The second vignette was actually taught by myself and published in a literacy journal (Turner-Bisset 2001). It is an example of good practice, and the reasons for this will be explained in subsequent sections of this chapter.

The Nature of History

When the National Curriculum came into being in the period 1988 to 1991, the two most debated subjects were English and history. The case of English is another story, which I am not concerned with here, but history has always been contested as a discipline, subject to paradigm shifts over the centuries. History was initially a chronology of events: it was seen in the early days of Christianity as the working out of God's purpose in the world. This gradually transformed into the basis for moral action. At the coming of the Enlightenment, it was regarded more scientifically, with the investigation and interpretation of primary evidence at the heart of historical processes. At the same time there was a Romantic view of history: that we could learn lessons from events in the past and not repeat the earlier errors of humankind. The past is fascinating because it concerns people, and therefore of great interest to children. All human life is there. Cooper (2000) characterized it as an umbrella discipline, concerned with the social, economic, scientific, technological, cultural, artistic, musical, aesthetic and religious aspects of past societies. History has been characterized as both an art and a science; sometimes as a mixture of both (Evans 2000). Traces of different paradigms of history can be found in the quotations about history in the National Curriculum documents, with the romantic view of history dominant, exemplified by Tony Robinson (a presenter of a popular history television programme) who cherry picks the romantic 'fun' elements of history.

It is of vital importance that teachers understand the nature of history. Sometimes teachers only 'learn' or research a selection of history 'bits', that then become fragmented in their teaching, and consequently, they are unable to provide children with a more rounded, fuller picture. Sadly, many of the student-teachers I have taught enter teaching with only a partial understanding. For several years, I asked at the beginning of a history module for students to write down a sentence or two on what they thought history was. Out of each group of 30 students, it was rare to have more than two students who mentioned evidence, enquiry and interpretation in their sentences. In order to teach history well, one needs three things: a deep understanding of the nature of history; a broad pedagogical repertoire; and a passion for the subject.

In my work with student-teachers, I draw upon the work of several scholars and historians to illuminate the nature of history. I start with my own definition given to students after they have investigated the contents of a bag 'left on the train' in order to find out information about the bag's owner:

> History is the imaginative reconstruction of the past using what evidence we can find from. We can state what we definitely know from the evidence. We can hypothesize about things we are unsure of, and we can use other knowledge and experience to inform our interpretation. (Turner-Bisset 2000b:171)

This definition was informed by several sets of ideas. Schwab (1978) argued that all disciplines have substantive and syntactic structures of knowledge. The substantive structures comprise two aspects.

1. First, there are the facts and concepts which go to make up the discipline: in history, for example, a fact that Henry VIII had six wives. There are overarching concepts such as time, evidence, cause, effect, continuity and change. Then there are lesser concepts such as the feudal system, the Black Death, rationing and the Blitz. Then there are concepts such as the Church (which is a body of people as much as it is that building on the corner of the road), power, authority, rights, monarchy, democracy, despotism and tyranny. These are the substance of the discipline.
2. Second, there are the frameworks or paradigms which we use to organize the facts and concepts in our minds. We do not just have a jumble of disconnected facts in our head. Just as, in science, the kinetic theory is used to explain a whole range of ideas about energy, force and power, in history, the Whig interpretation presents a view of history in which Britain progressed steadily to a better state. There are also paradigms such as Marxist and feminist interpretations of history, and frameworks such as history as a science or art. Unlike science where, from time to time, there are major paradigm shifts, such as the change from a Newtonian view of physics to Einstein's theory of relativity, in history, there tend to be several competing paradigms existing at the same time. This, in part, explains some of the contested nature of history. In addition, there are the syntactic structures, which are the processes by

which facts and concepts become established. In history, these are the processes of enquiry and interpretation of primary evidence, of questioning, which drives historical enquiry; and of using prior knowledge and experience to inform our interpretation. These are of fundamental importance in the study of history: however, these processes are those of which most beginning teachers are unaware To ignore these in teaching history in primary and elementary schools is in Schwab's terms a corruption of the discipline. If these terms seen too difficult or theroetical for the primary school, look back to the examples of teaching at the start of this chapter.

To teach history without questioning, enquiry and interpretation is corrupting the discipline and doing children a major disservice. Unfortunately, much history teaching in primary school omits the syntactic processes: furthermore it deprives teachers and children of opportunities for promoting equality.

The ideas of Collingwood (1946) are useful as a way of describing these syntactic processes. He likened history to detective work. Both the historian and the detective are carrying out enquiries ('a man is helping with our enquiries'). The historian might puzzle over how Tutenkhamun died, or who killed the Princes in the Tower: posing a question for enquiry is how a history topic should be approached – it provides the children with a clear focus and something which is quantifiable at the end of the topic. The nature of the evidence is different, but the processes of enquiry are similar. Hexter (1972) wrote about historical evidence and suggested some very powerful ways of understanding evidence and interpretation. He stated that history had two records. The first record was the primary evidence from the past, often incomplete or fragmentary. Primary evidence comes in many forms: artefacts, documents of all kinds, buildings, landscapes, pictures, photographs and sculpture, art, transport systems, music, song and dance. The second record is our own experience, knowledge and understanding, which informs our interpretation of the first record. We all have our own unique second record: the interpretation of evidence relating to the suffragettes might be different depending on our gender and experience of life. Children have limited second records and it is our job in history teaching to extend their second records through activities and sharing our second records with them. Nonetheless, even very young children can have experienced racial discrimination, family break-up, divorce, death, famine and war.

In addition, Hexter showed that history is a process. Fines and Nichol (1997) take from him the idea of 'doing history' and summarized the process thus:

- First, we must be examining a topic from the past and raising questions about it.
- Second, we must search for a wide range of evidence to help us answer our question.
- Third, we must struggle to understand what the sources are saying (and each source-type has a different language) so that we can understand them in our own terms.
- Fourth, we must reason out and argue our answers to the questions, and support them with well-chosen evidence.

- Finally, we must communicate our answers for the process to be complete.
(Fines and Nichol 1997:1)

Trevelyan stressed the link between hypothesizing and imagining. He stated that history is a combination of three aspects: the scientific aspect in enquiry and interpretation of evidence; the imaginative or speculative aspect in the exercise of the historical imagination; and the literary aspect in the presentation of history, or histories to others (Trevelyan 1913).

I have gone into some depth on the nature of history for these reasons: I wish to stress that the history we teach must be true to the nature of history; we must not teach it as a corruption of the discipline, or as a parade of facts and dates. A deep understanding of history is necessary to understand the National Curriculum document and interpret it for teaching. Finally, it will help us with the selection of subject content and processes to teach in promoting equality. Attention to the processes as well as the content of history will give children much broader opportunities for equality through the pedagogy employed, as well as through the topic.

The National Curriculum in History

This document, introduced in 1991, has been through two revisions. The first version had three attainment targets: Knowledge and Understanding of History; Interpretations of History; and Use of Resources. It was vastly overloaded: for example, at Key Stage 2, pupils were expected to study Romans, Anglo-Saxons and Vikings in Britain, a thousand years of history in about six weeks. The 1995 version saw a considerable slimming down of the history curriculum. The three attainment targets became one: history. The Key Elements which make explicit the syntactic processes of history were usefully set out separately in a box.

---

1. Chronological understanding
2. Knowledge and understanding of events, people and changes in the past
3. Historical interpretation
4. Historical enquiry
5. Organization and communication

FIGURE 1   The Key Elements

In the most recent document from 2000, these five elements are subsumed into the body of the document, which makes it all too easy for them to be ignored. The second and current versions of the history curriculum have been criticized for being too Anglo-centric. Most of the areas of study focus on British history. One unit on a past European society is the Ancient Greeks. Several possible areas of study are suggested for the world study unit on a past non-European society:

the ancient Egyptians, the Aztecs, the Indus Valley, the Benin, and the Maya. In practice, it is nearly always the first two of these which are tackled in primary schools.

There are two additional factors which exacerbate the problems in teaching primary history. The first is the lack of time for teaching history. Typically it is allocated about 4 per cent of curriculum time, although it is also true to say that some schools are now beginning to readdress this imbalance with more flexible timetables and connected curriculums. The lion's share of teaching time goes to literacy and numeracy. Thus, much has to be accomplished in a limited time, particularly if a focus in equality issues is to be achieved as well. The second problem is the ubiquitous use of the Department for Children, Schools and Families (DCFS) schemes of work for history. Because these schemes exist, hard-pressed teachers use them, often without consulting the curriculum documents. The net result is that, all over England in Year 2, you will find the same topics being taught to six- and seven-year-olds: Unit 3 – What were seaside holidays like in the past? Unit 4 – Why do we remember Florence Nightingale? Unit 5 – How do we know about the Great Fire of London? The schemes of work almost represent an alternative National Curriculum. The narrow selection of topics on these 'officially approved' schemes of work does not lend itself to promoting equality through subject content. For the lives of significant men, women and children drawn from the history of Britain and the wider world (for example, artists, engineers, explorers, inventors, pioneers, rulers, saints, scientists), which is one of the requirements for breadth of study at Key Stage 1, teachers could substitute Mary Seacole or Rosa Parkes (see endnotes for curriculum material), which would open up more opportunities for dealing with equality issues of race and class, as well as gender.

Equality, Citizenship and Controversial Issues

There are many ways in which adults and children can be unequal. All of them can be dealt with through history. The key aspects are social class, gender, sexuality, ethnicity, language, culture, disability, and environmental issues. That England is a deeply class-divided society is as true in the twenty-first century as it was in Victorian times. Despite our island heritage of absorbing new races, cultures and languages from the Romans, Anglo-Saxons and Vikings, through the Huguenots in the sixteenth century, successive waves of Jewish people from all over Europe fleeing pogroms and the more recent immigration of ethnic groups from south and eastern Europe, Asia, Africa and the Caribbean, our society still fractures along racial lines, as well as those of class. While we have new legislation, women are still paid less than men for similar work, their emotional labour in raising families is unrecognized financially or socially. New disability laws have been passed to improve the lives of disabled people; yet those with disabilities are not always seen as equal. A social reformist view of education sees education as the means by which society can be reformed. Education is not provided simply to maintain the status quo ('the rich man in his castle; the poor man at his gate'), but to promote equality and reform the worst of society's ills. McLaren (2000) extends the 'critical education' project into 'revolutionary pedagogy':

which is clearly based on a Marxist metanarrative. Revolutionary pedagogy would place the liberation from race, class and gender oppression as the key goal for education for the new millennium. Education ... so conceived would be dedicated to creating a citizenry dedicated to social justice and to the reinvention of social life based on democratic socialist ideals. (McLaren 2000:196) (See also, Hill 2009, in this volume).

This is in contrast to a utilitarian view of education as a way of preparing children for the world of work, which tends to be the dominant paradigm for the government. Nonetheless, there have been recent developments such as 'Every Child Matters' (DfES 2004) in which a focus on well-being aims to improve educational achievement and life chances:

> Pupil performance and well-being go hand in hand. Pupils can't learn if they don't feel safe or if health problems are allowed to create barriers. And doing well in education is the most effective route for young people out of poverty and disaffection. Every Child Matters: Change for Children will strongly support the principle of personalization and the work schools are already doing to raise educational standards by:
> - encouraging schools to offer a range of extended services that help pupils engage and achieve, and building stronger relationships with parents and the wider community; and
> - supporting closer working between universal services like schools and specialist services so that children with additional needs can be identified earlier and supported effectively.
>
> (DfES 2004:3)

This would appear to be a bridge between utilitarian and social reformist agendas, acknowledging the role education plays in lifting children out of poverty; yet there is little consideration of how the current nature of education, particularly in the core subjects and testing regime, can truly empower young people. I would argue that the substantive and syntactic knowledge bases of history taught through pedagogy for equality, can contribute significantly to empowerment and social reform. It means examining the citizenship curriculum to explore the links between history and citizenship, and it means not being afraid to tackle controversial issues.

In the Crick Report (DfEE/QCA 1998) there is a useful table which lists concepts, skills, aptitudes, values, dispositions and knowledge for children to learn through citizenship education. There is insufficient room to reproduce the table here, but I have selected below those which map on to the skills of history:

Skills and Aptitudes
- ability to make a reasoned argument both verbally and in writing
- ability to co-operate and work effectively with others
- ability to consider and appreciate the experience and perspective of others
- ability to tolerate other viewpoints
- ability to develop a problem solving approach
- ability to use modern media and technology critically to gather information

- a critical approach to evidence put before one and ability to look for fresh evidence
- ability to recognize forms of manipulation and persuasion
- ability to identify, respond to and influence social, moral and political challenges and situations.

(DfEE/QCA 1998:44)

Some of these, such as the critical approach to evidence and the ability to make reasoned argument are the very stuff of history. Through the imaginative reconstruction of the past, children can develop the ability to consider and appreciate the experience and perspective of others and to tolerate other viewpoints. The pedagogy of teaching through problem solving is integral to the process of doing history. The whole report is valuable reading for anyone wishing to promote equality through teaching history. Although there is not room to include all of them here, there are common concepts such as democracy and autocracy; if we could encourage children to develop all of the values and dispositions, such as for example, 'a willingness to be open to changing one's opinions and attitudes in the light of discussion and evidence' (DfEE/QCA 1998:44), we might really be able to change society. This willingness can be achieved through addressing controversial issues with children as young as six and seven years old, as Claire has demonstrated (Claire 2002). She described curriculum development work on famous men and women at Key Stage 1, using three people from the past whose personal actions contributed to changing discriminatory institutional structures and attitudes. These were Bessie Coleman, the first black woman aviator, Ruby Bridges, the six-year-old child who was part of integrating white schools in the Southern States in 1960, and Frederick Douglass, the slave who taught himself to read and became an important member of the abolition movement in the States in the mid-nineteenth century. The children surprised their teachers by their maturity and understanding of the issues. The teachers reported that the white children really took on the issues of justice and would remember it for a long time. The lesson for teachers here is not to underestimate what children can tackle.

How History can be used to Promote Equality

In this section, I give ideas for promoting equality through the teaching of history across the areas of study at Key Stages 1 and 2. Intrinsic to these examples is the notion of a broad pedagogical repertoire which uses both enquiry and interpretation and the exercise of the historical imagination. The wide pedagogical repertoire is essential for both good teaching and for purposes of social inclusion. History, all too often, can be a very text-based subject which can discriminate against those for whom literacy is difficult. By employing a wide range of teaching approaches, teachers create the opportunities for all children in their classes to access evidence and to learn. For example, storytelling, drama and role-play can open up pieces of primary evidence to those children with reading difficulties, and indeed these are good teaching approaches that are not just confined to history teaching but should be used in all subjects. There is no room here for a full discussion on children's learning in history, but I find the ideas of Bruner (1970) very powerful in understanding learning and teaching, and useful in evaluating teaching approaches. He stated that there are three characteristic ways of mental representation of the world: enactive representation involves understanding by doing; iconic representation is understanding through pictures, diagrams, drawings, maps and plans; symbolic representation is understanding through symbol systems such as mathematical symbols, spoken and written language, and musical notation. Young children tend to use enactive representation first (this can be seen vividly in children's imaginative play); then iconic representation, and finally symbolic representation. As adults, we move back and forth between each mode of representation. Thus, to take the lesson on Victorian maids at the beginning of this chapter, there were all three forms of representation. I have argued elsewhere (Turner-Bisset 2005) that storytelling functions simultaneously as all three forms of representation, through the lived dramatic experience of the story, through the creation of images in the minds of the storyteller and the listeners, and through the symbolic medium of spoken language. I added drama in the form of freeze frames to highlight certain points in the story of the maid asking for her first job. I used symbolic representation in the textual work on the three kinds of written evidence. I used singing as a way to tackle the last piece of evidence: music engages the emotions and helps us to experience the emotions of others. Thus the 10 and 11-year-olds were able to empathize with the maid in the song: an important aptitude for citizenship and equality education. At the same time we were 'doing history' in the way that Fines and Nichol, quoted previously, suggested. Handling the evidence enabled these children to draw their own conclusions about what it was like to be a maid in Victorian times. The suggestions which follow are brief and only examples of what might be done. In these examples, I am indebted to the late Hilary Claire (1996) in her book *Reclaiming Our Pasts*, who first opened my eyes as to what could be done teaching 'history from below' from the point of view of the 'lower' classes, women, racial and ethnic minorities and others at the fringes of society.

Key Stage 1 suggestions

There are four areas suggested in the breadth of study section. Of these, one lends itself particularly to promoting equality:

> Area c): the lives of significant men, women and children drawn from the history of Britain and the wider world [for example, artists, engineers, explorers, inventors, pioneers, rulers, saints, scientists]

For lives of significant people, one could adapt the current scheme of work on Florence Nightingale to include Mary Seacole. One starting point might be to ask the question: 'Why do we remember Mary Seacole? (I have found that many cohorts of student-teachers have never heard of her). For preparation, read her autobiography, *The Wonderful Adventures of Mrs. Seacole in Many Lands*, published in 1857, and visit the many websites on her. It is one of the first autobiographies by a mixed-race woman. From the book, one can prepare story-telling and drama using a range of techniques, and extracts for use as evidence. A comparison with Florence Nightingale, who received official sanction and support from the British government, while Mary Seacole did not, can serve to raise issues of race and class.

Claire (1996) offers many more suggestions of famous people to study, as well as a wealth of ideas for equality at Key Stage 1.

Key Stage 2

Local History

In many towns and villages there is a building which once was a workhouse. I have used this as a starting point for enquiry into social welfare in the nineteenth century in comparison with today. For preparation a useful starting point is the website: http://www.workhouses.org.uk/. Another excellent resource is the National Trust workhouse 'The Workhouse' near Southwell in Nottinghamshire. There are many possible pedagogical approaches, but I have used a story and drama technique of a modern family thrown into hardship by loss of work and injury. The children were encouraged to ask questions about how they might live and how society provides for people in such circumstances. We took a walk to view and photograph the workhouse (now a row of several smart terraced houses). On return to the classroom, children, working in pairs, had to devise three questions about the workhouse. They were given a selection of sources of evidence: an extract from a memoire of a workhouse childhood; photographs of Ormskirk workhouse; the daily routine and rules of the workhouse; and other sources of evidence. With photographs and pictures the pedagogical approach of: 'find three things which suggest that life was hard' was used; with textual materials highlighting text activities, the children were enabled to access sources. Songs, stories and drama were used to bring the materials to life. The presentation of their findings at the end of the project was a drama based on a family going into the workhouse. This was followed by discussions on how society treats its poor and outcasts and whether improvements could be made. The use of DVD and video sources does need to be highlighted as these are important and useful in teaching history. Another supportive approach is to visit the places of historical importance as it brings history to life for the children. For example, the Gaols of Nottingham provide children with an insight into the inequalities of the legislative system.

Anglo-Saxons

For this, I had the children form an Anglo-Saxon village. We used a photograph of a reconstructed village to site and plan our own. Using chance cards, we enacted the farming year, with all the problems such as injury, sick animals, crops failure and petty theft of tools. At the Thegn's court, all these issues were dealt with in open debate in role. Children learned that Anglo-Saxons were heavily dependent on each other and that they had rights and responsibilities in establishing fair treatment for themselves and others.

The Ancient Greeks

Using some of the ideas and approaches above, we considered how to answer the question: Did the Greeks have a democracy? The children found that women and slaves were excluded from the institutions and processes of democracy. This is a rich source for teaching about inequalities and for promoting equality.

The ideas provided above are all linked to the QCA schemes of work, and so location of resources will be easy, as will the implementation of the planning. However, many of the ideas and suggestions provided are stepping stones to addressing the issues of equality and racism in history. In order to embrace, challenge and deal with controversial issues, teachers need to look further afield than the confines of the QCA schemes. An integrated approach for tackling controversial issues can be helpful. For example, PSHE, literacy and art can all promote discussion.

Useful websites

Facing History – www.facinghistory.com
By studying the historical development and the legacies of the Holocaust, and other instances of collective violence, children will learn to combat prejudice with compassion, indifference with ethical participation, myth and misinformation with knowledge. The site is invaluable for teaching not only about anti-semitism, but also other forms of racism, and about current and recent issues such as the Danish cartoons about Islam.

Football Unites – www.furd.org
Campaigns against racism in and around football grounds are a significant development in recent years. Much valuable information is available from the Football Unites Racism Divides project, set up by Sheffield United. This brings equality and racism to the children's interest and deals with some very controversial issues.

Anne Frank House – www.annefrank.org
There are several websites teaching about anti-semitism and racism through the inspiration of Anne Frank's diary. Links to most of them are available through the site of Anne Frank House, based in Amsterdam.

Anti-Slavery – www.antislavery.org
This website hosts information about the Cross Community Forum, set up to promote discussion and debate about, and provide resources for, the bicentenary in 2007 of the abolition of the Transatlantic Slave Trade.

Further online resources:
- Hertfordshire Grid for learning provides free downloadable materials for teaching about the abolition of the slave trade – www.thegrid.org.uk/learning/mecss/achievement/resources_ks1-2.shtml
- Hertfordshire Grid for learning also provides free downloadable materials for

teaching refugee and traveller children. Resources include literacy hour plans, and aim high material for the education of the travelling community – http://www.thegrid.org.uk/learning/mecss/centres/traveller/resources.shtml

- Five full colour Black History timeline posters are available online at www.guardian.co.uk/uk/blackhistorymonth
- Ten colourful, and free, Black History month posters are available online at www.instantdisplay.co.uk/blackhistorymonth.doc
- Mary Seacole resources at
  www.100greatblackbritons.com/bios/maryseacole.html
  www.spartacus.schoolnet.co.uk/REseacole.htm
  www.black-history.org.uk/seacole.asp
  www.qca.org.uk/respectforall
- The BritKid website examines race, racism and growing up in Britain and focuses on nine young British people from different backgrounds. Children are invited into their homes to share experiences www.britkid.org/m.html
- A website for talking with children about terrorism is http://www.extension.-purdue.edu/purplewagon/

Acknowledgement from the Editors

We are sad to report that Rosie Turner-Bisset died unexpectedly, at an untimely early age of 58, in January 2009. Her obituary in *The Guardian* is at http://www.guardian.co.uk/theguardian/2009/mar/02/rosie-turner-bisset-obituary. We also thank Emily Beadle for doing the final tidying up, answering queries, and final additions to this chapter.

References

Bruner, J. S. (1970) 'The course of cognitive growth', in B. L. Klinz and J. Brunig (eds) *Research in Psychology*. Glenview, IL: Scott, Foresman and Co.

Claire, H. (2002) 'Why didn't you fight, Ruby? Developing citizenship in KS1, through the History curriculum'. *Education 3–13*, 30, (2), 24–32.

Claire, H. (1996) *Reclaiming Our Pasts: Equality and Diversity in the Primary History Curriculum*. Stoke-on-Trent: Trentham Books.

Collingwood, R. G. (1946) *The Idea of History*. Oxford: Oxford University Press.

Cooper, H. (2000) *The teaching of history in primary schools: implementing the revised National Curriculum*. London: David Fulton.

DCFS (Department of Children, Schools and Families) (2009) 'Scheme of work for history'. Online at: http://www.standards.dfes.gov.uk/schemes2/history/?view=get

DfEE/QCA (1998) *The Crick Report: Education for citizenship and the teaching of democracy in schools*. Final report of the Advisory Group on Citizenship. London: QCA.

DfES (2004) *Every Child Matters: Change for Children in Schools*. Nottingham: DfES Publications.

Evans, R. J. (2000) *In defence of history*. London: Granta.

Fines, J. and Nichol, J. (1997) *Teaching Primary History*. Oxford: Heinemann.

Hexter, J. H. (1972) *The History Primer*. New York: Basic Books.

Hill, D. (2009). 'Theorizing Politics and the Curriculum: Understanding and Addressing

Inequalities through Critical Pedagogy and Critical Policy Analysis'. In D. Hill and L. Helavaara Robertson (eds) (2009) Equality in the Primary School: Promoting good practice across the curriculum. London: Continuum

McLaren, P. (2000) *Che Guevara, Paolo Freire and the Pedagogy of Revolution.* Lanham, ML and Oxford: Rowman and Littlefield.

Schwab, J. J. (1978) 'Education and the structures of the disciplines', in I. Westbury and N. J. Wilkof (eds) *Science, Curriculum and Liberal Education.* Chicago: University of Chicago Press.

Seacole, Mary [1857] (2005) *The Wonderful Adventures of Mrs Seacole in Many Lands,* Sara Salih (ed.). London: Penguin Classics.

Trevelyan, G. M. (1913) *Clio, a muse: and other essays literary and pedestrian.* London, New York: Longmans Green and Co.

Turner-Bisset, R. A (2000b) 'Meaningful history with young children', in R. Drury, R. Campbell and L. Miller (eds) *Looking at Early Years Childhood Education and Care.* London: David Fulton.

Turner-Bisset, R. A. (2001b) 'Serving maids and literacy: an approach to teaching literacy through history and music'. *Reading, literacy and language,* 35, 1.

Turner-Bisset, R. A. (2005) *Creative Teaching: History in the Primary Classroom.* London: David Fulton.

Chapter 11

Geography

Gianna Knowles

Introduction

Geography is about people and place. However, places can only be truly understood in their political and cultural context. There is already considerable support available to teachers, in terms of helping them to plan meaningful geographical activities that enable children to undertake fieldwork and enquiry activities, in order to develop geographical skills, knowledge and understanding. Therefore, what this chapter encourages teachers to engage with, before they begin any work on place – or a particular place, is to examine whose version of that place are they teaching. If we are interested in promoting equality, we need to be aware of the actual experiences of people as they live their lives in any given place, rather than the received notion of what that place is like. This applies as much to the locality the children in the class live in, as well as those who live in distant localities.

Geography in the Primary Curriculum

The geography element of the Framework for the Early Years and Foundation Stage curriculum, and the Key Stage 1 and 2 National Curriculum programme of study, are some of the least prescriptive statutory curriculum documents from which teachers are required to plan the curriculum, and yet geography is currently one of the most poorly served subjects in early years settings and primary schools (OfSTED 2005a, 2008). There is considerable scope in geography for lesson activities that allow all children to be interested and motivated by their learning and to enable enjoyment and achievement (DfES 2004). Children of all abilities and learning styles (Knowles 2006) can access geography: it is a highly experiential subject, where personal enquiry and investigation is central to the programme of study (kinaesthetic learning), as is the use of visual material (photographs, maps, etc.), which are excellent for visual learners. It links well with all other subjects in the curriculum, particularly history, RE and citizenship and it has enormous potential in terms of promoting equality. In the same way, for those to whom a critical pedagogical approach to teaching is central to their work (see Hill 2009, in this volume), the geography curriculum allows far greater freedom to devise learning activities that 'contribute to increased equal opportunities and to lead to more equal outcomes between different social groups' (Hill and Cole 2001), than is perhaps true of other National Curriculum subjects.

Geography, as a statutory part of the school curriculum, is as well served as most subjects by curriculum support, ideas and resources both from government websites and educational publishers, and so diverse are the ways in which geography can be taught and linked to other subjects, there simply is not the space here to review the support material available and make coherent suggestions about planning schemes of work for your school. However, there is a list of recommended reading and websites at the end of the chapter to help you with this. Having said what this chapter does not do, what it *does* do is explore a fundamental concept that underpins the notion of geography, and one that is central to promoting equality in the primary school, that is, the power relationships inherent in our experience of, and our received knowledge and understanding of, place. Therefore, this chapter is about challenging the reader to consider the possibly unwitting assumptions they may have about their perception of place and to review where their notions of place come from, before designing a learning activity that may pass on these assumptions and perpetuate inequalities.

'The central purpose of geographical education is to give children a fuller, more rounded, structured opportunity to view, perceive, understand and respond to the world in which they live' (Carter 1998:16), and one of the most compelling aspects of geography is that geography is not 'an inherently ordered discipline where it is possible to pigeonhole particular ways of 'doing' geography into easy categories' (Holloway and Hubbard 2001:xi). True to this principle, the National Curriculum programme of study allows considerable freedom to plan learning activities that allow children to explore the world, people and places in a range of ways, building on the similarly unrestricted approach suggested in the Framework for the Early Years Foundation Stage (DfES 2007).

As OfSTED state, the strength and excitement of geography as a subject is that it:

> ...stimulates an interest in and a sense of wonder about places. It helps young people make sense of a complex and dynamically changing world. It explains where places are, how places and landscapes are formed, how people and their environment interact, and how a diverse range of economies, societies and their environments are interconnected. It builds on pupils' own experiences to investigate places at all scales from the personal to the global. (OfSTED 2008:8)

Places and spaces (the terms are used interchangeably) are central to the lives and well-being of children and their families (DfES 2004). Places inform identity and impact, both positively and negatively, on how lives are lived. However, places are also political and cultural constructs and can be 'taught' in ways that can promote equality and understanding about the world, its wonders and diversity and how different groups of people live in response to the places they find themselves in, or it can be taught in such a way as to reinforce the partisan political and cultural agendas that mitigate against social justice and notions of equality. Therefore, as teachers, before we begin to teach about places, and the natural and human characteristics and features that make a place distinctive, we need to be aware of where our understanding and information about that place has come from.

Traditionally, there has been a notion that place should be treated as something entirely objective, that places in geography could be 'conceptualized as an objective physical surface with specific fixed characteristics upon which social identities and categories were mapped out' (Valentine 2001:3). However, more recently, it has come to be understood that not only do places have a physical dimension with fixed characteristics, but also to be considered is how human beings live in those places. Furthermore, geographers have begun to understand that there is an almost symbiotic relationship between the characteristics of places and how people experience their lives and develop their sense of self within those places. This applies not only to human responses to the naturally occurring characteristics of a place, but also their response to those features that have been created by human beings. As Holloway and Hubbard (2001) state, in understanding what places are:

> ....geographers have begun to take into account 'other' voices: those voices which have been overtly or covertly silenced in an academic world which has so often been dominated by middle-class, white able bodied heterosexual men. Thus the voices and geographical experiences of (for example) women and people from different ethnic backgrounds and social classes have increasingly been influential in the development of geographical thought. (Holloway and Hubbard 2001:xii)

Therefore, before we begin to plan what we might teach in any given geographical activity, we need to understand what perception we might, ourselves, be bringing to geography and the study of place. We need to understand the subject of geography in the context of the notion of social justice and whose concept of place we are teaching.

While geography is about the study of people and place, more precisely it is about the examination of the type of relationship that exists between people and places (Holloway and Hubbard 2001:15). However, the tradition has been to study places in a way that seems almost to be a study of place without the people (Holloway and Hubbard 2001:15): to concentrate on the place, rather than how the people who live there interact with that place. In geography, it is usual to think of 'distinct but hierarchically ordered levels' of place (Holloway and Hubbard 2001:15). That is, beginning with the local, moving to the regional, the trans-national and finally, the global. Indeed, the National Curriculum programme of study for geography mirrors these distinctions, asking that children begin to investigate at a local level, and as they move through primary school, apply the geographical skills, knowledge and understanding they have developed to investigate places at a greater distance to them. Yet, because of what they have learnt about how people interact in their own place, and why people live in that place in that way, they can draw informed conclusions about how others live, in places distant to them and that they have no direct experience of. In this way, the ideas children form about others' places are informed, rather than received ideas.

However, for most people, and children, their lives are 'focused on a relatively clustered and localized set of places' (Holloway and Hubbard 2001:27). That is to say, most lives are 'structured around a set of local movements with only occasional forays further afield' (Holloway and Hubbard 2001:27). This has a twofold repercussion for children in terms of their developing understanding of what places are about. First, unless children are engaged in meaningful geographical learning and enquiry, they can grow up believing that all places are like the ones they are used to operating in and second, if they grow up believing all places are like their places they may feel other places, once they do begin to travel beyond their localized set of places, are alien and possibly hostile, including the people that live in these alien new places. In this way, children can develop a fallacious concept, not only of other places, but also of the people that live in them.

The ideas we form about a given place will also be influenced by the mode of travel we use; walking, using public transport, cycling or using a car, all affecting how we perceive place and distance between places. For example, travelling by car is, essentially, about travelling through places. Cars isolate those in the vehicle from direct experience with a place; in the way cycling or walking does not. In this way we can become distanced from experiencing and understanding what places might mean to the people who have more direct contact with them. As Holloway and Hubbard state: 'different people may experience the same place in very different ways according to their knowledge of that place' (Holloway and Hubbard 2001:38). As teachers we must be aware that it is possible to challenge the notion that places are objective realities that are 'experienced and understood in a similar manner by all individuals' (Holloway and Hubbard 2001:38).

In this way, if we are concerned to promote equality through the way we teach geography, we must explore not only what we mean by place, but *whose definition* of those places we are using. Increasingly, the body of research and writing in the area of social justice shows that 'particular people have the power to construct and impose their definition of reality on others' (Trifonas 2003:207). Therefore, when we consider a place or places we need to be thinking about who has constructed and defined those places. Holloway and Hubbard (2001:116) discuss how 'we understand places through socially constructed mythologies'. These are those powerful 'stories' which shape our physical (bodily) and imaginative journeys into both familiar and unfamiliar places and spaces (*ibid.*). Places are 'inscribed' with 'cultural and social values' (Holloway and Hubbard 2001:178). Therefore, before we do any teaching about place, we need to consider whose culture and values are underpinning our teaching, since we need to be mindful that 'the moral and aesthetic values of a society are configured in such a way that they reinforce its economic and political structures' (Shurmer-Smith 2002:29). That is to say, most 'everyday' landscapes can be read as the products of attempts by dominant cultural groups to inscribe their values into the geographic landscape' (Holloway and Hubbard 2001:178).

That we must be 'aware that places can encapsulate certain cultural values in the service of power' (Holloway and Hubbard 2001:179), is supported by the writing of Shurmer-Smith (2002), who in exploring Gramsci's notion of 'cultural hegemony' (Shurmer-Smith 2002:32), denotes this controlling of places, their use, construction and function, as being: 'the situation in which people subscribe to knowledge systems which are actually to the advantage of people with superior power and wealth,[1] rather than striving for their own interests' (Shurmer-Smith 2002:32). Not only does the 'cultural preferences of affluent and educated people lead to the appropriation of spaces which were formerly occupied by poorer people, who are then marginalized' (Shurmer-Smith 2002:33), but also, in this way, 'Social order and discipline can be instilled in place' (Holloway and Hubbard 2001:184). Therefore, 'places are potentially implicated in the reproduction of social orders ... a wide variety of places are characterized by power relationships that are based on control and discipline' (Holloway and Hubbard 2001:187). This applies to all and any space – city centres, the countryside, schools, workplaces, doctors' surgeries, car parks, shopping malls and the home. Further to this, places and how they are used and constructed are 'not merely an arena in which social life unfolds but ... a medium through which social life is produced and reproduced' (Rose 1993:18). Places are not always the product of the society that lives there, but actually impact on the society itself, its attitudes, values and behaviours.

This last point is important since, if places are created by powerful others, the people who use those places will take on various identities, ideas and value assumptions as a result of how those places have been created. 'Through their everyday interactions with people and objects, individuals develop certain kinds of knowledge – conscious, subconscious and ideological – and their subsequent actions based on these kinds of knowledge reproduce a social structure' (Rose 1993:20). Consequently, if those more powerful than you constructed for you a place to live that is badly insulated – both from cold and other peoples' noise – far away from shops and a transport system, requiring you to carry heavy shopping/pushchairs up and down flights of stairs because the lift is not well maintained, you take on a very strong cultural identity and understanding of how you are valued in that society, particularly when those very same powerful people may themselves live in gated and walled private estates.

In this way, we can see how exploring places, how they are used, their characteristics, features, the geographical patterns and processes, both human and natural, associated with how they have evolved (KS1 and 2 programme of study DfEE/QCA 1999:108–115), is central to understanding issues to do with equality and social justice; theories that explore notions that 'the forms of violence and "microaggressions"' (Davis 1995) 'experienced by dominated and exploited groups in the context of everyday life are both normalized and officially sanctioned by dominant ideologies and institutional arrangements' (Trifonas 2003:11). In explaining their theory of oppression, Adams, Bell and Griffin (2007) emphasize 'the pervasive nature of social inequality woven throughout social institutions as well as embedded within individual consciousness' (Adams, Bell and Griffin 2007:3; Griffiths 1998:13). As a result 'certain values are incorporated into the mainstream ... others are pushed to the margins as a result of the unequal power relations evident in Western societies' (Holloway and

Hubbard 2001:178). Simply stated, not all places are for all people and the dominant cultural group, usually that which is most economically powerful, will distribute places to other groups and define how they can be used.

To fully comprehend these ideas, let us explore them more thoroughly with respect to specific groups in society, bearing in mind the children we teach will be members of these, often marginalized, groups. One of the most powerful dominant groups in British society is the retail industry, who, according to official data from the Office for National Statistics, expects that their retail sales for the first half of 2008 will show an income for 2008 of £246.1 billion (Sehmi 2008). Compare this to the projected spending by the country of £74 billion on education and skills by 2010 (BBCa 2008). In May of 2005, this powerful lobby displayed the power they have in influencing values and behaviour by the banning of perceived undesirable – or undeserving groups – from retail centres, in particular young people wearing hooded tops, or hoodies. It was reported that 'hooded tops, baseball caps and swearing have been outlawed at Bluewater shopping centre in Kent as part of a crackdown on anti-social behaviour.' (BBCa 2008). Bluewater, as a privately-owned place, has a set of standards outlining acceptable behaviours in the place that is Bluewater. Traditionally, laws are made by a democratically-elected parliament and monitored by servants of the people, usually the Police service. Bluewater, as a private estate has established its own laws and enforces them through the '400 CCTV cameras at Bluewater which [are] being constantly monitored' by its army of security guards (BBCa 2008). Ironically, as Barkham also notes, hoodies, as a currently fashionable article of clothing are worn by a whole cross section of society 'from middle-aged women to teenage boys', and, just to underline the ruthless greed and hypocrisy of the retail industry, at Bluewater itself there 'were hoodies: on sale in the windows of dozens of other shops' (Barkham 2008). Bluewater sought to justify their actions by claiming they were trying to reduce incidents of 'anti-social' behaviour. However, statistically, youth offending is falling: between 1992 and 2002 the evidence shows a 'drop of almost 26%. Government research has found the most mentioned antisocial behaviour is speeding – an adult problem.' (Barkham 2008). Thus we have the 'replacement of open and democratic spaces by closed "sanitized" spaces in which certain groups and individuals are seen to be "out of place"' (Holloway and Hubbard 2001:189).

Such control over spaces can also be seen in controlling places with respect to other societal groups, for example, how people experience place is also determined by their gender. Most 'people tend to have a fairly restricted activity space, and do not venture far from home as a result of their day-to-day activities' (Holloway and Hubbard 2001:27). And if your day is centred around where you live, looking after children, shopping, using local parks or going to a local school, you will have a different perception of that place than if you routinely travel away from where home is to another place to work. For those whose life is spent close to home, still mainly women and children, their experience of such places is one that 'increases the isolation of domestic life from economic production', since women and children, as a group, are isolated 'not just inside the home, but inside a community far removed from offices, factories and civic spaces' (Holloway and Hubbard 2001:189; Rose 1993). In this way, women continue, literally, to be put in their place, on isolated housing estates, whether estates of private or social housing, and excluded from the important male concern of making money.

Other groups whose access to place is similarly controlled by powerful others are those who are discriminated against on the grounds of ethnicity. As the black educationalist Vini Lander writes: 'there are forces operating which, if left unidentified, can lead to disadvantage of black and minority ethnic groups' (Knowles 2006:57). How powerful groups in society have oppressed, and continue to oppress people with regard to place and ethnicity is a study in itself. Here, there is space only to consider two examples: that is, travelling people and refugees and asylum seekers.

It is possible to cite countless examples of travelling people being excluded from places: in the Czech Republic, in October 1999, residents of a town in the north of the republic built a two-metre-high wall to separate off the place where Gypsies were, from the place that was the rest of the town (BBCb 2008). In Britain, in 2005, at the same time as it was reported that a 'West Yorkshire council has created five no-go areas for travellers' (BBCd 2008), the 'Gypsy coalition called for reform' in the policy of site provision for traveller peoples, in view of the 'national shortage of sites for travellers and their families'. It was also stated that 'there had been "an increase in cases of harassment" of travellers in recent months' (BBCe 2008). While traveller people are excluded from places, asylum seekers and refugees are, by contrast, incarcerated in designated places. Although 'the law states quite clearly that people should be detained only as a last resort', and it is routine for those seeking asylum or refugee status in Britain to be contained in designated detention centres, where it is alleged asylum seekers and refugees have been subject to 'physical assault', and 'other forms of abuse' (Doward 2004).

In considering those groups whose access to places is controlled by others, there has been an implicit assumption that all these groups could access all places, should the cultural and political constraints be removed. We have not explicitly considered those who may, because of physical and sensory disabilities, be prevented from accessing places, as these places are, quite simply, inaccessible to disabled persons. Recent legislation, for example, The Disability Discrimination Act (DDA) 1995, the remit of which has been 'significantly extended' (Directgov 2008) by the Disability Discrimination Act 2005, has made provision for the access to more places for disabled children and adults, for example, 'it allows the government to set minimum standards so that disabled people can use public transport easily' (Directgov 2008). With regard to accessing schools, as places, disabled children 'should have the same opportunities as non-disabled people in their access to education' (Knowles 2006:127). As part of this legislation, schools should make necessary adjustments to the physical aspects of the school, as a place, as well as making any necessary curriculum adjustments.

Gilbert (in Knowles) states: 'if we are to consider that fostering independence in their learning and everyday life is vital for pupils with a disability, then we need to listen to the opinions of the children we teach. We need to provide opportunities for them to tell us about their experiences' (Knowles 2006:137). Indeed, we need to provide opportunities for all groups of children to tell us about their experiences, and in geography, before we begin any study of any place, we need to listen to the voice of those who live there and we should, as

Griffiths (1998) states, 'reckon to have ... [our] mind nurtured only or mainly by the oppressed' (Griffiths 1998:110).

The issues discussed so far are important concepts for schools and teachers to understand, not only in terms of what needs to be considered when undertaking geographical enquiry, but also in terms of meeting the well-being of children, young people and their families, as stated by the Every Child Matters (ECM) agenda. (DfES 2004). For the ECM agenda to succeed there needs to be greater understanding, on the part of teachers and schools, of the nature of their relationship with children's homes and families; that is, the places where children are when they are not in the place that is school. It is important because there exists between teachers and schools and children and their families an imbalance of power, where, in terms of interpreting and providing a curriculum and cultural steer, the teachers and schools hold the power; traditionally the teachers and the school have determined what will be taught, how it will be taught and the ethos of the school.

For example, before beginning a locality study, it is necessary for you to first conduct your own field enquiry into that locality and talk to the children and families that live there. In this way it is no accident that fieldwork is a significant part of geographical study and, equally, an important part of the National Curriculum. We learn about place – and about others – through first-hand experience, undertaking systematic investigations into what is actually there, not what we think is the case.

In undertaking geographical enquiry, pupils should be taught to:

- observe and record
- express their own views about people, places and environments
- use fieldwork skills
- identify and describe what places are like.

(DfEE/QCA 1999:110)

Once children have gained the geographical enquiry skills, knowledge and understanding, outlined in the National Curriculum, through the first-hand study of their own locality, they are in a more informed position to undertake study of a distant locality. While a field trip to a distant locality is not often a reality for primary schools, there are still many ways that direct links can be made with faraway places (see the websites at the end of the chapter), and resources that reflect the lives and experiences of the people in those places found and used.

Listening to children and their families when undertaking geographical locality studies is important as, particularly for young children who may still be developing notions of the world as being objective to them (Holloway and Hubbard 2001:53), the approach to the enquiry may bear no resemblance to the locality they know and, at best, fail to motivate and interest them; or, at worst, the teacher and school may be making negative value judgements about a place which is the children's home. For example, I have seen geographical locality study work undertaken where children have been investigating the varieties of houses that people live in. The children were taught that 'houses' may be detached, semi-detached, terraced or bungalows, and some of them may have thatched roofs: this was undertaken in an urban area where a majority of the children lived in social housing flats. 'Knowledge is constructed by individual human beings according to their own subjective understanding of surroundings' (Holloway and Hubbard 2001:43). Therefore, for there to be success in teaching, and for the ECM agenda to be met, teachers and schools need to work with children and families to construct a curriculum that is meaningful to the children.

Not only does the ECM agenda expect schools to work in closer partnership with children and their families, but there is the expectation that children should enjoy learning, as well as achieve at school (DfES 2004:1). We have seen already how important it is to consider, in terms of promoting equality, the assumptions we might have in our understanding about place that we might be teaching. Similarly, if we are to engage all children in enjoying their learning and, as a consequence, achieving the high expectations we have for them, we need to consider how what we teach interests and motivates them. Again, this may involve us in reviewing own assumptions and understandings of what that might be.

Sadly, there is OfSTED evidence that shows that in geography 'there is weaker provision ... than in any other National Curriculum subject' (OfSTED 2005a), and that there 'is some evidence of decline in provision in schools' (OfSTED 2008). Therefore, it is harder to find evidence, specific to geography, which supports the notion that children are more motivated to learn if what they are learning is more relevant to them, except by comparison with research into enjoyment and achievement in other areas of the curriculum. Let us, therefore, take the evidence that explores children's enjoyment and motivation by a comparison with another aspect of the curriculum. It is stated in the English programme of study, that children should read a range of literature that includes: 'stories, plays and poems by significant children's authors', (Key Stage 1) (DfEE/QCA 1999:47), and 'a range of modern fiction by significant children's authors and long-established children's fiction', (Key Stage 2) (DfEE/QCA 1999.54). While there is no specified 'list' of what might constitute significant long-established and more current children's authors, anecdotal evidence suggests that teachers and schools tend to provide children with a fairly traditional diet of British 'classic' fiction texts and poems and contemporary authors that reflect the teachers' background and interests with teachers relying on the same texts over a lengthy period (OfSTED 2005b:24), which is reflected in surveys into children's reading habits (OfSTED 2005b:9).

OfSTED inspection evidence (OfSTED 2005b, 2005c), also shows that teachers' interpretation of the literature aspect of the National Curriculum reading programme of study does not reflect children's interests nor encourage children to read for pleasure outside school, indeed there is a 'dissonance between school reading and home reading choices and experiences' (OfSTED 2005b:9), and in surveys asking children about influences on their reading choices, most children cited friends as influences on their reading choices. '[F]ewer pupils mentioned that their reading had been influenced greatly by teachers' (OfSTED 2005b:24). Furthermore, those children who most experience this dissonance are boys and particularly boys from socio-economically disadvantaged backgrounds and ethnic minorities (OfSTED 2005b, 2005c). Indeed, 'Children's own favourite books often disregard conventional notions of quality' (OfSTED 2005b:9).

Much OfSTED research (OfSTED 2005b, 2005c) into children's reading habits showed that both boys and girls enjoyed reading comics and multi-modal texts for pleasure, neither of which appear in the National Curriculum, or would seem to feature in the programme of study range of literature outlined above; children also felt that teachers didn't approve of comics (OfSTED 2005b:9).

This exploration of what is happening in reading is important because it provides evidence that there is a dissonance between what is taught at school and children's home life and interests which, in turn, leads to disaffection. If we continue to make narrow interpretations of the curriculum and impose our notions on children of what should be taught without thought to what might interest and motivate them, not only will children become more disaffected but we will fail to meet the outcomes of ECM.

Children's knowledge and understanding about place is, as is the knowledge and understanding of adults, acquired though our interaction with, and movement between, different places (Holloway and Hubbard 2001:48). However, some places we know about we may never actually visit, therefore our knowledge is acquired vicariously through representations, maps, atlases, videos, paintings, and so on (Holloway and Hubbard 2001:48). To ensure our knowledge and understanding is as informed as possible, what we must do, particularly if we are teaching this knowledge as 'facts' about people and places, is examine carefully where we have acquired our knowledge from. As Lander states in Knowles, if we are truly in the business of promoting equality 'the school curriculum needs to move beyond' tokenistic nods to social justice and 'examine the curriculum and develop a curriculum that allows pupils to examine other perspectives', and as teachers we should be able to identify, and remove from our teaching 'social bias which may favour some groups' (Knowles 2006:70). If we can do this with children, in a way that is meaningful to them, which enables them to enjoy and achieve at school, particularly through their geographical work exploring their own localities, we can, if we understand ourselves at the local level, better deal with the iniquities of the notions we perpetrate about other people in other places (Holloway and Hubbard 2001:21)

Note

1   The starting-point for Gramsci's concept of hegemony is that a class and its representatives exercise power over subordinate classes by means of a combination of coercion and persuasion ... Hegemony is a relation, not of domination by means of force, but of consent by means of political and ideological leadership. (Simon 2001:24) In the way education, health and other societal goods are held and controlled by particular classes, so, too, is the use and distribution of space.

References

Adams, M., Bell, L. A. and Griffin P. (2007) *Teaching for Diversity and Social Justice*, 2nd edn. New York & London: Routledge.

Barkham, P. (2008) *How a top can turn a teen into a hoodlum*. Online at http://www.guardian.co.uk/uk/2005/may/14/ukcrime.immigrationpolicy

BBCa (2008) *Mall bans shoppers' hooded tops*. Online at http://news.bbc.co.uk/1/hi/england/kent/4534903.stm (Accessed 23rd February 2008).

BBCb (2008) *Czech pledge to tear down wall*. Online at http://news.bbc.co.uk/1/hi/world/europe/478917.stm (Accessed 23rd February 2008).

BBCc (2008) *Main points: Darling statement*. Online at http://news.bbc.co.uk/1/hi/uk_politics/7036009.stm (Accessed 24th February 2008).

BBCd (2008) *Five no-go sites for travellers*. Online at http://news.bbc.co.uk/1/hi/england/bradford/4596723.stm (Accessed 2nd March 2008).

BBCe (2008) *Gypsy coalition calls for reform*. Online at http://news.bbc.co.uk/1/hi/uk/4517033.stm (Accessed 2nd March 2008).

Carter, R. (ed.) (1998) *The Handbook of Primary Geography* (10th impression 2002). Sheffield: The Geographical Association.

Davis, P. C. (1995) 'Law as Microaggression', in R. Delgado (ed.) *Critical Race Theory: the cutting edge*. Philadelphia: Temple University Press.

Directgov (2008) *Disabled People: the Disability Discrimination Act DDA* http://www.direct.gov.uk/en/DisabledPeople/RightsAndObligations/DisabilityRights/DG_4001068. (Accessed 23rd February 2008).

DFEE/QCA (1999) *The National Curriculum Handbook for Primary Teachers in England*. London: DFEE/QCA.

DfES (2007) *Statutory Framework for the Early Years Foundation Stage*. Nottingham: DfES.

DFES (2004) Every Child Matters: Change for Children in Schools. Nottingham: DFES.

Doward, J. (2004) 'Abuse is "systematic" at asylum detention centres', *The Observer*, May 23. Online at http://www.guardian.co.uk/politics/2004/may/23/immigration.immigrationandpublicservices. (Accessed 2nd March 2008).

Gilborn, D. (2008) *Racism and education: coincidence or conspiracy?* London: Routledge.

Griffiths, M. (1998) *Educational Research for Social Justice*. Buckingham, Philadelphia: Open University Press.

Hill, D. (2009). 'Theorizing Politics and the Curriculum: Understanding and Addressing Inequalities through Critical Pedagogy and Critical Policy Analysis', in D. Hill and L. Helavaara Robertson (eds) (2009) *Equality in the Primary School: Promoting good practice across the curriculum*. London: Continuum

Hill, D. and Cole, M. (eds) (2001) *Schooling and Equality: Fact, Concept and Policy*. London: Kogan Page.

Holloway, L. and Hubbard, P. (2001) *People and Place*. Harlow: Prentice Hall.

Knowles, G. (ed.) (2006) *Supporting Inclusive Practice*. Bungay, Suffolk: David Fulton.

Lehti, A. and Mattson, B. *Health, attitude to care and pattern of attendance among gypsy women—a general practice perspective*. Online at http://fampra.oxfordjournals.org/cgi/content/full/18/4/445. (Accessed 23rd February 2008).

Michael, K. and Pile, S. (1993) *Place and the Politics of Identity*. London: Routledge.

OfSTED (2005a) *OfSTED Subject Reports 2003/04 Geography in Primary Schools*. HMI/OfSTED. Online at www.ofsted.gov.uk (Accessed May 2008).

OfSTED (2005b) *English 2000–05*. HMI/OfSTED. Online at www.ofsted.gov.uk (Accessed May 2008).

OfSTED (2005c) *Informing Practice in English*. HMI/OfSTED. Online at www.ofsted.gov.uk (Accessed May 2008).

OfSTED (2008) *Geography in Schools: Changing Practice*. HMI/OfSTED.

Robertson, I. and Richards, P. (2003) *Studying Cultural Landscapes*. London: Edward Arnold.

Rose, G. (1993) *Feminism and Geography*. Cambridge: Polity Press.

Sehmi, J. (2008) *The Invisible Consumer*. Online at http://info.moneyweek.com/article.php? bbcam = adwds&bbkid = shop + profit&x = &jtid = 2330592&UID = JF + - + Google &p_id = 1419. (Accessed 24th February 2008)

Shurmer-Smith, P. (2002) *Doing Cultural Geography*. London: Sage Publications.

Simon, R. (2001) *Gramsci*. ElecBook.

Trifonas, P. P. (ed.) (2003) *Pedagogies of Difference*. London: Routledge Falmer.

Valentine, G. (2001) *Social Geographies*. Harlow: Pearson.

Useful resources and websites

http://www.oxfam.org.uk/education/

http://www.un.org/

http://www.geography.org.uk/ – this is the Geographical Association site, see also Scoffham, S. (2005) *Primary Geography Handbook*. Geographical Association

http://www.cafod.org.uk/resources

http://www.standards.dfes.gov.uk/schemes3/ – for the QCA schemes of work

http://www.actionaid.org.uk/index.asp?page_id = 100006

http://www.bbc.co.uk/

Chapter 12

Art

Jessica Haberman and Carole Hsiao

Introduction

This chapter will present two distinct but interlinked discussions of the art curriculum and its relationship to equality. In the first section, Carole Hsiao provides a brief, yet thorough, socio-political curriculum analysis of the art curriculum. In the second section, Jessica Haberman provides a brief history of art in English primary schools since 1988; an exploration of gender, ethnicity, special needs, social class and social exclusion as they relate to the art curriculum, and a discussion of the wider policy context within which the art curriculum finds itself and the challenges and opportunities this provides for the discussion of equality in the primary school setting.

Art – A Socio-Political Analysis by Carole Hsiao, PhD

Over the years, the role of the arts in schools has changed. Some of this is based on how schooling has changed and some of it is based on the way society's views on what constitutes art have changed. In this section, the idea that meaningful arts education resources can be found in the community will be explored. This work is built upon the premise that the arts are and have been based on the production of social forces and are inextricably linked to the influence of various social structures and social institutions (Wolffe 1981). I will identify how the community can play a positive and insightful role in arts education and how an arts curriculum can play a part in promoting issues involving social justice and, ultimately, empowerment for various constituencies. This examination will bring up issues of race and socio-economic factors as they play themselves out in the cultural and artistic realm of education and learning.

The school as an institution has arguably become dislodged from the very students it is asked to teach. The state has narrowed its focus on the demands of the market, rather than the students who are enrolled in its schools. Many scholars have written about this separation and how it impacts what is taught in the classroom. In *Ideology and Curriculum* (2004), Michael Apple discusses the significance of power in the world of education. In particular, his work on the official versus unofficial curriculum brings up important questions about what is considered legitimate knowledge and how that gets transmitted in schools. Dave Hill (1999, 2006) writes about how social class very strongly influences which students gain access to schooling, how that happens and what kind of schooling is made available to them. Due to these and other forces, the state then determines an official curriculum for arts and other education. These curricula may or may not be pertinent to the lived experience of all in the classroom and are not usually aimed at an education that fosters resistance or collective empowerment. But as Peter McLaren writes, 'We do not stand before the social world; we live in the midst of it' (McLaren 1989:63), and the reality is that the act of educating involves living players in a constantly shifting dialogue.

Within the classroom, Gloria Ladson-Billings' has determined successful strategies in the teaching of African-American students and it shows that an environment that respects the culture of students allows the students to prosper. In her theory, *Culturally Relevant Pedagogy*, she states, 'students must develop and/ or maintain cultural competence' (Ladson-Billings 1995:160). Her research shows that students ought to have some autonomy in their experience of culture. She asks for a cultural competence that will likely serve to ground students and orient them so that they can assert their ideas within a community of peers. And this is a contributing factor to the success of students.

Another reality that must be brought up in relation to arts curricula is the ever-present tension in the arts between what is called the art of the lived experience of people versus that which has been deemed significant by an exclusive portion of the population. Within this debate, there is a danger in over-simplifying the ideological argument and not spending time untangling some of the complex forces that influence art and popular culture, both in society at large as well as within the lives of the young. The educational system breeds a sort of 'high art' versus 'low art' mentality which can lead many to disregard the various rich insights we may have into our students' minds when they express themselves. The obvious but unfortunate aspect of this is that it is very much divided on class lines.

The work of Paul Willis is useful in developing the notion that the voices of young people ought to be heard on their terms. In *Common Culture* (1990), he examines the important role of the everyday aesthetic in understanding the lives and thoughts of the young. Willis dispels stereotypes that working-class youth don't have a legitimate culture or a valuable cultural capital. Pierre Bourdieu's work found that cultural capital is present within every segment of society with socio-economic class demarcating the habits between groups of people. Willis introduces many examples of how popular culture is a medium in which his students both live in the world and utilize its various outlets to express themselves. He provides an interesting discussion of how the viewing of television is an integral part of life. For an example, he utilizes the format of the soap opera to probe at its effects on youth. Some are able to reconcile their own feelings because they recognize them on the television. At the conclusion of this discussion, Willis suggests that given that so many young people are viewing television, their voice ought to be represented at the decision-making level for the programming and creation of TV shows.

In the book, *Learning to Labor* (Willis 1977), the lives of working-class lads and their sense of place are the foci. No matter how much they resent their position in society, they act and react in a way that keeps them in the same place, in part, because of their reaction against the status quo or those in power. Richard Johnson is another scholar who attests to the role of power in culture. His pioneering work in the field of Cultural Studies, *What is Cultural Studies Anyway?* (1983), supports the notion that culture is a medium in which power dynamics within society can be played out. An illustration of this phenomenon can be found in the medium of graffiti art, which expresses anger from the oppressed and disenfranchized within a system of visual symbols on the turf that they inhabit. Both the culture of hip hop (which covers an array of platforms) and the art form of graffiti are but a few venues which can be seen as creating opportunities for empowerment and liberation to spring from the confines of the cultural norms being imposed on them by the state; yet the roots of their cultural expression comes from their lived experience.

As schools and neighbourhoods experience a growth in immigrant populations, the art curricula that was created by the status quo no longer fits. Arts experiences that take place within the community can serve to inform educators of what has not traditionally been seen in the classroom. Further, the community offers social contexts that can provide greater understanding of students as a whole. Many groups arriving in their new homes soon establish networks formed around artistic experiences. For example, young female members of the Hmong community in the US participate in large numbers in dance *Hsiao, unpublished dissertation* (2005). As the population begins its transition to life in the US, the practice of dance has shifted from a ritual representing the coming of age to an artistic practice embedded in the Hmong community. It is also a communal activity for the youth. Migration of the Hmong to the US put an end to early marriage traditions (previously, the age of marriage was 11). Now, young women have opportunities to complete their high school education and work outside the home, which wasn't the case less than a generation ago. Ultimately, this has presented a shift in the identity of a Hmong young woman. By working with those in the Hmong community, educators can learn a great deal more about the context of their students' lives and the transition they are undertaking as a culture. At present, dance is not considered part of the school curriculum for these young women. In the example of dance, which had been practised as a coming of age ritual, the purpose of the art form has been altered as the role of the women in the society has changed. No longer does it serve as a courtship or pre-nuptial activity. Currently, it attracts and bonds Hmong families across regions of the US as a performance and community activity. Researchers who have examined the relationship between issues of cultural identity and their impact on schooling include Margaret Gibson (1998), Stacey Lee (1996, 2005) and Min Zhou and Carl Bankston (1998). Ann Fadiman has written a compelling account, *When the Spirit Catches You and You Fall Down* (1997), of the tension felt by a Hmong family as it deals with serious family illness.

How can we proceed? Here are some thoughts, in Peter McLaren's words,

> Knowledge is relevant only when it begins with the experiences students bring with them from the surrounding culture; it is critical only when these

experiences are shown to sometimes be problematic (i.e. racist, sexist); and it is transformative only when students begin to use the knowledge to help empower others, including individuals in the surrounding community. (McLaren 1989:80)

The example offered by the young Hmong females, particularly as expressed by their participation in dance, takes on new meaning when it begins to shed light on the complexity of the transitions they are facing as individuals and as a culture. All who are ready and interested in taking a critical look at the current state of education can begin by being open to, that is, watching and listening to, what is really taking place around us. It is through this sort of analysis that we can begin to see the ways in which the state inhibits the well-rounded education that each student deserves.

Without interrupting the current flow of a market-driven curriculum that determines what kind of art education is appropriate for the classroom, significant segments of the population will be left out and feeling disempowered. They will be left out of the aesthetic experience and there will be no space in which a culturally relevant milieu exists for them. As with the Hmong young women whose role in their families and society have changed dramatically in a short time, their continued involvement in dance is a significant way to express the complicated emotions they feel. Marked by race and class these young women tend to be segregated educationally from their white, middle-class counterparts at a very young age. The current system has chosen to relegate them to a path that will not lead to college prep courses or other mainstream educational choices and opportunities. Through dance, these young women are giving voice to life histories, struggles and an intelligent view of the world that deserves the hopeful future that should be shared by all young people.

The English Art Curriculum and Equality in the Primary School: Prospects and Problems by Jessica Haberman

Introduction

The English art curriculum is very well placed to promote equality within the primary school setting. However the position of art education in the English primary school has been placed under continued threat in recent years, which has grave implications for addressing wider matters of equality. This section will present a brief history of art in English primary schools since 1988; explore gender, ethnicity, special needs social class, and social exclusion as they relate to the art curriculum; and discuss the wider policy context within which the art curriculum finds itself and the challenges and opportunities this provides for the discussion and promotion of equality in the primary school setting.

Overview

Prior to 1988, there was no public policy for an art curriculum in English primary schools (Campbell 1993). With the Education Reform Act of 1988 the National Curriculum was established in England and Wales with attainment targets, programmes of study and assessment arrangements for all curriculum areas. Art was one of the last three subjects to be made statutory in 1992, protecting its position as an essential part of children's education (Hickman 2005). The inclusion of art in the National Curriculum made it statutory, protecting the entitlement of all pupils to have art comprise a part of their primary education. This introduction of art into the curriculum led to a great deal of subject training for teachers in the primary setting (Cox *et al.* 2007).

Art as a statutory entitlement for all children has led to a number of further developments in the arts education picture: art coordinator roles were created more widely; art policies were adopted by schools; in general, the profile of art in the primary school was raised. Support materials were devised for art, as for other National Curriculum subjects, such as the QCA scheme of work for Art & Design. This framework aims to enable a more broad and balanced approach to art education in primary schools in supporting teachers' planning for this. This scheme details units of work in art and design for all of the year groups in the primary school setting (DCSF 2009). They are a useful resource for the non-specialist art teacher in ensuring that pupils are exposed to a range of skills, knowledge and understanding about this subject area.

The National Curriculum for art has further improved the quality of teaching and learning in this subject area in that it has provided a common framework for building a more full account of good practice in art education. Galleries and museums are able to tailor educational programmes to the art curriculum for primary pupils and thus link more meaningfully with work done in schools. Initiatives have begun such as the Artsmark Award maintained by the Arts Council: an award that provides a benchmark for schools to strive towards having their work in the arts curriculum recognized (http://www.artscouncil.org.uk/artsmark/). Further developments from the art curriculum can be seen in the work that Creative Partnerships and similar organizations provide in schools around England (http://www.creative-partnerships.com/). Creative Partnerships was set up to promote creativity throughout the whole curriculum while forging partnerships between schools and artists/art organizations (Cox *et al.* 2007). The establishment of art as a statutory part of the National Curriculum has enabled many innovative people and organizations to work in tandem with schools to ensure that children are exposed to, and engage with, the broad and balanced opportunities that visual art can provide.

The importance of art as a subject enjoyed for its own sake, as well as for the 'richness' it brings to learning across the curriculum areas, is recognized in recent government policy (DfES 2003:9); '[a]s well as giving them the essential tools for learning, primary education is about children experiencing the joy of . . . being creative in . . . art' (DfES 2003:4). Art is identified in the Primary Strategy as a key factor in ensuring pupil enjoyment of education at the primary level (DfES 2003). This multi-faceted aspect of art as a subject that can positively contribute to the whole of a child's education is recognized across both policy-making and research circles (for example, DfES 2003; DfEE & QCA 1999; Stuhr *et al*. 1992; Freedman 2000, to name a few). Art is seen as a discipline that can provide for the spiritual, moral, social and cultural development of pupils (DfEE & QCA 1999). Despite the wide variety of support materials available, the coverage of art in the National Curriculum is less prescriptive than for other subjects, leaving it more open to adaptation and innovation on the part of the teacher. The utility of art in providing an engaging and accessible platform through which other skills can be developed is also of great value in the primary school setting. Skills of communication, the application of numeracy, working with others, improving learning and performance – and problem-solving skills are seen to develop and be promoted with the aid of art (DfEE & QCA 1999). The possibilities that work in art opens up for the development of a variety of skills and dispositions is of key importance in the discussion of equality in primary schools. With less prescription than other National Curriculum subjects, teachers are given greater freedom to select the content of their art programme as well as the links they choose to make with other curriculum areas. It is this freedom that enables the art curriculum to deal with matters of equality within the primary school in a powerful way and it is this freedom that places a greater emphasis on the sensitivities of teachers to really consider the content of the curriculum they teach.

Art for Equality

In considering art and equality in the primary school, it becomes clear that art can provide meaningful opportunities to discuss, develop and deconstruct issues of identity and stereotyping. Matters of gender, ethnicity, special needs, disability, social class, and social exclusion are all brought to bear in the art that is chosen for study and the pupils who are studying it. The following section will explore both the positive role for art and the important considerations required when addressing equality in the primary school classroom. In particular, gender, ethnicity, special needs, disability, social class and social exclusion will be looked at as they can be represented in the art curriculum, and how equal opportunity access to the art curriculum can be protected through pedagogical considerations on the part of the teacher.

Gender

Gender equality issues are brought to bear on the primary art curriculum largely through the particular works of art chosen to study, as well as the media chosen by the teacher to work with in class. The sensitivities of individual teachers are required to adapt the broad nature of the National Curriculum to their own classroom curriculum and ensure that both genders are represented by the subjects of art and the artists chosen for study. Fruitful discussion about the role of women in art history can take place through the careful selection of key works of art. Art that is displayed and used in the classroom can represent a range of male and female subjects as well as artists. Traditional patriarchal monopoly over art means that children are bound to be more familiar with male artists, as are teachers. Particular care needs to be taken in the selection of resources sought to redress the gender inequality in famous art (Cox *et al.* 2007). The work of women artists needs to be specifically sought out and brought into the classroom – and not just the half dozen or so famous women artists.

The conscious promotion of gender equality within the primary art classroom will involve discussions with children about the representation of women in art and how these have changed over time. Older pupils can be given investigative work to explore why the work of so many male artists is recognized and remembered. In this way gender equality can be made a tangible visual issue for pupils. Recognizing the gendered nature of particular media in art is important as well. Ensuring that more traditionally female media, such as weaving and knitting, and traditionally male media of woodwork and metalwork are encouraged for all pupils is another way in which teachers show their awareness of differences, and try not to give into their own gender stereotyping of appropriate art activities (Cox *et al.* 2007).

Race/Ethnicity

England is a multicultural nation and the art curriculum is very well placed to enable meaningful investigation and celebration of the cultural identity and heritage of pupils and citizens of the wider community and communities. The National Curriculum for art stipulates that art from both 'Western Europe and the wider world' should be studied in the classroom (DfEE & QCA 1999). Studying art from diverse cultural groups within the UK, and the world, can help to 'ensure that children do not acquire the kinds of prejudice that give rise to social injustice' (Cox *et al.* 2007:162). Once again the sensitivities of the teacher are required to ensure that the art that is represented and created in the primary school classroom reflects the ethnic background of the children in that class, school and community as well as the wider global community. Exposing pupils to the work of other cultures can help to build positive relations between members of different cultures and can promote a greater sense of connectedness with the local community. In this manner, racial and ethnic equality can be further promoted within the primary school classroom. A greater representation of minority cultures in the subject, artist and media that is presented in the primary classroom will also add to the feelings of self-worth and pride of many pupils from different backgrounds (Adejumo 2002). Furthermore, art can be a tool for challenging and correcting dominant ideologies of culture, ethnicity and race. Teachers' choice of focus in class can enable the promotion of racial equality through opening up opportunities to explore and discuss racism, prejudice and stereotyping.

Decisions about what kind of art to explore need to be taken very carefully to ensure that the representation of racial or ethnic difference is not one that actually encourages stereotyping. Practical considerations mean that only some cultures can be chosen to focus upon in class and this selection of one culture rather than another can cause difficulties. Utilizing community members to help in the presentation of cultural art and to contextualize the art is helpful in making the learning more authentic, especially if the culture chosen to focus on is different from the teacher's (Adejumo 2002). Specific practical considerations need to be taken by all teachers to ensure they are providing pupils with resources they can use to represent themselves in art, such as paints, pencils, crayons and pastels in a range of skin tones. Recognizing the variety of media used by different cultures is also an important consideration in the promotion of cultural equality. Broadening pupil awareness of art forms beyond the traditional dominant Western forms, and focusing on the traditional crafts and folk art of other cultures, is another way of encouraging equality in the multicultural classroom. By empowering pupils to provide their own cultural contexts for art education, teachers are enabling their pupils to communicate their own perspective on the world (Stuhr *et al.* 1992).

Special Educational Needs and Disability

The art curriculum is particularly well placed for ensuring equality of opportunity and access for pupils with special educational needs and/or physical disabilities. The notion that art is a subject without right answers is a crucial part of its role in promoting equality in the primary school: all answers are valid and relevant. Once again, this places greater emphasis on the teacher's sensitivities rather than on the curriculum. Ensuring that all pupils are encouraged to participate, and utilizing a variety of teaching strategies and media are some of the considerations crucial to equality in the classroom. Highly prescriptive activities are considered detrimental to the inclusive art classroom where risk-taking and creativity are what is valued (Cox *et al.* 2007). Teachers need to be able to provide opportunities and support pupils in the development of their own ideas without offering their own solutions.

Differentiation of work in the inclusive art classroom will focus more on outcome than process. In this way, all pupils are able to work on the same task at their own pace (Cox *et al.* 2007). Other practical considerations include making specific links with artists in the community who have special needs as this can help pupils to see the contribution that people from all walks of life make to art and wider society. Ensuring that pupils with disabilities have equal access to resources and work space are obvious considerations for art in any classroom: equipment and media can be altered in keeping with the needs of all pupils. Additionally, lessons can specifically focus upon a variety of sensory input in order to appeal to pupils with particular impairments (Karkou and Glasman 2004). Consideration of the needs of gifted and talented pupils is necessary to ensure appropriate challenge is built into teaching (Cox *et al.* 2007). The open-ended nature of art, its position as a mode of expression, and the opportunities it provides for critical and contextual analysis makes it an excellent subject for truly extending all pupils in a safe environment where risk-taking is valued and achievement is personal.

Social Class and Social Exclusion

Art can be seen as a subject optimally placed to encourage the socially excluded within schools to form a positive connection with education; where social exclusion is understood as 'people ... suffer[ing] from a combination of linked problems such as unemployment, poor skills, low incomes, poor housing, high crime, bad health and family breakdown' (SEU 2001:1.2). Arts are seen as a non-threatening educational interface that encourages participation among the socially excluded. The enjoyment that pupils get from creating and exploring art can be seen to 're-motivate and re-integrate pupils who are disaffected and disengaged' (Richey 2004:50). Art can be used across all curriculum areas to engage and inspire a greater sense of self-worth and esteem for those pupils considered socially excluded, while offering them greater opportunity for self-expression. There are many possibilities for using art to integrate pupils who may be socially excluded, however there are many possibilities for teachers to unwittingly uphold certain social stratifications that need to be considered. One such area for increased teacher sensitivity is in the use of art galleries and museums. Though galleries and museums provide opportunities for pupils to be exposed to the work of artists from a variety of backgrounds, teachers need to recognize that the positioning of big galleries and the art that they show has within it an implicit hierarchy of quality (Cox *et al.* 2007). Street or local art may be, unwittingly, presented as lower, or less valuable, than the art presented in a major national gallery. This can maintain notions of social positioning in communicating that value is somehow objective and defined by those with higher social status. Writers within the socialist/Marxist tradition such as Bourdieu, Bourdieu and Passeron, and Giroux, suggest that this 'symbolic violence' is far from accidental, it is a way of reinforcing and reproducing social class patterns of domination and subordination.

In terms of practical considerations, ensuring that the process in art-making is valued over the outcome is crucial in promoting engagement in the arts by those considered excluded or at-risk for social exclusion (Karkou and Glasman 2004). Visual communication rather than verbal communication is another key aspect of art that makes it a crucial subject area in the inclusion of at-risk pupils 'who may find verbal interaction unwelcome and/or threatening' (Karkou and Glasman 2004:61). Providing pupils with a quality arts programme in their class is one way in which teachers can ensure these pupils have a sense of inclusion and access in school. Connecting art to other curriculum areas can be seen as one way to increase participation in the learning process and further motivate and integrate those pupils identified as at-risk for social exclusion. In classrooms and communities with high levels of social exclusion partnerships with outside agencies can be sought to increase the access all pupils have to arts-based learning. Creative Partnerships is one of a number of initiatives currently working with the specific remit of increasing pupil participation in learning, through greater exposure to the arts (Balshaw 2004).

Art can be the subject through which pupils, from all backgrounds, can come to terms with their own world perspective and the perspectives of others. The art that is represented in the primary classroom can lead to discussions that actively promote equality by engaging children in understanding where their perspectives come from and in promoting empathy with others in their school, community and the world. The importance of a child's own socio-cultural context is key in art; this, along with the skills imparted through teaching, are how they will interact with the wider world (Cox *et al.* 2007). One role of the teacher in art education is to help mediate the wider society that children's artistic skills are being brought to bear on – a daunting task. Awareness of one's own prejudices and stereotypes is a crucial starting point in the development of a rich and meaningful classroom art curriculum.

Equality of Art

The foregoing outlines some of the important ways in which art can be seen to address inequalities within schools and the wider world. However, a closer look at the wider policy context within the English primary school setting reveals that the access pupils have to a quality art education is under grave threat. This threat against art in schools is, in some sense, a threat against equality for all participants in primary education. Specifically, a look at the standards agenda and the pressure this has placed on resources within schools, and a closer look at what has been called the 'economizing', will be shown to have marginalized art and lowered its status to the extent that it is incapable of promoting equality (Ozga 2000:233).

The Standards Agenda

The standards agenda with its focus on testing, published league tables and inspections is a weighty reality of English primary schools in the twenty-first century. While art is a statutory part of the National Curriculum, it is not considered a part of the core, or tested, curriculum. Tested, or core subjects, such as numeracy and literacy make up 50 per cent of the school week and leave the remainder of learning as 'trimmings' (Alexander 2004:27). Those areas of learning that are 'tested objectively and validated externally' are used to judge the effectiveness of schools (NACCCE 1999:109). As a result, '[t]he focus of teaching narrows, and so does children's learning and achievement' (NACCCE 1999:109). This has led to a lowering of the status of other areas of learning – including art. Narrowing of the curriculum in order to focus more thoroughly on the core subjects seems to be marginalizing art within schools; and this has grave implications.

> The Arts within the National Curriculum remain minority subjects at all levels for most children, and therefore despite the various government-funded Arts initiatives, the limited experience of the Arts in schools is likely to contribute to the social exclusion of some pupils: in effect they are being denied the opportunity to benefit fully from a range of cultural forms. (Sanderson 2007:4)

This marginalization of art within the primary school setting has been recognized by many (Cox *et al.* 2007; Brehony 2005; Jeffrey 2003). The drive for standards has resulted in a two-tiered curriculum where art, among other subjects, is given far less coverage in schools (Brehony 2005).

Allocation of resources can be seen to follow the areas of greatest concern within schools. As a result, school funds are often spent on inspection preparation, targets and performance management indicators rather than on art resources, subject knowledge training and community partnerships (Gewirtz 2000). If better art teachers come from greater investment in training and resources, as well as from greater curriculum time for their subject, then the standards agenda can be seen to strongly and negatively impact upon the art curriculum. If art is well placed to reach out to all students and to address matters of equality within wider society, then equality itself is being marginalized by the standards agenda currently in place within English primary schools.

Economizing of Education

The imposition of economic policy onto primary education policy in recent years can also be seen to negatively impact on the art curriculum (Ball 1999). 'Furthermore, schooling, in all its phases has become subordinated to the perceived requirements of the labour market' (Brehony 2005:31). Creativity has become the new catch phrase of primary education policy and this has been linked in policy documents and elsewhere to notions of employability (DfEE & QCA 2000; Gewirtz 2000; Brehony 2005). Art and creativity, in this light, become means to the end of economic innovation, rather than ends in themselves (NFER/QCA 2000). 'Autonomy, reflectivity [and] creativity .... are only valued, if at all, where they are seen to contribute to productivity' (Gewirtz 2000:362). This reduction of art to its instrumental value in encouraging the skills and dispositions required of the labour market threaten its ability to develop and promote deeper understandings of equality and connectedness to the wider world that pupils find themselves in.

Another concern about the nature of art in primary schools and its accessibility for all pupils is that this drive for creativity may lead to art being used, solely, as a tool for teaching other important skills. While cross-curricular teaching can help pupils to make important connections between subject areas, the current policy commitment to arts education seems to be based on the idea that it will improve other academic standards rather than on an appreciation for the intrinsic value of creative and art education (Sanderson 2007). If art continues to be justified as a tool for teaching other subjects or for inculcating productive behaviours required of the labour market, then art as a subject will remain marginalized within primary schools (Siegesmund 1998). Art as a subject needs to be given equal treatment within the National Curriculum. To marginalize art as an optional extra is to deny its potential to promote equality within the primary school classroom for the future citizens of a global society.

References

Adejumo, C. (2002) 'Considering Multicultural Art Education', *Art Education*, 55, (2), 33–39.

Alexander, R. (2004) 'Still no pedagogy? Principle, pragmatism and compliance in primary education'. *Cambridge Journal of Education*, 34, (1), 7–32.

Apple, M. W. (2004) *Ideology and Curriculum* (3rd ed.). New York: Routledge.

Ball, S. J. (1999) 'Labour, learning and the economy: a "policy sociology" perspective'. *Cambridge Journal of Education*, 29, (2), 195–206.

Balshaw, M. (2004) 'Risking creativity: building the creative context'. *Support for Learning*, 19, (2), 71–76.

Bourdieu, P. (1987) *Distinction*. Harvard: Harvard University Press.

Brehony, K. J. (2005) 'Primary schooling under New Labour: the irresolvable contradiction of excellence and enjoyment'. *Oxford Review of Education* 31, (1), 29–46.

Campbell, R. J. (1993) 'The broad and balanced curriculum in primary schools some limitations on reform'. *Curriculum Journal*, 4, (2), 215–229.

Cox, S., Watts, R., McAuliffe, D., Grahame, J. and Herne, S. (2007) *Teaching Art and Design 3–11. Reaching the Standard*. London/New York: Continuum International Publishing.

DCSF (2009) *Schemes of Work: Art and Design at Key Stages 1 and 2*. Online at http://www.standards.dfes.gov.uk/schemes2/art/ (Accessed January 28th 2009).

DfEE & QCA (1999) *Art and Design*. London: DfEE & QCA.

DfES (2003) *Excellence and Enjoyment: A strategy for primary schools*. London: DfES.

Fadiman, A. (1997) *When the Spirit Catches You and You Fall Down*. New York: Noonday Press.

Freedman, K. (2000) 'Social Perspectives on Art Education in the U.S.: Teaching Visual Culture in a Democracy'. *Studies in Art Education*, 41, (4), 314–329.

Gewirtz, S. (2000) 'Bringing the politics back in: a critical analysis of quality discourses in education'. *British Journal of Educational Studies* 48, (4), 352–370.

Gibson, M. (1988) *Accommodation without Assimilation: Sikh Immigrants in an American High School*. Ithaca: Cornell University.

Hickman, R. (2005) 'A Short History of "Critical Studies" in Art and Design Education', in R. Hickman (ed.), *Critical Studies in Art & Design Education*. Bristol: Intellect Books.

Hill, D. (1999) 'Social Class and Education', in D. Matheson and I. Grosvenor (eds) *An Introduction to the Study of Education*. London: David Fulton.

Hill, D. (2006) 'Class, Capital and Education in this Neoliberal/Neoconservative Period'. *Information for Social Change*, 23. Online at: http://libr.org/isc/issues/ISC23/B1%20Dave%20Hill.pdf

Hsiao, C. (2005) 'They Schools: The Price and Color of Popular Culture and the Arts in Public Education', Diss. University of Wisconsin-Madison, 2005.

Jeffrey, B. (2003) 'Countering learner "Instrumentalism" through creative mediation', *British Educational Research Journal*, 29, 4, 489–503.

Johnson, R. (1983) *What is Cultural Studies Anyway?* Birmingham: University of Birmingham.

Karkou, V. and Glasman, J. (2004) 'Arts, education and society: the role of the arts in promoting the emotional wellbeing and social inclusion of young people', *Support for Learning*, 19, (2), 57–65.

Ladson-Billings, G. (1995) 'But That's Just Good Teaching! The Case for Culturally Relevant Pedagogy'. *Theory In Practice*, XXXIV, (3), 159–163.

Lee, S. J. (1996) *Unraveling the 'Model Minority' Stereotype: Listening to Asian American Youth*. New York: Teachers College Press.

Lee, S. J. (2005) *Up Against Whiteness*. New York: Teachers College Press, 2005.

McLaren, P. (1989) *Life in Schools: An Introduction to Critical Pedagogy in the Foundations of Education*. Boston: Allyn and Bacon.

NACCCE (1999) *All Our Futures: Creativity Culture and Education*.

NfER/QCA (2000) *The Arts, Creativity and Cultural Education: An International Perspective*. London: QCA.

Ozga, J. (2000) 'Education: New Labour, new teachers', in J. Clarke, S. Gewirtz and E. McLaughlin, (eds) *New Managerialism, New Welfare?* London: SAGE.

Richey, S. (2004) 'Promoting social inclusion through the arts'. *Support for Learning*, 19, (2), 50–51.

Sanderson, P. (2007) 'The arts, social inclusion and social class: the case of dance'. *British Educational Research Journal*, 1–25. 15th November.

SEU (Social Exclusion Unit) (2001) *Preventing Social Exclusion*. London: Stationary Office.

Siegesmund, R. (1998) 'Why Do We Teach Art Today? Conceptions of Art Education and Their Justification', *Studies in Art Education*, 39, (3), 197–214.

Stuhr, P., Petrovich-Mwaniki, L. and Wasson, R. (1992) 'Curriculum Guidelines for the Multicultural Art Curriculum', *Art Education*, 45, (1), 16–24.

Willis, P. (1977) *Learning to Labour: How working class kids get working class jobs*. New York: Columbia University Press.

Willis, P., Jones S., Canaan J., and Hurd, G. (1990) *Common Culture: Symbolic work at play in the everyday cultures of the young*. Boulder: Westview Press.

Wolffe, J. (1981) *The Social Production of Art*. Hong Kong: St. Martin's Press.

Zhou, M. and Bankston C. (1998) *Growing Up American: How Vietnamese Children Adapt to Life in the United States*. New York: Russell Sage Foundation.

Chapter 13

Music

Curry Malott, Emily Beadle and Kate Blackmore

Introduction

One of the core aims of primary education is to provide children with a prosperous future in which all lives are enhanced and the educational prospects of all are met (Ofsted 2002). However, it is questionable whether or not all children's needs are met in the current educational system of the UK. This is a result of the limited cultural experience children are exposed to in the course of their school lives, where the focus is upon 'white middle-class' values rather than reflecting the diverse nature of the UK. This chapter recognizes that music is an extremely powerful vehicle in terms of social, spiritual and moral development and is, therefore, a necessary and vitally important way of creating a cohesive learning environment for all children. It provides a powerful and unique form of communication which all children can access, providing a means and potential to change the way pupils feel, act and think.

The chapter will be divided into two sections. The first section includes a theoretical outline regarding music teaching, while the second section will provide teachers with practical examples of how to encompass other cultures, ethnic groups and abilities into the primary music curriculum.

Music Education for Democratic Citizenship

In this chapter we argue for music education as part of the vital human interaction that contributes to democratic citizenship and against different forms of oppression. As an integral part of a creative curriculum, music will help to foster the creativity of children and contribute to the cultural development of society (Robinson et al. 1999). A passive engagement with music is not, however, conducive to musically articulate citizens. Critical literacy through music can serve as a pathway into the realm of emotion – a feeling that is too easily stifled, and in particular, stifled by the rigidity of scientific rationality. Scientific – as well as materialist or reductionist – modes of enquiry are complemented by engagement with the arts, which are holistic, additive, a-rational and creative, and each balances the other. When the balance is too far in one direction or the other, the outcome is impaired and biased. It is the knowledge produced through these creative, emotional and multi-sensory experiences that is particularly conducive to revolutionary shifts; in other words, when meaning is created both rationally through study and debate, and emotionally through an engagement with the arts and performance, levels of understanding and learning are deepened. This implies a sophisticated comprehension of self in context.

Part of music education should be to enable children to 'see through' the music industry; the way of promoting, selling, and in other words, 'commodifying' music into something to be bought, advertised and sold. All forms of culture industry, such as fashion, books, magazines and newspapers, are, of course, 'businesses'. Music serves as an excellent example of the twenty-first-century culture industry, as an example of capitalism, of big business and ferocious exploitation.

As a way of explaining this in theoretical terms, the Frankfurt School of thought – Adorno, Marcuse, Horkheimer, Habermas *et al.* – considered that the main problem of contemporary capitalism was that of over-production of goods. They theorized that this led to capitalist corporations continuing to create more and more 'needs'. As Longhurst writes:

> In contemporary capitalist societies the culture industry produces forms of culture which are commodities: that is, culture which is produced to be bought and sold on a market. It possesses exchange value and the companies that produce culture do so to make a profit from it. According to the Frankfurt School writers, such commodification had become increasingly widespread, penetrating all aspects of cultural production and social life. This led to a standardization of the products of the culture industries, which in turn induced a passivity in those who consume the culture industry products. Held (1980) explains that: The main characteristics of the culture industry reflect the difficult problem it faces. It must at once both sustain interest and ensure that the attention it attracts is insufficient to bring its produce into disrepute. Thus, commercial entertainment aims at an attentive but passive, relaxed and uncritical reception, which it induces through the production of 'patterned and pre-digested' cultural entities. (Longhurst 1954:4)

As radical educators we are deeply concerned that education can 'dumb down' critique and work against teachers and children asking deep and searching questions about the way things are, in their schools, local areas, country and world. Again, in theoretical terms this can be seen as teachers working and operating counter-hegemonically, against the main hegemonic 'commonsense view' that the way things are, is the way things should be and stay.

Our teaching must, therefore, be endowed with the courage and knowledge to successfully operate within this hostile environment. Paulo Freire's (2005) 'On the Indispensable Qualities of Progressive Teachers for Their Better Performance' provides a context for beginning to understand why a teacher *for* social justice and *against* oppression must have the necessary skills and dispositions to confront and overcome the fears that prevent teachers from fully embracing movement toward freedom.

Most people, especially those of us involved in primary and early years schools and education, are motivated by a love of children and a desire to help them make sense of the world, and one of the most important qualities in critical and progressive teachers is the understanding that many apparent 'truths' are, in fact, deeply embedded social constructs. In other words, the way it is, ain't the way it's gotta be! *People* make the world, and this is perhaps the greatest thing anyone can teach, along with the self-confidence to be creative and active rather than a passive consumer.

However, the difficulties of radicalizing music education is highlighted by veteran music teacher and teacher educator Estelle Jorgensen (2004) who acknowledged that 'many music educators are loath to engage in their task politically or to conceive of their role in political as well as musical terms' (Jorgensen 2004:5).

It is within this context that we can begin to understand the paradox of the learning standards. For example, content standards challenge music teachers to embrace a multicultural approach to music education by emphasizing the importance of children being able to identify and perform multiple *genres* and *styles* from *diverse cultures*. Conservatives tend to argue against such an approach, claiming a focus on difference is inherently divisive. Criticalists, or critical educators, on the other hand, critique the standards for perpetuating a superficial and static form of multiculturalism that does not consider the role power plays in privileging whiteness and European Western culture over others. This is most crudely obvious in any syllabus that speaks of 'world music' when referring to non-white and typically non-'classical' music.

In advocating education that is informed by critical theory, we might begin to discuss 'Critical Multicultural Music Education' (CMME) as Jorgensen (2004) suggests. CMME places special emphasis on the importance of the arts and their interrelationship with society and on culture transforming music, education and those who participate in it. CMME is understood as a political undertaking and music educators can be part of fostering what Jorgensen (2004:6) refers to as 'deliberative democracy' and a 'humane society'. Jorgensen makes the case that music teachers, are cultural workers because music, like other art forms, is the product of culture. Pointing to global capitalism as the number one threat to cultural diversity, she notes that:

the farther away from the people that decisions are made, the greater the difficulty in being heard in the public places and preserving one's 'local heritage' rendering it increasingly important for 'collective action' to be taken against capitalism and for the preservation of 'cultural distinctiveness. (Jorgensen 2004:8)

Music education can play a fundamental role here. CMME can help to create pupils who have increased awareness of others and a variety of cultures from within and from outside their community. All teachers are in the position of being able to offer different modes of interpreting the world, and passing on the idea that what *has been* and what *is* are not necessarily what *has to be* in the future. Peterson (2004) speaks directly to classroom teachers when he argues that, 'songs, like poetry, can be powerful teaching tools. The lyrical metaphors, rhythms, and stories in many songs motivate and educate students. It's amazing what students will remember from songs as compared to what they forget from a teacher talking' (Peterson 2004:133).

Music education can, therefore, become a critical element in assisting children in understanding and transforming the social world, as producers of music and musical knowledge. Presumably this is why the British National Party – the UK's ultra-Right group – set up their own record label called Great White records a few years ago. This is also why the German Nazi Party in Hitler's regime and later the Stalinist regime in the USSR imposed controls on the production and enjoyment of music.

Critical Multicultural Music Education in England

Although music is a discrete subject in the British National Curriculum (unlike other art forms such as dance and drama), it is often sidelined due to time and pressure from other subjects. In recent years, and especially since the introduction of literacy and numeracy hours (see Chapters 6 and 7 of this volume), the teaching of music has tended to be seen as less important than other foundation subjects in many English schools. This has led to a general lack of funding in respect of both resources and teacher training. Curriculum pressure and the use of a transmission model of teaching have often limited the creative and expressive potential of music.

However, in England music has been seen by many teachers, over the last ten years, as a way of engaging disaffected students through the creative use of cultural influences and the needs of the local community. In the course of these developments, pedagogic practices have changed under the influence of programmes such as Musical Futures and Creative Partnerships, which were influenced by community music practices springing from the 1960s and 1970s. Indeed, since the National Advisory Committee on Creative and Cultural Education report 'All Our Futures' (Robinson *et al.* 1999) 'creativity' has been a buzz word in UK education and has been seen as an essential aspect of preparing young people for the changing future. This creativity does not always focus on 'the arts', but rather that the arts are acknowledged as integrally creative and thus good models for creative practices which can be applied to other subjects. It also remains true that the so-called basics of literacy and numeracy continue to get the lion's share of the time and money.

Music is around us all of the time; we live in a diverse society that includes a rich culture of different musical styles. All of society, regardless of social class, cultural groups, ethnic community, age and ability have access to a wide range of cultural experiences through the infinite distribution of social and media outlets – radio, television, call centres, shopping centres – to name a few of the many ways we are bombarded with music in our daily lives (Paton 1997). Yet for some, music is only seen as either a savage expression of the *bewildered herd* or the superior culture of the European masters. The music of popular culture, which often appears to be informed by expressions of adolescent angst and frustration, is seen as inferior to classical music. Within our culture the classical, or high culture, musical expressions are portrayed as absolutely and objectively superior.

In terms of music education, teachers can either challenge or reinforce inequalities, either consciously or inadvertently, by the values they assign to different kinds of music. For example, by presenting the Western Classical tradition as the apex of musical achievement, the teacher devalues all other forms. Within the QCA schemes of work, the vast majority of examples and resources used stem from Western origins; many non-specialist teachers will follow these plans unquestionably.

Both popular and classical music has become a product which has been packaged and then sold back to the people. It is linked, via the multiplicity of media and advertising, to lifestyle, which in itself requires the consumption and display of particular brands and commodities. One of the outcomes of this is the assumption, at an increasingly early age, that music is something to be consumed, received, accepted or rejected. With the advent of a 'one click' culture to buy music on the internet, the consumption of music has been revolutionized on an international, indeed, global scale. This trend has increased to a level where we now spend more on the music industry than on the necessities of food, drink and keeping warm (Paton 1997). In the vast majority of cases, the product is presented as ready-made, externally 'perfect', with no mistakes of tuning, timing or intonation. It is, therefore, a struggle for the educator-musician to instil in children a love and understanding of music-making in all its human imperfection.

The ambiguous nature of the guidelines (such as QCA 2004) results in many non-specialist primary teachers feeling unsure and uneasy about the choices of curriculum materials that they have to make. A critical pedagogy, however, must be explicitly anti-racist and democratic and be based on the premise that real change can only come from people. A fundamental avenue for such an initiative is the use of popular music that reflects the music of the world in which we live. This tends to be relatively absent from music classes, especially in primary education. This absence has led educators such as Woody (2007) to note that 'although there are important reasons to preserve long-standing traditions of school music, one wonders why the content of our music curriculum doesn't better reflect the musical world in which we live' (Woody 2007:32). He goes on to argue that efforts to insert popular music into 'traditional school ensembles,' such as having marching bands cover rock songs, does not 'respect musical authenticity' (Woody 2007:32). Because popular music, for many students, represents their 'native music culture,' it is important to place it within its natural context. One of the complexities here is the fact that many children and young people enjoy their music exactly *because it is not school music* and is in some way anti-establishment, anti-authority. That is, the 'natural context' of pop music is not in schools.

At the primary level, it is difficult to find contemporary music that is age appropriate in terms of concept and language. The problem is that much popular music includes extremist statements promoting sexist, homophobic and racist attitudes, as well as the glorification of the 'money as power' aspect of capitalism. Songs from the radical folk traditions may, indeed, convey appropriate sentiments in suitable language – for example Si Kahn's song 'What you do with what you've got'. But as such, songs are likely to be new to children in primary education; if they are presented by teachers rather than discovered through social networks, they may be seen as 'school music' in any case!

Therefore, within the diverse culture of our classrooms teachers should be encouraged to:

- consider the benefits of taking note of the economic, social, and historical forces creating social inequalities within schools and the wider social world;
- recognize the urgency to develop critical forms of pedagogies for the purpose of ensuring that today's children are equipped to make sense of their world and understand the causes of oppression and injustice;
- take action as agents of change.

Music within the Primary Curriculum

Music is the most universal of all the arts. In any country, regardless of musical ability, children will always be able to discuss and provide an answer for their views of music. However, this power is not maintained or recognized within schools. It has been noted that despite liberal-democratic reforms in educational quality, educational opportunity and provision has never been achieved.

Within primary schools in England, music as a non-core foundation subject contains two sets of requirements; knowledge, skills and understanding and breath of study. It is this non-core subject status which often relegates music to being a 'poor relation' in comparison to the teaching of literacy and numeracy. This poor status emerges from lack of funding, pressure for results and lack of the professional development training of staff – who are often non-specialists and lack confidence in their abilities to teach effective and meaningful music lessons.

The Quality and Curriculum Authority outlines that teachers within music can aim to engage all children and to expose them to different cultures by a number of means:

1. Resources from a wide range of cultures
2. Teaching all children songs in various languages and different cultural backgrounds
3. Pictures and labels in different languages
4. Dual language books
5. Recognizing the contribution of musicians from different cultures.

Young children are naturally inquisitive in a quest to make sense of the world around them and the people within it. All young children love to listen and move to music and actively to participate in familiar songs and rhymes (Siraj-Blatchford 1994). From the outset of a child's education, the creative element of music is regarded as a key aspect of their development within the curriculum. Music then continues to remain a section of the curriculum, but the creativity is often lost. The failure to maintain the creative element is due to a number of reasons, namely; viewing music solely as the acquisition of knowledge about music; rigidity in the National Curriculum (1999); emphasis on literacy and numeracy; music can be seen as a luxury that, when the pressure is on, becomes expendable; and the fact that creativity creates noise (Hennessy 2005). But in order to facilitate the formation of rounded, well-grounded citizens, pupils' creativity needs to be fostered, which will enable the development of culture within which original ideas and actions evolve (Craft 2005). The adoption of a creative curriculum will facilitate the development of a cohesive learning environment within which all children are valued as equal. This equality should be regardless of gender, cultural, linguistic or ethnic background, class and ability. In the following sections we will consider each one of these issues in turn.

Gender

Music as a subject is particularly gender biased; it is still to a large extent male dominated in the workplace and within education. In the Western culture of traditional classical music, women are largely denied the key roles of composers, conductors and directors. Within schools, there is a clear gender stereotyping between the types of instruments studied, as nine times as many girls as boys learn the flute while twice as many boys learn the trumpet (Ofsted 2002). Male musicians dominate the QCA units schemes of work, for example, within Unit 10 'Exploring rhythmic patterns' all three suggested works are composed by men (Mike Oldfield, Dave Brubeck and Beethoven).

This pattern of male domination in music is replicated in many different cultures. This is particularly the case in Asian music where Indian classical music and also in Qowali (Muslim) singing are exclusively male (Paton 1997). Even in contemporary music such as jazz, hip-hop, punk and rock the scene is predominantly male.

To guard against the continuation of these prejudices against women, music teachers should:

- use a variety of music by both male and female composers;
- encourage girls to compose and direct performances in equal terms with boys;
- be aware of the historical context of discrimination against women in music;
- focus upon women artists who are successful in producing quality music, while providing positive role models, e.g. Ella Fitzgerald to Shakara, who have used their fame in a positive way;
- introduce and encourage girls and boys to play instruments that would not necessarily appeal to their gender group (adapted from Paton 1997)

Cultural, Linguistic and Ethnic Backgrounds

Cultural, linguistic and ethnic backgrounds should be celebrated within primary music. Music can transcend all cultural and linguistic barriers – it is accessible to all.

Throughout their primary education children need to be exposed to a wide variety of musical styles from around the world. In addition to this, there should be a wide range of musical instruments from different cultures. Musical instruments like tablas (Indian drums), maracas and castanets (South American), steel pans (Trinidad), congo drums (Congo) and singing bowls (India) can be available for children's experimentation. Building upon this, schools should seek to engage and involve parents by encouraging them to visit school and talk about and play any instruments from their musical heritage (Siraj-Blatchford 1994).

A core element of the early years curriculum is the use of rhyme and song – children can be taught these in a range of community languages, which provides another opportunity to involve parents (QCA 2004). In addition, teachers should seek to immerse children in music of different styles and different cultures. Potential examples include Ustad Salamat Ali Khan (who has had a huge impact on South Asian classical music), Nusrat Fateh Ali Khan (described as 'Elvis of the East' or 'Bob Marley' of Pakistan), Gilberto Gil (Brazilian Samba music), Thelonious Monk (African-American jazz music), La Havana (Cuban classics) and Fela Kuti (the 'African Bob Marley'). Care should be taken that children understand and respect the value of the music for its content rather than on solely tokenistic grounds where the music is perceived as being exotic and unusual (QCA 2004). Teachers need to be aware of children's prior cultural experiences as some new immigrants may have no education in music, while other children may come from strong musical traditions (such as Zimbabwe). Or, on the other hand they may have had little or no exposure to music as it was not an acceptable part of their culture (such as in Afghanistan) (QCA 2004).

To use music to its full potential of providing an effective means to value diversity, teachers should:

- involve parents in their children's musical education;
- expose children to a variety of musical styles from a range of cultures, and value the content not just the exotica;
- have instruments from a wide range of cultures available to the children;
- be aware of children's musical backgrounds;
- use examples of rhyme and song from other cultures.

Class

The vast majority of both classical and pop music is predominantly dominated by the middle classes. Therefore, teachers need to be aware of this and take into account the backgrounds of the children, so they do not focus exclusively on the massive resource of the music industry. For example, the classical music industry which is heavily subsidised by public funding but, in reality, is the domain of a relative minority of the public who reside in the upper classes (Paton 1997). A means of overcoming this would be for schools to make use of grass-roots musicians from within the local community. Schools should also aim to allow access for all children, regardless of ability to pay, to provide access to the local authority's music services, such as music lessons. This would be a small, yet significant, stepping stone for any child who wanted a chance to access the selection process regarding music set out by some secondary schools.

Teachers need to be aware of the different backgrounds of the children in their class and the families' perceptions of music, so that these can be recognized and addressed within the music lesson.

Suggested approaches to overcome class barriers:

- Inclusion of grassroots music in teaching
- Provide opportunities for all children to learn an instrument
- Invite a variety of musicians into the school, from within and outside the local community
- Instil within children the ability to value all music.

Ability

Music has a vital role in the education of children with special educational needs (Paton 1997). It is a subject that is accessible to all students, regardless of their literacy and numeracy skills, which are often used as the benchmark for assessing a child's ability. The creative element within music and the focus on musical improvisation removes barriers for those with special educational needs. Teachers need to be aware of and address children's specific needs and differentiate tasks as appropriate. The issues which hinder some children with the written recording of music also need to be addressed – teachers could use photographs, video and recording media to remove these barriers. Music can also provide a valuable outlet for children who experience emotional and behavioural issues. It is important to note that we are not talking in terms of levels of skill but rather in terms of equality of imagination and creativity.

We must not forget the gifted and talented when discussing music and equality. They must be equally challenged and given appropriate opportunities for their increased skill. Achievement of this can be met through looking at the level descriptors within the National Curriculum and working from an appropriate level to further their ability. This is regarded as normal practice in literacy and numeracy, yet is an area that is overlooked in many of the foundation subjects. Teachers must not be scared to use gifted children to enrich the curriculum and their lessons.

Within schools teachers can encompass all abilities by a variety of means;

- Creative use of improvisation
- Provide a range of means to record and evaluate music
- Provide opportunities for the gifted and talented to be stretched.

We have highlighted the main issues facing teachers within primary music. The art of teaching music can never be learnt or conceptualized through print. In reality, it is an art which needs to be practised, experimented with and refined through doing. Teachers should feel confident in moving forward and allowing the creativity of children to be developed. From this overall creative environment a unique classroom culture will be developed.

Resources

This list, far from being exhaustive, is intended to demonstrate the kinds of teaching materials which reflect the principles outlined in this chapter.

- Mantra Lingua – a range of resources, including books, in two languages that could be used in QCA scheme of work Unit 2 'Sounds interesting'. It provides a CD-ROM with multicultural songs and Asian nursery rhymes.
- Musica – the language of our colours – page found on the Arizona State University website. Links to websites that offer information on musical instruments used in different parts of the world.
- www.spirit-staff.co.uk/pakistan.arts.html provides information on Pakistani music, both current and classical.
- *Music Express* – www.acblack.com – although prescriptive it does provide a starting point for teachers and approaches the QCA documents in a different way.
- www.acblack.com – *Mango Spice, Phantasmogoria, Sing for Your Life, The Singing Sack, Tinder Box, Let's go Zudio,* etc. – a resource of songs in all styles and for many cultural and ethnic sources.
- Music QCA – www.standards.dfes.gov.uk/schemes/ – provides lesson plans for Key Stage 1 and 2 which are easily adaptable and accessible to all.
- Two Candles Burn – http://www.twocandles.com/ – this site could be of interest to teachers wanting to use Jewish songs as part of a multicultural approach within their music teaching. It could also be used to link to the teaching of Judaism within RE.
- The Virtual Javanese Gamelan – http://www.gamelannetwork.co.uk/virtual-gamelan.html – these materials offer a full 'hands on' practical exploration of an aspect of music through a 'virtual' environment. It offers a full course of study focused on one of the most joyful forms of Javanese music – the Lancaran.
- www.playmusic.org – musical resource for children and teachers – lots of information, things to listen to, fun activities to do.
- www.bbc.co.uk/radio3/makingtracks/games.shtml – this website is for teachers to use in the classroom with their pupils. It offers a range of music games and composing programs, including opportunities to compose, mix and edit tracks and send them off to the BBC directly. Suitable for children at KS2 upwards.
- www.childrensmusic.co.uk – activities and games to develop the children's musical and listening skills with stories and songs.
- www.kids-space.org – an educational learning site devoted to bringing out the creativity of kids of all ages around the world

Acknowledgement

We would like to thank Martin Milner for his comments on this chapter.

References

Craft, A. (2005) *Creativity in Schools: Tensions and Dilemmas*. London: Routledge.

Freire, P. (2005) *On the Indispensable Qualities of Progressive Teachers for Their Better Performance*. London: Taylor Francis Group.

Held D. (1980) *Introduction to Critical Theory: Horkheimer and Habermas*. Berkeley: University of California Press.

Hennessy, S. (2005) 'Creativity in the Music Curriculum', in A Wilson (ed.), *Creativity in Primary Education*. Exeter: Learning Matters Ltd., pp. 140–154.

Jorgensen, E. (2004) 'Pax Americana and the World of Music Education'. *Journal of Aesthetics Education*, 38, 3: 1–18.

Longhurst, B. (1995) *Popular Music and Society*. Cambridge, UK: Blackwell Publishers.

National Curriculum (1999) *Music: The National Curriculum for England*. London: Department for Education and Employment.

Ofsted (2004) *Provision of Music Services in 15 Local Education Authorities*. London: Ofsted.

Paton, R. (1997) 'Music', in M. Cole, D. Hill and S. Shan (eds), *Equality in Primary School*. London: Cassell. P. 260-287.

Peterson, B. (2004) 'The Power of Songs In the Classroom', in Kelley Dawson Salas, Rita Tenorio, Stephanie Walters, and Dale Weiss (eds) *The New Teacher Book: Finding Purpose, Balance, and Hope During Your First Years in the Classroom*. Milwaukee, WI: Rethinking Schools.

Robinson *et al.* (1999) *All Our Futures: Creativity, Culture and Education*. London: National Advisory Committee on Creative and Cultural Education.

QCA (2004) *Pathways to Learning for New Arrivals-Primary Music*. London: QCA. Available from: http://www.qca.org.uk/qca_7309.aspx

Siraj-Blatchford, I. (1994) *The Early Years: Laying the Foundations for Racial Equality*. Stoke on Trent: Trentham Books Ltd.

Woody, R. (2007) 'Popular Music in School: Remixing the Issues'. *Music Educators Journal*, 93, 4:32–37.

Chapter 14

Physical Education

Emma Whewell and Joanna Hardman

Introduction

This chapter will begin by exploring social inclusion and relate this to physical education (PE). It will then endeavour to explore the issues of equality which arise in PE and will offer practical ideas for combating inequality and promoting a more inclusive approach to teaching and learning in PE.

Social Inclusion

The concept of social inclusion is high on the political agenda and at the core of political planning and development. The Centre for Economic and Social Inclusion (CESI 2002) describes social inclusion as:

> a process by which efforts are made to ensure that everyone, regardless of their experiences and circumstances, can achieve their potential in life. To achieve inclusion income and employment are necessary but not sufficient. An inclusive society is also characterized by a striving for reduced inequalities, a balance between individuals' rights and duties and increased social cohesion.

The current government is focused on developing and achieving social inclusion in the UK, so that **all** individuals have the opportunity to reach their full potential. As highlighted in the National Curriculum Inclusion Statement, 'teachers should aim to give every pupil the opportunity to experience success in learning and to achieve as high a standard as possible' (QCA 1999a:28).

Meeting the unique needs of all individuals is central to inclusive practice. It is interesting to note that 14 years after The Salamanca Statement (UNESCO 1994) which brought to the forefront the principle of 'equality of opportunity' and the 'child-centred' approach, the recent Every Child Matters agenda (DfES 2004a) still actively promotes the concept that each and every child should have the opportunity to learn and develop according to their individual circumstances.

The Every Child Matters agenda (DfES 2004a), highlights the government's commitment to providing a social environment that fosters the well-being of children and caters for all. Pivotal to this policy is the belief that *every* child plays a role in the growth and advancement of society. The main goal of the current government's social inclusion policy is to create a society that evolves around the concepts of equity, inclusion and justice – a society that is embracing of all; one that is socially inclusive. If this social inclusion policy is to be actively promoted then individual differences need to be embraced and recognized. This can only be done if *all* individuals in society have a basic understanding of each individual's needs and act as advocates for each other.

In September 2002, 'citizenship' was introduced as a curriculum area on the National Curriculum, with the aim that pupils would 'become informed, active, responsible citizens contributing fully to the life of their school communities' (QCA 1999a:126). The QCA suggest that pupils should learn about 'their responsibilities, rights and duties as individuals and members of communities' (QCA 1999a:126). According to Laker (2000:92) PE has the potential to fulfil these QCA objectives since it is:

> ... a subject of expanded boundaries and possibilities. Those possibilities include the promotion of responsibility, the encouragement of personal development and a contribution to the education of a community of global citizens.

For young people to be 'global citizens' they need to be able to celebrate diversity. PE provides a vast array of opportunities to embrace, explore and understand different cultures. Dance is a required activity that has to be taught at Key Stage 1 and 2 of the primary PE curriculum. Dance and music have long been a part of many cultures and can promote a shared understanding of each other, through emotion, expression and communication. For example, in dance, Bhangra and the world of 'Bollywood', line dancing, Latin dancing, medieval dance and Scottish country dancing can all be introduced. Using movement to tell stories provides an opportunity to explore history and culture. Inviting dancers or story tellers from the local community to perform or use their stories as a stimulus for dance, for example, Gypsy storytellers, or myths and legends associated with African dance, can promote an understanding of different cultures and begin to break down barriers.

Addressing personal and global issues through dance is also a strong way of exploring how events such as war and famine can impact countries and individuals. A wide range of stimuli which reflect the impact of war (such as video, sculpture, art, clothing, poems and musical instruments) could be used as stimuli for creative dance. This form of critical pedagogy allows us to move beyond acknowledgment and tolerance of diversity, challenges the forces which maintain the status quo and can act as a starting point to clarify personal ethics, morals and values (see Hill 2009 in this volume, 2010; McLaren 2005; McLaren and Rikowski 2006).

PE can also challenge socially constructed views on beauty, appearance and ability. It is important to raise awareness of the subconscious prejudice that may take place towards people who look 'different' to these rules. *How* individuals react to each other can be affected by pre-conceived perceptions and bogus stereotypes, be they related to an individual's gender, race, (dis)ability, class, and so on. Groves (cited in Williams 1989) notes that both teachers and pupils exclude disabled children because they perceive them as incapable or they are worried that they will get hurt. The main focus of concern may be on the medical condition of the individual (disability), rather than what they can do (ability). This challenges one of the basic premises of inclusive education; that each individual should be valued and respected.

Care should also be taken not to categorize pupils; for example, black children as either sprinters or long distance runners, tall children as high jumpers, bigger children competing in throwing events; all assumptions and misconceptions that a teacher may bring with them into the classroom.

The National Curriculum Guidelines

Inherent in each of the review processes of the National Curriculum is the notion that the concept of inclusion is a central feature that informs and underpins practice. This is evident in the statutory statement for inclusion that was included for the first time in the National Curriculum in 2000 (QCA 1999a). The statement aims to address and promote fairness and justice in the delivery of education in schools. Three principles for inclusion are emphasized:

A) Setting suitable learning challenges
B) Responding to pupils' diverse learning needs
C) Overcoming potential barriers to learning and assessment for individuals and groups of pupils

(QCA 1999a:28)

The statement indicates that teachers have a duty to include all individuals in the learning process. For teachers to adopt a humanistic approach to learning they need to emphasize the development of the 'whole' person, encourage personal growth and awareness, and young people need to be provided with a range of opportunities to make responsible choices (Kyriacou 1997).

The Position of PE in the Primary Curriculum

PE employs a unique place in the primary National Curriculum in that it is 'the only area of learning that focuses on the body, its constituent parts, and the development of its movement potential' (Price 2008:2). Children can function in a PE environment without the need for language, indeed in the case of English as an Additional Language (EAL) a student's language can be accelerated by the notion that each action or skill they perform has a word associated with it (Kirk 2005). This can be valuable, allowing contact and communication with their peers, and pupils can be recognized for their skills and achievements, thus celebrating their abilities. The same can be said for young people with dyslexia; PE can provide an avenue for the expression of thoughts and feelings through physical movement.

PE also offers the opportunity for developing social, cognitive and affective skills that contribute to every child's health and well-being. Capel (2007:494) argues that one of the most important reasons for physical education '... is its unique contribution to the development of motor skills (particularly gross motor skills) ... and that ... recently the government has identified an important role for physical education in raising pupils' attainment and as a tool for whole school improvement.'

The Structure of the PE Curriculum

The National Curriculum seeks to offer a range of activities that promote a broad and balanced curriculum for all children in England and Wales between the ages of 5 and 16. At Key Stage 1, PE is taught via three programmes of study (dance, games and gymnastic activities) and at Key Stage 2 these have been extended into six programmes of study (games, gymnastics, dance, swimming and water safety, athletic activities and outdoor and adventurous activities). Within these programmes of study are four strands which allow learning on a developmental spectrum:

- Acquiring and developing skills – learning skills in isolation and building up a catalogue to use
- Selecting and applying skills – picking from their experience/catalogue depending upon the situation/challenge
- Evaluating and improving skills – evaluating the decision(s) made and challenging future decisions
- Key understandings for health – underlying and promoting the importance of a healthy and active lifestyle and lifelong learning.

The four strands have made a welcome change from the emphasis on performance (although still a part of the PE curriculum), as success can be recognized in many other ways, such as verbalizing your learning, evaluating your decisions, and interacting with other children. This challenges the idea that those who 'can do' are more worthwhile than those who cannot. By further questioning the content, knowledge, skills and understanding that are 'worthwhile', the curriculum reform represents a real opportunity to radicalize our primary PE pedagogy. Though critical theory has been explored throughout education in PE, there has been a lack of 'practical activism'. As Cuplan *et al.* (2007:3) highlight, 'critical pedagogy has emancipation and social justice at its central aims'. PE allows the building of cultural capital through reverence of the most able, is associated with clothing and footwear which are manufactured in developing countries, with concerns raised about 'poverty-level wages, forced overtime, no union rights, sexual harassment, excessively long working hours, child labour and poor health, and illness associated with working conditions' (Cuplan *et al.* 2007:3). Is this knowledge deemed 'worthwhile' enough to allow teachers to challenge learners in their class to question these practices and empower young people to consider social change and a critical approach to consumerism? Clearly curriculum content should never be devoid of context.

Since the review of the curriculum in 2000, teachers and schools have greater autonomy in selecting the medium of delivery and the content of the curriculum. The primary curriculum is currently undergoing a review aimed at designing a curriculum which 'promotes challenging subject teaching alongside equally challenging cross-curricular studies' (Rose 2008:5). PE is expected to fall under the umbrella of 'Understanding Physical Health and Well-Being'. The review takes into account the success of the early years foundation stage work, by developing a more flexible and up-to-date curriculum that moves away from the traditional 'activity centred approach' to a more 'child centred approach', that emphasizes the ethos of current educational principles – personalized learning. The 2020 Vision report (DfES 2006b), highlights that personalized education is seen as the central component in the development of modern schools in England.

By teaching children transferable basic skills (run, twist, throw, kick, catch, balance, strike), which can be used in a variety of different activities (cricket, rounders, rugby, handball, lacrosse, athletics), and other areas of the national curriculum, can improve confidence and limit motor elitism which exists in environments where physical prowess and athleticism are revered. Practices which 'also endorse competition, elitism and the privileging of winning and 'winners' ... normalize the domination of the curriculum by sports and games, where competition is used to structure activity and guide focus to the acquisition of techniques, skills and attributes associated with speed, strength and aggression.' (Garret 2007:27). Making the context less important and placing more emphasis on the skills will develop confidence and movement competence. It may also be worth considering exploring different games. For instance, some immigrants from Eastern Europe may be more familiar with games such as volleyball or handball, others such as Central American people may be more familiar with basketball and baseball.

The Role of the Teacher in Promoting Equality in Primary PE

According to the QCA (1999a:3), every child is to be provided with 'the chance to succeed, whatever their individual needs ...' but teachers need to recognize that political ideology is just the starting point in the development of inclusive practice. The process in which teachers unpack, translate and ultimately transfer policy into practice is crucial. Teachers are in fact 'key agents' in this process of change due to their role as facilitators of learning. The value that teachers place on including everyone in PE is vital in regards to the successful implementation of inclusive practice in PE. As facilitators of learning, teachers play a significant role in the development of an inclusive and equitable learning environment, and ultimately the personal development of each pupil. The stance or viewpoint that the teacher takes towards inclusive practice in PE will ultimately be affected by *how* they see and value each individual they are responsible for, and *how* they value PE as a curriculum subject.

To foster concrete foundations for inclusive PE environment, teachers need to recognize and appreciate the philosophical underpinnings of inclusion:

– The creation of an enabling environment

- The responsibility to meet all individual needs
- Recognizing and celebrating individuality and diversity
- Recognizing the right of all individuals
- Promoting equity and excellence for all
- Valuing and respecting the dignity of all individuals
- Providing suitable challenges for all, within an appropriate context.

Research by Dagkas (2007:434) further emphasizes the impact that teachers can have on cultural pluralism by '... their own modeling of positive attitudes, for example by greeting students in their native language or pronouncing names correctly'. Critical pedagogy aims to empower groups and individuals – to raise consciousness is not enough; 'for authentic change to occur at all levels of society, empowerment must incorporate change at institutional and social structural levels as well as change at the level of individuals and groups' (Kirk 2006:257). This means going beyond samosas, sombreros and saris to elicit a deeper understanding of cultures and faith.

Planning for Inclusion

If teachers are to actively engage in the inclusion process in PE and are to be proactive in accepting and implementing the principles of the statutory statement, then they need to consider:

A) *how* they set suitable learning challenges (by extending opportunities for all children)

B) *how* they respond to the diverse learning needs of pupils (through the adoption of a flexible approach)

C) *how* they enable all individuals to participate in the educational process (through the removal of existing barriers for all children).

(Adapted from the QCA 2007b)

A) Setting suitable learning challenges – extending opportunities

The statutory inclusion statement (QCA 2007b) highlights that it is the responsibility of teachers to promote and extend the learning opportunities available to **all** children, so that they have the opportunity to reach their potential:

When planning, teachers should set high expectations and provide opportunities for all pupils to achieve, including ... pupils from all social and cultural backgrounds, pupils of different ethnic groups including travellers, refugees and asylum seekers and those from diverse linguistic backgrounds.

(QCA Teaching Refugees and Asylum Seekers available at
http://www.qca.org.uk/qca_7281.aspx)

This can only be achieved by adopting a pedagogy that considers the diversity of the learners, while at the same time extends their knowledge and motivates them to perform to the best of their ability. There needs to be an element of flexibility in curriculum planning, and barriers to learning need to be removed in order for each individual to be extended and motivated to reach their potential. For example, when planning activities that are accessible for wheelchair users and mobility-impaired pupils think about:

- Seated throws, kneeling throws, standing throws
- 'Running' – view this as a means getting from A–B and open to interpretation
- Use modified equipment such as ramps instead of hurdles
- Plan 'alternative' athletic activities
- Encourage individual endeavour.

B) Responding to the diverse learning needs of pupils – increasing flexibility

Responding to the diverse learning needs of pupils requires thought and preparation. Teachers need to be flexible in their approach to learning and they need to be able to adapt and differentiate their lessons so that all pupils have the opportunity to perform to the best of their ability. When teaching a PE lesson to mixed ability pupils, teachers may want to consider incorporating elements of the STEP process (Haskin 2005) to ensure that all individuals are able to participate at the level they feel comfortable at.

The STEP principle encourages teachers to think about the way they adapt:

- the **S**PACE they are working in,
- the **T**ASK at hand,
- the **E**QUIPMENT the pupils might be using, and
- the **P**EOPLE who might be involved in the task.

For example, when teaching a football session to Year 6 girls of mixed ability, with a focus on heading the ball, the teacher may let the less confident girls work in a grid on their own (Space), where they practise individually, getting used to the ball and making contact with the ball on their forehead (Task). Meanwhile the more confident girls work in pairs in a grid, throwing the ball to each other and heading it back (Task and People). Pupils could choose the type of ball that they wanted to work with, for example, a soft ball or a football (Equipment), encouraging those less confident pupils to complete the task correctly, rather than worrying about making contact with a hard football.

According to Bailey (2001), the key to effective adaptation and differentiation is planning and commitment. Ensuring that all individuals in the class are included and individual needs are incorporated and accounted for does not mean that individual lessons should be planned for each and every young person. It might be the case that schools adopt 'one strong inclusive plan' (DfES 2006b), which enables teachers to account for individual differences, allows all children to engage in the activity, recognizes where and when support is needed and provides opportunities for individual choice. The parallel approach in the

Inclusion Spectrum (Stevenson and Black 1999) is a good example of this. In a mixed ability PE lesson, for example, it might be appropriate to split the class into smaller groups where children of similar ability work together to solve a specific learning objective. The whole class work towards a common goal (for example, spatial awareness in football) but they are involved in activities which are designed at different levels so that the needs of all individuals are met and any barriers to learning are removed. This process can be difficult to supervise since there is so much going on and it requires a range of equipment. In the long run, however, all pupils have the opportunity to access the activity at a level that they are comfortable with, and they also have the opportunity to progress into another group.

It is important to stress, however, that the process of adaptation is in itself flexible, in that it is a dynamic, multi-faceted process, which is always evolving. The young person is pivotal in the adaptation process and they need to be seen as key instigators in the promotion of personalized learning. Young people should be involved in the actual planning and shaping of their learning environment so that they recognize and appreciate their role in the learning process. They need to confront challenges to their learning and reflect on their learning process, so that they can suggest improvements to the process, thus encouraging pathways that promote the opportunity for success and progression. This recognition of 'personalized learning' (QCA 2007b) emphasizes the point 'every child will matter ... no child is to be left behind' (Rayner 2007:193).

This approach goes hand-in-hand with inclusive practice, in that the needs of the individuals are the quintessence characteristic of both. Rayner (2007) suggests that by moving towards personalized education 'schools are urged to begin by acknowledging that giving every single child the chance to be the best they can be, whatever their talent or background, is not compromising standards' (Rayner 2007:192).

The Qualification and Curriculum Authority (QCA) schemes of work (www.standards.dfes.gov.uk) can go a long way to assist with planning age- and developmentally-appropriate activities for PE lessons. They are clear in their expectations and give guidance about what 'most' children will be able to achieve by the end of that unit of work by use of a 'core task'. They offer extension and inclusion tasks for 'some' children to assist in differentiation within that activity and suggest that you can step up a unit or down a unit if children require further differentiation. The core tasks act as a starting point and offer a much-needed baseline of expectation and equality of opportunity. When delving deeper than curriculum content, it is important to question the messages the curriculum delivers in relation to context. A more holistic approach to delivery sees the potential to address the meaning behind physical activity, the importance of exercise, how children can use and view their bodies and how sport influences and reproduces power relations and privileges dominant groups in society' (Cuplan *et al.* 2007:5).

C) Enabling all individuals to participate – removing barriers

Even though the statutory inclusion statement was introduced in 2000, two years later the Audit Commission identified that there were still a number of challenges that impacted and acted as barriers to learning for young people with special educational needs, including:

- waiting too long to have their needs met
- being turned away because staff felt that they were not fully equipped to meet the wide range of needs
- special schools were unsure of their role
- variations in terms of support for families with children with disabilities.

(Audit Commission 2002)

This highlights the fact that although government policy recognized the need for a formal inclusion statement in the National Curriculum, barriers to learning still existed in schools.

Work by Ennis suggests that ' no curriculum in physical education has been as effective in constraining and alienating girls as that found in co-educational, multi-activity sports classes' (Ennis 1999:32). For many cultures, communal nakedness and modesty can be an anxiety for the child and the family. Some gypsy cultures and religious and ethnic cultures forbid undressing in public (Clark 2004), which raises issues about the practicalities of changing for PE. How can schools ensure adequate privacy (AfPE 2007a) and what arrangements can be put in place for cultures where communal nakedness is forbidden? Teachers need to be flexible and may need to consider making alternative options available for changing areas; modesty panels in changing rooms will provide privacy (Marley 2007), or full-length cloaks under which children can undress, may be a solution (AfPE 2007a).

Single gender classes may help to relieve anxieties, but in swimming lessons this is often unrealistic due to use of public swimming facilities. In this case, a discussion with the family and child about flexibility in swimming attire will be required. Perhaps for some Muslim girls, and for any pupils with low body image, discussions around body stockings or some other lightweight method of covering the arms and legs without hindering their progress may be necessary.

Having a 'PE day' where the pupils in your class come to school that day in the school PE kit eliminates changing issues but does little to tackle the concerns about hygiene!

Issues to Consider when Addressing the Principles of Inclusion in PE Lessons

Time

Since its introduction, the PESSCL Strategy, now PESSYP, has been improving the quality and provision of PE and school sport, with the intention of ensuring that children aged 5–16 were receiving two hours of high-quality PE and school sport. Are we, however, meeting these statutory requirements? This is an entitlement, but is it truly inclusive and accessible? Atkinson and Black (2006) concluded that only 50 per cent of the young people involved in a study ($n = 230$) that investigated the experiences of young disabled people participating in PE, school sport and extracurricular activities in Leicestershire and Rutland received the recommended time for PE (two hours per week). Considering this study was completed 18 years after the implementation of the ERA (that emphasized the point that all young people are entitled to access education) the issue that 50 per cent of the young people in this area are not receiving their entitlement of two hours of PE a week is worrying.

In many cases the requirement to meet two hours per week has meant a reduction in curriculum time for PE in preference of school sport. The five hour offer continues to promote physical activity but remains rooted in the school sport element of the PESSYP strategy. What role do extracurricular activities play in promoting equality in primary PE?

Extracurricular Activities

Will increasing the amount of extracurricular provision really improve access to the children already isolated from accessing it, or is it more of the same for the most privileged? This might well depend on the nature of activities that are offered after school and the purpose of these activities – are they to recruit for school teams or are they activities that promote lifelong physical activity? 'Allocating more time to physical activity does not take into account the limited social, educational and economic resources of lower income youth' (Azzarito *et al.* 2005:42)

Extracurricular clubs and community clubs can discriminate against those children whose families cannot finance transport or club/class fees such as, for example, the children of unemployed or low-paid parents, or refugee children. Social background, gender, ethnicity/'race', religion, and disability have a huge influence on a child's early experience of sport. Kirk (2005) highlights that white middle-class children are over-represented in club sport and, alongside, tradition suggests that the ability to pay for fees, transport and kit and flexibility of working hours can influence access. Kirk (2005) suggests that access to quality school experiences and sports clubs is limited to certain sectors of the population. Disabled children, groups of lower socio-economic status and girls miss out on quality physical activity and learning in comparison to able-bodied children, children from a higher socio-economic status and boys. Where possible, the school should consider clubs with no financial implication, perhaps at lunch-time or break-time, and have a supply of second-hand kit or equipment to be used if required. Building up a network of parents/carers who can provide a car-sharing team to help with transport to fixtures/clubs, or to act as volunteer helpers, can also increase access.

Use of extracurricular, break-time, breakfast activities and physical activity interventions, because of their voluntary nature, are not accessible to every child. Providing clubs which take place at the end of the school day may have implications for pupils who have family or religious commitments. Such issues highlight the need to have a flexible approach to the curriculum, accepting that, for example, during Ramadan, a child who is fasting would find vigorous physical activity exhausting.

Transport

Children with special educational needs for whom transport is provided by the Local Education Authority (LEA) may find it difficult to access after-school provision as their bus or taxi may leave immediately after school or early. Clubs which run at lunch- or break-times can provide an important informal social situation to interact with peers. Working with the LEA and transport team about flexibility of pick-up times may also allow after-school clubs to be attended and provide an opportunity to further develop skills and confidence.

Media

The media also play a large part in the misrepresentation of women and minority groups in sport. Women will find themselves largely appraised as a sex object rather than an athlete, thus marginalizing certain sports and groups. For example, due to this misrepresentation, you may be inclined to think that every Asian athlete is a badminton player or martial arts expert because of what they are normally portrayed as doing.

PE Kit

The AfPE (2008b) guidelines suggest that young people's clothing should be 'safe, suitable and comfortable' when participating in PE. With increasing concerns about body image in young girls, it is important to consider that participating in shorts and t-shirt may be upsetting for an obese child or one with poor body image. With this in mind, schools could be flexible in their approach to kit requirements, allowing tracksuit bottoms and sweatshirts to cover limbs and shoulders. Schools should try not to dictate kit which conforms to gender stereotyping, or which differentiates between boys and girls. Supplying kit with the school emblem can reduce the 'branded kit' which may be inaccessible to families with a low socio-economic status. Recent increases in supermarket clothing ranges means that school uniforms are more affordable and an option for many schools.

Jewellery

Removal of jewellery is recommended for safety reasons (AfPE 2008b) for the child and other participants. However, this may cause upset if one considers removal of the 'Kara' (bangle) in the Sikh religion; hence it can be taped over.

Curricular Activities

The National Curriculum for PE has been dominated by games, particularly those games deemed 'traditional', such as netball, hockey, rugby and football. A child who has not experienced these may be unfamiliar with these games and their concepts and struggle to engage with them.

The largely individual nature of athletics makes it a situation where individual skill and endeavour can be praised. Encourage children to evaluate and improve their own performance and not compare themselves with others in the group.

Outdoor and adventurous activities have much to offer pupils in terms of self-esteem and confidence. Activities which have a perception of risk can challenge pupils to use their thinking skills as much as their physical skills and place equal emphasis on process as outcome. Much of the outdoor and adventurous curriculum (orientation, problem solving and communication) can be adapted for pupils with physical difficulties. Initiatives such as the RYA 'Sailability' programme (see useful resources) are making progress in providing accessible and challenging activities for disabled learners. There are many opportunities to experience perceived risk and personal challenge within the setting of a primary school which may be much more accessible and can fulfil the curriculum requirements.

Schools may choose to complement their outdoor and adventurous curriculum by arranging a residential experience at an activity centre. Although this is likely to provide a quality, safe experience, it can raise issues associated with cost; having a scheme where trips can be paid for in monthly stages may lighten the financial load. Similarly, schools may have funds in reserve to assist in such cases or make use of grants or Big Lottery schemes. Teachers and their unions need to push hard for a massive increase in subsidized funding for residential centres.

Dietary requirements, prayer, access and medication are all issues that may need to be addressed and can have implications on staffing, time and funding. Every child, however, stands to gain a great deal from an experience away from home at an activity centre. Organizing 'parents meetings' to discuss and voice issues may help parents to see the value of such a venture and can help with any concerns by exploring the rigorous health and safety procedures which outdoor centres have to undertake to receive AALA (Adventure Activities Licensing Authority) recognition.

Outdoor and adventurous activities, by the nature of the curriculum content, do much to raise awareness of the environment the sports are conducted in and begin to challenge some of the practices which damage or pollute the local environment or on a more global scale. Talking about footpath erosion when walking, leaving litter, disturbing nesting birds when climbing; mountain biking, quad/trail biking and off-road driving damaging the tracks and bridleways they use. Golf courses represent gluttony in using natural resources, water, fertilizer and machines to maintain the look of a golf course (Fernandez-Balboa 1997); can the use of so much water be justified when globally some populations cannot access clean water? The effect of the fertilizers on flora and fauna is vast and run off from the courses will pollute water supplies in the locality.

Swimming is a part of the PE National Curriculum which causes schools many anxieties and throughout the United Kingdom there is an inequality of provision, in the most part stemming from access and training issues. Fulfilling the statutory requirements at Key Stage 2 is a difficult and ongoing issue, which challenges schools' budgets, timetables and staff. Rural dwellers and schools far from swimming facilities often suffer the most problems and time travelling is often longer than the time spent in the pool.

Swimming also highlights very obvious differences in ability; this is the case where children who can access swimming lessons will demonstrate more capability and confidence in the water. Groups in swimming need to be effectively differentiated to stretch the most able and support children who are beginners and non-swimmers. Providing suitably trained staff to meet the needs of all individuals can be costly.

Children with mobility impairment will find swimming beneficial and therapeutic, and hydrotherapy is often used in special schools to take the strain off joints and use the sensation of floating to aid movement development. This, however, has obvious implications for the support required in changing, getting in and out, and support in the water. Appreciation for each individual case and discussion with the LEA and Special Educational Needs Coordinator (SENCO) will explore issues of funding and support available. The severity of the disability will influence the extent to which the child can participate. But this can be established in discussion with parents, carers and the child. Swimming is particularly helpful for children with dyspraxia as it is a combination of repetitive movements that are predictable.

Gender and Sexualities

PE is an environment where heterosexuality and aggression has long been regarded as normal, if not compulsory; this has marginalized non-heterosexual identities and can further fuel discrimination on the basis of an individual's or group's sexual orientation. Lesbianism still impacts negatively on women's sport where a woman's sexuality is still questioned if she participates in classically 'male' sports such as rugby, football and boxing. The same discrimination (for men) is often seen in sports such as dance and gymnastics. Even when women compete on separate levels there is an implicit male standard to which they are compared. Scores, distances, times, heights and weights are recorded and compared, leading to claims of superiority. Garret (2007) builds upon this and argues that physical ability and being 'sporty' are determined by 'biology, gender, ethnicity and class', arguing that where 'race, sexuality, low socio-economic status and disability are significant factors students can be multiply marginalized, excluded and even alienated from physical education and sport' (Garret 2007:27). The physical nature of sport gives it special significance because of the fundamental link between social power, cultural capital and physical force.

An unconsidered statement or jibe can serve to reinforce stereotypes. PE provides an important context in which social stereotypes can be challenged. For example, the use of words and phrases such as 'sissy', 'throwing like girls' or 'big girls' blouse' is unacceptable. Schools can employ methods which confront, challenge and dismiss misconceptions of boys' athletic superiority or girls' inferiority. In theory, a mixed group should suit the diverse learning needs and interests of all students irrespective of gender. In reality, it often results in the space being dominated by some boys. McCaughtry (2006) suggests that sports such as dance, gym, aerobics, self-paced fitness and non-competitive activities meet the needs, interests and backgrounds of girls, whereas competition can alienate girls and low-skilled boys.

Some traditional dances require male and female partners; this does not have to be the case and can be overcome by using numbers one and two. Use both male and female pupils to demonstrate their work and feedback on all aspects of performance such as grace, suppleness, and empathy, encouraging them to watch and listen to each other. By its very nature, dance is a form of expression, is open to interpretation and can provide an open-ended, creative environment. It can challenge issues of stereotyping in relation to masculinity and femininity by using male and female role models, pictures and workshops and actively challenge preconceptions.

Risner (2007) in a study of masculinity and dance '... suggests various kinds of prevailing social stigma, including narrow definitions of masculinity, heterosexist justifications for males in dance, and internalized homophobia in the field' (Risner 2007:139)

Challenging views on stereotyping and gender bias and having a lively, modern and accessible curriculum will begin to change attitudes. 'While dance in many cultures has been, and continues to be viewed as an appropriate 'male' activity, the Western European cultural paradigm situates dance as primarily a 'female' art form,' (Risner 2007:140)

Gymnastics has, in the past, been subject to gender stereotyping. Challenging these views of girls and boys is a vital element of a safe and supportive learning environment. There is an emphasis on the aesthetic side of gymnastics, but this quality is achieved not only through flexibility and grace, but also through strength and power – all qualities which are equally achievable for boys and girls.

Outdoor and adventurous activities remain one of the few areas of the physical education curriculum which are relatively free from gender bias. There are male and female role models from adventure sports who show tenacity, perseverance and dedication in pursuit of their goals.

Assessment

Assessment in PE can cause anxiety or concern for staff and students. Lack of clarity or understanding of the levels of attainment, teacher confidence and training, and the largely subjective way that PE is assessed can make assessment in PE challenging. It is important to communicate success criteria with pupils and, in some cases, parents. Involving the parents further reinforces the communication channels and allows them to voice any concerns or raise questions about their child's PE, for example, teaching style, curriculum content and facilities.

It is important to be clear about the aims and objectives of lessons, refer to the levels of attainment or P scales and the task set. Using videos to show and explain the process and to reinforce a visual demonstration, or working with peers in a supportive environment, can boost confidence. Setting clear criteria for quality, time, and expectations and providing assessment opportunities over a range of contexts and time, and making the assessment process a two-way process to ensure the child understands and is comfortable with what they are being asked to do, are all helpful.

Strategies for Promoting Equality in Primary PE

The demands and needs of all children are wide ranging and quite individual. This section provides some general strategies for promoting inclusive practice in primary PE:

- Allow young people sufficient time to absorb instructions and complete work set, checking regularly for understanding.
- Use clear and achievable success criteria which are displayed throughout the lesson.
- Feedback on success criteria should be individualized and achievable to develop listening and communication skills.
- Adopt a flexible approach to your curriculum content, equipment and organization.
- Be realistic and clear in demands and rules.
- Challenge unacceptable behaviour by using a positive behaviour management approach.
- Keep instructions short and to the point and accompany them with a visual demonstration, cue card or sign.
- Break skills down, identify basic movements and tackle these one at a time.
- Place emphasis on effort, fun and participation.
- Establish a set routine for the start and end of activity/lesson so recognized patterns, are introduced.
- Use both boys and girls to demonstrate work – stereotypical views are challenged.
- Praise creativity and innovation – develop self-esteem and encourage freedom of interpretation, expression and ownership.
- Be sensitive to issues surrounding contact between children – in some cultures physical contact is discouraged.
- Displays, video and pictures of both male and female role models – dispel myths and stereotypes about gender and body shape.
- Develop good links with local junior teams and clubs – encourage progression into the community.
- Think carefully when picking teams and partners. Use innovative techniques to group young people (deck of cards, stickers, warm-up games, etc).

Conclusion

PE is both a diverse and specialist subject with much to offer in terms of individual and group development. It can provide cohesion and vibrancy in a school and local community, instilling passion and lifelong commitment to health and well-being, and individual and team success. Quality and innovative teaching in the field can have significant impacts on the schools and the individuals within it. Critical pedagogy in PE can go beyond creating a sensitive and equitable learning environment and begin to challenge the status quo, learning that what matters is learning that engages understanding and is an agent for change. Without challenging stereotypes, assumptions and prejudice change will not happen. Providing children with the skill to look beyond what they are presented with on the surface, to ask questions and explore issues with a socio-cultural critique will represent a step change in the learning and values behind that learning.

Acknowledgement

We would like to thank Northamptonshire primary schoolteacher Kate Blackmore for her comments on and contribution to this chapter.

Resources and Useful Addresses

The Dyspraxia Foundation – www.dyspraxiafoundation.org.uk/
Physical Literacy website – www.physical-literacy.org
The National Curriculum online – http://curriculum.qca.org.uk/
The Youth Sports Trust – www.youthsporttrust.org/
The Physical Education QCA schemes of work– www.qca.org.uk/pess/
The Healthy Schools website – www.healthyschools.gov.uk
The Paralympics website – www.paralympic.org
Cerebral Palsy Sport England – www.cpsport.org
Disabled Sailing/'Sailability'– www.disabledsailing.org
Safe Routes to Schools – www.saferoutestoschools.org
School Travel Plans – www.saferoutesinfo.org
QCA Physical Education Schemes – www.standards.dfes.gov.uk/schemes2/phe/?view = get

References

AfPE (2007a) *Guidance on changing in primary schools*. Online at www.afpe.org.uk (Accessed June 2007).
AfPE (2008b) *Safe Practice in Physical Education and School Sport*. Leeds: Coachwise.
Audit Commission (2002) *Special Educational Needs: A Mainstream Issue*. London: HMSO.
Atkinson, H. and Black, K. (2006) *The Experiences of Young Disabled People participating in PE, School Sport and Extra-curricular Activities in Leicester-Shire and Rutland*. Loughborough University: Peter Harrison Centre for Disability Sport.
Azzatrito, L. and Solomon, M. (2005) 'A reconceptualization of physical education: the intersection of gender/race/social class', *Sport Education and Society*, 10, (1), 25–47.
Bailey, R. (2001) *Teaching Physical Education: A Handbook for Primary & Secondary School Teachers*. London: Kogan Page.
Capel, S. (2007) 'Moving beyond physical education subject knowledge to develop knowledgeable teachers of the subject', *Curriculum Journal*, 18, (4), 493–507.
Clark, S. (2004) *Travelers*. Online at www.tes.co.uk (Accessed on 27th November 2007).
Cuplan, I. and Bruce, J. (2007) 'New Zealand Physical Education and Critical Pedagogy: Refocusing the Curriculum', *International Journal of Sport and Health Science*, 5, 1–11. Online at www.soc.nii.ac.jp/jspe3/index.htm (Accessed 22nd January 2009).
CESI (Centre for Economic and Social Inclusion) (2002) *Social Inclusion*. Online at http://www.cesi.org.uk (Accessed 11th January 2009).
Dagkas, S. (2007) 'Exploring teaching practices in physical education with culturally

diverse classes: a cross-cultural study', *European Journal of Teacher Education*, 30, (4), 431–443.

DfES (Department for Education and Skills) (2004a) *Every Child Matters*. HMSO: London.

DfES (Department for Education and Skills) (2006b) *Report of the teaching and learning in 2020 review group*. Online at http://www.teachernet.gov.uk (Accessed 11th January 2009).

Ennis, C. D. (1999) 'Creating a culturally relevant curriculum for disengaged girls', *Sport Education and Society*, 4, 41–49.

Fernandez-Balboa, J. (1997) *Critical Postmodernism in Human Movement, Physical Education, and Sport: Rethinking the Profession*. New York: SUNY Press.

Garret, R. and Wrench, A. (2007) 'Physical experiences: Primary student teachers conceptions of sport and physical education', *Physical Education and Sport Pedagogy*, 12, 23–42.

Haskin, D. (2005) *TOP Play and TOP Sport Handbook*. Loughborough: Youth Sport Trust.

Hill, D. (2009) 'Theorizing Politics and the Curriculum: Understanding and Addressing Inequalities through Critical Pedagogy and Critical Policy Analysis', in D. Hill and L. Helavaara Robertson (eds) *Equality in the Primary School: Promoting good practice across the curriculum*. London: Continuum.

Hill, D. (2010) 'Critical Pedagogy, Revolutionary Critical Pedagogy and Socialist Education', in S. Macrine, P. McLaren and D. Hill (eds) *Critical Pedagogy: Theory and Praxis*. London: Routledge.

Kirk, D. (2005) 'Physical Education, youth sport and lifelong participation: the importance of early learning experiences', *European Physical Education Review*, 11, (3), 239–255.

Kirk, D. (2006) 'Sport Education, Critical Pedagogy, and Learning Theory: Toward an Intrinsic Justification for Physical Education and Youth Sport', *Quest*, 58, 255–264.

Kyriacou, C. (1997) *Effective Teaching in Schools* (2nd edition). London: Stanley Thomas.

Laker, A. (2000) *Beyond the Boundaries of Physical Education: Educating young people for citizenship and social responsibility*. London: Routledge.

Marley, D. (2007) *Different strokes for different folks*. Online at www.tes.co.uk (Accessed 16th January 2008).

McCaughtry, N. (2006) 'Working politically among professional knowledge landscapes to implement gender sensitive physical education reform'. *Physical Education and Sport Pedagogy*, 11, (2), 159–179.

McLaren, P. (2005) *Capitalists and Conquerors: Critical Pedagogy Against Empire*. Lanham, MD: Rowman and Littlefield.

McLaren, P. and Rikowski, G. (2006) 'Critical Pedagogy Reloaded: An Interview with Peter McLaren (interviewed by Glenn Rikowski)', *Information for Social Change*, 23, (summer). Online at http://libr.org/isc/issues/ISC23/C3%20Peter%20McLaren.pdf

Price, L. (2008) 'The Importance of physical education in primary schools', in I. Pickup, L. Price, J. Shaughnessy, J. Spence and M. Trace (eds) *Learning to Teach Primary PE*. Exeter: Learning Matters.

QCA (Qualifications Curriculum Authority) (1999a), *The National Curriculum Handbook for Secondary Teachers in England*. London: QCA.

QCA (Qualifications Curriculum Authority) (2007b) *Teaching Refugees and Asylum Seekers*. Online at http://www.qca.org.uk/qca_7281.aspx (Accessed 6th February 2009).

Rayner, S. (2007) *Managing Special and Inclusive Education*. London: Sage.

Risner, D. (2007) 'Rehearsing masculinity: challenging the "boy code" in dance education', *Research in Dance Education* 8, (2), 139–153.

Rose, J. (2008) *The Independent Review of the Primary Curriculum: Interim Report*. Online at http://publications.teachernet.gov.uk (Accessed 26th December 2008).

Stevenson, P. and Black, K. (1999) *Including Disabled Pupils in Physical Education –Primary Module*. Manchester: EFDS (The English Federation of Disability Sport).

UNESCO (United Nations Educational, Scientific and Cultural Organization) (1994) *The Salamanca Statement and Framework for Action on Special Needs Education*. Salamanca: UNESCO.

Vickerman, P. (2007) *Teaching Physical Education to Children with Special Educational Needs*. London: Routledge.

Williams, A. (1989) 'PE in a multicultural context', *Issues in Physical Education for the Primary Years*. London: Falmer.

Chapter 15

Design and Technology

Jen Smyth and Steve Smyth

Introduction

Design and Technology (D&T) in early years settings and primary schools is one of the most liberating subjects on the curriculum. For teachers who believe in active learning and social constructivism – in terms that all learners construct their own knowledge frameworks in response to their environment and culture, and in interaction with others – D&T should be both exemplification and beacon. It is all about the *process of making*, creating something new, unique and personal, and for many learners this taps into their intrinsic motivation and excitement. It is about critical thinking and problem solving, such as making a vehicle of a right size and type to transport the class mascot, or making props for the school stage and the annual school play. It is about egg boxes and other recyclable materials, about glue, balsawood, straws, balloons and rolls and rolls of sellotape, but in essence it is much more than this. It is about creativity for its own sake – making a huge tower like Big Ben (a famous London landmark) simply because it is so fascinating – or about being able to identify a need and then working towards a solution. It does not depend on achievement in literacy or numeracy, subjects that in recent years have often been validated more highly than foundation subjects. Instead D&T offers learning opportunities of immediate relevance to *all* children and at all stages of their education. In D&T everyone can participate and achieve success.

And yet, often for the most part, D&T fails as a subject, and its implementation in schools leads to further inequalities rather than moving towards equality. The imagery of engineering and manufacture tends to turn girls away from it. The narrow choice of contexts serves to disenchant many children who may already feel that they do not quite belong to the school community; it may marginalize some children from disadvantaged or low socio-economic groups and those from black and minority ethnic groups and because the context of D&T does not build on their interests or prior knowledge and understanding of the world: not everyone is fascinated by or has seen Big Ben. Its relatively new status in schools means that there is a lack of understanding of the subject among communities that are less well informed about schools. This is coupled with the common misconception that 'those good with their hands' tend to be used as a euphemism for 'those who can't do anything else', which consequently leads to the ghettoizing of D&T further away from high-status subjects such as science and mathematics.

Consequently, in practice, D&T is often perceived as a low-status subject in primary schools. The current government thinking on advisory structures, where, for example, local secondary departments become the chief advisers to their feeder primaries through the notion of specialist status,[1] has a further deteriorating impact on the status quo.

How have we come to this situation and what can be done about it? How can we mitigate the current situation and at the same time consider equality? What can we do better? This chapter explores these three themes. It starts with a brief history of D&T as a primary subject, then presents a more detailed examination of present practice in schools, and finally concludes by providing some thoughts and suggestions for teaching for equality in D&T.

Part 1

How did D&T become a primary subject?

Was it an accident? For a subject that prides itself on its elegant solutions to problems, paradoxically the development of D&T has many elements of chance and farce, right from its conception and into a foundation subject of the primary curriculum. Prior to the Education Reform Act of 1988 (ERA), D&T did not exist in primary schools. To be sure, there was plenty of 'making' activity – and probably more than there is now that D&T is a formal subject – but this was done as part of the overall learning experience for pupils. One of the main purposes of the ERA (Tomlinson 1994; Hill 1997, 2001a, 2001b; Ball 2004; Lewis *et al.* 2009) was to create a framework for accountability for both teachers and schools, to control schooling and teachers. It introduced the notion of a ten-subject national curriculum, together with four Key Stages, with the intention of assessing each subject at each Key Stage. 'Languages' was quickly dropped from the primary curriculum when government ministers realized the cost of bringing specialist language teachers into primary schools, so a nine-subject curriculum was imposed on primary schools.

However, even in secondary schools, no one was actually certain what D&T was as a subject. It was a loose amalgamation of craft departments, comprising the metal-work, wood-work and technical drawing classes that had been thought so necessary for working class boys in the 1950s and 1960s, together with home economics and textiles that had been viewed as necessary for the future housewives of that era. At secondary school level, comprehensive schools had grouped these departments together under the banner of Craft, Design and Technology (CDT). This was partly in response to the more gender-aware atmosphere of the 1980s, but also in order for the mixed classes of comprehensive schools to be able to dip into these classes. But 'craft' is very much linked to 'arts', and to rather non-measurable ideas of personal enjoyment and empowerment, and so, in the 1987 version of the National Curriculum, and within this huge melting pot of different areas of knowledge, understanding and skills, the 'crafts' – and the 'C' – were dropped from the CDT and the subject became D&T.

Of all the subjects of the new National Curriculum none caused more confusion than D&T. What was this subject all about? What should teachers be preparing their pupils for? The working group that was set up to draft the specification for the subject produced a deeply philosophical justification for D&T and its place in the curriculum (DES/WO 1988). It suggested that it was all about the human products that pervaded the world, and that these could be categorized as artefacts, systems or environments, and that these existed within the realms of all of the component subjects. This document was one of the key items that sabotaged the whole assessment project within the ERA. The new National Curriculum was developed by Margaret Thatcher's Conservative government, and even the most ambitious of Thatcher's ministers could not countenance a subject in which each pupil would need to be assessed in 15 separate areas. Most of the D&T assessment project was quietly stalled during the following John Major's Conservative government of the early nineties, which resulted in a fuzzy, not-quite-defined area on the curriculum. Subsequently, all schools have to teach D&T but it is not one of their priorities.

The D&T process

One of the major outcomes of the intense critical appraisal of D&T as it became a curriculum subject was the emergence of a consensual view of D&T as a *process*. There had been attempts to identify such a process before, for example, with the design line (Williams and Jinks 1985). However, when D&T became a subject for all pupils between the ages of 5 and 16 years, the process skills were identified: Identifying Needs, Designing, Making and Appraising. These were perceived to form a cycle. We say 'consensual', but yet, it was a case of the then National Curriculum Council imposing its view. There is no agreement among D&T educators that such a process cycle exists, or that there are not other valid ways of analysing D&T (Johnsey 1998). In the early1990s, the concept of the D&T process also gave rise to the ludicrous notion that a pupil was only doing D&T if all four processes were in evidence. Fortunately, a more pragmatic guidance was issued in 1996, classifying D&T teaching into three areas: Investigating products, Focussed practical tasks (FPT) and Design and Make Assignments (DMA). This classification of activity is still in use today.

The D&T curriculum

D&T, since the third incarnation of the National Curriculum in 1996,[2] is considered to be about products. The study of systems and environments was considered far too complicated. Under the slightly more teacher-friendly regime since Labour assumed power in 1997 (though see Jones 2003; Tomlinson 2004; Hill 2006), some explicit guidance has been produced as to what D&T should look like in the classroom.

According to the most recent guidelines available from the Department of Children, Schools and Families (DCSF) it is stated that:

Design and technology offers opportunities for children to:
- develop their designing and making skills;
- develop knowledge and understanding;
- develop their capability to create high quality products through combining their designing and making skills with knowledge and understanding;
- nurture creativity and innovation through designing and making;
- explore values about and attitudes to the made world and how we live and work within it;
- develop an understanding of technological processes, products, and their manufacture, and their contribution to our society

(DCSF 2008)

And further exemplification is given in the units suggested as a whole school scheme:

Unit 1A. Moving pictures; Unit 1B. Playgrounds; Unit 1C. Eat more fruit and vegetables ;Unit 1D. Homes; Unit 2A. Vehicles; Unit 2B. Puppets; Unit 2C. Winding up; Unit 2D. Joseph's coat; Unit 3A. Packaging; Unit 3B. Sandwich snacks; Unit 3C. Moving monsters; Unit 3D. Photograph frames; Unit 4A. Money containers; Unit 4B. Storybooks; Unit 4C. Torches; Unit 4D. Alarms; Unit 4E. Lighting it up; Unit 5A. Musical instruments; Unit 5B. Bread; Unit 5C. Moving toys; Unit 5D. Biscuits; Unit 6A. Shelter; Unit 6B. Slippers; Unit 6C. Fairground; and Unit 6D. Controllable vehicles. (DCSF 2008)

The above list betrays the roots of D&T in separate craft departments. The list is less about a progression in skills and processes, but more about ensuring that visits to the areas of home economics, textiles and resistant materials are made on a regular basis. Most primary teachers would be able to take any of those titles and construct a teaching sequence that could be applied to any age group in a primary school. As an exercise, we have given these titles to PGCE students without the unit numbers and asked them to assemble the titles into a sequence – the results are always totally random, with the exception of '6D Controllable vehicles', which is always perceived as the most difficult, and therefore the last activity. We shall return to this unit later in the chapter.

Of course, as the government's website declares, the above scheme is not statutory and teachers are free to use as much or as little as they wish in constructing their own schemes of work. In reality, as it is extremely rare to find specialist D&T teachers in primary schools (DATA 2008), very few teachers have the confidence to challenge the accepted wisdom of the Quality and Curriculum Authority (QCA) that is responsible for developing these schemes of work, and consequently these units have gained the status of a defined curriculum. In surveying the school experiences of PGCE students in 150 North London schools between 2003 and 2008, no school had attempted to construct a D&T scheme of work that differed from the QCA guidance (Neonaki 2008).

Part 2

Teaching D&T for equality

Having provided a brief historical overview of D&T development in primary schools in England, and having examined some of forces that have impacted on this development, the question that needs to be asked at this point is what can we, as pragmatic educators, do to ensure that equality is promoted? Little has been written about equality and D&T. To find some guidelines to act as a starting point for this discussion, it is necessary to turn to a parallel curriculum area – science. The following is taken from a report by the Association for Science Education's multicultural education working party (Thorpe *et al.* 1991):

> Teaching and learning promotes equality when:
> 1. A variety of strategies is used
> 2. Children's own experience is valued and built on
> 3. Children are enabled to develop autonomy and responsibility for their own learning
> 4. Ideas and assumptions are challenged
> 5. Strategies are collaborative, not competitive
> 6. Control of learning is shared between teachers and pupils.

Valuing Children's Experience

Many teachers use the strategy of bringing in materials from home that children are already familiar with in order to start a project. This can be very effective, especially for the units that are implicitly toy- or book-based, such as 'Moving Pictures', 'Vehicles', 'Winding Up', 'Storybooks' or 'Moving Toys'. However, the 'toys-from-home' strategy also contains a huge potential trap for teachers, in that modern toy manufacturing and retailing has aggressively categorized toys as boys' or girls' toys. Many supermarkets now carry sections labelled 'Boys' Toys' and 'Girls' Toys'; the girl's section being instantly recognizable by the overwhelming use of pink, and pastel colours such as lavender and pale yellow, and the boys' section by the use of darker colours such as navy, dark green and black. Construction kits, which can be a useful adjunct for D&T teaching, are invariably categorized under boys' toys.

Over-reliance on materials brought from home may easily lead to and reinforce sexual stereotyping at a very early age. Teachers from the Foundation Stage onwards need to emphasize that toys can be interesting to and be played with by both sexes. Teachers at Key Stage 1 who use 'Golden Time' or 'Choosing Time' strategies (allocated times in the class timetable when all children are able to choose their own activities and self-direct their learning) will need to ensure that boys do not always choose the construction sets and girls do not always choose the home corner. Teachers of this age group will need to accept and discuss the sexual stereotyping that is forced on to young children, and to encourage their pupils to undertake different play experiences.

Autonomy and responsibility

One of the great features of D&T is that it is project-based. Most of the D&T units suggest a challenge, but that there is no right answer. Being successful in a D&T lesson is dependent on exploration, discovery, inventiveness and imagination. In fact, curiosity is a key motivator. Pupils are expected to follow a process, but as discussed previously, to promote a view that all D&T activities should include a neatly defined cycle – of identifying a need, planning and designing, making and finally apprising – is flawed. Instead, we believe good practice in D&T allows pupils to follow their own path to the final product. In this respect D&T offers more autonomy and responsibility than most other subject areas.

One of the flaws with the above received D&T process – and which seriously impacts on autonomy – is the insistence that a design phase *must* consist of a drawing (with pen and paper or on a computer screen) and that this *must* precede any making stage. It is an absolute nonsense that all children should be made to draw their designs every time before they embark upon their making. In fact this is cruel, and a hangover from the attempt to give D&T an intellectual base in the secondary curriculum. Children in primary schools do not possess the artistic techniques necessary for design drawing, nor do they possess the experience of materials to be able to envisage the outcome of their making activities. When asked to use a particular design for a product, typically completed in a separate lesson one week previously, by the time they come to make it, they have moved on and developed additional, further ideas. The design has ceased to be of any interest.

One of the most bizarre aspects of D&T that we see in visiting primary schools is this insistence of drawing a design. For pupils who are not ready for this aspect of D&T, it is highly counter-productive. What they produce inevitably looks different from what they initially drew, which leads to a loss of confidence by pupils (and sometimes leads to a negative evaluation of their project work by a teacher unfamiliar with D&T outcomes). The reason for the discrepancy in design drawing and product outcome may simply lie in the lack of graphic technique, but is more likely to result from lack of experience of materials. Pupils at primary schools will be exploring the materials they are working with; the outcome of their work may totally surprise them. So long as the outcome fulfils the initial brief, why should teachers worry that the product does not resemble the initial drawing? Too often, teachers kill the excitement generated by making activity by insisting on this valueless drawing stage. This is particularly true with some pupils – often girls – who may spend a long time in trying to please a teacher and then become frustrated when their making activity cannot match the design ambition. Similarly, some pupils, new to English schools, for example, or to schooling in general, or those from disadvantaged socio-economic backgrounds, may lack the easy familiarity with construction materials that other children have acquired.

Ideas and assumptions challenged

As stated in the previous section, there is no 'right' answer in D&T. If a teacher has set a genuinely open-ended challenge, then pupils may respond to that challenge in many different ways – ways that are unforeseeable to the teacher. Some of the solutions that pupils come up with may be superior to those proposed by the teacher. This may be a very difficult skill or approach for teachers to acquire and maintain – in their own classrooms they are used to being in charge and setting the agenda. The idea that pupils' ideas are an improvement on theirs may be difficult to accept, especially in a subject such as D&T where many teachers are struggling and lack confidence, and which they may have less time to develop.

One immediate consequence of this is that teachers may need a considerable amount of resources to deal with open-ended problem solving. If you make a balloon-driven buggy by giving out three pieces of wood, two straws, two pieces of dowel, four wheels, a piece of plastic sheet with a hole in it and a balloon, pupils may all make successful buggies, but essentially they will have been following a recipe. The recipe may not have been written out, but it is implicit in the limited quantities of materials distributed.

The recipe approach may be perfectly adequate if the teaching objective is to familiarize the children with techniques for joining wood and plastic, or for looking at how to create axles. But a better approach to the challenge of building a vehicle powered by a balloon is to demonstrate the jet principle with a balloon, and the technique of using straws as axles, then to allow the children choice over whether to use plastic, wood or card for the remainder of the vehicle, and to let them decide on size and shape. Of course, this involves a more liberal use of materials, which highlights one of the further problems of D&T; as a subject – it demands adequately resourced consumable materials. But allowing children to choose, and then to provide opportunities for them to compare the choices they have made, leads to far more effective learning (Smyth 2000).

It is also important to challenge the Eurocentric view of technology. So much of what children (and society) encounter under the label of technology is focused on Western high technology. Little status is accorded to either appropriate technology or to the history of technology in other cultures. Much of the technology used to build Great Zimbabwe, the Taj Mahal, or the Egyptian or Mayan pyramids was extremely advanced, and should be accorded status within the present account of D&T (Claire 2006). However, use of such examples needs to be done sensitively – many are historic examples, and we need to avoid giving the impression that Western technology equals new, while the technology of other cultures equals old and out-of-date. Similarly, while appropriate technology may be both far more understandable for children and far more useful for adults, teachers will not wish to imply that it is used by poor, third world countries, while Western countries can afford 'proper' high-tech solutions.

Collaboration, not competition

One of the worst features we encounter with D&T is that it frequently becomes reduced to a competition. As D&T has a low status in the curriculum, it is often easiest for senior management to make a big push in one of the designated weeks (National Science and Engineering Week in March, or Design and Technology Week in June), and then forget about it for the rest of the year. Then the theme

BALLOON BUGGIES

1. Cut 3 pieces of square section wood. Glue them together as shown in the diagram.

2. Cut out some card triangles to strengthen the joints between the wood. They should be glued to the upper side of the frame.

3. Glue 2 plastic straws onto the lower side of the frame. These will act as axle guides.

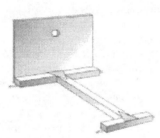

4. Cut a small hole, to take the end of an inflated balloon, in a square of correx. Glue the correx to the frame.

5. Tap a wheel onto a piece of wooden dowel.

   Push the wooden dowel through the straw axle.

   Tap a wheel onto the other end of the wooden dowel.

   Do the same with the other axle.

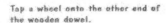
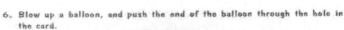

6. Blow up a balloon, and push the end of the balloon through the hole in the card.

Making and Selling Balloon Buggies

Balloon buggies are a good way of demonstrating the energy stored in a balloon full of air. They also show forces in action, and illustrate the principle of the jet engine. Children and parents really enjoy making them.

A lot of the fun is in making them, so it would probably be easier to sell them as kits, ready for people to put together.

Could you sell some at a school fair? Could they be an item for sale in science week in March? Would there be a market for them at Christmas?

1. Try making the buggy as shown on the activity sheet.

2. Can you improve the design?

3. Can you personalize the design? Perhaps you could make it in the school colours, or include pictures on the body.

4. Or could you find an opportunity for advertising? Perhaps a local business would like to have its name on the buggy or the balloon.

5. Try making up some kits together so people can make buggies to your design. Ask them for their feelings about whether it is a good product.

6. How will people fix their buggies together? Is sellotape best? How can you ensure that your kit is safe?

7. How much will your kit cost? There is an example spreadsheet in the pack, but you will have to check the prices. And, if you have changed the design, you may need to change the spreadsheet.

8. How much will you sell your kit for? You do not want to make a loss, so you will need to charge more than the cost of the pieces. You will need a fair reward for your effort. But if you charge too much, will people buy your product?

9. How will you advertise your product? Will you need to raise the price to include the cost of advertising?

of the week becomes a challenge; the challenge is judged on Friday with an award ceremony in Friday assembly to which parents and local community are invited and at which prizes are given out.

That format may bring a bit of local publicity and gives a good context for inviting parents into school. There is nothing wrong with celebratory activity. However, if that is all that D&T is reduced to, it obviates one of the guiding principles of the subject, namely that there is no right answer. It is, of course, possible to argue that the winner has not provided the right answer, merely the best answer, but primary children find this a pretty tendentious response. If their answer did not win, then it was the wrong answer, and their whole understanding of what the subject is about, and their confidence in it, will suffer.

Even worse practice is exhibited by many of the enrichment and enhancement schemes run by organizations that try to raise awareness of technology and engineering. There are many of these, as evidenced by the Shape the Future Directory (Royal Academy of Engineering 2007), which were set up to influence more children to follow careers in science, engineering and mathematics. The vast majority of these so-called enrichment and enhancement schemes are

From   *Principles of Diversity – a presentation to Organisations*
considering Enhancement and Enrichment activities
Steve Smyth
SETNET

3 do's and a don't

- Do produce something that schools want

- Do ensure that you have capacity to deliver

- Do get buy-in

- Don't make schools/communities compete for scarce resources.

Don't make schools/communities compete for scarce resources

- Don't do competitions – the usual suspects win.

- Don't do competitions – other schools don't take part because they expect the usual suspects to win.

- Don't do competitions – even if the usual suspects don't win, they will tell everybody they haven't won because of political

  considerations, and so the other schools feel belittled.

Don't do competitions......

- The only winners in competitions are the sponsoring firms. It is a cheap way for them to get publicity.

- There are other ways for the chairman to get his picture in the local paper.

- Why should pupils/students jump through hoops for companies? It should be the other way round.

competitions, offered to schools because competitions are cheap and easy to run and offer good publicity benefits for sponsoring companies. Such schemes tend to reinforce the right answer/wrong answer approach discussed above, but without the possible mitigation of a school that understands that competition must be placed in context. The sad fact is that such competitions are typically won by a small group of schools from affluent, middle-class neighbourhoods, who have long practice in finding acceptable winning lines or who have the resources and support to develop winning ideas. Children from schools with less affluent backgrounds tend to find that they are not winning such competitions and so decide that D&T is not for them. Far from achieving the stated aim of such schemes – to increase awareness of and participation in science, technology and engineering careers – the schemes may well be a factor in decreasing participation and closing the engineering professions off to all but a small cohort of middle-class children.

D&T teaching and D&T enhancement and enrichment do not have to be competitive at all. The activity inherent in D&T teaching is motivating enough in its own right – all age groups, but primary age children especially, love making things. It does not need the additional incentive of a book token for a winner. And the best D&T enhancement schemes concentrate not on competition but collaboration.

The photograph shows a group of Year 6 carrying out a D&T enrichment activity called Train (Smyth 2007). In this activity, a full class of 30 children is challenged to build a railway line from one end of the classroom to the other. The purpose is to show a way of transporting building materials (represented by marbles) safely and sustainably. The class is arranged into five groups, and tasks allocated as follows: a group to build the railway (shown above), a group to build loading equipment for the marbles, a group to build unloading equipment, a group to build signals and a level crossing, and a group to build a bridge over the line.

These are all fairly major tasks, so the groups rapidly learn that they need to collaborate between themselves to achieve targets. What also becomes apparent as the activity progresses is that collaboration between groups is also essential, to discuss setting of signals, height of bridges and the width of rolling stock. During the day that this activity is carried out, children are expected to report back to one another at regular intervals to discuss progress and problems. Many teachers have commented that this process of reporting is as valuable to children's progress against literacy targets as it is to their understanding of science and technology.

Shared control of learning

As discussed earlier, it may be difficult for a teacher to share control, and therefore power, in a classroom. But this is an essential facet of good practice in D&T teaching, and *all* teaching – teacher and pupil – are on a journey together. There is no right answer to the problem being solved, simply possible solutions to explore and evaluate, and the D&T context may provide more immediate opportunities for exploring this journey.

A teacher who makes a pretence of this partnership is likely to be found out. Step-by-step worksheets are a good example. How can a teacher maintain that the problem being solved is an open-ended one if the worksheet in front of the pupil guides them to an expected outcome? Printed worksheets have their place; often a pupil will require some support in accomplishing a task and a worksheet may provide some of this, but the way they are written must show the possibility for further input from the child, taking the project in new and unresearched directions.

A teacher who is genuinely willing to share this control will achieve a great deal, with pupils from all backgrounds. They will need to value ideas expressed, and not dismiss them as wrong or unworkable. They will need to praise all outcomes to problems, suggesting ways that all ideas could be taken forward, not just one or two solutions that reflect conventional thinking or expected outcomes. They will need to have access to a wide variety of resources, because they will never know what might be suggested by pupils.

Part 3

Developing the curriculum for equality

At the time of writing this, there are many proposed changes to the curriculum that will also impact upon D&T teaching. There is an intention to make the curriculum more integrated, especially in the area of STEM (Science, Technology, Engineering and Mathematics). Changes to the secondary curriculum scheduled for September 2008 will also impact on primary teaching, as will changes in the way subject specialist schools are expected to reach out to their community of feeder schools. There is also the ever-increasing clamour for more STEM graduates to feed the knowledge economy, impacting on schools through projects such as the London Engineering Project. This next section examines some of these and considers the implications for teaching for equality.

Enterprise

Enterprise has been a cross-cutting theme of the secondary curriculum since 2005 (Teachernet 2008). Although initially an area of secondary concern, many local authorities (Staffordshire 2008) have taken the step of extending enterprise education to primary schools. Given the liberal interpretation of enterprise and the foregoing discussion about collaboration and independent working, this is a welcome development. The Teachernet site goes on to define enterprise education as follows:

> Learners are expected to take personal responsibility for their own actions through an enterprise process that involves four stages.
> - Stage 1 – tackling a problem or need: students generate ideas through discussion to reach a common understanding of what is required to resolve the problem or meet the need.
> - Stage 2 – planning the project or activity: breaking down tasks, organizing resources, deploying team members and allocating responsibilities.
> - Stage 3 – implementing the plan: solving problems, monitoring progress.
> - Stage 4 – evaluating the processes: reviewing activities and final outcomes, reflecting on lessons learned and assessing the skills, attitudes, qualities and understanding
>
> (Teachernet 2008)

Most D&T projects could, therefore, be considered to also fall under the banner of enterprise, especially projects such as 'Slippers', 'Torches' and 'Photo-frames'. In some ways it is difficult to distinguish the enterprise process from the D&T process.

One difference that enterprise activity has, at least by implication, is that it can be more cross-curricular in scope. For example, the balloon buggy activity, discussed earlier, can easily be converted to an enterprise activity as shown by the earlier task sheet. From a teaching point of view, the activity now also explicitly covers mathematics and literacy.

There remains, however, a fundamental question – and an objection – to enterprise education. As Peter McLaren (2009) makes clear in his Preface, and as Dave Hill (2009) sets out in the concluding chapter concerning capitalist education and what it does to encourage and reproduce inequalities in education, teachers' embrace of enterprise education needs to be a critical one. Enterprise education needs to be critically interrogated. Critical and radical educators need to ask a question, and, furthermore, ask this question with and of their children: what is the concept of enterprise – as the fundamental building block of capitalism – when it is capitalism that has created the problems of inequality in the first place?

Engineering

As already mentioned, there is a persistent call from government and industry to place engineering more firmly in the minds of both secondary and primary children. In our view there is no doubt that engineering is a powerful ally in the quest for better teaching for equality.

To many primary teachers, engineering may well be a grey, hazy area. The public image of an engineer is a man in greasy overalls repairing cars, and engineering is, therefore, the grubby business of changing broken gaskets and replacing worn out tyres. There is little doubt that engineers are a vital component of our future, and it is a perverse outcome of the present education system that so few young people are encouraged, or even made aware, of the rich opportunities of engineering. The engineering professions in the UK remain a bastion of white, middle-class males.

Recognizing both the shortage of students taking engineering degrees, and the narrow clique from which students on engineering degrees were recruited, the Higher Education Funding Council for England set up the London Engineering Project in 2005 (London Engineering Project 2008). The scope of much of the project is beyond this book, but it is instructive to look at the projects that have been taken into primary schools.

The rationale behind taking such projects into primary schools is that many existing engineers have reported that they had decided to become engineers by the age of 11. The aim of the projects was to establish an awareness of engineering in the minds of children before entering secondary school, so that subject decisions at the end of Key Stage 3 and Key Stage 4 could be made with a fuller understanding of career implications. A secondary aim was to raise awareness of engineering among primary school teachers, so that a wider discussion of careers could begin at an early stage in a child's life.

Tram: An Engineering workshop for Year 5 or 6

Tram is a workshop designed to enhance both science and design and technology, and to reinforce the links between these two areas of the curriculum. It also links to numeracy, literacy, history and geography.

The workshop is designed for a class of Y5 or Y6 pupils for a whole school day. A workshop leader will be with the children for the whole of this time. There is, in addition, considerable follow-up work that could be pursued. It is not our intention to impose this upon teachers – it is our intention to provide this as a support. We will also endeavour to leave materials so that further project work can be undertaken without schools needing to use up their own resources.

The day is divided into three phases. During the first phase groups carry out electrical investigations that support Y6 work on electricity, especially the QCA unit 6G `Changing circuits'. Then each group builds a battery operated vehicle, guided by rails and track produced by themselves, and eventually build overhead electrification, so that the vehicle can be remotely controlled. This section supports the QCA DT unit 6D `Controllable Vehicles'.

Finally the pupils try out and evaluate their own and other groups systems, and organize presentations on what they have done. Some schools that have piloted the workshop have used this opportunity to present what they have done to the rest of the school in an assembly.

Tram can be organized as a workshop -- all the materials and tools are provided, and either sent in advance or brought by the workshop leader. Workshop leaders are fully trained teachers.

The projects also aimed to take a more holistic view of engineering activities, in an attempt to appeal to girls as well as boys, and to root the activities in a wider cultural context, to avoid giving the impression that engineering was Eurocentric. To reinforce the message to communities, the project leaders were recruited from the African and Asian communities (and were 100 per cent female).

One exemplar activity is 'Tram' (shown in Figure 2). This aims to explain the engineering of an urban railway in a way that links the task with both D&T and science. It takes as a context moving around in a city, with the problems that are familiar to inner-city children (noise, air pollution, unreliability) and looks at holistic, sustainable solutions (while electricity is not a sustainable energy option if generated from fossil fuel, it offers a realistic chance of harnessing sustainable production via wind, wave or solar energy; one of the extension activities of the Tram project is to run the children's models using solar panels).

The learning is collaborative, with children needing to work in groups in order to produce their designs. Groups can further collaborate together to produce larger, more extensive models (and the problems they encounter in that can be used to illustrate some of the historical problems that public transport systems have had in joining together). Learning proceeds as a dialogue between teacher and learner – there is no right answer, rather a series of improvements and extensions to designs. And the product is purposeful. It serves as a demonstration and call to action for the community in the provision of better and more sustainable forms of transport.

Conclusion: Towards a D&T Curriculum for Equality

In this concluding section we take some of the foregoing discussions and attempt to synthesize them into a curriculum for the future.

First, if we are to have a curriculum where teachers and children share the learning experience, we need to decouple the teaching of D&T from the exemplified content given in the QCA scheme of work. D&T work needs to be more spontaneous, organically growing from the needs of the class as learners, and the needs of the community. The curriculum needs to allow space for user-led innovation, where children's own ideas are explored. If the present scheme of work is to be retained at all, it should only be in a form where the activities are used as practical focused tasks, so that children can acquire familiarity with materials, and skills at handling them at a certain age.

Second, we need a system where primary teachers have a great deal more experience of D&T projects and techniques than at present. If learning is to be a shared journey, then teachers will need to feel comfortable about their role in that journey, and not be put off by the first suggestion that children make that takes them off the beaten track. This experience has to be gained by the teachers themselves, through their Initial Teacher Training or through Continuous Professional Development – external 'experts' can only do so much, and, in the long term, create the impression that D&T is only for a select few, whereas it is the entitlement of all.

Third, we need to review the overall context of D&T teaching much more critically. If D&T is about products, we need to be aware of exactly whose products? We need to be aware that teaching about products, production and enterprise gives implicit support for a market economy. Should we balance the recent rise in 'Enterprise Days' at school with 'Socially Just Production Days'? The critical pedagogy of Giroux (2005) and McLaren (2005) should be an important influence on such review.[3]

Finally, the D&T curriculum needs to be viewed as an entitlement to explore, and teachers need to be given the freedom and confidence to match genuine exploration with learning needs in other curriculum areas, such as literacy, numeracy and science. A far more flexible curriculum, such as a majority of primary schools in England and Wales experienced prior to the 1980s in the child-centred Plowden era of the 1960s and 1970s, is unlikely to be seen in England for a foreseeable future. If we are to justify a free exploration approach to D&T, it must be because it contributes to the achievement of targets in defined areas of the curriculum. Furthermore, in the light of what a critical approach to D&T can add in the quest for a more equal, more socially-just curriculum and schooling, an approach that highlights and contests labelling, discrimination and stereotyping that so often takes place in our schools on grounds of 'race', language, social class, ability/disability and sexuality of the children and their home backgrounds.

Notes

1 Specialist schools have their origin in the City Technology Colleges set up by the Conservative government in the late 1980s as a way of fragmenting local authority control. During the 1990s, they expanded to take on new specialisms in addition to the original specialism of technology – so there are now, for example, specialists in performing arts, sports, business and enterprise and science. Having a specialism brings additional funding to schools. The schools are expected to be beacons of excellence in their chosen specialism, and to act as advisers to other secondary schools and to primary schools that feed into them. This expectation is viewed by government as another way of reducing the size and remit of local authorities, as the schools act to replace the function of local authority specialist subject advisers. The problem is that, while this system looks tenable on paper, it is virtually useless for primary schools, as very few secondary teachers have any conception of how primary schools work, and so find advice difficult to give. This is particularly acute in technology (and engineering) specialist schools, where the teachers involved in the specialism tend to have expertise in only one area of technology (for example, textiles or resistant materials) and so find the broad-based approach of primary technology extremely difficult to advise on.

2 The National Curriculum has been through a number of revisions since first publication in 1989. D&T, in particular, has been revised a number of times in an effort by government to match what was specified for teaching with what was possible for teaching in schools and with what was possible for assessment. The first specification for D&T in 1989 was extremely broad, and, although welcomed by many teachers, was considered by government to be incompatible with the aims of assessment they had formulated. A second version, in 1991, was introduced with the aim of producing Standard Assesssment Tests (SATs) in D&T at KS1, 2 and 3 by 1996. In 1996, a third version was written, which recognized that SAT testing in D&T would not be implemented. This version has remained in force until now, although a fourth revision of the primary curriculum is in progress at the time of writing, and should be in primary schools by September 2010.

3 Suggestions about using schools and the curriculum to work towards a radical transformation of schooling and society – towards an egalitarian society – are typical of the writing of critical pedagogues such as Henry Giroux and Peter McLaren, both of whom have written/published more than 40 books. See, in particular, Peter McLaren's website at http://www.gseis.ucla.edu/faculty/pages/mclaren/. For a UK perspective, see Dave Hill's writing, for example, Hill 2007 and Hill and Boxley 2007. A summary of writing about critical pedagogy and education for equality can be found in this volume (Hill 2009).

References

Design and Technology Association (DATA) (2008) Online at http://www.data.org.uk/index.php?option = com_content&task = view&id = 99&Itemid = 171.

Department for Children Families and Schools (DCSF) (2008) The Standards Site. Online at http://www.standards.dfes.gov.uk/schemes2/designtech

Department of Education and Science/Welsh Office (1988) 'National Curriculum Science Working Group: Final Report'. London: HMSO.

Claire, H. (2006) 'Education for Cultural Diversity and Social Justice', in J. Arthur, T. Grainger, and D. Wray, *Learning to Teach in the Primary School*. London: Routledge.

Giroux, H. (2005) *Border Crossings: Cultural Workers and the Politics of Education*. Boca Raton: CRC Press.

Ball, S. (2004) *Education Reform: a Critical and Post-Structural Approach*. Buckingham: Open University Press.

Hill, D. (1997) 'Equality in British Schooling: The Policy Context of the Reforms', in M. Cole, D. Hill, and S. Shan (eds) *Promoting Equality in Primary Schools*, 15–47. London: Cassell.

Hill, D. (2001a) 'The National Curriculum, The Hidden Curriculum and Equality' in D. Hill and M. Cole (eds) *Schooling and Equality: Fact, Concept and Policy*, 95--116. London: Kogan Page.

Hill, D. (2001b) 'Equality, Ideology and Education Policy', in D. Hill and M. Cole (eds) *Schooling and Equality: Fact, Concept and Policy*, 7–34. London: Kogan Page.

Hill, D. (2006) New Labour's Education Policy, in D. Kassem, E. Mufti and J. Robinson (eds) *Education Studies: Issues and Critical Perspectives*, 73–86. Buckingham: Open University Press.

Hill, D. (2007) 'Critical Teacher Education, New Labour in Britain, and the Global Project of Neoliberal Capital'. *Policy Futures*, 5, (2), 204–225. Online at http://www.wwwords.co.uk/pfie/content/pdfs/5/issue5_2.asp

Hill, D. (2009) 'Theorizing Politics and the Curriculum: Understanding and Addressing Inequalities through Critical Pedagogy and Critical Policy', in D. Hill and L. Helavaara Robertson (eds) *Equality in the Primary School: Promoting good practice across the curriculum*. London: Continuum.

Hill, D. and Boxley, S. (2007) 'Critical Teacher Education for Economic, Environmental and Social Justice: an Ecosocialist Manifesto'. *Journal for Critical education Policy Studies*, 5(2). Online at http://www.jceps.com/index.php?pageID=article&articleID=96

Johnsey, R. (1998) *Exploring Primary Design and Technology*. London: Cassell.

Jones, K. (2003) *Education in Britain, 1944 to the Present*. Cambridge: Polity Press.

Lewis, C., Hill, D. and Fawcett, B. (2009) England and Wales: Neoliberalized Education and its Impacts, in Hill, D. (ed.) *The Rich World and the Impoverishment of Education: Diminishing Democracy, Equity and Workers' Rights*, 106–135. New York: Routledge.

London Engineering Project, 2008. Online at www.thelep.org.uk.

McLaren, P. (2005) *Capitalists and Conquerors*. Lanham, MD: Rowman and Littlefield.

McLaren, P. (2009) Preface, in D. Hill and L. Helavaara Robertson (eds) *Equality in the Primary School: Promoting good practice across the curriculum*. London: Continuum.

Neonaki, M. (2008) *Report to STEMNET 2008*. IHRP: London Metropolitan University.

Royal Academy of Engineering (2007) *Shape the Future*. London.

Smyth, J. (2000) *Inspire: Community Science and Technology Clubs*. Sheffield: Centre for Science Education.

Smyth, S. (2007) *Train, a CLUES project*. IHRP: London Metropolitan University.

Staffordshire County Council (2008) Online at http://www.staffpart.org.uk/enterprise.htm

Teachernet (2008) Online at http://www.teachernet.gov.uk/teachingandlearning/14to19/ks4/enterpriseeducation

Thorpe, S. (ed.) (1991) *Race, Equality and Science Teaching*. Hatfield: Association for Science Education.

Tomlinson, S. (ed.) (1994) *Educational Reform and its Consequence*. London: IPPR/Rivers Oram Press.

Tomlinson, S. (2004) (second edition) *Education in a post-welfare society*. Buckingham: Open
    University Press.
Williams, P. and Jinks, D. (1985) *Design and Technology 5–12*. London: Falmer Press.

Chapter 16

Religious Education

Ruth Mantin

Introduction

This chapter recognizes that the unusual and distinctive place of Religious Education (RE) in the curriculum brings with it a political and ideological legacy. As a result, there are particular challenges facing the effective, engaging and inclusive teaching of RE as part of an education which promotes equality. At the same time, however, the chapter argues that, when RE is explored in the light of the pedagogical approaches developed by theorists who challenge the confessional roots of the subject, it has a unique contribution to make to such an education. Multi-faith, enactive and engaging approaches to RE can introduce children to an understanding of a range of world views on their own terms. As such, they can encourage children to value all forms of difference and to question the narratives which legitimate oppression and inequality. They can also equip children with the attitudes and skills necessary to make a contribution towards constructing a socially just, radically egalitarian and anti-oppressive society.

RE has a distinctive and contentious position in any discussion of the promotion of equality through education. It has a unique place in the British curriculum.[1] It is therefore necessary to know something about its extraordinary history and the political and ideological legacies which this brings in order to appreciate the challenges facing the teaching of RE from a radically egalitarian perspective. At the same time, however, it is the argument of this chapter that, when taught effectively, this subject presents exceptional opportunities to promote equality and to provide children with positive strategies for approaching difference.

History of RE's Place in the Curriculum

Remarkably, when free state secondary education was first introduced into Britain in 1944 (free state primary/elementary education had been introduced in the 1870s and 1880s), the only subject which was compulsory by law was Religious Education, or 'Religious Instruction' as it was then called. There were several reasons for this. One was that in many cases, and especially in the case of primary education, the state was taking responsibility for schools which had previously been founded and run by churches (Barber 1994; Simon 1994). The churches agreed to this only if it was enshrined in the 1944 Education Act that state schools were obliged to provide a lesson of religious instruction every week and daily corporate worship for every child, unless the parents requested for them to be withdrawn. There were also other cultural factors which determined the place of religion in British state education. Britain was coming out of the experience of the Second World War and this had a profound effect upon the British self image. Apart from small dissenting voices from groups such as the British Humanist Association and from Britain's Jewish community, there was a general consensus that the state should provide 'spiritual education', by which it actually meant Christian instruction (Wedderspoon 1966:19–20). A quotation from an expression from the time of the aim of 'Religious Instruction' demonstrates this:

> The aim of the syllabus is to secure that children attending the schools of the country ... may gain knowledge of the common Christian faith held by their fathers for nearly 2,000 years; may seek for themselves in Christianity principles which give purpose to life and a guide to all its problems; and may find inspiration, power and courage to work for their welfare, and for the growth of God's kingdom. (Surrey 1945)

This extract illustrates how far it was regarded as an appropriate exercise for secular, state schools to attempt to nurture children into the Christian faith. It was decided that the content of religious instruction would be determined locally in each local education authority by a committee who would draw up an Agreed Syllabus. This committee was comprised of representatives from the Church of England, other Christian denominations, the local authority and teachers. Acknowledging its proselytizing nature, the 1944 Act gave parents and teachers the right of withdrawal from this subject. The reference in the extract above to a 'Christian faith held by our fathers' reflects the extent to which a notion of 'British heritage' was wedded to a very ethnocentric concept of 'Christianity'. This perception has dogged attempts to develop an educational, inclusive approach to RE, let alone one which promotes radical equality. It is possible to exercise some cultural relativity when appreciating the reasons why 'Religious Instruction' held this role in the 1940s. The issue for advocates of egalitarian education, however, is that this ideological legacy still influences debates about pedagogical approaches to RE in the twenty-first century.

During the 60s, amid radical cultural and social change, a growing number of teachers felt uncomfortable with their role as Christian evangelists. The arrival of increased numbers of members from black, Asian and other minority ethnic communities made Britain visibly multi-ethnic and multi-faith. For a growing number of educationalists this made the ideological perspectives of religious instruction in the 1944 Act untenable and anachronistic. Many theorists were now calling for the subject to be understood as religious education about a variety of faith traditions (Copley 1997). The upheaval of the 60s precipitated a wholesale reassessment of education in the form of the Schools Council Project which researched and reported on every aspect of the curriculum. The role of overseeing the examination of religious education was given to Professor Ninian Smart. Under his supervision, the Schools Council working Paper 36[2] was published in 1971 and brought about a paradigm shift in pedagogical approaches to religious education (Schools Council Project 1971). Smart had just established the new academic discipline of 'Religious Studies' at Lancaster University. Here, for the first time, he was advocating an approach to studying religions which was not theological or anthropological, but attempted to understand different faith perspectives on their own terms. He applied the same approach to the teaching of RE in schools. In the working paper, Smart identified four approaches to teaching RE which were current at the time. He coined the term 'Confessional 'to describe the traditional approach which viewed nurture into the Christian faith as the aim of RE in state schools. Smart argued that this approach was not legitimate outside a faith community and uneducational. He categorized as 'Neo-confessional' approaches where the attempt at Christian nurture was not explicit but an underlying assumption. Smart argued that if RE was to remain in the school curriculum, it should be there for educational reasons alone. Smart was passionate in his belief that learning about a range of different worldviews was an essential aspect of understanding the nature of human experience and vital to developing a peaceful and tolerant approach to religious pluralism. Smart argued that what he termed 'Anti-dogmatic' RE was also uneducational. This described the method where teachers, reluctant to adopt a confessional approach, provided only factual information about different religions. This unengaging 'naming of the parts' style of RE is, unfortunately, still very prevalent in many primary schools. Smart argued that unless the aim was to understand what the religions meant to their adherents, it was not educational. Instead he advocated a fourth option as the only truly educational approach to teaching RE. This was the phenomenological approach which he had pioneered in his work at Lancaster University. This approach, more popularly coined as the 'World Religions' approach, called for the aim of RE to be that of understanding the phenomenon of religion in all its diversity. Smart saw the distinctive role of RE to be understanding what religious ritual, doctrine and mythology meant to the followers of different faith traditions. This process involved educationally valid skills which were parallel to those required to study music, art or literature. Crucially, Smart was advocating a view of religious education which earned its right as an educational subject on the curriculum. The beliefs, religious or otherwise, of neither the teacher nor the pupils should, therefore, make any more difference to the delivery of this subject than to any other area of the curriculum.

This revolutionary pedagogical perspective transformed approaches to the educational aim of religious education in Britain. As the World Religions approach developed, its role in contributing towards an inclusive and anti-racist education was emphasized by some specialists. This was acknowledged specifically in the 1985 Swann Report which identified the phenomenological approach to RE as having a central role in countering the influences of racism (Swann 1985:496).[3]

This was further reflected in the development of Agreed Syllabuses produced by several Labour-controlled Education Authorities which underlined the function of multi-faith RE in 'developing positive attitudes towards, and a

sensitive understanding of, the demands of living in a multi-faith society'
(London Borough of Brent 1986). One of the many paradoxes of RE is that,
although specialists understand this revolution to have taken place several
decades ago, its implications still do not seem to have penetrated attitudes
towards this subject in many aspects of twenty-first-century elementary and
primary education.

The arrival of the Conservative government's 1988 Education Reform Act
was viewed by many RE theorists as an unrivalled opportunity to remove the
anomalies surrounding the role of RE and confirm its educational status.
Unfortunately, however, the decision making process about the place of RE in
the curriculum was hijacked by proponents of right-wing ideologies during its
passage through the House of Lords. Ironically, it was the intervention of the
Church of England which resulted in a compromise between right-wing attempts
to maintain the confessional role of religious education, along with 'collective
worship',[4] in promoting an ethnocentric notion of 'British heritage' and the
educationalists' desire to affirm the place multi-faith RE in a national
curriculum. This compromise was expressed in clause 8(30) of the Education
Reform Act:

> New local agreed syllabuses must reflect the fact that religious traditions in
> Great Britain are in the main Christian while taking account of the teaching
> and practices of other principal religions represented in Great Britain.
> (Education Reform Act 1988:6)

The government continued to provide 'guidance' to ensure the restrictive
interpretation of this clause and, despite a change of government, with the
election of New Labour in 1997, this and the application of a market-led
ideology to education, maintained 'the captivity of RE by the joint forces of
politicians and religionists each pursuing their own self interests' (Grimmitt
2000a:13).

More recently, however, a change in the culture of curriculum theory within
the Qualifications and Curriculum Association (QCA), has led to new
opportunities for the 'liberation' of RE. Replacing the Model Syllabuses, which
were devised in 1994 to reify the ideological presuppositions underlying clause
8(30) of the Education Reform Act,[5] the QCA has developed a National
Framework for Religious Education (QCA 2004). Because of the legislation that
RE must be determined locally in Agreed Syllabuses, this can only be non-
statutory guidance, but it presents an understanding of RE which is less content
driven and relates instead to skills, attitudes and process. The discussion of RE at
the Foundation Stage relates it to the early learning goals set out in QCA's
curriculum guidance (QCA 2000). In particular, the goal of acquiring
'Knowledge and Understanding of the World' requires the children to engage
with a range of faiths and cultures. At Key Stage 1 and 2, the framework presents
suggested 'themes, 'experiences' and 'opportunities' which allow the children to
explore their own responses to a range of issues, drawing on a plurality of faith
traditions and 'where appropriate', a secular worldview.

Because of the distinctive issues surrounding the nature of its place in the
curriculum, there continue to be complex pedagogical debates about the aims of

RE and what, precisely, is the nature of learning taking place (Grimmitt 2000). In his summary of these debates, one RE theorist argues that a continuing examination of these pedagogical issues is 'the first step in liberating RE from its captivity by self-interested politicians and religionists' (Grimmitt 2000a:15). Some protagonists in this debate, such as Trevor Cooling and Andrew Wright, place themselves firmly within the Christian tradition but defend themselves against their critics' claims that they are continuing neo-confessional approaches to RE. (Cooling 2000:163–165, Wright 2000:185). Others, such as Clive Erricker and Robert Jackson, were students of Ninian Smart.

It is the argument of this chapter that it is these latter approaches which enable a pedagogy of RE in elementary and primary education which is anti-oppressive and promotes social justice. Jackson's approach to religious education is influenced by his field research with children from different religious communities in Britain. He applies 'interpretive ethnography' to a pedagogy which recognizes that British children from ethnic minorities negotiate a plurality of cultural identities. The role of RE in schools is to help all children approach difference positively and learn how to recognize that, in understanding another's worldview, we need to reflect on the impact of our own (Jackson 1997). Jackson values the groundbreaking impact of Smart's phenomenological approach in ensuring that RE attempted to understand religions on their own terms. He does, however, question and challenge Smart's belief that the observer should 'bracket out' all presuppositions in order not to be judgemental. Instead, Jackson argues that we need to be very aware of the cultural assumptions we are bringing with us in an attempt to understand the 'other'. It is important to be aware of the power imbalance involved in such a process and the ethnocentric and colonial assumptions it brings with it. This can easily be carried into the primary or elementary classroom. In one observed example, the teacher involved the children in exercising a 'comparison' of Christian and Hindu notions of God. Her criteria for evaluation conveyed the view that Christian notions were positive and civilized while Hindu beliefs were primitive and threatening. Erricker also challenges Smart's view that it is possible or desirable to 'step out' of one's subjectivity. Erricker poses his challenge from a postmodern perspective and presents a pedagogy which focuses on children's own narratives (Erricker & Erricker 2000). He has been able to exemplify the practice of this pedagogical approach through his involvement in the development of the Hampshire Agreed Syllabus *Living Difference* (Hampshire County Council 2004).

Approaching Religious Diversity

In this chapter, I am arguing that an inclusive, learner-centred and multi-faith approach to religious education can present children with positive strategies for approaching diversity. This provides an environment in which their individuality is acknowledged and affirmed in line with the Every Child Matters agenda (2007) and in which differences of belief, practice and lifestyle are not considered threatening. This aims to help children to learn how to understand and respect a plurality of worldviews without feeling that they have to agree with them or accept them. In this way, children are also being taught to suspect definitions of the causes of inequality which attribute them to the teachings of 'someone else's' religion. They may, for instance, hear that 'Islam' is responsible for the oppression of women, or that 'Hinduism' is the reason for poverty and social discrimination. Not only are these over-simplistic definitions a convenient cover for racist attitudes, they also conceal the fact that situations of social injustice or inequality are created by the exercise of power by a dominant group over those they oppress. This is true regardless of faith and culture. Religion is used to legitimize such oppression. It is fundamental to this chapter's approach to learning about religious diversity that the children are introduced to the faith community in a manner which reflects the way in which the adherents themselves understand their religious tradition. It is, therefore, important to introduce children, at a level which is appropriate to their level of development, to the central concepts of a particular faith tradition. One reason, apart from the issue of religious commitment inherited from RE's distinctive history, why foundation stage and primary school teachers lack confidence in teaching multi-faith RE is the fact that many of them have not received effective multi-faith religious education themselves and therefore do not feel they have the relevant knowledge. For some, there is also the feeling that they are treading on someone else's 'sacred ground' and are therefore nervous about offending others. This is, of course, understandable. My response would be that the effective exploration of religious diversity is an essential aspect of an education for equality. There is a wealth of helpful material available to help teachers research multi-faith RE (see the suggested resources listed at the end of the chapter. I would particularly recommend Lindon (1999) to those working with very young children). Furthermore, if teachers approach faith traditions with the attitudes advocated here, it does not matter if they do not know every detail about the religions in question. Indeed, as has already been mentioned, it is important to view faith communities as internally contested, diverse and pluralistic rather than static and monolithic entities.

When teaching Islam, especially in the media-fed culture of post-9/11, we need to be aware of the powerful images which inform negative preconceptions of Islam and be prepared to address commonly-held misconceptions about Islam. Frequently used introductions to Islam reinforce negative and stereotypical images of Islam such as 'The five pillars of Islam'. Instead we need to consider the ways in which learning about Islam can be introduced through concepts which are central to a Muslim perspective such as 'Tawhid'. This expresses Muslim belief in the unity of all things. An immediate expression of this can be seen in Islamic art. Islamic patterns can be used to help children understand the idea that, for Muslims, Allah has made the world and people need to fit into the order that he has created. ICT software can be used to show how geometric designs have to follow a special order for the pattern to work. It is important to show that the concepts of Peace and Harmony are also central to Islam. The word Islam comes from 'salaam', the word for peace and, globally, Muslims greet one another with the phrase 'Assalum Alaykum' meaning 'Peace be upon you'.

The same sensitivity needs to be exercised with all faith traditions. When approaching Hinduism, for instance, we need to be aware that its cultural representation may seem very alien and 'other'. The colonial past of India makes some Westerners assume that Hindu traditions are inferior or 'primitive'. A good way of helping young children understand aspects of a Hindu worldview is through looking at Hindu art, which also helps them to develop positive attitudes to 'difference'. The younger the pupils, the easier this seems to be. Young children can recognize the 'specialness' in the rich colours, decoration and opulence. A careful interpretation of the images of deities can show that the divine can be represented in many different ways, including female, animal and aspects of nature. This expresses the important Hindu concept that God is in everything and everything is in God, therefore all forms of life are sacred. This then allows children to explore whether this perspective has something to offer a Western culture which has brought the world to the brink of ecological disaster.

It is important to note that when this chapter refers to 'multi-faith' or 'world religions', Christianity is included in these terms. Current legislation for England and Wales dictates that the primary curriculum spends more time on teaching about Christianity, but an effective and inclusive approach to RE ensures that the approach to teaching Christianity is the same as that used to teach any faith tradition (Cole and Mantin 1994). It is also important to show Christianity as a world religion which is very diverse and multicultural. Using Britain as an example of Christian practice is not always helpful. We need to appreciate that British Anglican Christianity is only a tiny aspect of global Christianity. Rather than present Christianity as a white, middle-class religion, we need to reflect the fact that the majority of Christians are black and live in the majority world. It is also important to ensure that children are not always presented with images of Jesus as a white European. There are many resources available now which provide representations of Jesus reflecting a rich plurality of cultures and ethnicities.

Teaching RE to Young Children

In too many schools, the failure to provide children with a wide range of cultural representations results in a hidden curriculum which teaches children to fear difference. Many of the topics popular at Foundation and Key Stage 1 help to reinforce this message. Unless handled carefully, topics such as 'Ourselves' or 'Homes' can present a stereotypical view of what 'home or 'family' means. Not only does this underpin social 'norms' with regard to concepts such as the patriarchal family, heterosexual relationships, middle-class values and the 'invisibility' of people with physical or mental disabilities, it can also alienate children whose experience does not allow them to identify with this 'norm'. It does not recognize the reality of looked after children or those who are primary carers. It also makes it much harder for children for whom 'home' is not a safe or secure place to disclose this to those who are delivering the dominant discourse about what home 'really' is. Instead, the multi-faith RE advocated in this chapter enables the teacher to present positive attitudes to diversity in which difference is welcomed and respected. For instance, at the foundation stage, children could have a Hindu shrine or a table set for the Jewish Shabbat meal as part of their 'home corner'.

As with all areas of the curriculum, it is, of course, important that children encounter these ideas in ways which are appropriate to their age. The teacher needs to start with these ideas in a way which is within the children's experience, for example, the concept of 'Specialness'. Children can discuss the objects, people, times and places that are special to them, then learn to appreciate and respect what is 'special' to others. In doing this, teachers need to avoid using terms such as 'us' and 'them' and using Christocentric[6] or Eurocentric examples, such as 'our Christmas', or describing Arabic as being written 'backwards'.

One of the most accessible ways into understanding faith traditions is through a focus on a particular child and his or her family. Books, videos, DVDs or the internet can be used to 'introduce' the class to a particular child and thereby to the particular objects, people, times and places that are special to 'her' or 'him'. Terms such as 'Hinduism' or 'the Jews' will probably be meaningless to young children but they can identify with 'Gaytri or 'Illana' who, like them, is a young person living in Britain today. On no account, however, should children in the class be used as 'examples' of different faith positions. They should not be 'spotlighted' and expect to explain their religious or cultural traditions to others. This only underlines the message that their 'difference' is being used to illustrate something which is not relevant to the class as a whole. Instead, the approach needs to convey the fact that the teacher and the children together are exploring something which is worthy of their attention, regardless of whether there happen to be any children from that faith tradition present or not. If this approach is adopted it is very likely that children who identify with the backgrounds being considered will want to express this, which is an invaluable contribution to the learning process. Of course, their contribution may well be something like 'Yeah we go there/celebrate that etc., ... but we don't do it like that!' In which case, there is no need to panic. The multi-layered, lived experience and skilled 'cultural navigation' of children from different faiths and ethnicities who live in Britain are often different from the images provided by text books (Jackson 1997). Creating an environment in which children can express and explore their narratives of difference is an essential aspect of providing an anti-oppressive and radically equal ethos.

Narratives from the faith communities can also provide fruitful sources for an education which promotes equality. Exploring the beginnings of some religious traditions allows children to appreciate the radically egalitarian nature of most of these early communities. The teaching and example of Jesus challenged the exclusions and prejudices of his day and promoted an equality of respect which could be discussed in relation to contemporary issues. Similarly the Medina community created by the Prophet Muhammad (*pbuh*) gave respect to women and slaves which was not available in the wider community. Key Stage 2 children can link this with the religious organizations which work to overcome poverty and campaign for social justice such as Christian Aid (www.christia-naid.org.uk) or the Red Crescent (www.ifrc.org). Children can also examine the lives of key figures in the struggle to promote equality, such as Martin Luther King Jr and Mohandas Gandhi, who were inspired and informed by their religious beliefs.

Since launching its new Primary National Strategy in 2003, the Department for Schools, Children and Families has revived an emphasis on the links between different subject areas and role of creativity in the Primary Curriculum. We need to ensure that this does not herald the return of approaches to 'thematic' teaching in which RE was presented through very tenuous links, often related to Bible stories. If implemented effectively, however, a holistic and creative approach to the primary curriculum offers real opportunities for teaching meaningful multi-faith RE. Teaching through 'Festivals' allows creative, engaging and enactive learning which automatically relates to a wide range of curriculum areas. Other appropriate themes include those which explore aspects of human experience such as 'Journeys', 'Buildings', and 'Clothes'. The central elements of life such as 'Food' 'Water' or 'Light' are also relevant focuses for exploration. There is a spiritual dimension to all of these for millions of people. If this dimension is omitted, not only is there a missed opportunity for some excellent RE, but also the themes themselves are not being fully explored. Unless children appreciate the symbolic, ritual and celebratory use of these factors and elements, they do not understand the essential aspects of the experience of millions of their fellow human beings.

Conclusion

It is the claim of this chapter that to create an environment in elementary and primary education in which religious and cultural diversity is respected is to lay the foundation for an education in which all forms of difference and individuality are respected. This does, however, still leave those who advocate an education which promotes radical equality with a dilemma. If a faith community is to presented 'on its own terms', how is this to be reconciled with the situation where most religious traditions have teachings on issues such as the position of women, the nature of sexuality and the status of mental and physical abilities which run counter to these notions of equality? I am arguing that if children learn to approach religious diversity with respect, they will be able to build on this foundation when they move into secondary education. Here, I would want them to be able to engage in meaningful debate about, for instance, whether indiscriminate terrorism can be reconciled with the teachings of Qur'an or whether culturally-embedded attitudes towards the role of women are compatible with the egalitarian teachings of religious leaders and founders. I would hope that then they would also be able to consider the validity of narratives which dehumanize people because of notions of difference such as sexual orientation or mental ability.

At the primary and elementary stage, the use of story can prepare children for such debate. An important aspect of understanding religious perspectives is an understanding of the role of story as a means of expressing truth as the storyteller perceives it. Storytelling is a powerful and central aspect of human experience in religious cultures. For many, the 'truth' of a story lies not in its historical accuracy but the extent to which it expresses 'the way the world is'. In helping children appreciate the power of story, however, RE can also help them understand something about the way in which power operates in society to create and sustain inequality. An exploration of story can help children appreciate that there are many different ways of perceiving the world, expressed in different stories, expressing different 'truths'. The story which is told most determines the way in

which the world is understood – 'history is written by the winners'. Those who
have the power can prevent others from telling their stories, so rendering them
'invisible' or 'demonized'. The reclaiming of their own stories, history and
'worldview' is therefore a vital aspect of all marginalized groups in their struggle
for equality. There are many picture books available for use with young children
which can prepare them for an exploration of these issues. The message of these
books can be over-sentimentalized but they deal with important issues about the
ways in which narratives of oppression are transmitted at a level that is relevant to
young children. For instance, at Key Stage 1, *Amazing Grace* (Hoffman 1991),
tackles 'head on' the effect of society's transmission of 'stories' about racism and
sexism. *The Whales' Song* (Sheldon and Blythe 1998), suitable for Key Stage 1–2,
allows consideration of the ways in which different 'worldviews' can determine
our treatment of others and of the world. These stories about story prepare
children to reflect upon the means by which powerful narratives determine the
'dominant discourse' about power relationships between different groups. The
aim of this approach to religious education is to promote the respect of a diversity
of faiths and cultures but also enable children to reflect critically upon them. The
intention is that if children begin by learning about different worldviews on their
own terms and thereby to respect difference, they will be enabled to examine the
ways in which faith traditions are sometimes used to disempower disadvantaged
groups. In this way, we can not only inform children about the religious diversity
in their local and global community but also equip them with the attitudes and
skills necessary to make a contribution towards constructing a socially just,
radically egalitarian and anti-oppressive society.

Notes

[1] In Britain, the situation is confused by the fact that some state primary schools are also
church schools. There are two types of Anglican 'church schools': 'controlled' church
schools are within the responsibility of the Local Authority and therefore are required
to follow the Agreed Syllabus; schools designated as 'aided' church schools, however,
receive some funding from the Local Authority but are under the educational
jurisdiction of the diocese. Subsequently, they are not legally obliged to follow the
Agreed Syllabus. Instead, they usually follow a curriculum determined by the Anglican
Diocese. In addition to this, there are also independently-funded schools which are
founded by faith communities. The role of religious education in these 'faith schools' is
beyond the remit of this chapter. The argument of this chapter is, however, that there is
a distinction between the process of nurturing into a particular faith community and
the role of multi-faith RE as an essential aspect of a child's education, which should be
part of the curriculum regardless of the distinctive religious ethos of the school. There is
considerable debate about the impact on social cohesion of the existence of these faith
schools. The White Paper *Schools Achieving Success* (DfES 2001) commended the 'ethos'
created by faith schools and called for an expansion in their numbers. At the same time,
however, the White Paper called for changes in the admissions policies of such schools
and sought to promote inclusiveness by setting a target of 20 per cent non-faith pupils
in the school's composition. (Gardner 2005:7). For further discussion of these issues see
Gardner, Cairns & Lawton (2005).

[2] Although this was the report on RE in Secondary Schools, it contained the rationale on
which the later report on RE in Primary Schools was also based.

3 The Swann Report, *Education for All*, claimed that RE had '... a central role in preparing pupils for life in today's multi-racial Britain and can also lead them to a greater understanding of the diversity of the global community ... RE can also contribute towards challenging and countering the influence of racism in our society.' It did, however, specify that for this to happen, a phenomenological approach had to be adopted (Swann 1985:496).

4 A discussion of the added complexity of the role of collective worship is beyond the remit of this chapter. Despite the tendency of government legislation to link religious education and collective worship they are, in fact, very distinct entities.

5 To explain further the role of these model syllabuses in buttressing right-wing educational ideologies, see Grimmitt 2000a:7–14.

6 This means a position which assumes the Christian worldview to be the 'norm' from which to evaluate all other religious perspectives.

References

Barber, M. (1994) *The Making of the 1944 Education Act*. London: Cassell.

Cole, W.O. and Mantin, R. (1994) *Teaching Christianity*. London: Heinemann.

Cooling, T. (2000) 'The Stapleford Project: Theology as the Basis for Religious Education', in M. Grimmitt (ed.) *Pedagogies of Religious Education*. Great Wakering, Essex: Mc Crimmons.

Copley, T. (1997) *Teaching Religion: Fifty Years of Religious Education in England and Wales*. Exeter: University of Exeter Press.

DES (1988) *The Education Reform Act*. London: HMSO.

DfES (2001) *Schools Achieving Success: Government White Paper*. London: DfES.

DfES (2007) *Excellence and Enjoyment: Learning and Teaching in the Primary Years*. London: HMSO.

Every Child Matters (2007) Online at www.everychildmatters.gov.uk

Erricker, C. & Erricker, J. (2000) *Reconstructing Religious Spiritual and Moral Education*. London: Routledge.

Gardner, R. (2005) 'Faith Schools Now: An Overview', in R. Gardner, J. Cairns and D. Lawton (eds) *Faith Schools: Consensus or Conflict?* Abingdon: Routledge/Falmer.

Gardner, R., Cairns, J. and Lawton, D. (2005) *Faith Schools: Consensus or Conflict?* Abingdon: Routledge/Falmer.

Grimmitt, M. (ed.) (2000) *Pedagogies of Religious Education*. Great Wakering, Essex: Mc Crimmons.

Grimmitt, M. (2000a) 'The Captivity and Liberation of Religious Education and the Meaning and Significance of Pedagogy', in M. Grimmitt (ed.) (2000) *Pedagogies of Religious Education*. Great Wakering, Essex: Mc Crimmons.

Hampshire County Council (2004) *Living Difference: the Agreed Syllabus for Hampshire, Portsmouth and Southampton*. Winchester: Hampshire County Council.

Hoffman, M. (1991) *Amazing Grace*. London: Frances Lincoln.

Jackson, R. (1997) *Religious Education: An Interpretive Approach*. Hodder & Stoughton.

Lindon, J. (1999) *Understanding World Religions in Early Years Practice*. London: Hodder Arnold.

London Borough of Brent (1986) *Brent Religious Education: Now and Tomorrow*. Wembley: London Borough of Brent Education Department.

Qualifications and Curriculum Authority (1994) *Religious Education Model Syllabuses*. QCA.

Qualifications and Curriculum Authority (1994) *Non Statutory National Framework for Religious Education*. QCA.

Schools Council Project (1971) *Schools Council Working Paper 36 – Religious Education in Secondary Schools*. London: Evans/Methuen.

Sheldon, D. and Blythe, G. (1998) *The Whale's Song*. London: Red Fox.

Simon, B. (1994) *Education and the Social Order 1940–1990*. London: Lawrence and Wishart.

Surrey County Council Education Committee (1945) *Syllabus of Religious Instruction*. London: HMSO.

Swann (1985) *Education for all*. London: HMSO.

Wedderspoon, A. G. (1966) *Religious Education, 1944–1984*. London: Allen and Unwin.

Wright, A. (2000) 'The Spiritual Education Project: Cultivating Spiritual and Religious Literary through a Critical pedagogy', in M. Grimmitt (ed.) *Pedagogies of Religious Education*. Great Wakering, Essex: Mc Crimmons.

Chapter 17

Community and Foreign Languages

Dina Mehmedbegovic

1. Introduction

This chapter will explore equality issues for children with skills in languages other than English and the way that languages themselves are positioned within the National Curriculum in England and Wales. It will also outline a set of recommendations for school practice, teacher training and policy development based on the author's own research and experience in London schools, case studies of good practice and relevant pedagogical theories. These recommendations have been developed with the aim of creating a school ethos which would lead to a shift from a culture of defining the educational experiences of bilingual pupils by the language skills they lack in English, to a culture of recognizing an all-encompassing communication competence developed by the use of different languages.

Raymonde Sneddon (2007) in a recent presentation of her research with bilingual children in mainstream primary schools referred to being 'privileged' to work with children using their first (non-English) languages and to witness their intellectual joy and challenge of 'solving the puzzle' that negotiating two languages presents to these children. The reality is that only a small number of bilingual children in schools will themselves be privileged to operate bilingually in their mainstream classrooms and to experience the excitement, joy and stimulus of bilingual learning. When something that is an integral and essential part of one's experience and cognition is exercised only as a privilege of the lucky few, who are selected for research purposes, or who are educated in bilingual schools such as the French Lycée in London, then it becomes a type of educational and, ultimately, social inequality.

This chapter will provide insights in issues relevant to children with skills in languages other than English, who will be referred to as bilingual/multilingual, and the issues relevant to positioning of languages themselves in the context of England and Wales.

2. Key Concepts

The key linguistic concepts this chapter engages with are: bilingualism, multilingualism and plurilingualism. The existence of multiple definitions of these concepts reflects the complexity and variety of approaches to relevant issues.

2.1. Bilingualism

The definition of bilingualism encompasses huge variations across different contexts. The common feature of all definitions available in theory and in practice lies in the recognition that bilingualism at the individual and societal level refers to the existence of two languages – meaning recognition that a number of individuals and communities use two languages in their everyday lives. In some cases, like the definition that is used in England and Wales for the purposes of collecting data and allocating the Ethnic Minority Achievement Grant (EMAG)[1] to schools and local authorities, the 'existence' of two languages is defined as 'exposure to two languages; living in two languages' (City of Westminster 2002). This is a very inclusive definition which avoids complex and, in some cases, hard-to-measure aspects of language use: competency, proficiency, fluency and literacy. The reasons why it is essential for England and Wales to have a broad, inclusive definition of bilingualism in education are explored below.

The criterion 'living in two languages' allows for the inclusion of a variety of profiles of bilingual pupils. These different profiles can be divided into three main categories. First are bilinguals born and educated in England and Wales. They are children from well-established immigrant communities, mainly originating from Commonwealth countries: India, Bangladesh and Pakistan. Lately, with the revival of Welsh, there are also children being educated bilingually in English and Welsh in Wales. Second, are recent immigrant bilinguals. They come from many different European, Asian, African and South American countries. They are mainly new to English and have various degrees of literacy in their first language. For example, children coming from countries in conflict may not have had any schooling prior to their arrival in England and Wales. The third group consists of settled immigrant bilinguals. These children were not born here, but have been immersed in an English-speaking environment for different lengths of time. They are at different stages of developing bilingualism depending on their backgrounds, support and abilities. They differ from bilinguals born here mainly by having had some of their formal education in a language other than English. Therefore, in many cases they have higher levels of literacy and background knowledge in that other language.

Having a definition that enables teachers and practitioners in education to identify all these different cases as types of bilingualism is essential in order to: collect data that accurately reflect the full range of societal bilingualism; to recognize experiences and language practices which children engage with outside school; to identify a variety of needs in terms of language development and language support that these children may have; and to allocate funds available for language support proportionally to identified needs, mainly by means of the Ethnic Minority Achievement Grant.

The application of an exclusive definition of bilingualism such as Bloomfield's (1933), which only recognizes bilinguals with 'native like control of two languages', also referred to in the literature as 'balanced bilingualism', would on the one hand produce a very narrow picture of a highly bilingual context such as England and Wales. On the other, it would leave practitioners dealing on an everyday basis with highly complex issues such as: what is meant by 'native like control'?; how is it measured?; what variety of a particular language is identified as standard?.

2.2. Multilingualism versus plurilingualism

The concept of multilingualism is relevant in the case of this chapter because it is used by practitioners and policy makers within the education system, in the context of 'multilingual classrooms'. In reality, this is a recognition of the fact that some, or many, pupils in these schools have a language other than English as a part of their lives, mainly outside the mainstream school. In Wales, the bilingual education agenda within the education system has far more presence than it does in England. However, bilingual education references in Wales are exclusively used in relation to Welsh–English bilingual schools. On the other hand, in continental Europe, policies engage with the discourse of plurilingualism, which I turn to next.

The main distinction between multilingualism and plurilingualism is that a multilingual approach is about having many different languages coexisting within individuals or society, with the ultimate aim of achieving the idealized competency of the native speaker (Council of Europe 2001:4). A plurilingual approach, on the other hand, places the emphasis on the process of learning the language of home, society, other peoples; developing communicative competencies as a life-long activity; and in different situations, flexibly calling upon different parts of this competence, in order to achieve effective communication. Plurilingualism recognizes an all-encompassing communication competence that is made up of different languages that one person has been exposed to and acknowledges the partial nature of the knowledge anyone can have of one language, be it their mother tongue or not. Therefore, plurilingualism removes the ideal of the native speaker as the ultimate achievement and replaces it with the aim of an effective pluralistic communicator who draws on his/her varied repertoire of linguistic and cultural knowledge in a flexible, creative and individual way (Council of Europe 2001:4, 5, 169). The emphasis in this process is on attitude formation and language and cultural awareness as essential to one's understanding of social and physical environment, and ability to function effectively in the local, national and international environment (Tosi and Leung 1999:17).

Apart from the European policy documents, this debate can also be identified in the concept of 'truncated multilingualism' (Blommaert, Collins and Slembrouck 2005; Blommaert 2005; Haviland 2003). The definition of this concept rejects the ideal of full and balanced competence in different languages as imposed by dominant ideologies and, instead, emphasizes competencies that are organized around topics or activities with which speakers engage.

A plurilingual orientation, outlined in the above-referenced European policy documents, provides a good starting point for rethinking communicative skills in education and practice. First, because it offers a tool to understand the linguistic reality in which most bilinguals operate. Based on my observations and personal experience, it can be compared with an image of a lively, bubbling, hot spa that feeds on all our linguistic experiences: different words for the same concepts; different ways of expressing one thought, one feeling; different jets of vocabulary and grammar always interacting, comparing, finding its way in the different languages used. And, sometimes, out of tiredness or in extremely emotional situations, this linguistic spa freezes and bilinguals or plurilinguals or truncated multilinguals struggle for words in any language. Interestingly, I have discovered after many years of using this metaphor that Jacquemet (2005) uses a similar one: 'whirlpool of electronic, communicative turbulence'. In my opinion a plurilingual orientation provides the most accurate conceptualization of the experience described.

Second, the concept of plurilingualism has important implications for classroom practice in terms of assessment. It implies that the linguistic or communicative competence of a bilingual cannot be reduced to a simplistic sum of linguistic competences measured in isolation in each of his/her languages. Grosjean (1982) pointed out that a bilingual person is not two monolinguals. Bilingual competence is not a sum of quantities but a qualitative difference.

Third, plurilingualism recognizes the reality of children and adults acquiring only partial knowledge of relevant languages. This reality need not be dismissed as a shortfall, but acknowledged as an important contributor to the enrichment of an 'all encompassing communicative competence'. This type of approach encourages language and cultural learning, appreciation and awareness, in formal and informal settings, for bilinguals and monolinguals alike. It places value on all of our linguistic experiences and provides a formal framework for their recognition – a Language Portfolio, as proposed by the Council of Europe. According to this proposition, every child in Europe would have a Language Portfolio in which to enter anything significant referring to their engagement with other languages and cultures. This means that even if a pupil cannot use a language in conventional ways, it is still valuable to recognize that s/he has, for example, done a project on it and has certain theoretical knowledge about it; or if a pupil has spent a certain period of time exposed to it, within the family, community or while abroad; participated in an oral discussion involving several languages; analysed a linguistic feature in one language in relation to another language and similar examples (Tosi and Leung 1999).

2.3. Parallel world: international and bilingual schools

Official research reports, government policy documents, and figures given for bilingual children in the context of education in England and Wales, refer always only to mainstream schools. When discussing bilingual/multilingual children and the positioning of other languages, one cannot help but notice that there is a visible parallel universe of private international and bilingual schools. In official discourse on bilingualism, there is an absence of acknowledgment that certain types of bilingual parents, able to choose private education, opt for schools which offer exposure to and learning in more than one language. In terms of research, professional development and teacher training these two worlds also never seem to meet. I would like to argue that without engaging with the elite layer of bilingualism/multilingualism that exists in our society, we are in danger of having a skewed picture of this phenomenon on the whole.

One of the first questions we may want to ask is: how big is this parallel universe? London International School Association (LISA) lists 16 international schools in London. There are also another nine schools in bigger urban centres throughout the UK such as: Cardiff, Manchester, Edinburgh and Aberdeen. Some of these schools have over 1,000 students on role. In addition there are bilingual schools supported by the governments of particular countries, such as the already mentioned French Lycée, which is heavily over-subscribed, German Grammar School, Norwegian School and a number of American schools. And there are also international schools supported by the European Union. Their curriculums and positioning of languages vary mainly depending on who their supporting body is: a national government or the European Union.

Insights into positioning of language skills of individuals and languages in these schools can be gained by looking into a selection of mission statements and curriculum programmes. ACS International School in Egham which caters for students from 40 different countries who speak 24 languages states that it 'encourages all students to maintain their native language proficiency as it helps their acquisition of additional languages' and it offers Native Language Enrichment programmes (www.acs-england.co.uk/schools/egham).

Southbank International School aims to develop 'able communicators' through English, MFL and Native Languages (www.southbank.org). The International School of London emphasizes on its website the contribution their leadership team made at the conference of the Alliance for International Education in Istanbul, in 2008. Their head and deputy heads gave presentations on: collaborative intercultural training among colleagues; using cultural diversity as a curriculum resource; and mother tongue programmes (www.i-slondon.com).

The following statement by a headteacher encapsulated well the aspirations of families who opt for international schools:

> 'Tomorrow's entrepreneurs will need exceptional interpersonal skills to relate to others and to work successfully within a mobile and multicultural society. Thus they will be able to work professionally in more than one language and will be trained to understand cultural differences, having studied alongside friends from many different countries.' (M. J. Cooper, Principal of the British School of the Netherlands, in Mejia 2002:249).

Now I will turn to the world that most of us know better: mainstream schooling.

3. Insights into Valuing Languages in Mainstream Schooling

3.1. How diverse are mainstream schools?

In terms of diversity and languages represented, every Inner London main-stream school boasts greater wealth in terms of its linguistic capital than the international schools mentioned above: around 40 different languages spoken is often registered. In terms of percentage of bilingual students, according to London Challenge[2] figures, 52 per cent of students in Inner London secondary schools are bilingual/multilingual, while in individual schools the percentage may vary from 30 to over 90 per cent[3] (London Challenge 2007). A figure used by the Greater London Authority (GLA), based on the data collection of Inner and Outer London local authorities, indicates that one-third of the London school population has English as an additional language (GLA 2006). Figures that are frequently quoted for the number of languages in all of London are based on a study published in 2000 (Baker and Eversley 2000). According to this study, which is in need of an update, there are 360 languages spoken by children in London schools.

At the national level, out of 17 per cent of the school population in mainstream schooling classified as ethnic minorities, 10 per cent are EAL pupils. The two single largest minority groups are Pakistani (3 per cent) and Indian (over 2 per cent) (DfES 2005).

An independent survey conducted by the National Centre for Languages (CILT) provides the figure of 702,000 bilingual children in England (CILT 2005:1). However, this figure needs to be taken as an underestimate because around one quarter of local authorities did not participate in the CILT's survey, and in terms of responses from complementary and mainstream schools, which provide tuition in community languages, the response rate was only 18 per cent (CILT 2005:4).

The DfES has not so far published the national data on minority languages, even though many individual authorities collect this type of data on an annual basis. For example, the City of Westminster recorded 108 languages spoken by its pupils, with Arabic and Bengali each featuring as the home language of over 11 per cent of Westminster's school population (City of Westminster 2008). *Language Trends*, a study published by CILT, uses the figure of 'at least 300 languages', but again considering the return rate of their survey, this must be significantly below the actual number (CILT 2005:1). With the introduction of the new DfES *Guidance on the collection and recording of data on pupils' languages* (DfES 2006a), it is expected that more authorities will be collecting individual languages data from January 2007. However, the collection of languages data remains voluntary for schools and local authorities. Therefore, complete data returns are not guaranteed even under the new Guidance, especially during the initial period.

In Wales, there are 93 languages registered in use by around 15,000 children, which is around 3 per cent of the total Welsh school population (EALAW 2003). This figure does not include children who are bilingual in English and Welsh. Prior to this study, there was no national data collected. Two years on, the CILT study (2005) documents an increase in the number of languages, from 93 to 98, but their figure for the number of bilingual children is almost halved in comparison with the EALAW figure: 'at least 8,000 children'. The most likely explanation is missing data, due to incomplete data returns. However, there is a possibility that this may be due to bilingual children increasingly opting to identify English as their first language without identifying the use of other languages as well. This occurrence has been noted by practitioners and researchers in England.

3.2. 'They just want to be like the others.'

These observations that bilingual pupils self-identify as monolingual are often accompanied by teachers' comments: 'They just want to fit in and be like the others.' Having encountered these comments in schools where over 60 per cent of pupils were on records as bilingual, I started looking for the explanation of who these 'others' were. This search has led to researching attitudes to bilingualism in mainstream schooling. I have interviewed bilingual parents, headteachers, lead professionals, politicians and pupils. The following are some key insights into positioning of languages and language skills, linked to relevant theories.

At the beginning of this section, I would like to emphasize that there are pockets of outstanding practice when it comes to the use of other languages in school life. Indeed CILT's website (www.cilt.org.uk) is an excellent resource for keeping up to date with the development of good practice driven either by the Government's national initiatives such as Languages Strategy or CILT's project Our Languages, which focuses on community languages. The evidence collected in these projects in support of arguments that use of other languages positively impacts on learning across the curriculum, enhanced skills in English, better school performance and improved parental and community involvement, is extremely encouraging and optimistic (CILT 2009). However, in this section I will not be focusing on what is available and accessible in the public domain. My aim is to dig deeper and explore equalities through the voices that can only be heard in anonymized circumstances. My attempt is to address the reality of mainstream schooling where bilingualism is still very widely seen as a deficit and obstacle to learning.

The following statement provides a glimpse of the dominant myths of intellectual confusion associated with bilingualism:

> In the classroom, my feeling is, that it could potentially be confusing to children who come to the school knowing or at least having an implication that the school is where English is spoken to find that the people are trying to speak in their language or trying to communicate in their language. I can't quite honestly see that. Although we do it here in sign form (welcome signs), I'm not sure ... I think it's playing the game. We have notices all around the school saying welcome in different languages – well they could say anything to be honest. They could be rude words, for all I know. Nobody is saying you can't speak another language or that we don't respect your other language, but when you come to school English is the language you expect to hear, that's the language you expect to use. And that way they would develop their bilingualism I think.' (Headteacher of a London school, in Mehmedbegovic 2008)

This view can be seen as one of the fundamental monolingual fallacies. The idea that more than one language causes confusion, translates into practice implication that the best way is to keep the languages in separate boxes, one for school and learning and one for home and 'culture maintenance'. This kind of monolingual dictatorship, underpinned by 'monoglot ideologies' as defined by Blommaert, Creve and Willaert (2005), confines the natural use of two languages by bilinguals into the domain of inner dialogue. In the invisible and inaudible moments of thinking bilinguals will still be drawing on both of their languages in a preparation for a disciplined monolingual language output, expected from their environment.

As argued by Baetens Beardsmore, there is a 'deep-seated and widespread fear of bilingualism, mainly among monolinguals'. His suggestion that this fear is only overtly about language, culture and education, but, in fact, it is of politico-ideological nature (Baetens Beardsmore 2003:10, 20), is visible in the sample of views I collected in the interviews while researching attitudes to bilingualism. The interviewed MPs and lead professionals referred to great fear of immigration, fear of difference, fear for the National Curriculum, fear of the British identity being subsumed into the European Union, fear of children who can speak a language a teacher cannot, and fear of people who have a foot in two different cultures (Mehmedbegovic 2008).

Leaving aside primarily political issues such as immigration and Britishness, I would like to concentrate on the pillar of most centralized systems of education in nation states: the National Curriculum.

What does the National Curriculum need protecting from? One interviewee referred to 'not having problems with segments of the school day being used to promote or teach community languages, but within the context of protecting the National Curriculum' (Labour MP, Interview data).

This statement opens many questions. Are minority languages seen as something that can be merely tolerated as long as the National Curriculum is not endangered in any way? Why is the set of knowledge and skills validated as the National Curriculum of higher importance than one's first language? Who makes these decisions on behalf of minority groups?

These decisions are often dressed up in the rhetoric of good intentions: achieving on National Curriculum levels opens up prospects of social mobility, economic well-being and access to power. But is 'protecting the National Curriculum' discourse about giving individuals the skills and knowledge to change power relations fundamentally on a wider scale, or about protecting the system that serves to reproduce existing power relations?

The theory of cultural reproduction (Bourdieu 1998) dismisses education as the neutral 'transmitter' of knowledge and skills. Instead, education is the instrumental force in class and inequality reproduction. When it comes to the acceptance of first languages not being a part of official learning, school environment and curriculum, Bourdieu's (1998) conclusions that the groups lower down the hierarchy of power accept a social construct like marginalization of first languages as a necessity of the same order as the law of gravity, seem to correspond to reality very well (see Hill 2009, in this volume).

It is interesting to look at the case of Welsh. According to the interviewees, it is within the memory of their living family members that there was the acceptance that: 'it (Welsh) wasn't a language that you would get on in life with' and 'was not on a par with English' (Interview data, Bilingual Welsh professional). In many ways this minority, but indigenous, language was exposed to much harsher means of oppression than any minority language of present day immigrant communities. With the Act of Union in 1563, Welsh lost the use and status of the official language, and domination of English remained unchallenged until 1942. However, it was not until the 1960s that the first Language Act restoring the status of Welsh was adopted. It took another 30 years for a significant process of language revival to develop (Ager 2003:69). One interviewed Welsh speaker reflected on this history in the following way: 'it is surprising that we (Welsh speakers) have survived at all' (Interview data, Bilingual Welsh professional). The same interviewee identified that Welsh people were glad to be 'regarded as European rather than just British', because it gave them 'more status as a nation and as a language' (Bilingual Welsh professional, Interview data). It was interesting to notice that the context of a United Europe was seen by this interviewee as supportive and affirmative to her language and national identity, while one of the interviewed English politicians expressed the view that:

> ... the British are worried about their identity being subsumed within the European Union. ... and I also don't think British people have had their say or that there has been a proper debate about the implications of mass immigration for our culture. And until we are able to have that debate in a sensible and mature fashion there will be a sort of culture of fear and concern to which politicians will respond in a fashion which is to say, while there is immigration they are in favour of integration. If we can, as it were, have immigration under control and people feel a bit more relaxed about it, then we can also have a much more relaxed and mature discussion about the benefits of multiculturalism, which I think includes benefits of bilingualism. (Conservative MP, Interview data).

Considering the fact that English is one of the twenty official languages of the European Union and the most dominant one (Phillipson 2003), while Welsh is not one of the official languages, this difference in attitudes does not seem to correspond to the relevant facts. Possible explanations could be explored along the lines of possibly xenophobic feelings among native English speakers, identified by another interviewee:

> Xenophobia is implicit in the indigenous population of Britain. It is based on the fact that different is dangerous. They've had a 'diet of difference', not a diet of what is similar, what is similar about people, and then what is unique about them. British National Party type of people talk about difference. (English lead professional, Interview data).

Or perhaps another explanation could be in the changes of power balance through the protected status of minority languages within the larger entity of the United Europe. European language policies emphasize preserving and promoting language diversity in Europe as essential to the success of European integration (Vienna Manifesto on European Language Policies, Principle a) 2001).

The approach that 'unease about language is almost always symptomatic of a larger unease' (McArthur, in Dewaele, Housen and Wei:20) seems relevant to the views presented above. The fact that immigration, xenophobia, Europhobia, the need to protect the National Curriculum and British identity were addressed by interviewees demonstrated identification of this 'larger unease' as directly linked to bilingualism/multilingualism.

This brief insight into attitudes to bilingualism and practices influenced by them exposes some of the discourses that create environments in which bilinguals self-identify as monolinguals. The argument that children 'just want to fit in and be like the others' is at odds with the growing number of schools where the 'others' are also bilingual/multilingual. It is also at odds with the increase of multilingualism at the global level. Therefore, I would like to suggest that these children are more likely trying to fit in with the only affirmed profile in their learning environment: the monolingual one.

3.3. The issue of choice

One of the main arguments that I have been confronting when promoting encouragement of first language maintenance and its use in learning has been the issue of choice. Some teachers argue that children and parents 'don't want it', while some academics suggest to me that loss of first language is a 'natural language shift' and that addressing it as language loss results in 'romanticizing bilingualism'.

This view was also championed by one of the MPs I interviewed:

> There will be certain families that will integrate and leave behind their home language and there will be others that will take it seriously and continue to speak it at home. I think we should allow the individuals the freedom to decide which culture they are going to inherit and take on board. (Conservative MP, Interview data)

I find these arguments especially damaging to any attempts of achieving equality in the domain of languages. Their danger is in the fact that they mask the issues of social injustice, with the rhetoric of civil liberties, freedom, integration and choice. Bourdieu's (1991) concepts of 'cultural capital' and 'misrecognition' are essential in understanding how misleading these arguments are. Cultural capital is a category that encompasses past and present experiences, histories of communities an individual is linked to, languages, customs, system of beliefs and lifestyles. The domination of cultural capital of certain groups is often perceived by the dominated groups, whose cultural capital is devalued in the context of education and society in general, as natural, without recognizing it as a social and political construct. Bourdieu terms this process 'misrecognition'. The end result of this process is symbolic violence, which minority groups often comply with and, in a way, even support, due to the misrecognition that their cultural capital is of a lesser value and that it is natural to lose it and replace it with the one that has more value.

The interview data I collected revealed an interesting polarization of two sections of society who relate differently to the experience of symbolic violence.

One consists of speakers of non-indigenous minority languages such as Bengali or Bosnian. Statements like 'you are nobody if you don't speak English' (Bosnian parent) or 'Bengali has no value' (bilingual pupil) are delivered without hesitation by members of minority groups and communicate that they are currently experiencing what Bourdieu defines as symbolic violence. The other group are the interviewees who are either bilingual English–Welsh speakers or have Welsh as a part of their background. Their responses reflect the fact that Welsh speakers are surfacing out of a period of partly misrecognition, partly open oppression. Statements like 'in the past people didn't regard Welsh as being on a par with English' or 'Welsh was not seen as a language that you would get on in life with', in contrast to statements like 'there is actually economic benefit in speaking Welsh' and 'Welsh is valued among employers' – represent the shift in values that has happened during their lifetime, as a result of the Welsh Assembly-led, strategic and well-resourced Welsh revival programme. Another layer that adds to this polarization of experiences among different groups is the fact that these interviewees, who work as lead professionals, are aware that symbolic violence continues for other groups in their own environment:

> Because Welsh is given such a high level of importance within the Government of Wales Act ... community languages are left to ... they are almost third status, they are given a lower status than English and Welsh'. (Interview data, Welsh civil servant).

Therefore, I would like to argue that the issue of choice needs be considered within the context of society that predominantly communicates low-value messages in relation to non-indigenous minority languages and provides no information for parents on how to bring up children bilingually and what the benefits are. The exception is the initiative Twf (Growth) launched in Wales in 2002 which resulted in health visitors responsible for visiting mothers and newborn babies providing basic information on benefits of bilingualism, free packs with further information and toys (Edwards and Pritchard Newcombe 2005). The only criticism of this excellent initiative is that it only refers to English–Welsh bilingualism.

In England, bilingual families have no access to crucial information needed for making sure their children enjoy a healthy linguistic diet and a supportive environment. Research done by the Qualification and Curriculum Authority (2005) acknowledged that 'bilingual parents have little or no awareness' what benefits come with first language maintenance (QCA 2006:2).

The 'experience of choice' for me is best summed up by an adult who reflected on the decision her father made several decades ago upon the arrival of their family in England, which was to 'leave behind their Punjabi' and communicate in English only. She describes as the consequence of that choice – the feeling of 'being disinherited'. In Wales an interviewee talked about 'a generation in Wales who did not learn Welsh and now regrets it' .

These reflections highlight another very complex issue to do with choice, which is the responsibility of adults who make language choices for young children. By this, I mean the decisions about what language is used at home, if a child attends a mother tongue school or not, whether a child will have opportunities to acquire fluency and literacy in first or home language, whether s/he will be encouraged to produce school work bilingually, whether s/he will be encouraged to take exams and other formal assessments in that language, and similar choices which will collectively contribute to the development of plurilingual competencies.

The questions we need to ask are: How informed are these choices? Are they in agreement with the principle of supporting children to develop their full potential? Are their maximizing or curtailing equality of opportunity? And most important of all, will these choices stand the test of time and appear to be the best choices in ten or twenty years' time? Will they 'create tomorrow's entrepreneurs with exceptional interpersonal skills' or will they result in feelings of regrets, disinheritance, deprivation and social injustice?

My suggestion is that this is the choice that educators need to discuss, not the false choice of freedom to devalue and abandon one's language.

4. Modern Foreign Languages

The impact of England's monolingual culture on economy and society was well documented in the Nuffield Enquiry Report which revealed that 20 percent of potential orders were lost due to a lack of skills in languages. A 1 per cent increase in export is worth £2 billion to the UK economy. In terms of specific industries, tourism relies on nearly 20 millions customers a year from non-English speaking countries who have sufficient proficiency in English, while key staff at a London airport were found, not only unable to respond to a request in another language, but unable to distinguish if the request is in French or Spanish (The Nuffield Foundation 2000:23).

The Nuffield Report initiated a cycle of parliamentary debates that eventually resulted in the introduction of the National Languages Strategy in 2002. The following are a sample of views debated in the House of Lords:

> ... language, not the mythical fog, will isolate the Continent from us and us from the Continent. Seriously, I believe that our failure to play our full part in Europe during the past half century stems in substantial part from linguistic inadequacy.' (Lord Watson of Richmond, Lords Hansard 2002)

> We found that there was demand from pupils and parents and from employers and business. It is hard to get the statistics together. It is a mark of lack of seriousness with which we regard this matter that good statistics are not available. But there is an enormous amount of evidence of language learning at considerable inconvenience and expense to families outside the educational structures.' (Baroness O'Neill of Bengarve, Lords Hansard 2002)

> Our young people are talented as any. But they are being denied the opportunity, the encouragement and the basic provision. A child can be keen as he or she may be, but if the basic provision is lacking, nothing substantial happens.' (Baroness O'Neill of Bengarve, Lords Hansard 2002)

I argue that there are probably very few young people who really understand the different opportunities within the different professions and jobs, and their potential to enhance their careers as a consequence of language ability.' (Baroness Ashton of Upholland, Parliamentary Under-Secretary of State, Department for Education and Skills, Lords Hansard 2002)

This selection of views represents interests of different sections of society: young people, parents, employers, businesses and the interest of the state and its place in Europe. The lack of language skills impacts on all of them, resulting in some type of loss. However, a point specific to children and young people is that their loss is based on a lack of opportunities and provision. It is the policy-making mechanism and the system that are responsible for their disadvantage, rather than their own actions or lack of them.

In the case of bilingual young people, the lack of opportunities to use and further develop their knowledge and talents translates into an even more problematic loss of already existing linguistic capital. However, the fact that bilingual young people can take GCSEs in almost all languages represented in the UK is a big advantage in the existing system. This is further improved by the recent introduction of the Languages Ladder assessment. This assessment allows children and young people who are speakers of a particular language, but have no literacy or a low level of literacy in that language, to have the skills they do possess recognized. This is achieved by separating assessments and grades for different skills: speaking, reading and writing (CILT website, www.cilt.org.uk).

Another significant development is the National Language Strategy in the primary sector (DfES 2002). This opens up the possibility of having languages available in primary schools and this time schools can decide which language they will offer. All languages are seen as equally appropriate for achieving the language learning aims of the Strategy. Giving a language the status of a mainstream subject taught within the National Curriculum will positively impact on the status of that language in the wider society. Therefore, communities that use that language will be more motivated in terms of language maintenance.

A welcome pointer to the future is that with the change of the Cabinet in June 2007 it has been proposed that schools will be given more flexibility to shape their curriculum and will be encouraged to offer languages perceived to be of economic importance to Britain, such as Mandarin and Urdu (www.dfes.gov.uk).

5. Recommendations for practice and policy

The following recommendations have been developed with the aim of creating school ethos which would lead to a shift from a culture of defining the educational experiences of bilingual pupils by the language skills they lack in English. My argument is that seeing a child through a 'he has no English' lens only leads to low expectations and ultimately to committing educational and social injustices.

5.1. School practice

The language diversity in England and Wales, further complicated by the uneven and fluctuating numbers of speakers of particular languages, represents real obstacles to developing provision for minority languages in terms of tuition. However, I argue that an awareness of the issues linked to the benefits of bilingualism and the importance of language diversity and language main-tenance should be built into the mainstream curriculum. The type of awareness and respect towards other religions currently communicated within mainstream education can be used as a starting point in developing language awareness. Alternatively, if schools engage with the ecological approach to language diversity, these issues can be taught alongside environmental awareness.

The systematic lack of engagement, throughout key institutions, with the bilingualism of children going through the system leads to drawing parallels with the criticism of policies and practice that have failed to engage with the racial and ethnic differences labelled as 'colour blind' or what Blommaert terms 'normative monoglot ideologies' (Blommaert, Creve and Willaert 2005). This blindness to diverse linguistic profiles imposes a fallacy that not only is monolingualism the norm, but that everything else is undesirable or even embarrassing.

The crucial question is: how do schools that have speakers of 40 or more languages represented provide 'an affirmative mirror' (term after Cummins 2003) to all of them? How do they communicate to bilingual children that their bilingualism is a resource? First of all, bilingual children and their parents need to be given a clear, affirmative, consistent message by the school and their teachers in terms of a healthy bilingual linguistic diet. It should be a part of the Healthy Schools Initiative, currently implemented in schools focusing on healthy eating and lifestyle. As well as using every opportunity to say: 'It is good for you to eat fruit and vegetables every day'; it should also be said: 'It is good for you to speak, read and write in other languages'. In terms of Modern Foreign Languages, as a matter of urgency, the issue of categorization needs to be addressed. The fact that England, unlike any other European country, has categorized languages into Modern Foreign Languages, with high status and educational value, and world languages/minority languages/community lan-guages, with low value, has been one of the main obstacles to remedying the under-utilization of the existing linguistic skills. It is increasingly obvious that abandoning this division on MFL and other currently spoken languages makes sound economic and social sense and would be a significant step towards having an equal opportunity system applied to languages. That does not mean that some languages will not be seen in a particular time frame or setting as more favourable, which is not an issue. The issue is the institutionalized hierarchy and ultimate discrimination of languages, which needs to be removed.

5.2. Teacher training

Currently, there is widely varying provision for new headteachers and teachers, especially London teachers, on race, ethnicity, culture and religion, although language is not identified as a category in its own right. One can argue that it can be assumed with certainty that language will feature and be covered under culture and possibly ethnicity. Based on my research findings (Mehmedbegovic 2008), I would like to challenge this assumption and suggest that culture and language awareness and appreciation do not develop jointly. Fostering positive and informed attitudes to bilingualism and linguistic diversity, in general, needs to be addressed as an area in its own right with sufficient time allocation.

Again, it is helpful to look at our parallel universe: how is the independent sector equipping teachers to work with EAL learners? University of Cambridge provides an internationally-recognized course and accreditation: International Teacher Certificate (ITC). Teaching EAL is one of the five standards on which this course is based. Therefore, international teachers of all types are required to demonstrate skills to teach EAL. This is very much the idea underpinning the mainstream model of working with EAL pupils, but the difference is there is no core compulsory training for all mainstream teachers.

In addition to making explicit language awareness a part of the compulsory modules for headteachers' training, I would like to suggest that requirements in terms of understanding bilingualism and its implications in education should be built into the recruitment process and person specification for headteachers applying for headships of schools with one third or more bilingual children on roll. It should be a reasonable expectation that candidates can demonstrate knowledge and commitment to the specific needs of such a significant proportion on their school roll.

5.3. Policy development

May (2001) argues that there 'appears to be a high correlation between greater minority participation in the governance of education and higher levels of academic success by minority students within that system'. Minority participation in decision-making processes, rather than being just a debate among political classes as suggested to me by the interviewed Conservative MP, leads to a closer match between minority aspirations and subsequent educational provision (May 2001:181).

Fishman (1989) advocates the concept and practice of ethnolinguistic democracy where minority languages are recognized and present in schools and education alongside each other and without representing a challenge to a common, core curriculum and official language. This concept can be recognized in the approach of the European Council to language policy and planning, emphasizing inclusion and encompassing the standard state language, home languages, European languages and world languages (Council of Europe 2001:5, 169).

One of the key public debates centred around the European language framework and policy, but in fact questioning much wider issues of the European Union, was: can Europe speak in one voice in so many different languages? The answers to this question are not only found in manifesto statements that preserving and promoting language diversity are essential to European integration (Vienna Manifesto 2001), but also in a very complex concept of plurilingualism. In my opinion, plurilingualism is the final qualitative step that for individuals removes the fallacy of different languages they use as separate competencies and entities, while for societies it opens new perspectives on all different languages as contributors to the overall communication, learning and development in those societies. This type of approach is liberated from either majority or minority languages being threatened. It recognizes that every language has its own distinctive contribution to make and, therefore, it communicates messages of value attached to all of them. For a society committed to racial equalities and recognition of contributions of different racial groups, recognizing languages as a significant part of that equality is essential.

Notes

1   Ethnic Minority Achievement Grant (EMAG) is currently part of the Standards Fund and its allocation to schools and local authorities is based on a 'needs formula'.
2   London Challenge is a regional strategy for London launched by the Government in 2003.
3   Examples of schools with over 90 or over 90 per cent EAL pupils: Hallfield Infants, Westminster, Kensington School, Newham, Gateway, Westminster (City of Westminster 2009)

References

Act of Union (1563)
Ager, D. (2003) *Ideology and Image*. Clevedon: Multilingual Matters.
Baker, P. and Eversley, J. (eds). (2000) *Multilingual Capital*. London: Battlebridge Publications.
Baetens Beardsmore, H. (2003) *Who is Afraid of Bilingualism*, in J. M. Dewaele, A. Housen and L. Wei (eds) *Bilingualism Beyond Basic Principles*. Clevedon: Multilingual Matters.
Blommaert, J. (2005) *Discourse: A Critical Introduction*. Cambridge: Cambridge University Press.
Blommaert, J., Collins, J. and Slembrouck, S. (2005) 'Spaces of Multilingualism'. *Language and Communication*, 25, 197–216.
Blommaert, J., Creve, L. and Willaert, E. (2005) 'On Being Declared Illiterate: Language Ideological Disqualification of Dutch Classes for Immigrants in Belgium'. *Language and Communication*, 25.
Bloomfield, L. (1933) *Language*. New York: Holt, Rinehart and Winston.
Bourdieu, P (1991) *Language and Symbolic Power*. Cambridge: Polity Press.
Bourdieu, P. (1998) *Acts of Resistance*. Cambridge: Polity Press.
CILT (2005) *Language Trends*. Research Report. London: CILT.
CILT (2006) *Positively Plurilingual*. Report. London: CILT.
CILT (2009) 'The Business of Languages', *CILT Newsletter*. London: CILT.
City of Westminster (2002) *Language and Basic Skills Service Handbook*. London: City of Westminster Local Authority Documents.
City of Westminster (2008) *Key Statistics 2008*. London: City of Westminster Local Authority.
City of Westminster (2009) *Key Statistics 2009*. London: City of Westminster Local Authority.
Council of Europe (2001) *Common European Framework of Reference for Languages: Learning, Teaching, Assessment*. Cambridge: Cambridge University Press.
Cummins, J. (2003) *Bilingual Education: Basic Principles*, in J. M. Dewaele, A. Housen and L. Wei (eds) *Bilingualism Beyond Basic Principles*. Clevedon: Multilingual Matters.

Dewaele, J.M., Housen, A. and Wei, L. (eds) (2003) *Bilingualism Beyond Basic Principles*. Clevedon: Multilingual Matters.

DfES (2002) *National Languages Strategy*. London: DfES Publications.

DfES (2005) *Ethnicity and Education: The Evidence on Minority Ethnic Pupils*. Research Report. London: DfES Publications.

DfES (2006a) *Guidance on Collection and Recording of Data on Pupils' Languages*. London: DfES Publications.

EALAW (2003) *The Achievement of Minority Pupils in Wales*. Research Report, Wales.

Edwards, V. and Pritchard Newcombe, L. (2005) *Language Transmission in the Family in Wales: An Example of Innovative Language Planning*, 29, (2), 135–150.

Fishman, J. (1989) *Language and Ethnicity in Minority Sociolinguistic Perspective*. Clevedon: Multilingual Matters.

Greater London Authority (GLA) (2006) *A Profile of Londoners by Language*, DEMAG Briefing, 2006/26.

Grosejean, F. (1982) *Life with Two Languages*. Cambridge: Harvard University Press.

Hansard Records (2002) Lords and Commons Hansard. Online at http://www.publications.parliament.uk/cgi-bin/semaphoreserver.

Haviland, J. (2003) 'Ideologies of Language: Reflections on Language and US Law'. *American Anthropologist*, 105, 764–774.

Hill, D. (2009) 'Theorizing Politics and the Curriculum: Understanding and Addressing Inequalities through Critical Pedagogy and Critical Policy Analysis', in D. Hill and L. Helavaara Robertson (eds) (2009) Equality in the Primary School: Promoting good practice across the curriculum. London: Continuum.

Jacquemet, M. (2005) 'Transidiomatic Practices: Language and Power in the Age of Globalisation', *Language and Communication*, 25, 257–277.

London Challenge (2007) *Annual LCLL conference*. London: IOE.

May, S. (2001) *Language and Minority Rights: Ethnicity, Nationalism and the Politics of Language*. England: Longman.

Mehmedbegovic, D. (2008) 'Leading Increasingly Linguistically Diverse Schools'. *Educate*, IOE online Journal, Special London Issue.

Meija, de A.M. (2002) *Power, Prestige and Bilingualism: International Perspectives on Elite Bilingual Education*. Clevedon: Multilingual Matters.

The Nuffield Foundation (2000) *Languages: The Next Generation*. Report. London: The Nuffield Foundation.

Phillipson, R. (2003) *English Only Europe? Challenging Language Policy*. London: Routledge.

QCA (2006) *Community Languages in the National Curriculum*. Report and Guidance.

Sneddon, R. (2007) *London Seminar*. London: IOE.

Tosi, A. and Leung, C. (1999) *Rethinking Language Education: From a Monolingual to a Multilingual Perspective*. London: CILT.

Vienna Manifesto on European Language Policies. Vienna, 2001.

Chapter 18

Citizenship Education

Gavin Baldwin, Linda Whitworth and Philip Kovacs

Introduction

This chapter focuses on two main elements of citizenship education as it has developed in primary schools: first, the relationship between citizenship education and equality in school and second, the essential relationship between citizenship education, equality and the outside world.

It also allows us to address what we see as one of the major challenges facing education at the beginning of the twenty-first century – the development of a more equal, inclusive pluralist society that is reflexive enough to support and nurture the identities of individuals and groups while exploring the alliances and tensions that will inevitably develop from such a project through the development of a more equal, socially just, and democratic society. In part, we are reducing citizenship education to (or celebrating it as) identity politics in *practice*. In our context, this practice must be democratic. For that to happen, all identities must be respected equally and given an equal voice, but equal respect will not promote equality enough. In itself, it does not challenge unequal institutional and systemic practices.

'Voice'

We wish to define voice in a particular way, using the work of Peter McLaren. 'Voice,' he explains, 'suggests the means that students have at their disposal to make themselves "heard" and to define themselves as active participants in the world' (2003:245). The second half of McLaren's definition is essential. Being heard and being included is one matter; being able to actively participate in social reconstruction when one is ignored or left out is quite another. We absolutely do not wish to leave the reader with the impression that citizenship education ends with hearing and tolerating. Students and teachers learn citizenship skills when they listen to one another about the worlds they live in, identify issues and injustices in their lives, and then act together to create conditions more suitable to democratic living. Voice without action is meaningless, and citizenship education that ends with being heard and tolerated mere tokenism, as it leaves the causes of silence and intolerance unchallenged and unchanged.

Improving social equality requires recognition, understanding and celebration of diversity, and action in the face of injustice and in the face of practices that are discriminatory, for example, on grounds of social class, 'race', sex/gender, sexuality and disability. Recognition, celebration and action lie at the centre of our view of citizenship education. For people to make a full contribution to a democratic society they have to feel that they are valued, that they belong, and that they have the power to work with others to create conditions where humans can value each other and develop a sense of belonging despite differences. Citizenship education must, therefore, be committed to all aspects of equality of opportunity, particularly in terms of race, gender, class, disability and sexual orientation. Equally as important, citizenship education, as explored in this chapter, must help students develop the capacities and skills to be actors, citizens who identify injustice and oppression of any sort and act to end them. This means:

1. making these sociological categorizations and the oppressive relationships within them a focus of the curriculum
2. developing an analysis of the contributory causes of inequality between various categories
3. developing strategies to overcome those inequalities, and
4. putting those strategies into action.

Paulo Friere helps us begin the task with a challenge:

We must dare to say scientifically and not as mere blah-blah-blah, that we study, we learn, we teach, we know with our entire body. We do all these things with feeling, with emotion, with wishes, with fear, with doubts, with passion and also with critical reasoning. However, we never learn, teach or know with the last only. We must dare so as never to dichotomize cognition and emotion ...We must dare to learn how to dare in order to say no to the bureaucratization of the mind to which we are exposed ever day. (cited in Foreword, Freire 2005:xxiv–xxv, see also, Hill 2009, in this volume; 2010).

This challenge is particularly appropriate for primary school citizenship education, which allows for the combination of Personal Social and Health Education (PSHE) and Citizenship Education in a way that the secondary curriculum does not. This combination enables the development of the individual in both a private and public context without artificial distinction (as may occur at secondary) and further encourages the development of a citizen as a rational/emotional being with a fluid social/political identity. Moreover, at the primary level there is a clear emphasis on *practising citizenship*. The curriculum has not been developed to analyse alone, but to teach ways of taking effective action through democratic processes.

Importantly, as citizenship educators, Freire's challenge has particular resonance because it reminds us that citizenship education can serve bureaucratization and compliance as easily as it can serve democracy, equality and liberty. This is especially the case at the time of writing as tension between groups is fuelled by inequalities (local and global) and the rhetoric of national security is used to plead cooperation and conformity. Agreeing with McLaughlin's model of 'maximal' citizenship (1992) we argue that citizenship education should be an opportunity to develop pupils' critical faculties, understanding and knowledge of issues such as equality and justice and, through such education, become democratically empowered actors rather than passive subjects who witness injustice but are incapable of ending it.

To promote democracy there needs to be a recognition of the worth of each individual, while at the same time, an understanding of the values and actions which create a society sympathetic to social negotiation. Such processes are often seen as serving the cause of social harmony or social cohesion but we are uneasy about terminology here – the vision may be for social harmony but that implies a degree of agreement that is probably impossible and may even be undesirable if it leads to social stagnation. Cohesion may be a better term if it can tolerate the social friction that is inevitable and leads to challenge: the recognition of new and alternative possibilities and enriched social development. To achieve a truly democratic society, the whole citizen (rational/emotional) must develop the knowledge, skills and attitudes to recognize and engage in a 'cultural navigation' (Ballard 1994) of multiple identities through social negotiation with other identities (individual and group) that they encounter. This negotiation must be multi-voiced and all identities empowered to speak, be heard, and act.

Schools as Democracies

Having rehearsed some contextualizing ideas, we now wish to focus on schools as one environment in which democracy can be experienced by children. In a primary school, the ethos can be controlled with some success to provide a supportive setting for democratic experiment. Diversity can be celebrated and multiple voices can be heard. It is also possible to enable children to negotiate tensions between each other and begin to understand and confront the inequalities that shape their lives in the outside world. Their awareness of these issues and ability to articulate their concerns is richly and movingly illustrated in *Not Aliens*, Hilary Claire's wonderful study of two London primary schools (2001). Her interviews with primary-aged children reveal their concerns about social injustice: they were worried about racism, violence and crime and wanted to be protected by adults from issues such as war.

Akosua (7 years old) talked about her mother being left short of money when her father left, and suggested the council should provide homes for the homeless. In her words:

> I'm worried about the world ... the way that people are treated, like they're treated like flies and everything, and they haven't got nothing to eat, and like some people are rich and they don't even spend money, and the people who are poor, and I don't even like that about the world. I'm worried about whatever's going to happen, like I think it's gonna be bad. (*ibid.*:98–99)

The study further shows that young children can engage emotionally in the suffering of others as a result of social injustice. Chrissy talked about the guilt she feels,

> I feel guilty because whenever people like say, people pick on people, I feel really guilty and stuff, because I feel sorry for them, and I care, I care about it, really, all the people who have something wrong and people in hospital and things like that, blind people and things like that, that's me, why I feel guilty. (*ibid.*:34)

David Sehr argues that schools are places where pupils structure their own beliefs in a cultural context (Sehr 1997:85). They can, therefore, be 'incubators of citizens' democratic values and their capacities for thinking, discussion and debate.' (*ibid.*:64); and 'at their best, schools will provide opportunities for students to take this journey of discovery and formation of self in its interaction with society. They can do this through focused study of, and experiential learning in, the social world outside the school' (*ibid.*:64).

To construct a more equitable and inclusive society, however, we need to develop new understandings of social reality – a reality that allows those who are marginalized to contribute their voices (see, McLaren 2003) to their construction of the world in a way that can influence and enrich the lives of everyone. According to Manning Marable (1992) such projects can transform society by reinvigorating a materialistic and oppressive system with humanism; in short, to restore humanistic values to marginalized and oppressed groups. For us, such a debate needs to begin at an early age. There needs to develop a 'habit' of critical discourse – a natural development of the young child's almost obsessive 'why?' – in order to challenge the monolithic orthodoxies that may limit social 'negotiation.' In order to encourage such critical discourse development, and the challenging of monolithic orthodoxies, students should understand that democracy has evolved because of people asking the 'obsessive why.' As Zygmunt Bauman explains:

> Democracy expresses itself in a continuous and relentless critique of institutions; democracy is an anarchic, disruptive element inside the political system; essentially, a force for dissent and change. One can best recognize a democratic society by its constant complaints that it is not democratic enough. (2001:55)

Understanding democracy as an idea constantly in flux, Giroux argues, 'helps to redefine the role of the citizen as an active agent in questioning, defining, and shaping one's relationship to the political sphere and the wider society.' (2005:29) Said differently, if we raise children to understand that the world has been made and can be remade, which, in fact, democracy requires us to do so, they are far more likely to develop into adults with the skills, capacities, beliefs, and desires to remake the world.

Working from this general consideration of democratic education we will now trace the development of citizenship education in schools and suggest that the most appropriate model of citizenship to underpin our teaching and learning is that of the 'cosmopolitan citizen' (Osler and Starkey 2005). This concept will then be allied to Lord Parekh's analysis of Britain as a 'community of communities'. The implication of this for the identity of a citizen will then be explored, and we will argue for an engaged citizenship, where students work together to address pressing issues in their lives.

The Argument for Cosmopolitan Citizenship

In such aspiring democratic schools, teachers construct their teaching within the framework of the National Curriculum. The Framework for Personal, Social and Health Education and Citizenship at Key Stages 1 and 2 requires teachers to develop knowledge, skills and understanding about becoming informed citizens. These include skills of enquiry and communication, participation and voluntary action. Emphasis is placed in both Key Stage 1 and Key Stage 2 on 'developing good relationships and respecting the differences between people' (DfEE/QCA 1999:138, 140). Some authors have argued for more emphasis to be given to human rights and anti-racism and that children be recognized as citizens not just citizens in waiting (Osler and Starkey 2005). Nonetheless, although limited in scope, National Curriculum Citizenship provides opportunities both as a separate subject, and across the curriculum, to focus pupils' learning on issues that might help develop a robust pluralist and inclusive society. It also facilitates democratic forms of teaching and learning as implied in David Sehr's analysis above.

This project can be pursued even more effectively if we accept the model of 'cosmopolitan citizenship' developed by Audrey Osler and Hugh Starkey (2005). Seeing citizenship as made up of status, feeling and practice they argue thatL

> Cosmopolitan citizenship is a *status* deriving from equal entitlement to human rights. Importantly, it is based on a feeling of belonging and recognition of diversity across a range of communities from the local to the global. It is a practice involving negotiation, equitable resolution of differences and work with others to promote freedom, justice and peace within and between communities. Cosmopolitan citizenship requires consideration of the meaning and the implications of belonging to a world community and an appreciation of the nature and scope of common human values. It also requires an understanding of equality and diversity in local communities. Learning for cosmopolitan citizenship therefore requires the development of global awareness, an understanding of and commitment to human rights, and opportunities to act with others to make a difference. (*ibid.*:78)

They see this in the spirit of the *United Nations Convention on the Rights of the Child* as helping young citizens 'to recognize their common humanity, make connections between their own lives and those of others and operate effectively in contexts of cultural diversity and change' (*ibid.*:78).

This model is not, however, static. Citizenship is seen as a process of becoming. As Armstrong (2004:114–15) argues in his study of the life stories of adults with learning difficulties:

Far from being a state of *being*, 'citizenship is perhaps better understood as a process of *becoming*. As such it is constantly being contested and negotiated in social practice. It is concerned with the endeavours of individuals and groups to participate on equal terms and with dignity in the life processes of which they are part ... It is about belonging and being accepted on terms that are fair, humane and dignified.' (Osler and Starkey 2005:77)

As a response to globalization, cosmopolitan citizenship provides a positive model for developing an awareness of the interconnectedness of the world while investigating and challenging inequality and exclusion locally and globally. In short, it demands the study of the development of a range of communities and an understanding of change over time. The model is particularly attractive to us as it reflects the reality of the best practice that we see developing in schools that we value by enabling cultural navigation and social negotiation. It enables young people to develop their identity in relation to the responsibilities owed to them and that they owe to others, and it requires respectful, critical dialogue as rights and responsibilities intersect and conflict. Importantly, cosmopolitan citizenship education teaches children that action can be used to bring about social change, ultimately increasing social and political opportunity and equality.

The idea of community is central to much discussion of Citizenship as communities are often seen as places where people develop and express their identities. Without offering an analysis of communitarianism (Arthur 2000, for example) it is important to critically consider the model of community on which cosmopolitan citizenship is based.

The Parekh Report

Lord Parekh in his report on *The Future of Multi-Ethnic Britain* (2000) wrote that:

> Citizens are not only individuals but also members of particular religious, ethnic, cultural and regional communities, which are comparatively stable as well as open and fluid. Britain is both a community of citizens and a community of communities, both a liberal and a multicultural society and needs to reconcile their sometimes conflicting requirements.' (Parekh 2000:ix)

This draws attention to the complexity of citizenship as it is lived and felt in Britain. We have our rights and responsibilities as citizens and feelings of belonging to other communities both within and beyond geographic boundaries, for example, a community with particular religious or ethnic affiliations. Although beyond the scope of Lord Parekh's report, we see no reason why these categories of community should not also relate to political, class, gender, disability or sexual affiliations.

This is important because it is often within communities that people explore and develop their identities: where they feel secure and empowered, committed and included. These communities must, therefore, be valued and included by the state in a community of communities so that as Osler and Starkey point out 'the

state guarantees the freedom for individuals to determine their own identities.'
(Osler and Starkey 2005:82)

It is important, however, that Parekh's ideas don't lead to a cosiness that
ignores the political realities of those communities with power and those without.
As suggested above and developed below, citizenship must develop this political
understanding, investigating how the world impacts identity negotiation and
navigation, paying attention to unequal power relationships children experience
from an early age.

Citizenship in the Primary Curriculum

We now turn our attention to the realization of these ideas in the primary
classroom.

Citizenship and PSHE are non-statutory at the primary stage and citizenship
is relatively new in the curriculum. This inevitably means that it is competing for
space in an already crowded curriculum. Citizenship is, however, more than a
subject; it is an empowering approach which gives context to pupils' experience
and learning. We would argue that many of the ideas underlying the citizenship
curriculum have long been part of the ethos of many, though not all, primary
schools. Promotion of the whole child's development, including social and moral
understanding, self-esteem and community identity, has been central to the
primary vision for many years. The advent of citizenship as a subject has enabled
greater focus on the skills and understandings pupils need to understand and
participate in local and global contexts. As mentioned above, a particular
strength of the primary curriculum for citizenship is that it blends the
development of the private individual with the public citizen. This is potentially
enabled by the combination of two subjects that are treated separately in the
secondary phase: PSHE and citizenship. A considerable advantage of this
combination is that it enables teachers to help young people articulate their
personal and public identities and learn to recognize and value those of others.

From the Crick Report (1998) (QCA 1998) onwards, citizenship education
has focused on the three elements of social and moral development, community
understanding and political development. In primary school terms this means
from an early age engaging pupils with their individual identities and, through
growing confidence in self, learning to understand and negotiate with those
around them. In The Early Years Foundation Stage documentation, children's
status as citizens, rather than citizens 'in waiting' is affirmed.

All children are citizens and have rights and entitlements. (DCSF 2007)

The Framework indicates the importance of developing individuals who are
'resilient, capable, confident and self-assured,' and who are engaged in positive
relationships with others. (DfES 2007:9). Pupils' diversity is valued and
respected and learning environments which are rich and stimulating are
expected.

These qualities are developed in the primary curriculum through the teaching
and learning of PSHE and citizenship education. This is divided into four strands:

1. Developing confidence and responsibility and making the most of their abilities
2. Preparing to play an active role as citizens
3. Developing a healthier, safer lifestyle
4. Developing good relationships and respecting the differences between people.

(DfEE/QCA 1999:136–140)

Within this structure children can learn to culturally navigate and socially negotiate.

They can be made aware of their own and others' multiple identities from an early age. They can see that they operate in a variety of contexts in their daily lives and that in different situations certain identities are more dominant and others rendered more powerless than others. Celebration of diversity by pupils and teachers encourages everyone to see themselves as significant and equal members of a community which is interested in what individuals contribute.

Seeing one's self as a significant member of a community is not possible without being able to act in, with, and upon communities. Included in this view of citizenship is a recognition of the values needed by children to support them in their developing role as active citizens. These values include feeling good about themselves, being open-minded about diversity, showing respect or tolerance for others, and acting in the face of disrespect, intolerance, and other forms of injustice. Osler and Starkey base their 'Cosmopolitan citizen' on the United Nations Convention on the Rights of the Child. These rights have the potential to transcend religious or cultural teaching and as such provide a global context for the values which underlie them. By being taught about their rights and schools operating as examples of how these rights are lived out in practice, pupils can become attuned to expressing their own views fluently and practising active citizenship in the school context. By developing their awareness of their relationships with others locally and globally, students realize the interconnectedness of their identities and their common humanity.

Examples of this approach can be found in a report commissioned by UNICEF, *Rights, Respect and Responsibility Initiative to Hampshire County Education Authority*. This highlights how a group of primary schools developed an emphasis on human rights which has impacted on school ethos, pupil and staff empowerment, behaviour and 'a notable change from confrontational and adversarial approaches to conflict resolution to rights-based explanations' (Covell and Howe 2005:10).

Developing from this, UNICEF UK has developed a 'Rights Respecting School Award' for schools (2008).

This is based on four strands:

1. Leadership and management for embedding the values of the UNCRC in the life of the school.
2. Knowledge and understanding of the UNCRC.
3. Rights respecting classrooms.
4. Pupils actively participate in decision-making throughout the school.

Millfields Community Primary School in Hackney, London is an example of such a school (http://www.unicef.org.uk/features/feature_detail.asp?feature = 39). The pupils' understanding of human rights was promoted through teaching in PSHE and other areas of the curriculum. Class Charters were drawn up which matched rights with a responsibilities. 'Friendship finders' and 'peer mediators' were established to help pupils experience a more inclusive atmosphere in the playground. The global dimension was also included, 'Pupils are encouraged to empathize with, not sympathize, with their counterparts elsewhere' (UNICEF 2009). The reports make it clear that the impact of this teaching has been instrumental in improving pupil relationships in the schools who have embraced the scheme.

There is a tension between developing a group identity among children, which emphasizes what is shared in common and the identification of difference which marks one individual or group identity out from others. Teachers who provide authentic decision-making opportunities in the classroom are enabling children to express their own preferences and helping them to realize that within a group theirs might not be the only or indeed the popular choice. Teachers who support pupils by encouraging them to voice reasoning behind their decisions are helping them to develop their skills of argument while also modelling an approach to coping with conflict. Self-esteem is central to the development of citizens but those who are confident that they have a right to be heard also need to balance this right against their responsibility to consider others.

> The PSHE and citizenship guidance advocates developing confidence in oneself, good relationships and respect towards others. The ability to withstand abuse and to refrain from using it against others is, at least in part, dependent on self-confidence and self-esteem ... Self-confidence and self-esteem develop with relation to the world in which the children are growing up, a world beset by serious inequalities and difficulties. It is not just that children have to negotiate and come to terms with these difficulties in their own lives, but that they also provide the ammunition which they can use against each other so effectively. (Claire 2004:25)

Claire recognizes the realities of the classroom and playground. Teachers have to become skilled in helping staff, parents and pupils to create and sustain the type of school ethos in which self-esteem and celebration of difference can flourish. This is a political stance where equality is active within the confines of the school. But it also inevitably spills over into the multiple identities of the pupils operating in forums beyond the school itself.

The Role of the Teacher

There is a need for teachers not only to develop their own classrooms as inclusive and equable, but also to be conscious of the types of negativity pupils may be encountering outside the classroom and actively seek to counteract them. Part of this awareness needs to be self-awareness, as teachers consider how their own experience influences their decision-making and the types of resourcing and examples which they promote in class.

If our efforts to enhance self-esteem and mutual respect are to be realistic, relevant and lasting, we need to educate ourselves about children's actual experience and what they know and care about in their personal lives outside school. (Claire 2004:39–40)

This indicates the depth of knowledge and understanding that is required of the professionally- and ethically-charged teacher. How do teachers understand the experience of the children themselves, help them to function in the world they have to negotiate, and inspire them to attempt change in those situations where they recognize injustice and inequality?

To begin with teachers need to learn to be social negotiators. Many teachers have developed and continue to navigate their identities in worlds very different from the people they teach. How do they pay more than passing reference to diversities which they may not have experienced in their own lives?

In her examination of her own experience as a white teacher teaching mostly South Asian pupils in *YOU wouldn't understand*, Sarah Pearce clearly charts her realization that her 'life experience was structured by the fact that [she] was white' (2005:27). Her writing explores not only racial but also gender and class differences, investigating how differences impact on children's perceptions and their behaviour in school. Pearce discusses how, at an early stage of her research, her pupils felt uncomfortable talking about race because they felt it was a taboo subject. She acknowledges that she failed to challenge their silence or their thinking because she saw racism as an individual's problem and she did not want to cause controversy.

I felt that it was inappropriate for me to push the children if they did not want to pursue certain topics. I now feel there are times when this is precisely the teacher's role. I already had ample reason to suppose that they did not want to discuss the matter because they had picked up subtle messages that the issue of race is to be avoided. I wanted to challenge this way of thinking. How could I do so without asking the questions and pressing for answers? (Pearce 2005:31)

The responsibility of the teacher is to analyse their own position and understanding and then take steps to change their teaching to make it more truly inclusive. This does not mean ignoring or playing down racial or gender issues but providing pupils with strategies to challenge and cope with them, moving from reaction to proaction in helping pupils become comfortable with their own identity and capable of challenging stereotypes. Pupils need to be aware not only of their own perceptions of themselves but also need ways of recognizing and dealing with how others see them.

Importantly, teachers need to tune in to the experience that their pupils are having, helping students make connections between their personal experiences and the socio-political factors shaping them. In the words of Henry Giroux:

This presupposes that teachers familiarize themselves with the culture, economy, and historical traditions that belong to the communities in which they teach. In other words, teachers must assume a pedagogical responsibility for attempting to understand the relationships and forces that influence their students outside the immediate context of the classroom. (Giroux 2005:199–200)

We cannot underscore enough the importance of teachers bridging the gap between schools and communities. Students come into classrooms with plenty of material for discussion and examination, so that the teacher can familiarize himself/herself with the worlds his/her students inhabit. As Giroux explains, when teachers ignore the experiences students bring into classrooms from their communities, they are depriving their students of a 'relational or contextual understanding of how the knowledge they acquire in the classroom can be used to influence and transform the public sphere.' (*ibid*:201) When this happens, citizenship education becomes something studied at school but not practised at home. Moreover, as Ira Shor argued some time ago, 'the teacher who does not seek to learn from the class will not listen carefully to what students offer, and hence will condition students in non-speaking' (Shor 1987:105). 'Non speaking' in the primary grades often marks the beginning of 'non speaking' throughout schooling, a silence that many children carry with them after graduation. Finally, as Freire (1996) reminds us, pedagogies which seek to end injustice 'must be forged *with*, not *for*' the individuals facing that injustice. Teachers who don't begin teaching citizenship with their students' lived experiences become banking educators, ultimately serving to further marginalize their students by teaching them that their needs are ancillary to those of the teacher or school.

A pedagogic model for teaching about diversity

Developing confident, socially aware, and active pupils requires pedagogies which engage them in dialogue with the diversity around them. In developing a classroom which respects this diversity, classroom teachers need to ensure that the way they represent the world outside the classroom is not reinforcing stereotypes or culturally divisive perceptions. One of the areas many teachers are anxious about is the representation of religions and the religious/cultural interface. There is anxiety about causing offence unwittingly, or misrepresenting religious belief or practice, because of ignorance or lack of understanding. The Interpretive Approach (Jackson 1997, 2004), questions the teaching of religions as reified systems and instead has a more fluid, layered approach which sees religious believers as individuals, experiencing their own personal belief, as members of groups within religions and as members of the religious traditions themselves. By being introduced to information about British children who are, for example, Ukrainian Catholic Christians (Barrett 1994a), Orthodox Jews (Barrett 1994b) or Theravadan Buddhists (Barrett 1994c), pupils can explore variety within, as well as between, traditions. This approach to diversity within and between religions is significant in encouraging pupils to negotiate their understanding with reference to their background and perceptions. Rather than seeking to study religion from a neutral position, pupils are encouraged to recognize their own position in relation to the material studied and extend and challenge their perceptions in the light of their increasing understanding. Through the use of questions and critical thinking, pupils and teachers ask questions about religious and non-religious belief, enabling them to explore what it might mean to individuals to have faith rather than presenting religions as uniform in belief and practice.

By building respect for the experiences held within the class community, teachers enable their pupils to recognize, reflect on and share their own perceptions through the process of enquiry. It develops a more subtle understanding of communities, moving from 'dominant' to 'demotic discourse' (Baumann 1996, cited in Jackson 2004). This changes the representation of, for example, 'the Muslim community' to a richer understanding of the range of practice within Muslim communities which also reflects cultural and linguistic differences. This more negotiated and dialogic approach has much to offer when considering Parekh's community of communities. Moving from dominant to demotic discourse enables a more equal balance between communities and the classroom can be a more neutral location for pupils to discuss on a more individual and less representative level.

> At the social level, religion is approached in relation to its cultural context and the attendant debates about concepts such as community, ethnicity, nationality ... At the level of individual identity, each person's religious or secular beliefs or outlook can be positioned in relation to such factors. Thus religious education as a subject of study ... ha[s] a great deal to offer to overlapping fields such as multicultural or intercultural education, antiracist education and citizenship education. (Jackson 2004:126)

This pedagogy has particular relevance in citizenship because it emphasizes dialogue and enables pupils to see the negotiation individuals and groups make to practise their religion or culture in a multicultural society. This approach, respectful as it is of learners as experts in their own lives and teachers as co-learners, has much to teach us about the social negotiation we wish to foster through citizenship education as explored in this chapter.

It also reminds us of Freire's emphasis on the effect of dialogue:

> Through dialogue, the teacher-of-the-students and the students-of-the-teacher cease to exist and a new term emerges: the teacher-student with student-teachers. The teacher is no longer merely the one-who-teaches, but one who is himself taught in dialogue with the students, who in turn while being taught also teach. They become jointly responsible for a process in which all grow. (Freire 1996:61)

This model of the teacher-student, who is reflective and recognizes the authenticity of pupils' voices, is an important one for our vision of the citizenship-based school as well as for citizenship as a subject. Demotic dialogue is a political experience in the classroom. It requires a teacher to provide an environment where children feel trusted and where there is a belief that change is possible. For demotic dialogue to occur the teacher needs to be a flexible facilitator, conscious of the process as well as the outcome of learning and ready to assist young pupils in creating and navigating such dialogue. This is not an easy process. It should be a consistent approach, influencing all teacher-pupil interactions and extending further into all relationships in the school community.

If we are to empower people to hope and dream of a different reality, we must engage the important question of convincing them that real freedom is not an individualistic pursuit but one predicated on the fostering of a community. (Van Heertum 2006:50)

Developing teaching and learning about controversial issues

If we accept the challenge laid down by Freire to engage wholeheartedly in developing a new order which rejects 'the bureaucratization of the mind' we need to see citizenship education as an opportunity to extend pupils' engagement in and experience of political processes. Pupils developing a growing confidence in their own abilities to speak and act and a growing awareness of their own identity in relation to others, need to exercise these in authentic situations where they can change and challenge outcomes. Many schools use the structure of schools' councils to enable pupils to experience decision-making as representatives and on behalf of others, but in some circumstances this can be tokenistic and limited to those pupils who are articulate or popular. More fundamental to pupils' experience are the opportunities created by the teacher for pupils to exercise real choice in everyday decision-making.

This leads us to consider how teachers and pupils can employ citizenship skills and understanding to tackle controversial issues, both in the classroom and in relation to the wider world. Controversial issues are a much greater test of cosmopolitan citizenship than exercises in class cohesion, but it is in these more stressed circumstances that teachers and pupils can consider their progress in terms of respect for diversity.

Controversial issues such as what to do about global warming, human rights or conflict and peace in various areas of the globe all affect the pupils in our schools and they affect them in different ways. Pupils need exposure to diversity in opinions and opportunity to argue from a basis of equality and fairness. There can be a danger in primary schools of over-simplification or a desire to reach conclusions when the process is the significant learning.

Steiner (1992) cited in Ross (2007) concludes that:

Most teachers concentrate on the self-esteem building, interpersonal skills and cooperative element of the world studies approach. They also engage in work that questions stereotypes such as racism or sexism. The environment, local or 'rain forest', is a common theme. Global issues, such as those to do with the injustice inherent in the current systems of the global economy, or highlighting the cultural achievements and self-sufficiency of Southern societies... receive far less attention. (Steiner 1992:90)

While some primary teachers may feel engagement with the political dimension which underlies many global issues is too complex for young pupils, as Claire and Pearce argue, children are already exposed to political dimensions in their everyday lives. Therefore, teachers need to help students understand and challenge situations which reinforce injustice. Very young children understand fairness and it is important for them to see that injustice and inequality can be successfully challenged in their own experience. The classroom community which develops and abides by its own rules, and where children are engaged in the process of deciding what is just, can provide the safe, structured situation where controversial issues can be deliberately explored, as well as providing a forum to deal with issues as they arise in the class or playground. We turn now to examining a few models of classroom practice that show promise for helping children develop the skills and capacities necessary to act as respectful and engaged citizens.

Turning Theory into Practice

We have attempted to make the theoretical case for a robust understanding of citizenship education. However, knowing the path and walking the path are two different experiences, and we wish to offer readers three ways of 'doing' citizenship education with primary pupils. Following Freire, dialogue is central to each of these lessons, and these lessons require teachers to help children think more critically about themselves, the texts they encounter, and the worlds they co-create. The lessons that follow were adapted from six texts that cover a decade worth of research (Bigelow, *et al.* 1999; Christensen 2000; Michie 2005; Ginwright, Noguera, and Cammarota 2006; Singer 2006; Adams, Bell and Griffin 2008; Griffen-Wiesner and Maser 2008).

1. Identify '-isms.' Teachers can work with pupils to help them identify racism, sexism, heterosexism and classism in books, in films, in commercials, in music, or on television. The Council on Interracial books for Children offers ten ways children and teachers can identify various 'isms' in the texts they read (Bigelow, *et al.* 1999), and their model can be used with any 'text' children encounter. Ideally, children who practise identifying injustice in texts will become adults who identify injustice in their lives. Working with their pupils and respecting their experiences and voices, as called for by Freire, teachers can use texts to explore tokenism, stereotypes, loaded words, the roles of women or people of colour, and the lifestyles celebrated or condemned inside various texts. Questions teachers might use while helping children explore these texts include: Are the women in the story all stay-at-home mothers? Do the women do all the housework and look after the children while the men pursue exciting and often practical careers? Are the heroes all white or all male? Do the criminals in the film have a certain accent and come from similar groups of people (ethnic minorities, social classes, etc.)? What type and why? How does the text or film support or undermine the roles that we play in our real lives? What problems do you see with the people and events in the text or in the film? Do the texts or films present conflict from different points of view? What could we/you do differently than the characters in the text to make conflict resolution more equitable and just?

2. Studying the world of work. Matt Witt (Bigelow *et al.* 1999), offers a compelling case for teaching citizenship through exploring what pupils' parents do for a living:

If a goal of education is to teach students to think critically about how our society is organized, their study of work-related issues cannot be limited to learning the difference between 'goods' and 'services,' memorizing a few names ... and soaking up donated corporate propaganda that paints an incomplete picture of the country's economic life (*ibid.*:70).

At the primary level, pupils and teachers can begin studying work by asking children to create pictures or stories about their parents' or carers' jobs. In an effort to bridge the gap between classrooms and communities, teachers might invite parents/guardians to come into school to discuss their work. Teachers should invite pupils to engage in dialogue regarding a number of related issues: How has work changed over time? Are some people better suited for some jobs than others? Why don't women earn as much as men in all jobs? How much should we be paid for our work? What makes work satisfying and important to society? What causes unemployment? What should our society do about unemployment? Could/should the class help someone who is unemployed?

3. Use children's books to teach children about others who have worked to change the world for the better. While Jessica Singer (2006) uses children's books with secondary students to study individuals who effect positive change in the world, her work can be adapted and used with primary students. As she explains, 'Children's books often address sophisticated and politically charged topics and include many of the qualities of great literature.' (*ibid.*:4) After compiling a number of children's books which contain themes of social action, she asks her students to respond to questions which help them compare the texts to their own lives. Teachers might ask students to identify the character that acts to change their world, describing what made the character decide to take action, and listing the hurdles the character had to overcome to succeed. Importantly, Singer asks her students to identify and discuss the individuals who helped the character succeed. Finally, students should be asked to compare what they read to what they live, reflecting on how they can use elements of the story in their own lives. Singer also invites her students to write their own stories, describing a time when they were the victim of discrimination or injustice, a witness to discrimination or injustice, or a time when they treated someone else unjustly. Both of these exercises help primary educators legitimate students' lived experiences, resulting in classroom practice that is less banking and more problem posing, as called for by Freire.

4. Identify and solve problems. Ask students to discuss real problems they see in school or the local community. Either by voting or negotiating some form of consensus, have students select one problem and create an action plan for solving it. Students may decide that the stream adjacent to their building is polluted and needs to be cleaned. This is an opportunity for the teacher to combine science, ecology, writing and citizenship education as pupils collect information on the water source and usage. They might campaign for the collection of water samples, develop an action plan which they may send to elected officials or local news agencies, and then monitor and record the clean-up of the stream, ideally with the help of local volunteers contacted by the school. This would enable

children to see the procedure for local environmental campaigning, the stages of a campaign (with possible fund-raising opportunities), and hopefully a satisfactory conclusion which impacts directly on their local environment. At the end of the process students should be invited to reflect on what went right and wrong, discussing how their experience with one stream could be shared with other pupils (perhaps via a class-maintained website) who want to clean up the areas around their schools. The critical teacher should ask students how rivers become polluted and who pollutes in the first place, creating the opportunity for further research and discussion. What, for example, can pupils do if the pollution in a local stream results from a large corporation? Why does asthma and lead poisoning occur more frequently in some places rather than others? How can we work together to reduce or eliminate pollution?

Yes We Can

Our response to our opening question is therefore based on promoting 'the development of an inclusive pluralist society that is reflexive enough to support and nurture the identities of individuals and groups through the creation of a more equal, socially just, and democratic society.' Citizenship education, as explored in this chapter, offers opportunities for establishing just such a community within school. The nature of primary education and its emphasis on developing the whole child offers an opportunity to explore expressions of identity and diversity respectfully and actively, develop a community where inequalities based on diversity can be recognized rather than swept under the carpet, and can be addressed and challenged. By developing individuals' self-esteem through positive celebration of difference, pupils are challenged to consider and, as appropriate, change their views and embrace opportunities to participate in democratic decision-taking, and in recognizing and challenging inequalities. Recognition is given to the cultural navigation which many pupils are engaging in, and developing social negotiation is seen as a necessary skill in participating in democratic structures.

Experience of a community which operates in this way influences children's understanding and practice of the values and attitudes which underpin it. Such practice reinforces teaching and learning about diversity, can develop attitudes to and commitment to equality, and paves the way for pupils to develop skills which are relevant beyond the school gate. Experience of primary classrooms has convinced us that these can be stepping stones towards a more just and equal society because it is here that the pupil can explore the interface of the private and public self.

References

Adams, M., Bell, L., and Griffin, P. (eds) (2008) *Teaching for Diversity and Social Justice*, 2nd edn. New York: Routledge.

Armstrong, D. (2004) *Experiences of Special Education: Re-evaluating Policy and Practice through Life Stories*. London: Routledge Falmer.

Arthur, J. (2000) *Schools and Community: the communitarian agenda in education*. London: Falmer Press.

Ballard, R. (1994) *Desh Pardesh: the South Asian Presence in Britain*. London: Hurst and Co.

Barrett, M. (1994a) *An Egg for Babcha*, 'Bridges to Religions' Series. *The Warwick RE Project*. Oxford: Heinemann.

Barrett, M. (1994b) *The Seventh Day is Shabbat*, 'Bridges to Religions' Series. *The Warwick RE Project*. Oxford: Heinemann.

Barrett, M. (1994c) *The Buddha's Birthday*, 'Bridges to Religions' Series. *The Warwick RE Project*. Oxford: Heinemann.

Bauman, Z. (2001) *The Individualized Society*. London: Polity Press.

Bigelow, B. *et al.* (eds) (1999) *Rethinking Our Classrooms: Teaching for Equity and Social Justice*. Milwaukee: Rethinking Schools.

Baumann, G. (1996) *Contesting Culture: Discourses of Identity in Multi-Ethnic London*. Cambridge: Cambridge University Press.

Christensen, L. (2000) *Reading, Writing, and Rising Up: Teaching About Social Justice and the Power of the Written Word*. Milwaukee: Rethinking Schools.

Claire, H. (2001) *Not Aliens: primary school children and the Citizenship/PSHE curriculum*. Stoke on Trent: Trentham.

Claire, H. (2004) (ed.) *Teaching Citizenship in Primary Schools*. Exeter: Learning Matters.

Covell, K. and Howe, R.B. (2005) *Rights, Respect and Responsibility Initiative to Hampshire County Education Authority*. Online at http://www.unicef.org.uk/tz/teacher_support/assets/pdf/rrr_research_fullreport_05.pdf (Accessed 21st January 2009).

DfEE/QCA (1999) The National Curriculum for Primary Teachers in England. London: DfEE/QCA.

DfES (2007) *Statutory Framework for the Early Years Foundation Stage*. London: DfES Publications.

DCSF (2007) Online at http://www.standards.dfes.gov.uk/eyfs/site/1/2.htm (Accessed 21st January 2009).

Freire, P. (1996) *Pedagogy of the Oppressed*. London: Penguin Books.

Ginwright, S., Noguera, P., and Cammarota, J. (eds) (2006) *Beyond Resistance! Youth Activism and Community Change: New Democratic Possibilities for Practice and Policy for America's Youth*. New York: Routledge.

Giroux, H. (2005) *Schooling ant the Struggle for Public Life: Democracy's Promise and Education's Challenge*, 2nd edn. Boulder: Paradigm Publishers.

Griffen-Wiesner, J. and Maser, C. (2008) *Teaching Kids to Change the World: Lessons to Inspire Social Responsibility for Grades 6-12*. Minneapolis: The Search Institute Press.

Hill, D. (2009) 'Theorizing Politics and the Curriculum: Understanding and Addressing Inequalities through Critical Pedagogy and Critical Policy Analysis', in D. Hill and L. Helavaara Robertson (eds) *Equality in the Primary School: Promoting good practice across the curriculum.* London: Continuum.

Hill, D. (2010) 'Critical Pedagogy, Revolutionary Critical Pedagogy and Socialist Education' in S. Macrine, P. McLaren and D. Hill **(eds)** *Critical Pedagogy: Theory and Praxis*. London: Routledge.

Jackson, R. (1997) *Religious Education: an interpretive approach*. London: Hodder and Stoughton.

Jackson, R. (2004) *Rethinking Religious Education and Plurality*. London: RoutledgeFalmer.

McLaughlin, T. H. (1992) 'Citizenship, diversity and education: a philosophical perspective', *Journal of Moral Education*, 21, (3), 235–50.

Marable, M. (1992) *The Crisis of Color and Democracy*. Monroe, ME: Common Courage Press.

Macedo, D. and Freire A. M. A. (2005) Introduction in P. Freire *Teachers as Cultural Workers*. Colorado: Westview Press.

McLaren, P. (2003) *Life in Schools: An Introduction to Critical Pedagogy in the Foundations of Education*, 4th edn. Boston: Allyn and Bacon.

Michie, G. (2005) *See You When We Get There: Teaching for Change in Urban Schools*. New York: Teachers College Press.

Osler, A. and Starkey, H. (2005) *Changing Citizenship: democracy and inclusion in education*. Maidenhead: Open University Press.

Parekh, B. (2000) *The Future of Multi-Ethnic Britain: Report of the Commission on The Future of Multi-Ethnic Britain*. London: Runnymead Trust.

Pearce, S. (2005) *YOU wouldn't understand*: White Teachers in Multiethnic Classrooms. Stoke on Trent: Trentham.

QCA (1998) *Education for Citizenship and the Teaching of Democracy in Schools* (The Crick Report). London: QCA. Online at http://www.qcda.gov.uk/library/Assets/media/6123_crick_report_1998.pdf.

Ross, A. (2007) 'Political learning and controversial issues with children', in H. Claire and C. Holden, *The Challenge of Teaching Controversial Issues*. Stoke on Trent: Trentham.

Sehr, D.T. (1997) *Education for Public Democracy*. New York: State University of New York Press.

Shor, I. (1987) *Critical Teaching and Everyday Life*. Chicago: University of Chicago Press.

Singer, J. (2006) *Stirring Up Justice: Reading and Writing to Change the World*. Portsmouth: Heinemann.

Steiner, M. (1992) *World Studies 8-13: evaluating active learning*. Manchester: Manchester Metropolitan University, World Studies Trust.

UNICEF (2008) *UNICEF UK Rights Respecting Schools in England briefing paper*. Online at http://www.unicef.org.uk/campaigns/publications/pdf/RRSbriefing.pdf (Accessed 21st January 2009).

UNICEF (2009) *Class Act*. Online at http://www.unicef.org.uk/features/feature_detail.asp?feature=39 (Accessed 21st January 2009).

Van Heertum, R. (2006) 'Marcuse, Bloch and Freire: reinvigorating a pedagogy of hope', in *Policy Futures in Education*, 4, 1, 45–51.

Chapter 19

Sex and Relationships Education

Gillian Hilton and Gavin Baldwin

Introduction

This chapter discusses sex and relationship education (SRE) and whether primary schools, by offering SRE, can promote equality in society, in particular for those children who are lesbian, gay or bisexual (LGB). The controversial nature of SRE and the history of the confused legislation are discussed together with considerations of how provision is affected by the recipient's gender, culture and religion, age and the varied expertise of teachers. The problems of equal access such as the parents' right to withdraw children from lessons are examined. The reasons for the patchy nature of sex and relationships education are considered and the conclusion drawn is that the pleas for the compulsory statutory provision of PSHE and SRE should be heard so as to use these subjects to demonstrate commitment to equality, particularly in the areas of gender and sexuality. This would aid the lowering of teen pregnancy rates, prevent a further rise in the spread of sexually transmitted infections and stamp out homosexual abuse in schools.

Sex and Relationships Education

Sex and Relationships Education (SRE) has been a controversial issue in English schools from its inception to the present day. Much of this controversy stems from uncertainty about what we want sex and relationships education to achieve: is it about knowledge, health, or stopping unwanted teenage pregnancy? It is difficult enough to agree on what knowledge and at what age this should be 'imparted' but once we see sex in a broader socio-political context, SRE can become an issue of group identity conflict that typifies a central problem of living in contemporary, pluralist, Britain; the friction between a modern, liberal, secular democratic state and the values and traditions of some of the communities of which it is constructed.

As social mores change so does the role which sex plays in defining ourselves and our communities. Central to our personal, often private, identities, sex and particularly sexual orientation, has become increasingly significant to our public identities as well. As such, it has a political dimension that can empower the traditional domination of heterosexuality, and marginalize alternative sexualities or liberate oppressed groups. sex and relationship education, therefore, also has a parallel political function – it can reinforce a more or less heterosexual view of the world (heterosexism) or it can support the struggle for equality by Lesbian, Gay, Bisexual and Transgendered (LGBT) people.

Controversy surrounding SRE is made more complex when knowledge and politics are aligned with moral and religious teaching. These elements are a potent mix, often seen by communities as the touchstones of their group identity, and central to this identity are a cluster of ideas, traditions, prohibitions, liberalizations and values, etc., about sex. Arguments about SRE can therefore be illustrative of a major challenge of living in a 'community of communities', as Parekh has described modern Britain (Parekh 2000). How can we respect the identities and sensitivities of different groups while upholding our commitment to equality and social justice?

Explicit sex education in English schools was first delivered in the 1920s (Mort 1987), but in reality very few children received any sex education, and what was on offer tended to be patriarchal and targeted towards girls (Reiss 1998). Limond (2005) points out that during the designing of the 1944 Education Act discussions on the need for sex education did occur. However, at the same time the National Union of Teachers (NUT) raised the problem of teachers' reluctance to address sex education issues, leading to pupils receiving fragmented or incomplete information (NUT 1944). In more recent years, successive government acts have led to the issuing of guidance documents and now SRE is part of the curriculum in science and PSHE (since 2000), ostensibly available equally to all children.

There are many examples of the constantly recurring public and political debates that have, over the last decades, surrounded the provision of sex education, including the notorious primary school 'blow job' (a health visitor answered questions from primary children on using Mars Bars to practise blow jobs, resulting in a press outcry) controversy in 1994 (Stears *et al.* 1995) and the concerns in the twenty-first century over the appointment of a practising Catholic as Secretary of State for Education (fears were expressed about her membership of a Catholic society and whether this would lead her to restrict teachings about alternative sexualities. She has long since been replaced by a succession of other politicians). Thorogood (2000) points to the ever-increasing statutory regulation of SRE from the 1980s onwards, but also to the effects of changing social values and beliefs about what should be taught. She argues that sex education has received so much attention because it is underpinned with the idea of introducing heterosexual sexual relationships and accepted forms of masculinity and femininity as the norm. Due to a variety of reasons, therefore, the opportunities for learning in SRE are not equable for all children in the system and this may be one of the reasons for the UK's high rates of sexually transmitted infections (STIs) and teenage pregnancy rates, which are the second highest in the world after the USA and about six times higher than those in The Netherlands (DfES 2006). Nor is it just a matter of equable access to information. SRE also gives us a valuable forum to address identity equality issues around gender and sexual orientation and begin to tackle the prejudices that enable sexism and homophobia to flourish in schools.

The 1986 Education Act was the first legislative attempt to regulate the teaching of sex education in schools. However, Stears *et al.* (1995) place the establishment of sex education for all as a result of the National Curriculum Science order, the Cross Curricula theme of Health Education (1990) and the 1993 Education Act, which made sex education compulsory for every school. However, this Act removed all but biological aspects, including HIV/AIDs, from the National Curriculum, placing this area and relationship issues within Personal Social and Health Education (PSHE). Subsequent Acts have followed this split presentation, resulting in patchy and varied provision.

The question of equality of access in the provision of SRE is problematic. First, the manner in which SRE is organized, controlled and taught raises issues related to equal access to information and second, the divide between biologically based sex education and sexuality education, covering relationships, thoughts, attitudes, feelings and values, presents challenges for teachers. The DfEE (2000a) guidelines clearly set SRE within the boundaries of PSHE as well as in National Curriculum Science. The objective of sex and relationship education is to help and support young people through their physical, emotional and moral development. (DfEE 2000a:3).

The guidelines continue to point out that SRE includes not only knowledge and understanding, but the attitudes, values and personal and social skills of children. However, the whole area has remained controversial in the eyes of many parents, teachers and the media in a manner not experienced in other countries. Attitudes, elsewhere in Europe, to sex and sexuality are more matter of fact and it is accepted that children now are sexually aware much earlier than in previous generations (Lewis and Knijn 2001; Bartz 2007). Hemmin *et al.* (1971) argue that one of the original main errors in this country had been the limiting of the availability of SRE, or even totally excluding knowledge about sex from the curriculum, while Went (1995) points to the changes in school sex education in the 1970s which became more biologically explicit in text book diagrams. Relationships, particularly sexual ones, however, still did not feature strongly in the curriculum.

According to the National Children's Bureau (NCB), SRE in English schools suffers from confused legislation (NCB 2007). The 1996 Education Act consolidated all earlier acts and subsequent legislation has followed the same themes with the split nature of provision between science (statutory) and PSHE (non-statutory). All schools are required to have a policy on SRE, generally within the PSHE policy, or for primary schools intending to deliver only the statutory element of SRE in NC science, a Statement of Intent so to do. The school governors are in charge of the policy and what is taught in this area of the curriculum and are obliged to give details of the curriculum to, and consult parents about, the courses they offer. Parents have the right to withdraw their children from non-NC science aspects of SRE. This creates a divide between schools who take a restricted stance and other schools offering a broader approach to SRE. Children, therefore, may or may not receive full SRE teaching, depending on their parents' choice of school. This leads to inequality in the kind of SRE children receive (NCB 2007). The 2000 guidelines on SRE which replaced an earlier Circular 5/94 (guidance for schools following the 1994 Education Act) advised that primary schools need to tailor their SRE to the 'the age and the physical and emotional maturity of the children' (DfEE 2000a:(1.3)12). They reiterate the NC science syllabus with regard to learning about puberty and how a baby is conceived and born, while the contribution of PSHE is to aid children in preparation for puberty, naming parts of the body and developing confidence in discussing emotions. The Guidelines appear to make the teaching of this area problematic for teachers, as it suggests that the NC science element be 'rooted in the PSHE framework' (DfEE 2000a:(1.12)9). This produces a dilemma as parents are allowed to remove children from PSHE but not NC science.

Government's justification for the non-statutory nature of PSHE is to allow for flexibility and for schools to 'develop a curriculum relevant to their pupils connecting with their interests and experiences' (QCA 2005:1). Unfortunately, therefore, some children in primary school may receive no education relating to the feelings and emotions engendered by sexual relationships or their changing bodies, though anecdotal evidence tells us that these children receive information second-hand from friends who have attended classes. Whether this information is entirely accurate is difficult to tell. Ofsted (2002), however, profess that only small numbers of students are withdrawn from SRE PSHE lessons.

The non-statutory nature of SRE is also indicative of the tension that exists in these matters between different social groups. On the one hand, this status may allow for the sensitivities of some communities to be respected. On the other hand, however, with regard to the socio-political dimension of SRE and the promotion of equal opportunities, pupils may not receive an open-minded and inclusive approach that can challenge sexism and homophobia. They may not also, for instance, consider the many configurations of gender, and therefore sexual orientation, that can constitute a family. This seriously misses an opportunity to support those children of LGBT couples and to broaden an understanding of what might constitute personal and family love. Statutory content would at least be a first step towards enabling these discussions in the classroom.

The Teenage Pregnancy Advisory Group (2004) and Ofsted (2002, 2007) point to the patchy provision of SRE, which is often under-resourced and in some schools is taught by untrained staff. This may be contrasted with other countries where SRE is a right for every child, as in Norway where sex education begins at age seven and continues till the age of 16, while in the Netherlands nationally-set attainment targets are used (Lewis and Kinjin 2001, Bartz 2007). So, from the beginning of schooling, English children's experiences of SRE are not equal due to the lack of conviction from successive governments to override the conservative pressure groups and religious lobbies over parental rights and retain the right of parents to withdraw children from SRE in PSHE. These groups do not seem to have such a strong influence in other European countries. This makes England's attitudes to SRE closer to those held in the USA where abstinence education has been gaining ground in recent years (SEF 2004). Some groups supported by certain elements in the press strongly profess that SRE should be in the hands of parents and not given over to schools and teachers who may not have the 'right' approach. The objections are often focused on discussions of alternative sexualities, sex outside marriage, and abortion: these being perceived as sinful or even corrupting. This sits oddly with government directives that schools should address such questions, particularly in the light of Ofsted reports on homophobic bulling (DfEE 2000b). It can also deny children knowledge of the real world in which they are living where LGBT people are represented in the media children encounter and where same sex relationships can now be recognized in civil partnerships akin to marriage. Added to this debate on equality of access to information, are considerations of the children being educated, their gender, ages when SRE occurs, those with Special Educational Needs and the training of teachers.

Gender

Children enter nursery classes already aware of their sex and quickly adopt the genderized behaviours attributed to that sex to ensure they continue to develop as that sex (Bee and Boyd 2007). Boys are slower in both their physical and emotional development than girls, reaching puberty about two years later. This slower development has led to negative stereotypes of young men being perpetuated, boys in some cases being seen as problems in the classroom (Hilton 2001; SEF 2006). SRE lessons in schools have been criticized as being too female oriented, making boys feel that SRE has little to do with them (DfEE 2000a; TPU 2001; Hilton 2003; SEF 2006). Boys feel that they are presented as difficult and uncontrollable, while girls are perceived as being more mature in their response to SRE. Boys' behaviour in SRE classes is often negative; they fool around and show off to the girls. SEF (2000) and Hilton (2003) claim that this is generally due to embarrassment and worry over losing face before their classmates. Boys believe that they have to know everything about sex without having to be told (Hilton 2007).

There has been much discussion, therefore, over the need to teach boys and girls separately for SRE, particularly in primary schools. This approach would satisfy the needs of some religious groups and could accommodate the different development rates of the two sexes. However, it is essential that boys and girls know about the development of the other sex, particularly in primary school, in relation to changes at puberty. In some schools there has, in the past, been a prevalence for talks on menstruation being given to the girls, while the boys play football or discuss wet dreams (Nobel and Hofman 2002). Young people themselves express a strong preference for some lessons apart and some together which appears to be a sensible way of meeting needs and ensuring equality of access to information (Hilton 2007).

It is essential that pupils examine the stereotypes of each sex that are commonly presented in the media, particularly those related to class, religion or race. Boys need to be encouraged to talk about feelings, relationships and caring while girls, who may find bodily changes embarrassing, be given a safe environment in which to discuss these matters (Measor *et al.* 2000; Hilton 2007). However, although boys are generally proud of the changes to their bodies, research has shown that males find it difficult to discuss sex and growing up with boys, so the input of fathers at home is often limited (Bidulph and Blake 2001). Many boys are growing up without a male role model, so giving them the time and space to discuss concerns and fears in school lessons is essential.

It is clear that to ensure equality of provision for the two sexes some differentiation of approach is needed with especial care being given to the needs of boys, who, in the past, have often been neglected. However, it is essential that the two sexes are brought together, to ensure they learn to listen to the points of view and perspectives of the opposite sex.

Cultural, race and religious issues

As the SRE Guidelines (DfEE 2000a) point out, some children's parents do not adequately prepare them for sexual relationships. This is particularly so in some minority communities or religious groups where discussion of such topics outside marriage is considered indelicate or against religious practice. The result is that these children rely heavily on good school SRE, but it is often these children who are withdrawn from PSHE lessons. Hilton's (2004) research in London boroughs on the delivery of sex education by local health providers showed in some cases a 25 per cent or more withdrawal rate from SRE in PSHE. To attempt to avoid this it is suggested that schools consult local parents and faith leaders before designing SRE courses. DfEE (2000a:12) guidelines suggest that SRE should be 'culturally appropriate', but in multicultural classrooms this is a difficult challenge for a teacher. Whose culture and accepted practices should be presented and should some accepted practices, which are illegal in this country, be discussed? In any case, the biological aspects of SRE are supposed to be compulsory. Splitting the biology from the attitudes and feelings is bad practice, nigh on impossible, and can lead to lessons that merely describe the facts rather than explore the feelings involved in sexual relationships.

Suggestions have been made by some minority wing Christian groups (for example, The Plymouth Brethren) that the SRE curriculum is unsuitable, and this belief was echoed in 1994 by the Muslim Parliament of Great Britain (Halstead & Reiss 2003:23) These authors and Gerouki (2007) point out that there is an underlying assumption here that 'facts' can be separated from 'values' and also point to the concerns that uninformed children are more likely to be in danger from sexual abuse. It is essential that all children receive the same input and information, not only that seen as appropriate by one particular group. All points of view should be examined and discussed openly so that children can understand the diversity of opinions and be free eventually to accept or reject the views of their community. This is highly controversial and one of the reasons why successive governments have failed to make the whole of SRE statutory. The Sex Education Forum (SEF 1996) points to the importance of good consultation with parents to ensure that misunderstandings do not occur and controversial issues are dealt with sensitively. For example, there will be no acceptance that sex outside of marriage is the norm for all, or that the only way to protect one's self from sexually transmitted infections is by using a condom.

Sexuality and Homophobia

One particular area of controversy is sexuality education, as some minority communities or religious groups perceive homosexuality as sinful. The NUT in

1999 asked that explicit references to different types of family patterns and lifestyles should be included in the new PSHE curriculum for the primary school and the Qualifications and Curriculum Authority responded to this request to some extent. The guidelines (DfEE 2000a) and Ofsted (2002) clearly state that this aspect of SRE should be addressed and that homophobic bullying, which is common in many schools, should always be challenged.

Many may argue that addressing issues of sexuality and homophobia in primary schools is inappropriate because of the age of the children, but to remain silent is to perpetuate 'The Last Prejudice'. If sexuality is seen as a factor in the matrix of the identity factors (race, gender, class, etc.) that make us who we are, then to fail to address homophobia is to condemn young people to a system where their identities cannot flourish (Baldwin 2004).

> The aim must be to allow young people to develop fully and confidently, valuing who they are and recognizing the equal value of others. It is only in this way that they will achieve educationally and socially. These issues are of an absolutely fundamental nature at the heart of what it is to be human. (Baldwin 2004:82)

Young people in schools are growing up in an environment of almost endemic homophobia. There are pockets of good practice but recent surveys have shown that many young people are subjected to homophobic abuse and violence and are living in LGBT-hostile environments. Taking a long-term view, if homophobia is to be tackled in society as part of a strategy for improving human rights and social justice, strategies must be developed in schools to address this flourishing prejudice. In 2006, Stonewall, the gay rights campaign and pressure group, sponsored a survey conducted by the Schools Health Education Unit of the experiences in school of LGB pupils (or those who thought they may be) (Hunt and Jensen 2007).

In summary, the survey found that 65 per cent of young LGB pupils experienced direct bullying, with the percentage rising to 75 per cent in faith schools. Even if not directly bullied, they are being educated in a homophobic atmosphere where 98 per cent hear 'gay' used in a derogatory way ('that's so gay', 'you're so gay'). 96 per cent hear other insulting homophobic remarks (poof, dyke, rug-muncher, queer, bender) and 70 per cent hear them frequently. Of those bullied, 92 per cent have experienced verbal homophobic bullying, 41 per cent physical bullying – including stabbing – and 17 per cent have received death threats. The negative impact on attainment is explored, with 70 per cent of bullied pupils reporting an impact on their school work and half skipping school (20 per cent more than six times). The report also shows that school responses are patchy at best and often negligent, with such bullying being ignored or even condoned by some teachers.

> Less that a quarter (23%) of young gay people have been told that homophobic bullying is wrong in their school. In schools that have said homophobic bullying is wrong, gay young people are 60% more likely not to have been bullied'. (Hunt and Jensen 2007:2)

Furthermore:

> Over half of lesbian and gay pupils don't feel able to be themselves at school. Thirty five per cent of gay pupils do not feel safe or accepted at school. (Hunt and Jensen 2007:2)

This survey has been quoted at length because it paints a detailed picture of the extent of homophobia in our education system. If we add to this the unreported misery many LGBT young people suffer, even leading to the taking of their own lives, we sense something of the seriousness and urgency attendant on tackling homophobia in schools. Nor is homophobia confined to secondary schools. It may become more acute as pupils advance through adolescence but there is plenty of evidence that it is rife in primary schools as well. Moreover, in the words of 'Stand up for us: Challenging homophobia in schools' (DfES 2004):

> All schools, particularly early years settings and primary schools, are ideally placed to challenge homophobia because they make a significant contribution to the development of values and attitudes in young children that are likely to be highly resistant to change in later life. (DfES 2004:4)

Reynolds (2002) describes the nature and extent of bullying by primary school boys, of girls and of other boys, using swear words, sexually explicit phrases and homophobic harassment which must be addressed in the school curriculum and behaviour policies. Without addressing same sex relationships within SRE then girls and those whose interest is in such relationships, can feel excluded and marginalized.

Furthermore, Atkinson (2005) reports that a survey conducted by the charity Beatbullying among some 1,200 primary and secondary children showed that 81 per cent of the primary age respondents saw the use of the word 'gay' as a way of attacking or making fun of someone.

> That young children use the term 'gay' consciously as a term of abuse perpetuates the view that being gay is a bad thing: even where primary teachers challenge the use of the term, it is often only to silence it, rather than to unpack and address its negative connotations. (Atkinson 2005)

She goes on to argue that the silence and absence of an LGBT perspective leads to school becoming 'a very lonely place indeed' for some pupils (Atkinson 2005). In her Report on the General Teaching Council GTC online forum: 'Challenging homophobia: Does every child matter?' she explains this silence further as arising from teacher's reluctance to address same sex relationships because of an 'implicit conceptual link between sexual <u>orientation</u> and sexual <u>activity</u>.' (Atkinson undated:4).

The same report project came to five significant themes that can help us develop policy and curriculum strategies in primary schools.

1. The invisibility of lesbian, gay, bisexual and transgender parents

2. The emotional energy expended by lesbian and gay teachers in concealing their sexual orientation through fear of adverse reactions
3. The lack of representation, for children in families with same-sex parents of their everyday life experiences within and beyond the school curriculum
4. The tendency of teachers to take a reactive rather than a proactive approach to addressing sexualities equality, where it is addressed at all
5. Underestimation of the significance of homophobic bullying in primary schools. (Atkinson undated b)

So what can primary teachers do?

The major challenge for primary teachers is to end the silence: to include discussion of different patterns of family relationships – who can make a family and how children can fit into these models. They can tackle homophobic bullying in ways similar to tackling any other equal opportunities issue, through policy, through intervention and through curriculum materials. There are many children's stories that challenge gender stereotyping and an increasing number that can be used to illustrate same-sex friendship and love. There are also a growing number of organizations and projects aimed at supporting primary teachers. The No Outsiders Project (www.nooutsiders.sunderland.ac.uk), co-ordinated by Elizabeth Atkinson cited above, undertakes and disseminates research and resources for schools, and the DfES 'Stand up for us' guidance, also cited above, has an online resource list of storybooks for primary school-aged children (www.wiredforhealth.gov.uk/Word/additional_materials_04.doc)

As shown above, LGB children report negative attitudes from teachers and other children to alternative forms of sexuality. Heterosexuality is seen as the norm and many LGB children report that they receive little support from school staff. The NCB (2005) points to recent legislation changes that should help these children, such as the equalization of the age of consent, new employment law and same-sex partnerships. However, these are of little help to the primary school child who may be LGB or have parents from those groups, if a homophobic culture is rife in the school. It has been clearly demonstrated that such a culture can seriously affect attainment, self-esteem and the happiness of children, and all schools must address alternative sexualities in the SRE curriculum and actively promote equality and diversity within the school (NCB 2005).

Age

One specific area of controversy is when to teach SRE. Blake (2002) points out how children worry about growing up and how information about sex surrounds them from an early age. Protecting our children from a sexualized society is only possible by giving them correct information and the chance to discuss their concerns, not pretending that sex does not exist. A news report in 2005 pointed to research about the numbers of girls under 13 (2 under 10) who were being prescribed the contraceptive pill, underlining the need for an early start to SRE (BBC News 2005).

The age at which lessons on puberty and birth occur also needs careful consideration. Many girls are now reaching menarche earlier than in previous years, one in eight starting periods at primary school (BBC News 2001). Puberty preparation left till the end of Year 6, after NC tests, is for some girls too late. Schools decide when to cover this area of the curriculum during Key Stage 2, but to ensure that most girls are properly prepared for menstruation in time it is advisable that teaching about this begins in Year 5. Arguments for boys' preparation to be left later, because of their slower emotional maturation than girls', needs consideration and a two-stage approach could be discussed. Girls are further disadvantaged, in many primary schools, because early menarche is not catered for. Few primary schools have coin-operated machines in girls' lavatories and many girls have to ask a teacher for sanitary protection. Only 43 per cent of schools, in a survey undertaken by Bath and NE Somerset Primary Care Trust, were found to provide disposal facilities for sanitary protection in girls' toilets (BBC News 2001).

Research by Liverpool John Moores' University (BBC News 2006) pointed to the need for earlier SRE, as lack of response to earlier development can cause sexual health problems. There is, too, the danger that uninformed children are more prone to become victims of sexual abuse. Many groups such as The Independent Advisory Group on Teenage Pregnancy (IAG 2003) and the Liberal Democrats (Curtis and agencies 2003) have urged that SRE should start earlier and be compulsory, in order to help with the government target of halving the teenage conception rate by 2010. The Institute of Public Policy Research (2006) further underlined this appeal with a call for the need to inform children in their last year of primary school about the importance of contraception. At present, it is felt by these groups that primary sex education starts too late and its non-statutory status disadvantages many children.

Teaching SRE

SRE has to be taught within the concept of family life (DfEE 2000a) which can prove difficult for teachers who work with children from many different family types and those in the care of local authorities (see above). The whole area is very controversial and the concerns raised by the Local Government Act of 1988 preventing the promotion of homosexuality, though repealed in this century, still colour feelings about how to work in SRE. This Act, though having nothing to do with schools (it concerned Local Authorities and governing bodies who, by law, decide on the content and delivery of SRE), created confusion and fear among teachers as to whether they could discuss sexual orientation. Government guidance now (DfEE 2000a) clearly states that teachers should discuss different sexual relationships and that attitudes to them should be explored. Teachers also need to explore and challenge their own attitudes so as to ensure they are ready to challenge homophobic behaviour and language. The delicacy of approach needed and the requirement to obtain parental consent for material outside of NC science add to teachers' dilemmas. In addition are the strong beliefs held about the purpose of SRE, ranging from the need to shield innocent children from evil, to the need to empower children's decision making, acknowledging their experiences and aiding them in making their own choices (Thorogood 2000). The main problem appears to be the lack of adequate training in what to teach in SRE and how to teach it. Teacher education is firmly allied to the TDA standards and concentrates on preparing primary teachers for the core areas of literacy, numeracy and science. It has been often documented that the other subjects in the curriculum have been marginalized in the push for good league table results. Consequently, many teachers in both primary and secondary schools are still required to teach SRE with little or no training. All other subjects in the NC have teachers with specific training in the area, but SRE in many initial teacher training courses is limited to the odd lecture or short course. The non-statutory nature of PSHE gives the impression of it being of less importance in the curriculum. In an attempt to counteract this, Ofsted have repeatedly pointed out that SRE is best taught by specialists, but in primary schools they rarely exist (IAG 2006). The result is that often other adults, such as health visitors, are brought in to work with groups on aspects such as puberty. However, though these individuals are well informed, they are not trained as teachers and may not use the requisite language or active learning approaches to enable pupils' understanding and participation in lessons.

The government has introduced a Certificate for the teaching of PSHE to be undertaken by PSHE co-ordinators in schools, but the question must be asked is this too little, too late? To ensure good SRE teaching, all teachers who work in the area, and that is all primary teachers as SRE should start in infant school, should be properly trained. Lack of proper preparation can lead to inexperienced teachers using materials such as videos to cover the required content, but failing to follow this up with question and answer sessions, discussion and other work to ensure that values and attitudes have been questioned and explored. The result as reported by Ofsted (2002) is that only one-third of lessons on factual aspects of SRE are good or better, and assessment of SRE is weak, with monitoring and evaluation of SRE learning often poor. This variation between schools, coupled as it is with schools being able to choose whether to deliver any SRE outside of the NC science, obviously leads to inequality of provision.

Lewis and Knijn (2001) found that teachers interviewed in English primary schools were worried about adverse comments about SRE teaching and threatening parents who disagree with content. Under this kind of restraint not all children will receive the relevant supportive introduction to SRE they need. SRE needs to be taught in a climate of safety to ensure no child feels threatened or marginalized. Clear rules of behaviour and respect for others must be established and no personal remarks made or personal questions asked (QCA 2005). Resources used must be up-to-date and suitable for the ages of the children being taught and all these must be available for parents to see before teaching occurs. The use of techniques such as the anonymous question box, where children can ask questions without their classmates knowing their identity, and teachers having control over what questions to address, needs to be explored during pedagogy sessions in initial teacher training. Good and sufficient exposure to suitable teaching methods, assessment techniques and class management for controversial subject areas for all primary teachers is, therefore, essential.

Conclusion

The needs of children for SRE have changed over the years. Young children are nowadays exposed to sexually explicit media images and material much earlier than formerly occurred. Popular 'soap operas' shown before the nine o'clock watershed have storylines about issues such as pregnancy, rape and homosexual relationships and have been used in material prepared for SRE in secondary schools. Primary children watch these programmes and also experience events such as birth (either pets or new babies) in their families. It is impossible to 'protect' children from this information despite the wishes of some parents, and giving all children clear and correct information, helping them to discuss this sensitively and take into account different opinions, is essential.

To achieve equality of access to information and to allow all children the opportunity to discuss issues in a safe environment and to ensure that inadequate home teaching is enhanced, SRE must be made compulsory and the right of every child. The confused situation between government, individual school governing bodies, parents and teachers, differing perceptions of morality and the need for clear health education messages needs to be addressed and simplified. The present situation is untenable and looked at with disbelief by many of our European neighbours. Added to this is the need to adequately train teachers for this work, as poorly prepared teachers give lower standard lessons and pupils hate being taught by embarrassed staff (Hilton 2007). Many bodies have called for a compulsory, stepped, planned and implemented programme from age five to nineteen (Ofsted 2002; IAG 2006). The Independent Advisory Group on Teenage Pregnancy, in their report of 2003/4, put forward a strong case for statutory PSHE and included within it SRE, in order to improve knowledge, sexual health and relationships, and further underlined this plea in their 2006 joint report with the Independent Advisory Group on Sexual Health and HIV. The present state of affairs, in their opinion, has contributed to the high levels of teenage conceptions, sexually transmitted infections and emotional distress (IAG 2006). This group also profess that children lack the skills to discuss feelings and needs in their relationships. Many do not know from where they can obtain advice and help and do not want to turn to parents through embarrassment or fear. Consequently, children worry unnecessarily over natural occurrences such as menstruation, wet dreams and masturbation, uncontrollable erections and breast growth. In 2008, the government in its response to the Report by the Sex and Relationships Education (SRE) Steering Group announced that PSHE and, within it SRE, are to be made statutory, but as yet no new guidance has been issued (DCSF 2008). However, it is not likely that the right of parents to withdraw their children from SRE in PSHE will be removed, so some children will still be denied access to good sexuality education where relationships and feelings are addressed and stereotypes challenged.

Somers and Eaves (2002) undertook research with American adolescents to determine whether earlier sex education is of harm or benefit to its recipients. Earlier SRE seemed to increase boys' communication about sexuality, which is a positive result and to be encouraged. Some parents fear that early SRE can lead to a higher engagement in sexual intercourse, but no such evidence exists. In reality, it can delay the onset of intercourse. Starkman and Ranjani (2002) point to the fact that countries with compulsory sex education in primary school have rates of sexually transmitted infections, teen pregnancy and abortion lower than countries which do not offer a specifically designed programme, taught to all children. Furthermore, giving children equal access to effective SRE can provide protection from abuse.

In this chapter many of the controversies and social implications have been explored. It seems clear that consensus about SRE will be difficult to achieve given its strong relationship with group identity through espoused values and religious beliefs. This should not be seen as an excuse, however, but a challenge to enter into a dialogue with those of different cultural and religious views about sex and particularly alternative sexualities, in order to build a society more equitably committed to social justice. We live in a society where the state is formally opposed to homophobia and recognizes same-sex relationships through civil partnerships. To that extent the law is clear. It is time that the same clarity was applied to SRE. Possibly it is even time to remove the debate about SRE from the political arena, and place it firmly into the hands of health professionals. Ofsted (2007) claimed that too much time is being wasted on whether PSHE, and therefore SRE, should be statutory. One cannot but fail to disagree with this viewpoint and repeat the pleas of SEF and IAG for SRE to be made an equal right for all children whatever their gender, faith, ethnic group or age. The Health Development Agency (2001) describes effective SRE as that which is provided before puberty, empowers all pupils regardless of their sexuality, offers a positive viewpoint on sex, meets children's needs and ensures both pupils and teachers are clear in what they are aiming to achieve, thereby reducing risk. To ensure that this is available to all children, SRE needs to be taught by specialist trained teachers to all children as a right. It should be part of the NC from age five or even the earlier Foundation Stage where practitioners can answer children's questions with honesty and stress the importance of loving relationships, so it becomes just another part of the school curriculum constantly revisited on a Brunarian curriculum model, seen as a normal part of human life and removed from the 'nudge, nudge, wink, wink' approach to sex for which the British are so well known.

References

Atkinson, E. (2005) *Homophobia for Beginners*. Online at http://www.guardian.co.uk/education/2005/dec/07/schools.uk.

Atkinson, E. (Undated) *Report of the GTC online forum: Challenging homophobia: Does every child matter?* Online at http://www.spectrum-lgbt.org/downloads/safety/Challenging _homophobia_Does_every_child_matter.pdf (Accessed 5.8.09).

Atkinson, E. (Undated). *Executive summary of report: Challenging homophobia: Does every child matter?* Online at http://www.gtce.org.uk/documents/publicationpdfs/mag_sum05_p-magz0605.pdf..

Baldwin, G. (2004) 'Combatting Homophobia and Heterosexism – the last prejudice', in H. Claire (ed.) *Gender in Education 3–19: a fresh approach*. London: ATL.

Bartz, T. (2007) 'Sex education in multi-cultural Norway'. *Sex Education*, 7, (1), 17–33.

BBC News (2001) 'Young girls not helped with periods'. Online at http://news.bbc.co.uk/hi/english/health/newsid_1494000/1494998.stm (Accessed 24th April 2006).

BBC News (2005) 'Girls aged 10 are taking the pill'. Online at http://news.bbc.co.uk/1/hi/health/4523129.stm (Accessed 12th May 2006).

BBC News (2006) 'Children need sex advice sooner'. Online at http://news.bbc.co.uk/1/hi/health/6062670.stm (Accessed 15th June 2007).

Bee, H. and Boyd, D. (2007) *The Developing Child* (11th edn). USA: Pearson International.

Bidulph, M. and Blake, S. (2001) *Moving Goalposts: Setting a Training Agenda for Sexual Health working with boys and Young Men.* London: FPA.

Blake, S. (2002) *Sex and Relationships Education: A Step by Step Guide for Teachers.* London: David Fulton Publishers.

Curtis, P. (2003) 'Lib Dems propose sex education for primary schools'. Online at http://education.guardian.co.uk/education/2003/sep/24/schools.uk2.

DCSF (2008) *Government Response to the Report by the Sex and Relationship Education (SRE) Review Steering Group.* London: DCSF.

DfEE (2000a) *Sex and Relationship Education Guidance* (0116/2000) London: DfEE.

DfEE (2000b) *Bullying: don't suffer in silence.* London: DfEE.

DfES (2004) Stand up for us: Challenging homophobia in schools. London: DfES.

DfES (2006) *Teenage Pregnancy Next Steps: Guidance for Local Authorities and Primary Care Trusts on Effective Delivery of Local Strategies.* London: DfES.

Gerouki, M. (2007) 'Sexuality and relationships education in Greek primary schools – see no evil, hear no evil, speak no evil'. *Sex Education,* 7, (1), 81–100.

Halstead, M, and Reiss, M. J. (2003) *Values in Sex Education: From principles to practice.* London: Routledge/Falmer.

Health Development Agency (2001) *Key Characteristics of Interventions Designed to Reduce Teenage Pregnancy: An Update.* London: Health Development Agency.

Hemmin, J., Menzie, M., Proops, M. and Farder, K. (1971) *Sex Education of School Children.* London: Royal Society of Health.

Hilton, G. L. S. (2001) 'Sex Education – the issues when working with boys'. *Sex Education,* 1, (1), 31–41.

Hilton, G. L. S. (2003) 'Listening to the Boys: English boys' views on the desirable characteristics of teachers of sex education'. *Sex Education,* 3, (1), 33–45.

Hilton, G. L. S. (2004) *Breaking the Macho Mould: what boys want from sex education lessons and how they want to be taught.* Unpublished PhD thesis submitted to Middlesex University.

Hilton, G. L. S. (2007) 'Listening to the boys again: an exploration of what boys want to learn in sex education classes and how they want to be taught'. *Sex Education,* 7, (2), 161–174.

Hunt, R. and Jensen, J. (2007) *The School Report: the experiences of young gay people in Britain's schools.* London: Stonewall.

IAG (2003) *Annual report 2002/3.* London: Independent Advisory Group on Teenage Pregnancy.

IAG (2004) *Annual report 2003/4.* London: Independent Advisory Group on Teenage Pregnancy.

IAG (2006) *Time for Action Personal Social and Health Education (PSHE) in Schools.* London: Independent Advisory Group on Teenage Pregnancy.

Institute of Public Policy Research (2006) Press Releases, 'Sex education in primary schools needed to cut teenage pregnancy and unprotected underage sex'. Online at http://www.ippr.org/pressreleases/?id=2387 (Accessed 27th October 2006).

Lewis, J. and Knijn, T. (2001) 'A Comparison of English and Dutch Sex Education in the Classroom'. *Education and Health,* 19, (4), 59–64.

Limond, D. (2005) 'Frequently but naturally: William Michael Dunae, Kenneth Charles Barnes and teachers as innovators in sex(uality) education in English adolescent schooling c. 1945–1965'. *Sex Education,* 5, (2), 107–118.

Measor, L. Tiffin, C. and Miller, K. (2000) *Young People's Views on Sex Education: Education Attitudes and Behaviour.* London: Routledge/Falmer.

Mort, F. (1987) *Dangerous Sexualities: Medico-Moral Politics in England since 1830*. London: Routledge, Kegan Paul.

NCB (2005) *Sexual Orientation, sexual identities and homophobia in schools. Sex Education forum Fact sheet 33*. London: NCB.

NCB (2007) 'Beyond biology'. Online at http://docs.google.com/gviewa=v&q=cache:kGhOpiMuld0J:www.ncb.org.uk/dotpdf/open_access_2/beyond_biology_p9.pdf+Beyond+biology&hl=en.

NUT (1944) *Sex Teaching in Schools: Statement by the Executive of the National Union of Teachers*. London: NUT.

Ofsted (2002) *Sex and Relationships Education in Schools*. London: Ofsted.

Ofsted (2007) *Time for change: Personal Social and Health Education*. London: Ofsted.

Parekh, B. (2000) *The Future of Multi-Ethnic Britain: Report of the Commission on the Future of Multi-Ethnic Britain*. London: Runnymead Trust.

QCA (2005) *Sex and relationships education, healthy lifestyles and financial capability*. London: DFES.

Reiss, M. (1998) 'The History of School Sex Education', in M. J. Reiss and S.A. Mahud (eds) *Sex Education and Religion*. Cambridge: The Islamic Society.

Reynolds, E. (2002) '(Hetero)sexual, heterosexist, homophobic harassment among primary school girls and boys'. *Childhood*, 9, (4), 415–434.

SEF (1996) *Forum Factsheet 10 Developing partnerships in sex education: a multi-cultural approach*. London: SEF.

SEF (2004) *Abstinence-only education. Forum Briefing*. London: SEF.

SEF (2006) *Boys and young Men; Developing effective sex and relationships education in schools*. London: Sex Education Forum.

Somers, C. L. and Eaves, M. W. (2002) 'Is earlier sex education harmful? An analysis of the timing of school-based sex education and adolescent sexual behaviours'. *Research in Education*, 67, 23–32.

Starkman, N. and Ranjani, N. (2002) 'Commentary: the case for comprehensive sex education'. *AIDs Patient Care and STDs* 16, (7), 313–318.

Stears, D., Clift, S. and Blackman, S. (1995) 'Health Sex and Drugs Education Rhetoric and Realities', in J. Ahier and A. Ross (eds) *The Social Subjects within the Curriculum*. London: The Falmer Press.

Thorogood, N. (2000) 'Sex Education as Disciplinary Technique: Policy and Practice in England and Wales'. *Sexualities*, 3, 435–438.

TPU (2001) *Guidance for developing contraception and sexual health advice services to reach boys and young men*. London: TPU.

Went, D. (1995) *From biology to empowerment: how notions of good practice have changed*. Paper presented at Sex Education in School: Working towards Good Practice Conference. London.

Chapter 20

Theorizing Politics and the Curriculum: Understanding and Addressing Inequalities through Critical Pedagogy and Critical Policy

Dave Hill

Introduction

In this theoretical chapter, in Part One, I want to look at the political nature of the National Curriculum, indeed, the political nature of any curriculum; the political nature of pedagogy and the hidden curriculum; and at how a curriculum – any curriculum, such as a national curriculum, or Every Child Matters, or a classroom curriculum – can be analysed critically.

In Part Two, I also want to look at education for equality. Here, I summarize and examine one specific approach to education for equality, critical pedagogy, referring to writers such as Paolo Freire, Antonio Gramsci, Henry Giroux and Peter McLaren. I then suggest what the task for critical, radical and socialist educators should be, and delineate a set of radical left, egalitarian, principals for education to guide such tasks.

I conclude by revisiting and refining a framework for Critical Education Policy Analysis, a series of questions which critical, radical and social justice educators should ask of education policy – any education policy – such as the/a national curriculum, or a change in teaching/learning methods, or in education policy proposals or change at the micro- (classroom or school level), meso- (local authority/school district level) or macro- (national, or global levels).

PART ONE: The National Curriculum, the Hidden Curriculum and Equality[1]

Introduction

This chapter examines the political nature of the construction of the National Curriculum for England and Wales. One central issue addressed is whether the current national curriculum does – or could – contribute to increased equal opportunities, or even to more equal outcomes between different social class/ social strata or different ethnic groups.

A second central issue, and site of labelling, stereotyping and discrimination, is the hidden curriculum, which includes the values, attitudes, and culturally loaded expectations expressed through school/institutional arrangements, through pedagogic relationships, and through rewards and punishments typical of the daily life in schools. With exceptions, and despite the best efforts of many teachers and schools,[2] the hidden curriculum serves, in general, to reproduce the educational, social and economic inequalities in classrooms, schools and in society, rather than to expose, challenge, and contest those inequalities.

Thus, this chapter considers the formal (subject) curriculum and the hidden curriculum and their impact on equality in schooling. I discuss how the National Curriculum part of the (Conservative) 1988 Education Reform Act was developed. There are a number of concepts that are highly useful here, such as Pierre Bourdieu's (1976, 1990; Bourdieu and Passeron 1977) concepts of 'cultural capital', 'symbolic violence' and 'cultural arbitrary', and Louis Althusser's (1971) concepts of education as an 'Ideological State Apparatus' (ISA) with some characteristics of a 'Repressive State Apparatus' (RSA).[3]

Such concepts can, firstly, illuminate the political and ideological nature of the selection of knowledge in the formal curriculum, and, secondly, what is formally valued by teachers and schools in terms of 'know-how' and factual knowledge that comprise cultural capital. Below, I expand on these two types of knowledge, 'knowledge how', and 'knowledge that'. Different cultural behaviours, different 'knowledge that' and 'knowledge how' are privileged and rewarded through both the formal and the hidden curricula. Some school students/pupils, and their particular cultures and behaviours are negatively labelled, others positively.

Together with Marxist concepts of class (Marx and Engels, 1848) and social class reproduction (for example, in Bowles and Gintis 1976; Rikowski 2006; Hill 2006c, 2007), these concepts provide insight into how schools and schooling systems reproduce inequalities, replicate community disfranchisement, and structure social exclusion and alienation. Education, despite the wonderful motives of many teachers, in general can be seen to serve to advantage or disadvantage particular pupils/students – and indeed, teachers and other workers – with different, 'low-status' cultural characteristics. In other words, to embed and to confirm 'raced' and gendered social class inequalities in education, jobs, power and society.

Awareness, of how Capital and of how reproduction works in schools and classrooms – and in broader educational systems – can, of course, aid us in working against inequality in schooling, and in striving for more equal outcomes – a more equal, egalitarian classroom, school, schooling system, and society.

The Political Nature of the National Curriculum – and of the Conservative National Curriculum that resulted from the Education Reform Act of 1988

The National Curriculum is clearly a political creation. Any curriculum is, though some curricula are clearly more openly partisan than are others.

Curricula do not arrive on spaceships from outer space uncontaminated, unmediated, by the ideologies and beliefs and value systems and political agendas of the curriculum makers. Those who decide what 'knowledge' and 'skills' are to be compulsory in schools – and for whom – have their own political and ideological agendas. The National Curriculum of 1988 created by the Conservative Government attempted to create a Conservative hegemony in ideas, and remove liberal progressive and socialist ideas from schools and from the minds of future citizens (see Hill 1989, 1997a; Jones 1989, 2003; Tomlinson 2005).

In the process of developing and writing the separate subject guidelines for the National Curriculum, the National Curriculum subject Working Parties were pre-selected on ideological grounds – they were overwhelmingly packed with right-wingers, and were certainly not representative of the education profession. Duncan Graham, the first Chair and Chief Executive of the National Curriculum Council (appointed by the Conservative Government), accused Ministers of 'a wilful distortion for political ends'.[4]

Within public education, the ideas and personnel of the Radical Right seized power at national level. Some of these ideologues were installed at the higher levels of education power. For example, Anthony O'Hear was a member of CATE (the Committee for the Accreditation of Teacher Education), and became a member of its successor body, the Teacher Training Agency. John Marks, a writer of the right-wing Black papers of the late 1960s and the 1970s, and member of the influential right-wing Hillgate Group of writers on education, became a member of the National Curriculum Council. Brian Cox, erstwhile radical writer of the right-wing Black Papers of the 1960s and 1970s wrote:

> Since the general election a persistent rumour has been going round in education circles that the Prime Minister has agreed to a deal with right-wing Conservatives. They will go quiet in their opposition to Maastricht if he will allow them to take control of education. What truth there is in this I do not know, but it certainly fits the situation which has emerged in the last few months. (Cox 1992; cited in Hill 1994. See also, Graham and Tytler 1993; Blackburne 1992)

The radical Right was able to work itself into a central, powerful position. Activists of the radical Right – such as Martin Turner, John Marenbon and John Marks – were appointed to the National Curriculum Council and the Schools Examination and Assessment Council (SEAC) or its sub-committees and to its replacement Schools Curriculum and Assessment Authority (SCAA) (see Simon 1992; Graham 1993a, 1993b; Lawton 1994). The radical Right consistently and controversially overruled 'professional' opinion (Jones 1989; Lawton 1994; Tomlinson and Craft 1995). In this conflict, the arbitrary powers awarded to the Secretary of State by the 1988 Act became all too visible. History was been brought to a stop at 1972, lest more recent history become a licence for radical approaches (Graham 1992); science was redefined in a way that jettisons curricular attention to the social implications of scientific activity (Dobson 1992); English was reorganized so as to give priority to the Right's main cultural themes, which involve making fetishes out of 'Standard English', a literary canon, 'traditional grammar' and spelling. Indeed, various of the chapters in the predecessor to this book (Cole, Hill and Shan 1997) referred to this political selection of knowledge in particular subject areas (see Hill 1997a for more detail on this).

Questioning a Curriculum

The political nature of any curriculum becomes apparent when it is subjected to particular questions about the power relations it defines.

Questioning a Curriculum

1. Whose curriculum is it?
2. Who actually selected the content (e.g.) of the National Curriculum for England and Wales? And who chose them to do the selecting, and why were they chosen?
3. Whose culture(s) is/are validated and empowered? and how? Is the National Curriculum culturally elitist with emphasis on history, music, literature of the ruling upper and upper middle classes (and with a dismissal or downgrading of working class and minority ethnic cultures)? Or, conversely, and to what extent, is it an appropriately eclectic curriculum? (Or even, is a proletarian curriculum praising and validating only working-class achievements and histories and culture?)
4. Who wins and who loses?
5. What ideology does it represent (e.g. an individualistic competitive ideology, or a collective, collegial, ideology for social responsibility).[5] What values and attitudes are affirmed? For example, does it represent and affirm the ideology, the values and attitudes, of a particular social group of people?

The Conservative National Curriculum of the 1988 Education Reform Act is widely criticized as overwhelmingly elitist[6] returning to more formal, test-driven methods and incorporating specific *dis*advantages for particular groups, such as working-class and minority ethnic groups.

Clearly a *national* Curriculum is, to a large extent, operationalizing the belief that the same body of formal curriculum content should be available to all (at least within the state sector – it is not compulsory for the private sector of schooling) within the primary and secondary state school systems.

The political principles behind a curriculum for 'national' education, whether it is overtly egalitarian or anti-egalitarian, support the wider objectives of governmental policy and these are, of course, not only social but also economic. The National Curriculum has aims beyond the controlled reproduction and re-validation of particular cultural forms and elites. It is also 'a bureaucratic device for exercising control over what goes on in schools' (Lawton and Chitty 1987:5). Michael Barber noted about the 1988 Act that it 'not only provided for a market, but also a standardized means of checking which schools appeared to be performing best within it' (Barber 1996:50).

The National Curriculum and its effect on equality

The child-centred, 'liberal-progressive' curriculum that was typical of very many primary schools in the 1960s and 1970s, recognized and stimulated by The Plowden Report of 1967 (CACE 1967), was expressed both in terms of 'relevant' curriculum content, a general lack of 'intimidating' assessments, and in terms of more democratic pupil (student)/teacher (tutor) relationships. Here, both the formal and the informal curriculum attempted to validate, to welcome, a whole range of home cultures and experiences. This child-centredness (typical of liberal-progressive ideology) was in reaction to the subject-centred curriculum, teacher-centred pedagogy and authoritarianism of schooling and pedagogic relationships that characterized most state education of the pre-World War Two and immediate post-war era.[7]

In contrast, the post-1988 National Curriculum, in all three of its versions (1991, 2000, 2006), asserts the centrality of particular socio-economic/social class definitions of national culture against the increasing tendencies to both *ethnic and social class pluralism* that were at work in many schools and local education authorities in the 1970s and 1980s, for example, in radical, socialist LEAs such as the Inner London Education Authority (ILEA) (abolished as part of the 1988 Education Reform Act). With respect to 'race' and ethnicity, the Blair and Brown New Labour governments' emphases on 'integration', and away from 'multiculturalism' are a confirmation of a disavowal of the pluralism represented, in rhetoric at least, by policies for cultural diversity and multiculturalism. The National Curriculum is driven more by a project of cultural homogeneity than by the rhetoric of equal opportunity. Hatcher suggests:

> What was crucial about equal opportunities in the 70s/80s was that a 'vanguard' of progressive teachers had been able to reach a much wider layer of teachers in the 'middle ground' – the role of *LEAs and school policies* was important here, and so was the prevalence of *working groups* on equal opportunities. At school and LEA levels these were the key organizational forms feeding equal opportunities into the wider arena. . . . Once we had equal opportunities working groups in schools, now we have National Curriculum or SATs working groups, or none. (Hatcher 1995)

With the National Curriculum, and standardized testing, now in place, there is a greater degree of comparability attaching to student experience across the country – in purely curriculum terms, and more information regarding school performance for parents. There is now a considerably greater check, and surveillance (by parents, media, the Office for Standards in Education (Ofsted) on the standards of teachers and schools.

Bourdieu and the National Curriculum as Cultural Reproduction

The work of Pierre Bourdieu[8] analyses the relationship between education and cultural formation. Bourdieu criticizes the desirability of a curriculum which is culturally elitist, culturally restorationist. The concepts of *culture* and *cultural capital* are central to Bourdieu's analysis of how the mechanisms of cultural reproduction function within schools. For Bourdieu, the education system is *not*, in practice, meritocratic. Its major function is to maintain and legitimate a class-divided society. In his view, schools are middle-class institutions run by and for the middle class. In summary, Bourdieu suggests that this cultural reproduction works to disadvantage working-class students in three ways.

1. It works through the formal curriculum and its assessment. Exams serve to confirm the advantages of the middle class while having the appearance of being a free and fair competition. Examinations and the curriculum clearly privilege and validate particular types of 'cultural capital', the type of elite knowledge that appears the natural possession of middle- and, in particular, upper-class children, but which is not 'natural' or familiar to non-elite children and school students, both white and Black and Ethnic Minority (BEM) children.[9]
2. Cultural reproduction works through the hidden curriculum. This hidden curriculum categorizes some cultures, life-styles, ways of being and behaving (for Bourdieu the *habitus*), attitudes and values as praiseworthy, as being 'nice', as being characteristic of the child for whom one can more likely expect and encourage academic aspiration and success. Thus, middle-class way of walking, talking, accent, diction, vocabulary, and ways of interacting with teachers and authority figures, tend to be welcomed, praised and validated by schools (and universities).
   In contrast, other ways of being and behaving, language, clothing, body language, and attitudes/values, attitudes to teachers and authority figures, are not viewed quite as tolerantly or supportively. 'Loud-mouthed' (i.e. assertive) girls/young women, or large African-Caribbean young men or boys, or shell-suited, cropped-headed, working-class, white young men/boys tend to be regarded as regrettable, 'nasty', alien and/or threatening – indeed, suitable subjects for exclusion, if not from school itself, then from academic expectation and success. People who walk and talk like Prince Charles are likely to be viewed very differently by teachers and schools than the children who appear in *Shameless, East Enders*, or who are mocked in *The Catherine Tate Show* (popular television programmes in 2009 in England), those who speak with what Bernstein described as a 'restricted code' (rather than the 'elaborated code' typical of the middle class.[10]
3. Cultural reproduction works through the separate system of schooling for the upper- and upper-middle classes, nearly all of whom, in a form of educational apartheid, send their children to private (independent) schools. Such schools attract around 7 per cent of the school population in England and Wales, but monopolize power positions in society.

Cultural Capital

Bourdieu argues that the culture transmitted by the school, and that expected by the schooling system, confirms, values and validates the culture of the ruling classes. At the same time, and as a consequence, it disconfirms, rejects and invalidates the cultures of other groups. Individuals in classrooms and school corridors bring with them and exhibit different sets of linguistic and cultural competencies

The significant aspect of cultural capital is that school pupils/students (and, indeed, individuals in the workforce, such as teachers in schools or lecturers in colleges seeking promotion, or seeking a permanent instead of a temporary contract), stand to benefit from if they possess or show the 'right sort' of cultural capital.

This dominant cultural form is expressed in two ways. First, there is *actual knowledge*, of facts and concepts, acquaintance and familiarity with particular forms of historical, musical, artistic, literary, geographical, etc., culture. The current form of top/Premiership soccer clubs, of the latest spat between pop stars or glamour models, or the love-life of reality television personalities, or of contemporary *argot* tends to be viewed as less important, of lower status in the hierarchy of knowledge than the selection of knowledge represented in the formal curriculum. This type of knowledge, *knowledge that*, is presented, and rewarded, (or rejected and penalized) for being part of, or not part of, the formal curriculum. In addition, lots of 'elite' knowledge and experiences not represented in the National Curriculum are rewarded through the hidden curriculum – the praise, estimation and expectations of teachers and of schooling. Some types of learning experiences of educational visits within the family, peer group or school – trips to the theatre, museums, exhibitions – are more highly validated and recognized than, say, a seaside holiday on the beach in Benidorm or Blackpool.

A second type of cultural capital is *'knowing how'* – know-how – how to speak to teachers, not only knowing *about* books, but also knowing *how* to talk about them. It is knowing *how* to talk with the teacher, with what body language, accent, colloquialisms, register of voice, grammatical exactitude in terms of the 'elaborated code' of language and its associated *habitus*, or code of behaviour.

> In a number of social universes, one of the privileges of the dominant, who move in their world as a fish in water, resides in the fact that they need not engage in rational computation in order to reach the goals that best suit their interests. All they have to do is follow their dispositions which, being adjusted to their positions, 'naturally' generate practices adjusted to the situation (Bourdieu 1990:109, quoted in Hatcher 1998).

Some topics and ways of talking about them have more value in the eyes of schools in general. The 'nice child' is one who appears to be middle class, or who appears to be able – and willing – to cease exhibiting working-class, or Islamic or Rasta characteristics, and to adopt those of the white or assimilated middle class. In other words, the 'nice child' is usually one who also meets stereotypes of social class, gender, ethnicity and sexuality. To take one (true) example of what was perceived by some teachers as a descent from 'acceptable' cultural capital, to 'unacceptable', once a Moslem girl used to dressing in 'Western' clothes takes the decision to wear the Moslem scarf (hijab), then she is liable to be regarded as 'less acceptable' by many teachers, to be regarded as 'not as sensible as I thought you were' (quoted in, and from the experiences of, Khan 1998).

The Arbitrariness of the National Curriculum: Bourdieu and 'the Cultural Arbitrary'

Bourdieu's concept of the *cultural arbitrary* refers to school education being arbitrary in that the cultural values offered are not intrinsically *better* than any other, but are the values of the dominant class. In this sense, the selection of knowledge represented in the National Curriculum can be seen as arbitrary, as one selection of knowledge among many possible selections. The arbitrariness of the National Curriculum is far from random. It is fundamentally and primarily the imposition of ruling-class knowledge over working-class (and other subaltern cultural) knowledge.

Bourdieu and Symbolic Violence

The National Curriculum did not arrive by accident. Its content, as indeed virtually any national curriculum content, was keenly fought over. By *symbolic violence*, Bourdieu is referring to the way in which symbolic forms of communication such as language and culture are used as weapons to maintain power relations. The success of symbolic violence depends on the way that it is commonly unrecognized. Most accept the loaded rules or the game. Most 'buy in', at least on a conscious level, to the elitist model by which they have a deficit. As a result, many working-class children tend to become either submissive or to opt out from school academic achievement, to become alienated from and/or resistant to/dismissive of 'official' school culture. In contrast, middle-class children are familiar and at ease with 'desirable' symbolic forms. To legitimate what are, in fact, *imposed* meanings is a form of *symbolic violence*. There is a relationship between the pedagogic work of schools and the capital advantages associated with particular cultural attributes. Importantly, the school in this relationship is not neutral: it embodies the *'cultural arbitrary'*, the interests of the dominant class. Cultural capital is not conceived of as an individual attribute but as a 'relational concept to institutionalized class power' (Hatcher 1998:17). To appreciate the institutional role of education as part of this process, it is useful to refer to specific concepts within Althusser's work.

Althusser and Schooling as Ideological Reproduction

Althusser's analysis of schooling concerns a particular aspect of cultural reproduction, namely, ideological reproduction – the reproduction of what is considered 'only natural', or as 'common sense'. Here he drew, to some extent, on Gramsci (1978) who distinguished between 'common sense' which is a more or less chaotic and incoherent set of beliefs affected by the mass media, and 'good sense' which is critical, and sees through the 'common sense' that the ruling capitalist class is happy for people to believe. 'Good sense' in contrast, in Gramsci's terms, is superior to 'common sense', it is 'critical' and enables political action to contest the rule of 'the bourgeoisie' or capitalist class.

Althusser (1971) defines and shows the means by which a small but economically, politically and culturally powerful (capitalist) ruling class perpetuates itself in power, and can reproduce the existing political and economic systems that work in its favour. He distinguishes the Repressive State Apparatuses (RSAs), such as the Law, the Police and the Armed Forces, from the Ideological State Apparatuses (ISAs) such as the Family, Schooling and Education, Religion and the Media. The term 'State Apparatus' does not refer solely to apparatuses such as Ministries and various levels of government. It applies to those societal apparatuses, institutions and agencies that operate on behalf of, and maintain the existing economic and social relations of, production. In other words, the apparatuses that sustain capital, capitalism and capitalists. So, private schools, although not run by the state, can be regarded as ideological state apparatuses, just as much as state schools. Similarly, the mass media, owned by millionaire/billionaire capitalists and their corporations, act as ideological state apparatuses in terms of the ways they work to 'naturalize capital', to make competitive materialistic individualistic acquisitiveness seem 'only natural', rather than a product of a particular economic system – capitalism.

States, governments, and the ruling classes in whose interests they act,[11] prefer to use the second form of state apparatuses – the ideological state apparatuses (ISAs) rather than the repressive state apparatuses, the RSAs. Changing the school and initial teacher education (ITE) curriculum, or the law on strikes or picketing, is less messy than sending the troops onto the streets or visored baton-wielding police into the strike-bound mining villages or picket lines (such as at Orgreave in 1984) of Britain during the Great Miners' Strike of 1985 – or indeed, any strike or anti-government/anti-capitalist demonstration. As Bourdieu has also noted, schooling and the other sectors of education are generally regarded as politically neutral, not as agencies of cultural, ideological and economic reproduction. The school, like other institutions in society such as the legal system and the police, is always presented in official discourse as neutral, non-political, and non-ideological. All ISAs play their part in reproducing 'the capitalist relations of production', that is, the capitalist/worker *economic relationship* based on the economic power of the former over the latter, and the *social relationships* (of, for example, dominance and subservience) that are produced by those economic relationships.

For Althusser, the dominant, the most important ISA in developed capitalist societies/economies/social formations is the educational ideological state apparatus. In this are included all aspects of the education system, from schools, to further (vocational) and higher (university) education, to (what is of particular importance in ideological and in cultural reproduction), the 'teacher training' and education system. For Althusser, School (or, to use Althusser's phrase, the Educational ISA) and Family have replaced the Church and Family ISAs as the dominant, most powerful ISAs. Church and family were the dominant structures in ideological reproduction in previous centuries. Schools are particularly important since no other ideological state apparatus requires compulsory attendance of all children for eight hours a day for five days a week.

How does the school function as an ISA? Althusser suggests that what children learn at school is 'know-how'. But besides techniques and knowledge, and in the course of learning them, children at school also learn the 'rules' of good behaviour, 'rules of respect for the socio-technical division of labour and ultimately the rules of the order established by class domination.' The school

> takes children from every class at infant-school age, and then for years in which the child is most 'vulnerable', squeezed between the family state apparatus and the educational state apparatus, it drums into them, whether it uses new or old methods, a certain amount of 'know-how' wrapped in the ruling ideology in its pure state (Althusser 1971:147)

Ideological and Repressive State Apparatuses in Schooling and Initial Teacher Education

Althusser suggests that *every Ideological State Apparatus is also in part a Repressive State Apparatus*, punishing those who dissent:

> There is no such thing as a purely ideological apparatus ... Schools and Churches use suitable methods of punishment, expulsion, selection etc., to 'discipline' not only their shepherds, but also their flocks. (Althusser 1971:138)

The education ISAs engage in repressive activities. Thus they often sideline, dismiss, or render likely to be dismissed, teachers and lecturers who are trade union and/or socialist activists, and those who teach subjects derided by the government. School and college/university subjects can be made invisible, as is explained below: the potentially 'critical' subjects of sociology, philosophy and politics can be virtually exorcized from the teacher education/teacher training curriculum, for example, and their protagonists made redundant (see Hill 1997b, c, d). And it affects school students and university students too. Resistant, 'stroppy', pupils/students who challenge the existing system, either individually, or by leading/joining 'walkouts' over local or national political issues are liable to be excluded from school. And resistant, counter-hegemonic teachers/lecturers are likely to be excluded from promotion.

Schooling and the Reproduction of Existing Society and Economy

The particular theoretical insights of Bourdieu and Althusser (among others) referred to in this chapter show how the current National Curriculum, a political construct ultimately designed by politicians, and the hidden curriculum, which just as ideological even though hidden, are central to a grossly unequal schooling and education system; a system that in very many ways reproduces and justifies the economic inequalities of an elitist hierarchy, along with the cultural and ideological discrimination that support it.

Detheorized Initial Teacher Education in England and Wales

The amount of freedom/autonomy, the space for individual (or group) 'agency', available to teachers, teacher educators, schools and other educational institutions is particularly challenged when faced with the structures of capital and its current neoliberal project for education (as argued in Hill 2001a, 2004, 2005a, 2006c, 2007, 2009). How much agency, autonomy, freedom of manoeuvre and action we have, as educators, has always been circumscribed. Critical Marxist voices and critical organizing always have been. In England and Wales, since the 1988 Education Reform Act and National Curriculum for schools, and with the 1992/1993 restructuring of teacher education (renamed 'training'), with its heavily circumscribed and monitored tick-box list of 'standards' that trainee teachers have to reach, spaces within the subject curriculum and within pedagogy – the methods we use – have been narrowed – though not removed!

Of course, many teachers and students do resist, and, by virtue of the material conditions of their own and their families' and communities' existence, do see through the capitalist 'common sense' acceptances of capitalist society and a quietist schooling system. But many do not.

PART TWO: Critical Pedagogy, and Education for Equality[12]

What does education do in unequal Capitalist Britain (indeed, in any capitalist country). Recognizing the limitations – but also the opportunities – of our efforts as socialist and critical and radical educators and teachers, as people who try to work, in Gramscian terms (Gramsci 1978), as critical organic public transformative intellectuals[13] where should we, as teachers in different sectors of the education state apparatuses, put our efforts?

There are considerable constraints on progressive and socialist action through the ideological and repressive apparatuses of the state, such as schooling and 'the academy'/universities. Non-promotion, sidelining, denigration, threats, even dismissals, are common among socialist activist teachers, among egalitarians who 'rock the boat'.

Education for Equality, or (one version of it) Critical Education for Economic and Social Justice – or socialist education – is where teachers/educators try to act as Critical Transformative and Public Organic Intellectuals within and outside of sites of economic, ideological and cultural reproduction. Such activity is both deconstructive and reconstructive, deconstructing and critiquing the aims, workings and effects of capitalism, including capitalist schooling. It also embraces utopian politics of anger, analysis, action, and hope that recognizes, yet challenges, the strength of the structures and apparatuses of capital, that challenges the current system of education for inequality.

Educators have a privileged function in society – or can have. Within classrooms, critical transformative intellectuals – socialist educators – seek to enable student teachers and teachers (and school students) to critically evaluate; that is, from a Marxist perspective, to evaluate a range of salient perspectives and ideologies – including critical reflection itself – while showing a commitment to egalitarianism and socialism. There are other arenas: in/with local communities, and in national and global arenas.

In the next section, I suggest that it is useful to recognize that capitalism – transnational and national business corporations – wants particular services from schools (and from education in general). The particular agendas that business has regarding education – including primary schools – are set out below.

The Business Agenda *in* Education

The capitalist agenda *for* education is that education should produce a labour force that is structured into different tiers in a hierarchy of skill, pay and power. A labour force that has its labour powers (its skills, personality characteristics, knowledges) developed (or restrained and moulded) to fit the hierarchically-tiered labour market. This substantially reproduces the existing social class relations in the labour market, in incomes, wealth, life chances, life quality. Most working-class children/young people get working-class jobs (whether in the blue collar or white collar strata of the working class), most so-called middle-class kids[14] (which in Britain is taken to signify the sons and daughters of the managerial and supervisory strata of the working class, whereas in the USA middle class also refers to skilled workers) get middle-class jobs; most upper-class kids, the scions of the capitalist class, learn to rule and boss. Rich kids in the USA get to Ivy League, and there is a social class/strata-based tiered system of universities, as there is in Britain. 'Rich kids' get to Oxbridge, middle strata to the Russell Group (old) universities, and a proportion of the lower supervisory and skilled (blue collar manual and white collar) sections of the working class get to the 'new' universities, the former polytechnics – pretty much vocationalized skill development factories. And the same is true in most countries. [Is this the capitalist agenda for education?] This is the capitalist, or business agenda *for* education, to, by and large, produce a hierarchically skilled and tiered labour force that substantially reproduces not only the capitalist system, but also reproduces patterns of class inequality; that is, reproduces ('raced' and gendered) social class advantages and disadvantages.

The Business Agenda *for* Education

The other aspect of the capitalist agenda *for* education is to reproduce ideological conformity and acquiescence – to restrict and define 'youth rebelliousness' as under-age drinking, having sex or wearing 'yoof' clothes or piercings.

Reproducing ideological conformity means accepting those forms of 'yoof rebellion' that do not threaten the existing social and economic (capitalist) system. But this agenda, of reproducing ideological conformity, means that schools (and the media) do not allow children/young people to be 'exposed to', listen to, question, develop *seriously alternative* ideas, such as socialism. So here, schools and universities (and the mass media) function as what Althusser (1971) termed 'Ideological State Apparatuses', reproducing, more or less, the prevailing individualistic, materialistic, competitive, acquisitive, hedonistic ideology of contemporary neoliberal capitalism.

As noted earlier, one way in which this ideological reproduction has been strengthened in England and Wales – the confirmation of the existing state of affairs, and the sidelining of opposition – has been by the 'conforming' of teacher education, the ideological straight jacketing of 'those who teach the teachers'.

Critical Pedagogy: The Resistant Role of Critical Cultural and Education Workers and Critical Pedagogy

Paolo Freire

The Brazilian educator and political activist, Paulo Freire, argued that while there are exceptional academics and a handful of organizations dedicated to conducting research which serve egalitarian ends, not enough academics are working as critical 'cultural workers' who orient themselves toward concrete struggles in the public and political domains in order to extend the equality, liberty, and justice they defend (Freire 1998). He maintained that '[t]he movements outside are where more people who dream of social change are gathering', but points out that 'there exists a degree of reserve on the part of academics in particular, to penetrate the media, participate in policy debates, or to permeate policy-making bodies' (Shor and Freire 1987:131).

Freire argued that any curriculum which ignores racism, sexism, the exploitation of workers, and other forms of oppression at the same time supports the status quo (Heaney 1995). For Freire, critical educators attempt to develop 'conscientization', a process through which learners develop critical consciousness, becoming (more) aware of oppression, and of becoming a subject rather than an object of politics, of history. Through becoming conscious of becoming a subject in common with other oppressed subjects, this leads to becoming part of a process of changing the world. This is a very different concept of the teacher than 'teacher as technician', delivering someone else's curriculum, as de-theorized and thereby de-skilled. Leena Helavaara Robertson's Chapter 1 in this volume (Robertson 2009) exposes the very different ideological agendas and values regarding early years curricula in England, citing the Freirean-type principles in the Reggio Emilia model of pre-school education, and the 'Every Child Matters' agenda in England, with its opening statement 'Every Child Matters is all about improving the life chances of all children, reducing inequalities and helping them achieve what they told us they wanted out of life'. This is not Freirean in the sense that this statement would seem to accept children's (and their communities') current state of desire and expectation, which is commonly rather less than challenging the existing macro-economic and political structures that reinforce and reproduce their inequality, rather than challenging it, and working to overcome/replace it. (But it is more progressive than the rival National Curriculum KS1 and 2, and the Early Years Foundation Stage).

Freire argued that if scholars, researchers, or educators want to transform education to serve democratic ends, they cannot simply limit their struggles to institutional spaces. They must also develop a desire to increase their political activity outside of the schools. To engage as critical cultural workers would require academics to politicize their research by becoming social actors who mobilize, develop political clarity, establish strategic alliances, and work closer to the nexus of power, or the 'real levers of transformation' (Shor and Freire 1987:131).

Antonio Gramsci

The Italian communist leader and theoretician of the 1920s and 1930s (until his death in one of Mussolini's Fascist jails) wrote extensively about the role of intellectuals, especially concerning their potential, as transformative intellectuals, in developing 'good sense', a critical analysis of society, as differentiated from 'common sense', fairly akin to 'folklore' . He wrote that educators have a privileged function in society – or can have. In this sense, as Gramsci put it, '[a]ll men [sic] are intellectuals ... but not all men have in society the function of intellectuals' (Gramsci 1971:10), maintaining that the notion of intellectuals as being a distinct social category independent of class was a myth. By 'organic', Gramsci was referring to those intellectuals – such as school teachers – who remain or become part of the social class they are working with, linked into/part of/participating in, local struggles, campaigns and issues, and who work towards developing critical consciousness – class consciousness and analysis. Many teachers do this, taking on the issues and experiences and demands of the local community, of the community from which their children are drawn. This is in contrast to those 'traditional intellectuals' who see themselves as a class above and separate from class struggles, or who ally themselves with the dominant (pro-capitalist) ideology.

United States Critical Educators/ Pedagogues[15]

The writings of leading US critical educators, Henry Giroux, Peter McLaren, and Ira Shor, were all inspired in part by Paolo Freire and his Marxist inspired/ Marxian (though not Marxist) theories and also by Gramsci (and by the Culturalist Marxism of the Frankfurt School, themselves affected by Gramsci's work). These stressed the need for ideological intervention in the perennial 'culture wars' between the ideas of the capitalist class and the ideas of 'subaltern' oppressed social groups such as minorities, women, workers.[16]

For critical pedagogy, teachers and lecturers should be critical transformative intellectuals who seek to enable student teachers and teachers (and school and university students) to critically evaluate a range of salient perspectives and ideologies – including critical reflection itself – while showing a commitment to egalitarianism. For Peter McLaren, 'critical pedagogy must ... remain critical of its own presumed role as the metatruth of educational criticism' (McLaren 2000:184). This does not imply forced acceptance or silencing of contrary perspectives, but it *does* involve a privileging of egalitarian and emancipatory perspectives; not, in liberal fashion, sitting on the fence. Critical pedagogy espouses a metanarrative (a story), a critique of oppression and a hope and call for emancipation. It has an ethical, moral, ideological component – and an activist demand.

Critique of liberal versions of critical pedagogy

Critical pedagogy can be vapid, pluralistic, identitarian, a mish-mash of 'now let's sit down and discuss this in a non-threatening and non-authoritarian manner' with 'now let's all choose what we want to do classroom projects on'. It can dissolve into the liberal-progressive/child-centred individualism and feel-good practice that was typical of much of primary schooling in England and Wales of the sixties and seventies. While for many, this liberal-progressivism, and the Plowden Report (CACE 1967) that legitimized it, was a very welcome advance on the traditional teacher-centred teaching methods and rigid subject-centred curriculum of the fifties and before, and while it did actually prioritize schools being happy places, it did tend to ghettoize working-class and minority ethnic children into their social class communities, and tried to make the curriculum 'relevant', without critiquing or seeking to go beyond felt needs of relevance.

Critical pedagogy might call for liberation, emancipation, the ability to critique and deconstruct the individual, social, media and political world, and to actively organize and work for a more equal world. It isn't socialist or Marxist, nor does it claim to be. It does not seek to change society radically, by replacing capitalism with socialism. As Rikowski notes,

> critical pedagogy becomes a form of Left liberalism, where social justice, equality, social worth etc. (in general, and in relation to education specifically) can be solved or resolved within the existing framework of capitalist society. The solutions appear to rest on equalizing resources and rewards, and on changing attitudes towards certain groups (Rikowski 2007).

Of course, many or most people reading this chapter will be quite satisfied with reforms, making existing society a bit better. Others (such as me) want more radical change. While welcoming reforms – little steps – in classrooms, schools, and at Local Authority (LA) and national level, they can have, of course, major life-enhancing impacts on the children and young people we teach.

Critical Revolutionary Pedagogy

In the USA a new, and Marxist, development in critical pedagogy, is critical revolutionary pedagogy. Some of their work, and some of their theorized praxis in schools and colleges and in wider arenas, is published in online journals such *the Journal for Critical Education Policy Studies* (www.jceps.com) that I edit, *Cultural Logic* (at http://clogic.eserver.org/) and *Workplace, a Journal of Academic Labor* (at http://www.cust.educ.ubc.ca/workplace/). Of course these are drops in the ocean of racist, sexist and pro-capitalist individualistic imperialist capitalist media and schooling.

McLaren (2000) extends the 'critical education' project into 'revolutionary pedagogy', which is clearly based on a Marxist metanarrative. Revolutionary pedagogy

> would place the liberation from race, class and gender oppression as the key goal for education for the new millennium. Education ... so conceived would

be dedicated to creating a citizenry dedicated to social justice and to the reinvention of social life based on democratic socialist ideals. (*ibid.*:196)[17]

Revolutionary Critical Pedagogy, which sounds very un-English and very American, so I prefer to anglicize it as Socialist Education, must remain self-critical, and critique its own presumed role as the metatruth – the gospel – of educational criticism. It has to critique itself, not just the existing system. It is not a gospel, immune from criticism.

The task of radical educators/teachers

As I see it, radical educators and teachers who are socialist or Marxist seek equality – more equality of outcome – rather than simply equal opportunities to get on in a grossly unequal society. The task of democratic Marxist/Socialist teachers, and of resistant egalitarian Socialist and Marxist counter-hegemonic teachers, students, cultural workers, policy makers and activists is:[18]

1. to expose and organize and teach against the actual violence by the capitalist state and class against the 'raced' and gendered working class;
2. to expose the ways in which they perpetuate and reproduce their power, that of their class, through the ideological and repressive apparatuses of the state (such as the media, the schooling, further education and university systems);
3. in particular, the way they do this through demeaning and deriding the 'cultural capital' and knowledges of the ('raced' and gendered) working class through what Pierre Bourdieu termed 'cultural arbitrary' and 'symbolic violence'; the way working-class kids are largely taught they are worth less – or worthless – and upper-class kids are taught they will control and inherit the earth, and some middle-class kids are taught how to manage it for them;
4. to argue for, propagate, organize, agitate for and implement democratic egalitarian change and policy.

Some Radical Left Principles for Education Systems: Part of an Eco-Socialist Manifesto[19]

One of the academic/educational/propagandizing roles I try to play is by developing, collaboratively, with other socialists/Marxists/radicals, suggestions, ideas, and codified ideas as draft manifestos for education, for what a Marxist education would be like. What education could be! Here, in developing democratic Marxist proposals for an egalitarian education system, the following nine aspects of education need to be considered:

The Aims of Education

1. Curriculum/Curriculum Content, e.g. what is selected, who by, how it is organized – in subjects, as interdisciplinary learning, as problem solving?
2. Pedagogy, the hidden curriculum, our relationship with pupils/students, e.g.

democratic or authoritarian classrooms and schools – what patterns of rewards and expectations are there for the different ('raced' and gendered) social class groups of children/young people in our classrooms and schools?

3.   Relationships with the Communities we serve, e.g. are we open or closed to parents and local school communities, for example, in connection with questions of 'really useful knowledge' for the local communities; are we keeping the communities out or in?

4.   The Macro-Organization of Schooling e.g. who controls the school system at local or national level, what are the different types of schools, who do they serve (which 'raced' and gendered social class groups or strata), what is their funding, are there private schools alongside state schools, or not?

5.   The Organization of Pupils/Students within Schools, e.g. how should school students be organized – as mixed ability, or 'banded' or 'streamed'?

6.   The Organization of Education Workers and the Forms of Management within Schools, e.g. what is the degree of collegiality, of shared decision-making, the degree of 'brutalist managerialism' typical of 'new public managerialism'?

7.   The Control of Education at National and at Local and at School Levels, e.g. who controls schools – is there democratic control, private control, workers' control, pupil/student control, central government control, business control, religious leaders' control, police control?

8.   The Resourcing and Funding of Education, e.g. is more spent on education than defence, or less? Is more money given to funding disadvantaged areas/groups of pupils/students, or is there no positive discrimination re funding, or is mostly given to to the most advantaged?

9.   Evaluating How We Are Doing with all the above . . . who is gaining what and who is losing what? And How?

In connection with – indeed, as some answers to – the above questions, here are some suggestions for schooling for equality:

Schooling for Equality: 20 Policies

1.   Vastly increased funding for education, resulting in, for example, smaller class sizes, better resources and hugely improved low-environmental-impact school buildings, set in grounds conducive to children's development of a love of nature as well as of their communities;

2.   A complete end to selection and the development of fully comprehensive schooling, further and higher education;

3.   A complete ban on private schools;

4.   Schools and colleges on a 'human scale' within or as local to communities as possible;

5.   Greatly increased provision of free school transportation, including, where possible, 'walking buses';

6.   Free nutritious school food, prepared on site with the use of locally-sourced produce where possible;

7.   Cooperation between schools and local authorities, rather than competitive markets;

8. Greatly increased local community democratic accountability in schooling and further education, rather than illusory 'parental choice';

9. Increased powers for democratically elected and accountable local government to redistribute resources, control quality and engage in the development of anti-racist, anti-sexist, anti-homophobic policies and practices;

10. The enactment of egalitarian policies aimed at achieving greatly more equal educational outcomes, irrespective of factors such as social class, gender, 'race', sexuality or disability, while recognizing that what education can achieve is limited unless part of a thoroughgoing social transformation to eliminate poverty and discrimination;

11. An anti-elitist, anti-racist, flexible common curriculum that seeks to support the transition from current social relations to those based on socialist cooperation and ecological justice, to be negotiated by local and national governments in cooperation with workers' representatives and communities;

12. The curriculum to be rich and varied, allowing themes, natural and human processes to be explored in a range of ways – artistically, musically, scientifically, politically, ecologically;

13. Place-based learning, concerned with the meaning of everyday life: critical studies of environmental impacts of capital on local scales alongside historical injustices arising out of the circuits of capitalist social, political and ultimately economic relations;

14. Teaching and learning to foster critical awareness, sensitivity towards and confidence and ability to challenge ecological and social injustice – a planetary consciousness rooted in an internationalist global citizenship, and empowerment to act in defence of the oppressed, of other species and ecosystems;

15. The abolition of punitive testing regimes and the exploration and establishment of alternative creative assessment practices;

16. Teachers educated to exercise authority in democratic and anti-authoritarian ways, engaging in critical ecopedagogy, with a commitment to developing their school and community as sites of ecological and political awareness and activism;

17. A breaking down of boundaries fixed within educational systems e.g. between childhood dependency and adult responsibility and between subject specialisms;

18. Teachers and administrators who act as role models of integrity, love, care and thoughtfulness in institutions capable of embodying ideals in all of their operations, avoiding hypocrisy in a separation of academic and theoretical ideals from reality;

19. A recognition on the part of teachers and officials that all knowledge acquired in schools and FE and HE institutions carries with it the responsibility to see that it is well used in the world;

20. A fostering of cultures within classrooms and schools and further/vocational education and higher education institutions which is democratic, egalitarian, collaborative and collegiate, promoting an educational system the aim of which is the flourishing of society, collectives, communities.

Some might say that under the existing system, this is all a bit overwhelming, and, can this be done under the existing system? To which I respond: do teachers wanting equality want the above? Any of the above? Some of them? So, is it better to try or to shrug our shoulders and say, 'we can't do anything. Let's just be lovely teachers and work to develop the best we can from our children'. Which is what many wonderful teachers, committed to the children they teach, to 'doing their best', say and do. But how much better to try to create a system that allows, and encourages – and demands – education for equality, so the system works with egalitarian teachers, and does not hinder – or suffocate – those noble aims!

Others might say, 'but how can we possibly achieve all of the above? Won't we be dissipating our energies trying for all of that? To which my response is that piecemeal reforms, victories on one front or another are hugely important. But without dreaming of, and articulating, an overall education (and social) utopia, we will never reach it.

Conclusion

Critical education policy analysis

In helping us reach education for equality, the following form of policy critique may be useful – a list of questions that can be applied to any education policy – for a change in classroom practice, in school admissions, in the curriculum, in school meals policy, in funding policy within a school, or between schools, a policy of academy schools, or of privatization, or of relations with the community/communities, of headteacher or governors' powers, for example.

Thus, one way of analysing policy (any education policy, any policy, at global, or national, or local education authority/school district level, or school/college or classroom level) is to ask about any policy the following questions:[20]

Critical Policy Questions to Ask

The Policy Itself
1. What is it?
2. Who/what does it impact on/regulate/deregulate?
3. What are the policy features/changes?
4. Who proposed/originated the policy?
5. Who opposed it?
6. Who carried it out?
7. When? And when does/did it become operational?

Aims
8. What do its originators (e.g. the government, their ideologists/news media/think tanks, or, e.g. the school governors/headteacher/principal/administration) claim are the reasons for it? What problem(s) is the policy intended to 'solve'?
9. What do they claim are its *intended aims* (what it is intended to do, or solve) and what are its *likely effects*?

10. What do others (e.g. its opponents, critics) say are the *aims* of the policy?
     (i.e., are/were there hidden alternative additional aims?)
11. What do others (e.g. its opponents) say are the *likely effects* of the policy?

Context

12. How does the policy relate to wider social trends, in ideological
     developments and in government policies – does the policy form part of
     an overall policy of, for example, redistributing power to, or from,
     particular social groups, particular class strata? Or is it part of a broader
     project of privatization, or 'rolling back the state'? What is the wider
     context, nationally and internationally (e.g. is there 'policy borrowing', e.g.
     copying a US policy, or a British policy)?

Impacts

13. *Who actually wins and who loses* as a result of the policy – which ('raced' and
     gendered) social class, or social class layers (or ethnic group, gender,
     religious or other group) gain, or, alternatively, lose power/wealth/income/
     educational and economic opportunity as a result of the policy? In other
     words, 'who gets the gravy, and who has to make it'?
14. *Who resists the policy, how and why, and how successfully* -- in the short term
     (policy proposal stage), medium term (policy legislation stage) and the long
     term (the policy implementation and consolidation stages)?
15. What, if any, are the *unintended consequences* of the policy?

Asking critical questions such as these, in particular, the question, 'who wins
and who loses', of any education (or other) policy can enable us to better
evaluate what is going on at local (classroom/school) level, at local authority/
school district levels, and at national level. Without such critical questioning, the
rampant inequalities that exist in education systems will continue to be
reproduced. Critical questioning, critical analysis is not enough. It needs to
lead to action and activism/action within the classroom, within teachers'
associations, trade unions, social and community groups and movements. But
within the classroom is a good start, teaching against racism, sexism,
homophobia, disablism, and against social class inequality and discrimination
and labelling, and modelling that egalitarianism in our own behaviour in the
classroom and staffroom.

The two Promoting Equality in Schools books of the late 1990s (Cole *et al.*
1997; Hill and Cole 1999a), and the first two books in the 2009 series of books
(Hill and Robertson Helavaara 2009 (this publication); Cole 2009), do attempt
to show how each curriculum subject can be used to promote equality in schools
and classrooms, and also (in many cases) enable teacher, student teachers and
teaching assistants, to evaluate how subjects can and do work against promoting
equality. A new curriculum, or an interpretation of the existing curriculum
subject, could be validating, speaking to, speaking about and representing a
range of cultures, rather than being restricted – overwhelmingly and
fundamentally – to the cultural forms traditionally associated with those who
rule our society.

Teachers and schools can use and can creatively develop or 'subvert' the
formal and the hidden curricula, to develop critical reflection in pupils and
students. At a wider level, radical teachers, teachers promoting equality, can

themselves work towards a wide-ranging comprehensive restructuring of the schooling and education systems so that they can maximize both equality of opportunity and a far greater degree of equality of outcome. In this way, the negative labelling of millions of children in our primary schools, with its ('raced' and gendered and other types of) social class-based stereotyping, discrimination, hurt and inequality, can be replaced by a loving, egalitarian and emancipatory system of schools, classroom experiences, and, ultimately, society.

Notes

[1] An earlier version of sections of this chapter appeared as 'The National Curriculum, the Hidden Curriculum and Equality', in Hill and Cole (2001).

[2] This is not to be over-deterministic. Tens of thousands of teachers who are aware of such issues, do try to make sure that class, race and gender stereotypes and labelling do not happen in their classrooms and schools. Within Marxist educational theory, see Giroux 1983 for a succinct summary of the work of 'reproduction theory' writers, such as Althusser, Bowles and Gintis, and Bourdieu. Giroux, as a 'resistance theorist' was contesting what he saw (and sees) as the over-determinism of reproduction theory, the theory that sees schooling and state apparatuses as reproducing the existing capitalist system economically (as in Bowles and Gintis), culturally (as in Bourdieu) and ideologically (as in Althusser) (for a similar set of views, see Cole 1988). My own writing is as a structuralist and classical Marxist, accepting reproduction theory, but not as deterministic. My own theoretical analysis of the relationship between the state, ideology and the curriculum is contained, for example, in Hill 1989, 2001a, 2005a, also Hill 2004 and Kelsh and Hill 2006.

[3] Althusser 1971; Hill 1989, 2001a, 2005a.

[4] Cited in Docking (1996:10). Various of the subject by subject chapters in Cole, Hill and Shan (1997) and Hill and Cole (1999a) and in this volume (Hill and Robertson 2009) and in Cole 2009, detail some of these disputes. Several of the Programmes of Study were manipulated by Prime Ministerial and ministerial diktat. This is clearly set out in Margaret Thatcher's autobiography (Thatcher 1993) and in those of Minister of Education, Kenneth Baker (1993), and the first Chair of the National Curriculum Council between 1988–1991, appointed by Kenneth Baker, Duncan Graham (see Graham 1992, 1993a, b; Graham and Tytler 1993).

[5] In Hill 2001b, I set out characteristics of five ideologies in Western education, child-centred 'liberal-progressivism', redistributionist and moderately egalitarian 'social democracy', competitive, individualistic 'neoliberalism', traditionalist and hierarchical 'neo-conservativism', and radical egalitarian socialist 'radical left' ideologies.

[6] See, for example, Davies *et al.* 1992; Hill 1997a; Hillcole Group 1997; Hill and Cole 1999b, and comments in Jones 2003; Tomlinson 2005.

[7] There is a Left-wing critique of liberal–progressive and socially differentiated schooling and curricula. It draws primarily on the work of Gramsci (see Epstein 1993; Hill, Cole and Williams 1997). Gramsci considered that schooling is and should be hard work, that while developing a critical perspective and attitude, working-class children need to study and become inducted into and familiar with the elite, dominant culture. Sarup's summary and discussion of Gramsci (Sarup 1983) is very clear.

[8] Bourdieu 1976, 1990; Bourdieu and Passeron 1977; Lareau 1997; Grenfell *et al.* 1998; Reay 2004; Mehmedbegovic 2009)

[9] See Robertson and Hill 2001, for a discussion of how some minority ethnic groups are, in relative terms, excluded from the Literacy Hour.

[10] Bernstein 1971. For a brief summary, see Atherton 2008.

[11] The Marxist analysis of social class and society is most famously, perhaps, expressed in the following quote:

> The history of all hitherto existing society is the history of class struggles ... oppressor and oppressed stood in constant opposition to one another, carried on an uninterrupted, now hidden, now open fight, a fight that each time ended, either in a revolutionary re-constitution of society at large, or in the common ruin of the contending classes ... Our epoch ... has simplified the class antagonisms ... into two great hostile camps, into two great classes directly facing each other: Bourgeoisie and Proletariat. (Marx and Engels 1848)

In the footnotes to *The Communist Manifesto*, it is explained that 'By bourgeoisie is meant the class of modern capitalists, owners of the means of social production and employers of wage labor' and that 'By proletariat, the class of modern wage laborers who, having no means of production of their own, are reduced to selling their labor power in order to live. [Note by Engels – 1888 English edition]. The *Communist Manifesto* was first published in February 1848 in London. It was written by Marx and Engels for the Communist League, an organization of German emigré workers living in several western European countries. For documents/ data relating to Marxism, see http://www.anu.edu.au/polsci/marx/marx.html, or read (British) Marxist online newspapers and journals, such as those by The Socialist Party at http://www.socialistparty.org.uk/, The Socialist Workers Party at http://www.swp.org.uk/, The International Socialist Group at http://www.isg-fi.org.uk/ and its international review at http://www.isg-fi.org.uk/spip.php?rubrique27

[12] Parts of this section are a summary of and taken from Hill (2009).

[13] This is a Gramscian phrase, used widely in critical pedagogy. See, in particular, Giroux 1988; Hill 1989; Aronowitz and Giroux 1993; Borg, Buttigieg and Mayo 2002; Fischman and McLaren 2005; Hill and Boxley 2007; Hudson 2009.

[14] The common classification of social class in the UK is that used by the census, national statistics, formerly the Registrar-General's classification of social class. It is a series of classifications based on education, income and lifestyle/consumption patterns. It is based on Weberian sociology which emphasizes patterns of consumption rather than what Marxists do, which is to look at the relationships of people to the means of production – i.e., are they members of the capitalist class, the owners of labour power relate people, or are they the proletariat, those who sell their labour power. As a Marxist, my own analysis, when referring to 'middle-class kids' is that in Marxist terms these are the middle strata of the working class. See Rikowski 2006, and for a more extended discussion, Kelsh and Hill 2006.

[15] Socialist resistance to capitalism and to capitalist education is not new. There is an impression that there was little radical education, little socialist, communist, Marxist schooling, or teaching, before the critical pedagogy in the USA that started in the 1970s and 1980s with the impact of Freire on such North American radical educators such as Henry Giroux, Peter McLaren and Ira Shor. But there have been hundreds of thousands, if not millions, of such teachers and pedagogues within and outside official education systems, throughout Western and Eastern Europe, Russia, Latin America, India, for example, since *The Communist Manifesto* (see Neary 2005). Socialist/ Marxist education has a long history. So does communist education (e.g. see Morgan 2003).

[16] Because of the particularly virulent anti-communism and anti-Marxism of the US government and state apparatuses – from the times of HUAC (the House UnAmerican Activities Committee) of the 1950s to the Patriot Act of George W. Bush – many radicals in the USA (other than small groups, parties and sects) preferred to call themselves 'radical' or critical, sometimes a euphemism for Marxist.

[17] See also McLaren 2005, McLaren and Farahmandpur 2005; McLaren and Jaramillo 2007; McLaren and Rikowski 2006. For a commentary on McLaren and Revolutionary Critical Pedagogy, see Martin 2006. Peter McLaren's website is an excellent

introduction to critical pedagogy, at http://www.gseis.ucla.edu/faculty/pages/mclaren/. A simplified introduction to critical pedagogy is the 'Rage and Hope' website at http://www.perfectfit.org/CT/index2.html

[18] The key task, for Marxist educators – indeed Marxist – is class and class consciousness. In *The Poverty of Philosophy* [1847] Marx distinguishes a 'class-in-itself' (class position) and a 'class-for itself' (class consciousness) and *The Communist Manifesto* (Marx and Engels 1848), explicitly identifies the 'formation of the proletariat into a class' as *the* key political task facing the communists.

[19] This is a summary of Hill and Boxley 2007; see also Hill 2005b.

[20] I have carried out some sample policy analyses, addressing various of these questions, in the following: Hill 1997a, which analysed Conservative education policy 1979–1977; Hill 2006a, which analysed New Labour's education policy 1987–2008; Hill 1989, 1990, 2004, 2006a, b, 2007b and Hill, Cole and Williams 1997, which analysed the restructuring of teacher education into teacher training by the Conservatives in 1992/1993 and the maintenance of that technicizing and detheorization by New Labour; and Hill 2006b, for the ILO, analysing global neoliberalism and its impacts on education and on education workers. Lewis, Hill and Fawcett 2009 does the same for England and Wales.

References

Althusser, L. (1971) 'Ideology and state apparatus', in *Lenin and Philosophy and Other Essays*. London: New Left Books.

Aronowitz, S. and Giroux, H. (1993, 2nd edn) *Education Still Under Siege*. Westport, CN, USA: Bergin and Garvey.

Atherton, J. S. (2008) *Doceo; Language Codes* [On-line] UK. Online at http://www.doceo.co.uk/background/language_codes.htm

Baker, K. (1993) *The Turbulent Years: My life in politics* London: Faber.

Barber, M. (1996) *The Learning Game: Arguments for an education revolution*. London: Victor Gollancz.

Bernstein, B. (1971) *Class, Codes and Control Vol 1*. London: Paladin.

Blackburne, L. (1992) 'Government attacked by its old trusties'. *Times Educational Supplement*, 20 November.

Borg, C., Buttigieg, J. and Mayo, P. (2002) *Gramsci and Education*. Lanham, MD.: Rowman and Littlefield.

Bourdieu, R. (1976) 'The school as a conservative force in scholastic and cultural inequalities', in R. Dale (ed.) *Schooling and Capitalism*. London: Routledge, Kegan Paul.

Bourdieu, R. (1990) *In Other Words*. Cambridge: Polity Press.

Bourdieu, R. and Passeron, J. (1977) *Reproduction in Education, Society and Culture*. London: Sage.

Bowles, S. and Gintis, S. (1976) *Schooling in Capitalist America: Educational Reform and the Contradictions of Economic Life*. New York: Basic Books.

CACE (Central Advisory Council for Education) (1967) *Children and their Primary Schools* (The Plowden Report). London: HMSO.

Cole, M. (ed.) (1988) *Bowles and Gintis Revisited*. London: Falmer Press.

Cole, M. (2009) *Equality in the Secondary School: Promoting good practice across the curriculum*. London: Continuum.

Cole, M., Hill, D. and Shan, S. (eds) (1997) *Promoting Equality In Primary Schools*. London: Cassell.

Cox, B. (1992) Curriculum for Chaos. *The Guardian*, 15 September.

Davies, A-M., Holland, J. and Minhas, R. (1992) *Equal Opportunities in the New ERA*. London: Tufnell Press.

Dobson, K. (1992) *The Guardian*, 21 March.

Docking, J. (ed.) (1996) *National School Policy: Major Issues in education Policy for Schools in England and Wales, 1979 onwards*. London: David Fulton.

Engels, F. [1888] Preface to the English Edition of the Communist Manifesto, in K. Marx and F. Engels *The Communist Manifesto*. Online at http://www.anu.edu.au/polsci/marx/classics/manifesto.html

Epstein, D. (1993) *Changing Classroom Cultures: Anti-racism, politics and schools*. Stoke-on-Trent: Trentham

Fischman, G. and McLaren, P. (2005) *Rethinking Critical Pedagogy and the Gramscian and Freirean Legacies: from Organic to Committed Intellectuals or Critical Pedagogy, Commitment, and Praxis*. Online at http://amadlandawonye.wikispaces.com/2005, + McLaren + and + - Fischman, + Gramsci, + Freire, + Organic + Intellectuals

Freire, P. (1998). *Teachers as cultural workers*. Boulder, CO: Westview Press.

Giroux, H. (1983) 'Theories of reproduction and resistance in the New Sociology of Education: a critical analysis', *Harvard Educational Review*, 53, (3), 257–293.

Giroux, H. (1988) *Teachers as Intellectuals: Towards a Critical Pedagogy of Learning*. Westport, CN: Bergin and Garvey.

Graham, D. (1992) *The Guardian*, 13 October.

Graham, D. (1993a) *A Lesson For Us All: The Making of the National Curriculum*. London: Routledge.

Graham, D. (1993b) 'Reflections on the first four years', in M. Barber and D. Graham (eds) *Sense, Nonsense and the National Curriculum*. London: Falmer Press.

Graham, D. and Tytler, D. (1993) *A Lesson For Us All: The making of the National Curriculum*. London: Routledge.

Gramsci, A. (1971). *Selections from the prison notebooks of Antonio Gramsci*. London: Lawrence and Wishart.

Gramsci, A. (1978) *Selections from Prison Notebooks*. London: Lawrence and Wishart.

Grenfell, M. and James, D. with Hodkinson, P., Reay, D. and Robbins, D. (1998) *Bourdieu and Education: Acts of practical theory*. London: Falmer Press.

Hatcher, R. (1995) 'The limitations of the new social democratic agendas: class, equality and agency', in R. Hatcher and K. Jones (eds) *Education After The Conservatives*. Trentham Books: Stoke-on-Trent.

Hatcher, R. (1998) 'Class differentiation in education: rational choices?' *British Journal of Sociology of Education*, 19, (1), 5–24.

Heaney, T. (1995) *Issues in Freirean Pedagogy*. Online at http://www.paolofreireinstitute.org/Documentsfreiren_pedagogy_by_Tom_Heaney.html.

Hill, D. (1989) *Charge of the Right Brigade: The radical right's attack on teacher education*. Brighton: Institute for Education Policy Studies. Online at www.ieps.org.uk/PDFs/hill1989.pdf.

Hill, D. (1990) *Something Old, Something New, Something Borrowed, Something Blue: Teacher Education, Schooling and the Radical Right in Britain and the USA*. London: Tufnell Press.

Hill, D. (1994) 'Initial Teacher Education and Ethnic Diversity', in G. K. Verma and P. D. Dumfrey (eds) *Cultural Diversity and the Curriculum, Volume 4, Cross-Curricular Contexts, Themes and Dimensions in Primary Schools*. London: The Falmer Press.

Hill, D. (1997a) 'Equality and primary schooling: the policy context, intentions and effects of the Conservative "reforms"', in M. Cole, D. Hill and S. Shan (eds) *Promoting Equality in Primary Schools*. London: Cassell.

Hill, D. (1997b) 'Reflection in teacher education', in K. Watson, S. Modgil and C. Modgil (eds) *Educational Dilemmas: Debate and Diversity: Teacher Education and Training, 1*. London: Cassell.

Hill, D. (1997c) 'Critical research and the death of dissent'. *Research Intelligence*, 59, 25–26.

Hill, D. (1997d) 'Brief autobiography of a Bolshie dismissed'. *General Educator*, 44, 15–17.

Hill, D. (2001a) 'State theory and the Neo-Liberal reconstruction of schooling and teacher education: a structuralist Neo-Marxist critique of Postmodernist, Quasi-Postmodernist, and Culturalist Neo-Marxist theory'. *The British Journal of Sociology of Education*, 22, (1), 137–157.

Hill, D. (2001) 'Equality, Ideology and Education Policy', in D. Hill and M. Cole (eds) *Schooling and Equality: Fact, Concept and Policy, 7–34*. London: Kogan Page.

Hill, D. (2004) 'Books, Banks and Bullets: Controlling our minds – the global project of Imperialistic and militaristic neo-liberalism and its effect on education policy'. *Policy Futures in Education*, 2, 3–4 (Theme: Marxist Futures in Education). Online at http://www.wwwords.co.uk/pfie/content/pdfs/2/issue2_3.asp

Hill, D. (2005a) 'State Theory and the Neoliberal Reconstruction of Schooling and Teacher Education', in G. Fischman, P. McLaren, H. Sünker and C. Lankshear (eds) *Critical Theories, Radical Pedagogies and Global Conflicts, 23–51*. Boulder, CO: Rowman and Littlefield.

Hill, D. (2005b) 'Critical Education for Economic and Social Justice', in M. Pruyn and L. Huerta-Charles (eds) *Teaching Peter McLaren: Paths of Dissent*. New York: Peter Lang.

Hill, D. (2006a) 'New Labour's Education Policy', in D. Kassem, E. Mufti and J. Robinson (eds) *Education Studies: Issues and Critical Perspectives, 73–86*. Buckingham: Open University Press.

Hill, D. (2006b) 'Education Services Liberalization', in E. Rosskam (ed.) *Winners or Losers? Liberalizing public services, 3–54*. Geneva: ILO.

Hill, D. (2006c) 'Class, Capital and Education in this Neoliberal/Neoconservative Period'. *Information for Social Change*, 23. Online at http://libr.org/isc/issues/ISC23/B1%20Dave%20Hill.pdf.

Hill, D. (2007) 'Socialist Educators and Capitalist Education'. *Socialist Outlook*, 13. Online at http://www.isg-fi.org.uk/spip.php?article576

Hill, D. (2007b) 'Critical Teacher Education, New Labour in Britain, and the Global Project of Neoliberal Capital'. *Policy Futures*, 5, (2), 204–225. Online at http://www.wwwords.co.uk/pfie/content/pdfs/5/issue5_2.asp

Hill, D. (2009) 'Critical Pedagogy', in S. Macrine, P. McLaren and D. Hill (eds) *Critical Pedagogy: Theory and Praxis*. London: Routledge.

Hill, D. and Boxley, S. (2007) 'Critical Teacher Education for Economic, Environmental and Social Justice: an Ecosocialist Manifesto'. *Journal for Critical Education Policy Studies*, 5, (1). Online at www.jceps.com

Hill, D. and Cole, M. (eds) (1999a) *Promoting Equality in Secondary Schools*. London: Cassell.

Hill, D. and Cole, M. (1999b) 'Introduction; education, education, education – equality and 'New Labour' in government', in D. Hill and M. Cole (eds), *Promoting Equality In Secondary Schools*. London: Cassell.

Hill, D. and Cole, M. (eds) (2001) *Schooling and Equality: Fact, Concept and Policy*. London: Kogan Page

Hill, D., Cole, M. and Williams, C. (1997) 'Equality and primary teacher education', in M. Cole, D. Hill and S. Shan (eds) *Promoting Equality In Primary Schools*. London: Cassell.

Hillcole Group (1997) *Rethinking Education and Democracy: Education for the twenty first century*. London: Tufnell Press.

Hudson, M. (2009) *Education for Change: Henry Giroux and Transformative Critical Pedagogy*. Online at http://www.solidarity-us.org/node/1734.

Jones, K. (1989) *Right Turn: The Conservative Revolution in Education*. London: Hutchinson Radius.

Jones, K. (2003) *Education in Britain, 1944 to the Present*. Cambridge: Polity.

Kelsh, D. and Hill, D. (2006) 'Class, Class Consciousness and Class Analysis: a Marxist Critique of Revisionist Left and Weberian derived analyses'. Online at http://www.jceps.com/index.php?pageID = article&articleID = 59

Khan, Z. (1998) *Multicultural Education*, Final Year NA Hons. Education Studies Dissertation, Nene University College, Northampton, Unpublished.

Lareau, A. (1997) 'Social class differences in family-school relationships: the importance of cultural capital', in A. Halsey, *et al. Education: Culture, economy, society.* Oxford: Oxford University Press.

Lawton, D. (1994) *The Tory Mind on Education 1979–94.* London: Falmer Press.

Lawton, D. and Chitty, C. (1987) 'Towards a National Curriculum'. *Forum*, 30,(1), 4–6.

Lewis, C., Hill, D., and Fawcett, B. (2009) 'England and Wales: Neoliberalized Education and its Impacts on Equity, Worker's Rights and Democracy', in D. Hill (ed.) *The Rich World and the Impoverishment of Education: Diminishing Democracy, Equity and Workers' Rights.* New York: Routledge.

McLaren P. (2000) *Che Guevara, Paulo Freire and the pedagogy of revolution.* Lanham, MD: Rowman and Littlefield.

McLaren, P. (2005) *Capitalists and Conquerors: Critical Pedagogy Against Empire.* Lanham, MD: Rowman and Littlefield.

McLaren, P. and Farahmandpur, R. (2005) *Teaching against Global Capitalism and the New Imperialism.* Lanham, MD: Rowman and Littlefield.

McLaren, P. and Jaramillo, N. (2007) *Pedagogy and Praxis in the Age of Empire.* Rotterdam: Sense Publishers.

McLaren, P. and Rikowski, G. (2006) 'Critical Pedagogy Reloaded: An Interview with Peter McLaren (interviewed by Glenn Rikowski)'. *Information for Social Change*, 23, (summer). Online at http://libr.org/isc/issues/ISC23/C3%20Peter%20McLaren.pdf

Martin, G. (2006). 'Remaking critical pedagogy: Peter McLaren's contribution to a collective work', *International Journal of Progressive Education*, 2, (3). [Reprinted in M. Eryaman (ed.) (2007) *Peter McLaren, education, and the struggle for liberation: The educator as revolutionary.* New York: Hampton Press.]

Marx, K. [1848] *The Poverty of Philosophy.* Online at http://www.marxists.org/archive/marx/works/1848/poverty-philosophy/

Marx, K. and Engels, F. (1977) [1848] The Communist Manifesto, in *Karl Marx & Frederick Engels: Selected Works in One Volume.* London: Lawrence and Wishart. Online at http://www.anu.edu.au/polsci/marx/classics/manifesto.html

Morgan, J. (2003) *Communists on Education and Culture.* London: Palgrave MacMillan.

Neary, M. (2005) 'Renewing Critical Pedagogy: Popular Education as a Site of Struggle', *Asian Labour Update*, 54 (March). Online at http://www.amrc.org/hk/alu_article/popular_education/renewing_critical_pedagogy_popular_education_as_a_site_of_struggle.

Mehmedbegovic, D. (2009) 'Community and Foreign Languages' in D. Hill and L. Robertson Helavaara (eds) *Equality in the Primary School: Promoting good practice across the curriculum.* London: Continuum.

Reay, D. (2004) 'Education and Cultural Capital: The implications of changing trends in education policies'. *Cultural Trends*, 13, 2, 1–14.

Rikowski, G. (2006) 'Ten Points on Marx, Class and Education'. *A paper presented at Marxism and Education: Renewing Dialogues IX Seminar, University of London, Institute of Education, 25th October.* Online at http://www.flowideas.co.uk/print.php?page=195

Rikowski, G. (2007) 'Critical Pedagogy and the Constitution of Capitalist Society'. Online at www.flowideas.co.uk/?page=articles&sub=Critical%20Pedagogy%20and%20 Capitalism

Robertson, L. (2009) 'In the Crossfire: Early Years Foundation Stage, National Curriculum and Every Child Matters', in D. Hill and L. H. Robertson (eds) *Equality in the Primary School: Promoting good practice across the curriculum.* London: Continuum.

Robertson, L, H. and Hill, R. (2001) 'Excluded voices: educational exclusion and inclusion', in D. Hill and M. Cole (eds) *Promoting Equality in Secondary Schools.* London: Cassell.

Sarup, M. (1983) *Marxism/ Structuralism/ Education.* Lewes: Falmer Press.

Shor, I. and Freire, P. (1987). *A pedagogy for liberation: Dialogues on transforming education.* South Hadley, MA: Bergin & Garvey.

Simon, B. (1992) *What Future for Education?* London: Lawrence and Wishart.

Thatcher, M. (1993) *The Downing Street Years.* London: Harper Collins.

Tomlinson, S. (2005) (2nd edn) *Education in a post-welfare society.* Maidenhead, Berks: Open University Press.

Tomlinson, S. and Craft, M. (1995) 'Education for all in the 1990s', in S. Tomlinson and M. Craft (eds) *Ethnic Relations and Schooling.* London: Athlone.

Index